Diary of an
EDWARDIAN SCHOOL

Diary of an
EDWARDIAN SCHOOL

SLADE SCHOOL THE FIRST 100 YEARS

Maurice R. Western

HISTORY INTO PRINT

First published by
History into Print, 56 Alcester Road,
Studley, Warwickshire B80 7LG in 2008
www.history-into-print.com

ISBN: 978-1-85858-320-4

A Cataloguing in Publication Record
for this title is available from the British Library.

Typeset in Bembo
Printed in Great Britain by
Cambrian Printers Ltd.

CONTENTS

LIST OF ILLUSTRATIONS

SPORTS TABLES

ACKNOWLEDGEMENTS

Birmingham Evening Mail
Birmingham Post
Erdington News
Ex-pupils Slade School
Central Library
Radio Times
Sporting Mail
Sports Argus
Sutton Coldfield News
Sutton Observer
Warwick Record Office

DIARY OF AN EDWARDIAN SCHOOL

Owing to the development of the Gravelly Hill district at the beginning of the 20th century, the Aston School Board authorised the building of a new school in Slade Road, Erdington. The site of Broomfield Farm was selected and work commenced.

1903

TUESDAY, JUNE 30th

The foundation stone was laid by County Councillor Robert P. Yates, J. P. chairman of the last Aston School Board, who was ably assisted by Councillor C. H. Machin, chairman of the Sites and Buildings Committee. The architect was one, William Jenkins, and his design followed the religious stereotypes that had been so evident over the previous decades, and whose pattern was soon to change in favour of more simpler designs as the church played a lesser role in their running. Only a mile away, in Aston, one can find Yew Tree School, which was opened 10 years earlier in 1894, and to which Slade School bears a striking resemblance. It took 12 months for Thomas Johnson, the builder, to lay all the foundations and erect the initially-approved buildings, which comprised those fronting Slade Road, and others in Broomfield Road, up to and including the caretaker's house.

1904

MONDAY, JUNE 27th and WEDNESDAY, JUNE 29th

The Headmaster, Mr Henry Page, attended at the school to receive the names of the intending scholars. He had trained at Saltley College from 1881 to 1883 and had greatly distinguished himself in the theory and practice of teaching. On leaving college, it hadn't been very long before he had been appointed headmaster at St. Anne's (Church of England) School, which was in Devon Street, Duddeston. Owing, however, to adverse reports concerning the structural unsuitability of the school, whilst on the threshold of a most promising scholastic career, he had found himself without either a headship or a school. With great courage, he had started life again as an assistant teacher at the Aston Lane Schools before, four years later, being appointed chief assistant at Osborne Road Schools where, for many years, he served as Mr Charles Smith's right-hand man. Now, at the age of 42, he was once again fully in command of a school.

MONDAY, JULY 4th

It was recorded that two things were at once apparent – viz. the commodious, comfortable and complete character of the schools themselves and the necessity which existed for them in the populous and growing neighbourhood, as manifested by the large and encouraging attendance of scholars on the school's opening day. A total of 282 children were admitted. Present on that opening day were the following managers: Mr C. H. Machin (chairman) accompanied by Mrs Machin;the Reverend E. A. Anthony M. A. (correspondent); Councillor J. Dawson J. P. (chairman of the District Council); Dr Evans J. P.; Mr Tranter and Mr Warder. After prayers had been read by the headmaster, Councillor Machin, addressing those present, declared the school open and gave some words of advice to the children. The Reverend E. A. Anthony also addressed the children, urging upon them the great necessity for good behaviour. They were then marched to their classrooms to commence work. On that very first day Mr Page was assisted by Miss Clara Baum, Miss Ada Butler and Mr G. Phillips. Miss Nellie Bryan took charge of the infants. Except for Mr Phillips, who left within two years, the other four teachers put in nearly 100 years of service at the school between them. This would have been even more, but for the premature death of Mr Page, and the removal of girls over the age of eleven in 1931, which necessitated Miss Baum and Miss Butler to seek employment at other schools.

A typical morning started with registration, following which there would be fifteen minutes devoted to the scriptures. Arithmetic would then last for 35 minutes, with 20 to 25 minutes each of Handwriting and Poetry to conclude the session before break, which would take place at a quarter to eleven. After recreation, at eleven o'clock, there followed Geography and Art until eleven forty. Up to this point, each standard had been taking Drill for the duration of one of the lessons. For the final twenty minutes, before the children broke up for lunch, each standard had its own activity, which consisted of more of what they had just been doing. At midday, all the children were given two hours in which to go home for lunch before re-assembling back in school for the afternoon session. By this time, Warwickshire County Council had taken over control of the school.

FRIDAY, JULY 15th

Mr Page, the Headmaster, attended at the school this evening between 7 and 8p.m. to take the names of intending pupils. Parents were expected to bring their child's birth certificate with them. Within two weeks of opening the number of children on the books had risen to 300, before the school closed on July 28th for the summer vacation.

MONDAY, AUGUST 29th

Four weeks later, the school re-assembled. There had been 64 new admissions and the number of children attending the school had now risen to 350. Attention was being drawn to the size of the classes and a decision had been taken by the managers to appoint two new teachers. On that Monday, at the morning assembly, there was no military command, but there were the scarcely less impressive ones: Stand Up! Attention! Eyes Closed! Then, the headmaster, in reverent, impressive tones, thanked God for "The mercies of creation and preservation and all the blessings of this life." He invoked the divine blessing on the work of the school and asked for a Christlike spirit of kindness to be shown to each other by the scholars of the school. Then, not mumbled irreverently, all joined with heart and voice in the Lord's Prayer. A youth at the piano struck the key and then, in musical monotone, such as one could have heard at a cathedral service, there rolled out right-gloriously from the children's lips the grand old words of the prayer. The first full term had begun.

Within a short time, a Sunday School had been organised at the school, under the auspices of the All Saints District Church in George Road.

WEDNESDAY, SEPTEMBER 14th
18 girls from Fentham Road School commenced cookery lessons in the cookery classroom at Slade Road.

FRIDAY, SEPTEMBER 16th
A half-day's holiday was granted, because the children had achieved 95% attendance for the month of July.

FRIDAY, SEPTEMBER 30th
An assessment was made of the children's progress during the previous week. Spelling and multiplication tables were considered weak, though it was considered that a fair amount of progress had been made.

FRIDAY, OCTOBER 7th
The school was becoming congested and 52 children were sent back to the Infants to help relieve the situation.

MONDAY, OCTOBER 31st
As no improvement had been seen, a further 47 were returned to the Infants. This helped to free up accommodation in the upper school, so that classes could be divided into more manageable units.

Further half-day holidays were given in October and November due to the attendance level not falling below 95% in the preceding months.

FRIDAY, NOVEMBER 11th
The school was closed as it was the occasion of the King's birthday. However, by the middle of November, sickness was becoming rather prevalent and, by the end of the month, a heavy fall of snow had reduced attendances further.

TUESDAY, NOVEMBER 22nd
Concern, at this time, was equally being expressed with regard to the cold nature of the school as the heating was not working properly. This appeared to take some weeks to rectify.

Both photographs were taken in front of the entrance to the vault, the top one in 1904, whilst the lower one dates from 1905.

THURSDAY, DECEMBER 22nd
The Christmas vacation commenced. During the holiday, the heating apparatus was overhauled and improved.

1905

MONDAY, JANUARY 9th
The school re-opened. The heating apparatus appeared to work more satisfactorily during the first week back.

FRIDAY, JANUARY 13th

Mr Page was informed that the school year had changed. It now ran from January 1st to December 31st. Consequently, a new school year had begun and examinations were held to determine those children who should be promoted to higher standards. At this time, children did not automatically move classes each year according to age but ability.

FEBRUARY

The Warwickshire County Council gave notice that they were proposing to build an extension to the current school, in order to accommodate more children. This extension was intended to provide for 300 boys, whilst the girls and infants would occupy the current building.

FRIDAY, MARCH 3rd

220 pupils were awarded certificates for never being absent during the month of February.

TUESDAY, MARCH 7th

A further half-day's holiday was given on the morning for making 95% of attendance during the month of February. As it was Shrove Tuesday, the afternoon was also given as a holiday. These practices continued for many years to come.

THURSDAY, MARCH 30th

By this time, Mr Clegg, Miss Hillis and Miss Ada Carpenter had joined the teaching staff, with the assistance of Edith Mounsey, who was in her first year as a pupil teacher.

FRIDAY, MARCH 31st

Because of the closeness of the Erdington Cottage Homes in Fentham Road, children from there had attended Slade School from its inception. They didn't go to Fentham Road School which was even nearer because, at the time, fees of 3d. for juniors and infants and 6d. for girls were required. Any illnesses in the Homes could adversely affect attendance, as the illness of one child would close that Home to prevent the spread of disease. By the end of March, several Homes were closed because of an outbreak of measles. Throughout March and April the attendance fell steadily to 75%.

FRIDAY, APRIL 14th

The measles epidemic had even caused the Infants' department to be closed completely for more than a week.

WEDNESDAY, APRIL 19th

The Easter vacation arrived.

APRIL

During April the plans for the proposed extension to the school were submitted for approval. It was already anticipated that this new department, intended to be occupied by

310 boys, would become a Junior Mixed department when the last block was built. The current plans were approved and work duly commenced on the buildings that would continue up Broomfield Road from the caretaker's house.

MONDAY, MAY 1st
Re-opening after the holiday, there were 8 Cottage Homes (16 children per home) closed due to the outbreak of measles.

FRIDAY, MAY 12th
There were now 12 Cottage Homes closed.

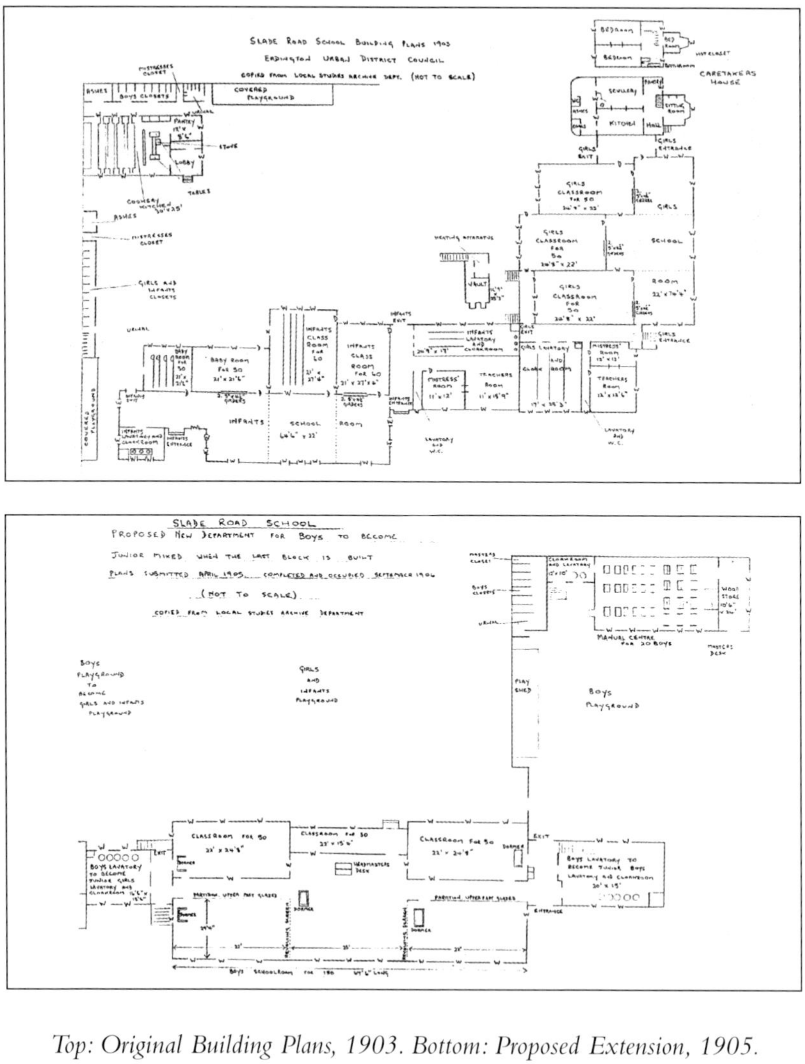

Top: Original Building Plans, 1903. Bottom: Proposed Extension, 1905.

THURSDAY, MAY 18th
The school was advised by the Board of Education that the average attendance of the Mixed School must not exceed 300, otherwise a deduction might be made from the following year's grant!

WEDNESDAY, MAY 24th
Empire Day arrived and was celebrated with some panache. The schoolroom was tastefully decorated with the aid of flags, flowers and plants. After the scripture lesson, each teacher gave a lesson on the growth and development of the British Empire. Afterwards, all the children were brought together, whereupon they gave a rendering of a selection of patriotic songs and recitations. The Reverend E. A. Anthony, then, gave an interesting and instructive address urging them to make the most of their present opportunities, in order that they might be able, in the future, to take their places and ably do their share towards maintaining and extending the glorious Empire to which it was their privilege to belong. A large number of parents attended the celebrations, expressing their appreciation in a most vocal manner. With the singing of *Great Britain, Our Native Land* the proceedings concluded with hearty cheers for the King and the Empire. A holiday was, then, given in the afternoon.

FRIDAY, JUNE 9th
The school closed for the Whitsun holiday, rather later than nowadays.

MONDAY, JUNE 19th
Having re-assembled after the holiday, for the first time it was reported that a number of children from the Cottage Homes had been sent to Canada. Despite this, it would appear that the school was suffering from having too many children in the lower classes.

FRIDAY, JUNE 30th
Mr Page held an examination during the week in order to determine how many children could be promoted to higher standards.

FRIDAY, JULY 14th
During the week, two Sunday School treats considerably reduced the attendances, as a large number of children went off for the day to enjoy themselves with their respective Sunday Schools.

FRIDAY, JULY 21st
A noteworthy occasion for the first-ever pupils from the school were successful in gaining scholarships. Polly Mainwaring and Ethel Morgan were granted £10 minor scholarships by the Warwickshire County Council, and went on to attend Aston Grammar School, which still catered for girls at that time.

FRIDAY, JULY 28th
The summer holidays were upon us once again.

MONDAY, AUGUST 28th
The school re-opened again four weeks later.

THURSDAY, OCTOBER 19th
The school closed for the afternoon, in order that all the teachers could travel to Leamington, so that they could have an opportunity of attending an exhibition of students' and scholars' work. Slade School, itself, exhibited and was awarded four first class, one second class and one commended certificates. These were given for needlework, kindergarten work, arithmetic and writing.

SATURDAY, MONDAY and TUESDAY evenings, OCTOBER 21st, 23rd and 24th
Only just over a year after the school had first opened its doors, it held its first of numerous successful concerts. This one was intended to provide pictures to be hung around the school in order to make it look more pleasant. It was a great success, realising £19.3s.7d., and the pictures were duly purchased in late November. The schoolroom was tastefully decorated with evergreens, flowers and flags. The infants, whose ages ranged from 3 to 9 years of age, supplied the first part of the programme, which went as follows:

Speech: *A Welcome* – Leonard Francis
Song: *Union Jack* – Children
Song: *Roly Poly* – G. Showell and Children
Kindergarten game: *Mousie* – Babies
Song: *Peppercorns* – Children and ten boys
Recitation: *A Pocketful* – J. Dolman
Musical play: *Nursery rhymes* – Children
Recitation: *The Chicks* – Children
Ribbon Drill: Standard 1 girls
Kindergarten game: *The Seasons* – Children
Song: *Gay Little Japs* – 3 girls
Kindergarten occupation: *Flowers* – Standard 1 girls
Song: *Influenza* – Children
Song: *Goodnight* – Babies and Children

After a short interval, the chairman of the proceedings gave a speech, congratulating everyone at the school for what they had achieved in such a short span of time. Altogether, in the school's first year, a pupil-teacher scholarship and seven other scholarships had been gained – five of these at the Whitehead Road School; whilst many pupils had passed the examination qualifying them for admission to grammar schools in Birmingham and Aston.

The second part of the programme commenced with the mixed department presenting a cantata entitled *The Musical Village*. The whole scene was intended to represent a May Day Festival. There were milkmaids, blacksmiths, tailors, farmers and soldiers, all dressed in keeping with their characters. They all took their turn to sing songs to a pianoforte accompaniment played by Mr Henry Page, the Headmaster. Miss Baum and her lady colleagues had prepared some excellent scenery to fit the occasion and the ten main characters performed wonderfully. There was Nellie Lile, resplendent in her most artistically-designed court dress as the May Queen; George Sanders as the Duke Goldcoin; and Frank Dolman as Captain Kindheart. The other principal parts were played as follows: Foster Father – Oscar Royce; Foster Mother – Edith Fry; Master of Ceremonies – Horace Jarvis; Timothy Twaddle – Clement Goldsby; Moses Lee – Alfred Jeffs; The Beadle – Charles Garner; Principal Farmer – George Goodby.

The occasion was honoured by the presence of the Reverend E. A. Anthony as chairman on the Saturday evening, whilst Dr Paget Evans J. P. (chairman of the Erdington District Council) and Councillor G. H. Machin (chairman of the local managers) found time to chair the other two performances respectively.

FRIDAY, NOVEMBER 10th

The King's birthday arrived once again lending itself to a day's holiday.

FRIDAY, NOVEMBER 17th

Another half-day was given, because there had yet again been a 95% attendance level over the previous four weeks.

MONDAY, NOVEMBER 27th

A schools' inspector paid a visit and made an assessment of the school, for which the report alongside was submitted.

MONDAY, DECEMBER 18th

A sale of needlework was held.

THURSDAY, DECEMBER 21st

The school closed for the Christmas holidays.

1906

MONDAY, JANUARY 8th

The school re-opened with the teaching staff taking charge of different classes. The children were likewise affected by promotions to higher classes.

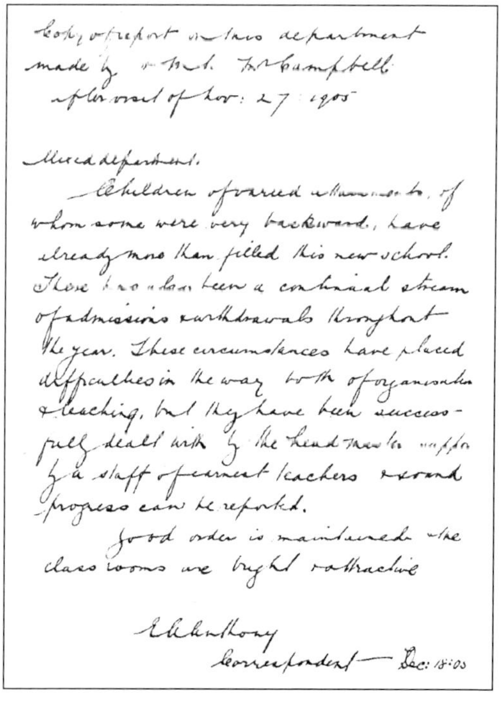

Copy of report on this department made by H. M. I. Mr Campbell after visit of Nov: 27 1905

Mixed department.

Children of varied attainments, of whom some were very backward, have already more than filled this new school. There [illegible] been a continual stream of admissions & withdrawals throughout the year. These circumstances have placed difficulties in the way both of organisation & teaching, but they have been successfully dealt with by the head master supported by a staff of earnest teachers & sound progress can be reported.

Good order is maintained & the class rooms are bright & attractive

E A Anthony
Correspondent — Dec: 18:05

School Inspector's Report, 1905.

FRIDAY, JANUARY 19th

For the first time, the school closed its doors for the day as it was taken over to be used in connection with the General Election. Ever since then, it has been used for all the Local as well as General and European Elections.

WEDNESDAY, JANUARY 24th

The school was visited by Mr W. Stanton, one of the schools' lecturers appointed by the United Kingdom Band of Hope Union. He delivered a lecture to the older children of Standards 4 to 7 on 'Alcohol and the Human Body'. Subsequently, they were expected to write out a report of what they had learnt.

FRIDAY, MARCH 2nd

78 children received certificates of excellence from the Reverend Anthony this afternoon for the reports they had written on 'Alcohol and the Human Body'.

WEDNESDAY, MARCH 7th

The girls were able to undertake cookery with the new heating apparatus, which had been installed in the building known as the Cookery Kitchen.

MONDAY, APRIL 9th

Permission having been requested and granted, for the first time prizes were given out. The Reverend E. A. Anthony and Mr Stoker, two of the managers, came into school to distribute them. 52 prizes were given out, 26 for attendance and 26 for conduct and efficiency. Another annual event had started.

WEDNESDAY, MAY 16th

Miss Boulton, H. M. Inspectress of Cookery, paid a visit to the Cookery Kitchen this afternoon.

THURSDAY, MAY 24th

Empire Day arrived again and, after the usual lessons on the subject, the older children (Standards 4 to 7) were taken to the Erdington Park (Rookery Park). They were not the only ones to go, for the children from Osborne Road and St Thomas' also took part in the joint festival. Shortly before eleven o'clock in the morning, a total of 1500 children marched, with flags and banners flying, from their schools to the new public park, where the massed children sang the National Anthem. A total of four trees was planted, that on behalf of Slade Road by Councillor Joseph Dawson. It was to be referred to as the Slade Road Council School Oak Tree. Mr Dawson gave an excellent address to the children, after which they sang patriotic songs, the proceedings terminating with hearty applause for the tree planter and three cheers for the King.

FRIDAY, JUNE 15th

Another 12 children from the Cottage Homes were sent to Canada this week.

THURSDAY, JUNE 28th

The school was closed today so that 80 teachers and scholars could go to Warwick to witness a preliminary performance of the Pageant. Despite the fact that it rained all day, for many of the children it must have been a unique experience.

THURSDAY, SEPTEMBER 6th

The new school building having been completed, the girls and boys separated. There were 220 boys names on the books when they moved into their new department, which could cater for up to 310. Mr Henry Page continued to take charge of the boys, whilst Miss Clara Baum now assumed leadership of the newly-formed girls' department. The infants were unaffected.

FRIDAY, SEPTEMBER 14th

During the week, the boys commenced their manual instruction in the purpose-built accommodation provided for them. The boys of Deykin Avenue School were also allowed to use the premises on specific days of the week. Woe betide them if they should cross the playground in order to reach the building when the boys of Slade Road were about – for you could imagine the catcalling that took place!

FRIDAY, NOVEMBER 2nd

Parallel and horizontal bars were fixed up, to enable the children to better undertake physical exercises.

FRIDAY, NOVEMBER 9th

The school was closed for the day as it was the King's birthday.

FRIDAY, DECEMBER 14th

Half-day holidays continued to be granted fairly regularly as the attendance level did not drop below 95%. Despite all this, however, a report was required to be prepared showing the attendance levels of the children from the Cottage Homes for the year ending March 31st, 1906. It was a dismal 52.9%, although, to be fair, a proportion of this could be put down to contagious illnesses, which resulted in the closure of a Home although not all the children were necessarily ill.

During the week, the children had a collection on behalf of the *Poor Children's Xmas Party* and the sum of 10s.7d. was sent to the promoters.

1907

The building regulations in force at this time required that schoolrooms and classrooms must show an average of not less than 10 square feet of floor space for each older scholar, and not less than 9 square feet of floor space for infants. The curriculum, in the case of infants, stated that physical exercises should take the form of games involving free movement, singing, and breathing exercises, rather than of set drill. Younger infants were encouraged to employ their eyes, hands and fingers in suitable free occupations, whilst the teacher should, by talking with them, encourage them to ask questions, and, by telling them stories, lead them to form ideas and express them in simple language. The teaching of older infants should be supplemented by short lessons in which the children were trained to listen carefully, speak clearly and recite easy pieces, reproduce simple stories and narratives, cultivate their powers of observation, do simple things with their hands, begin to draw, begin to read and write, acquire an elementary knowledge of number, practise suitable songs and sing simple musical intervals. Instruction could be given in sewing and knitting to older infants, but care should be taken to avoid fine work and injury to eyesight. Other scholars were to be taught the English Language, Handwriting, Arithmetic, Drawing, Geography, History, Music, Observation and Nature Study, Hygiene and Physical Training, whilst, for girls only, there would be the teaching of Domestic Subjects, which included Needlework, Cookery, Laundry Work and Housewifery. Moral instruction was expected to form an important part of the curriculum, though this could be incidental, occasional or as fitting opportunities arose. This instruction should be specially directed to the inculcation of courage, truthfulness, cleanliness of mind, body and speech, love of fair play; gentleness to the weaker, kindness to animals, temperance, self-denial, love of one's country and appreciation of beauty in nature and art. In the case of staff, where a vacancy arose for an ordinary teacher, a young person employed as a monitor could be recognised temporarily for a period not exceeding three months as part of the school staff. In no case could staff be considered sufficient if it was not equivalent to an average attendance measured on the following scale: Head Teacher 50; Certificated Assistant Teacher 60; Uncertificated and Student Teachers 45; Provisional Assistant and Pupil Teachers 30. Equally, the number of pupils habitually present at any one time under the instruction of any one teacher should not exceed 15% of these totals.

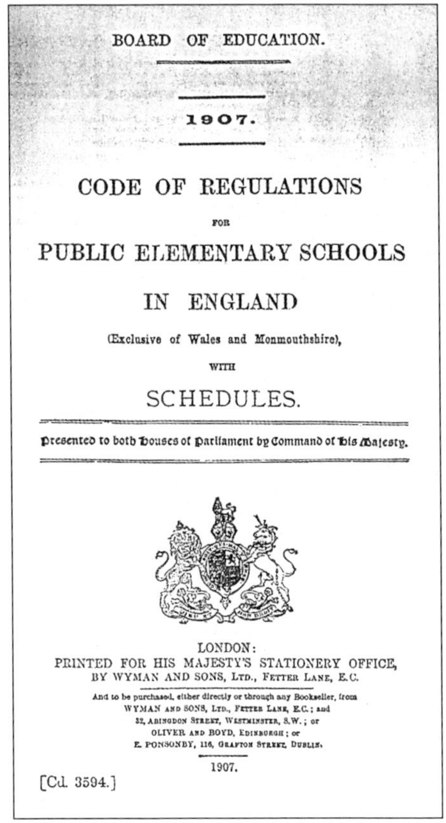
BOARD OF EDUCATION.

1907.

CODE OF REGULATIONS

FOR

PUBLIC ELEMENTARY SCHOOLS

IN ENGLAND

(Exclusive of Wales and Monmouthshire),

WITH

SCHEDULES.

Presented to both Houses of Parliament by Command of His Majesty.

LONDON:
PRINTED FOR HIS MAJESTY'S STATIONERY OFFICE,
BY WYMAN AND SONS, LTD., FETTER LANE, E.C.

And to be purchased, either directly or through any Bookseller, from WYMAN AND SONS, LTD., FETTER LANE, E.C.; and 32, ABINGDON STREET, WESTMINSTER, S.W.; or OLIVER AND BOYD, EDINBURGH; or E. PONSONBY, 116, GRAFTON STREET, DUBLIN.

1907.

[Cd. 3594.]

Code of Regulations – Public Elementary Schools, 1907.

FEBRUARY and MARCH

Many children were away in consequence of an outbreak of mumps and measles. It was May 3rd before everything was back to normal!

THURSDAY, MAY 16th

Prizegiving and 50 books were given away, 28 for attendance and 22 for efficiency and conduct.

WHIT MONDAY, MAY 20th

The Erdington Charity Sports were held on the grounds of the Sir Josiah Mason's Orphanage. Slade Road, together with Osborne Road, performed for the benefit of the large crowds. It must have been a joy to watch the children as they gracefully twined the coloured ribbons around the maypole and performed Scottish dances as well as wand and musical drills.

SATURDAY, JUNE 22nd

In appreciation of the efforts of the children who performed at the Charity Sports, they were entertained at Sutton and, despite the unsettled weather, a very enjoyable time was had by all.

THURSDAY, AUGUST 29th

It would be untrue to say that everything was sweetness and light for two boys, William Allen (10) and Edwin Cotterill (11), inmates of the Cottage Homes, were arrested and charged with stealing a silver watch and chain (value £3), the property of Mrs Mary Jane Ward, who had only started as a teacher at the school on March 14th. They had removed the article from her desk, and had disposed of it by throwing it into a field in George Road, from where the police later recovered it. They appeared at Aston Police Court on Monday, September 2nd, where the magistrates adjourned the case for further reports, as the ten and eleven-year-old lads had admitted their guilt.

FRIDAY, SEPTEMBER 13th

Another noteworthy event occurred when the school decided, for the first time, to enter into the competitive spirit of sports by forming a football team. The Aston Manor Schools' Football Association held its last meeting during the evening. They were, henceforward, to be known as the football section of the Aston Schools' Sports Association. In addition to the ten already-competing teams, Slade Road, along with Albert Road, were accepted into membership. Christopher Kerton, an uncertificated assistant, took charge of this first-ever school football team.

WEDNESDAY, SEPTEMBER 18th

The two lads from the Cottage Homes, who had been remanded three weeks earlier on a charge of theft, were brought before Aston Police Court again today. The clerk of the Aston Guardians, Mr John North, made an application to the bench that the boys should be committed to the Harborne Industrial School until they were 16 years of age. The Guardians had fully considered the matter and thought this the best way to deal with them. The bench granted the application and it is to be hoped that the lads learned a salutary lesson.

SATURDAY, SEPTEMBER 21st
Slade Road played their first-ever football match today, the result being a one-all draw with Alma Street.

FRIDAY, OCTOBER 18th
One of the classrooms was taken over for the purposes of staging a concert. A platform was erected and rehearsals began. The production was a cantata entitled *Princess Zara* and a superb presentation it was too.

SATURDAY, MONDAY and WEDNESDAY, OCTOBER 26th, 28th and 30th
There was a crowded and enthusiastic attendance on each of the three nights. The large audiences meant money, and all the net proceeds of £18.2s.4d. were aptly dedicated to the adornment of the school in the form of pictures of a suitable character. Not only was it an eminently pretty story, admirably calculated to catch the imaginations and stir the enthusiasm of the young people taking part, but the music, though simple, was of a tuneful and expressive character; and admirably played by the Headmaster of the Boys' School, Mr Page. The superintending and cutting out of all of the costumes was undertaken by Miss Baum, the Headmistress of the Girls' School, and her staff. The costumes of the young actors and singers were extremely pretty and effective and the scenery, though not elaborate, was sufficient to illustrate the plot of the story. When one considers that there were seventeen main characters and upwards of fifty members of the supporting cast, it is not difficult to understand the tremendous amount of work that must have been involved in putting the production on. The plot of the piece, whilst not too heavy, was amply sufficient to comprise all that, under such circumstances, was required of it.

King Buonocora resigned his throne in favour of his sixteen-year-old daughter, Princess Zara, and preparations were made for the coronation. The Queen Butterfly, disguised as an old woman, warned the Court of disaster, but the warning was disregarded. The King, who had offended the witches by ridiculing their cherished traditions, was threatened with some very terrible things. The Butterflies, however, resolved to circumvent the fell purpose of the witches. The coronation took place, and when the crown was placed upon her head, the Princess fainted amid the general confusion. Act two showed the working of the witches' curse during which Zara changed and treated everyone very harshly and cruelly. Eventually, with the intervention of the fairies, Zara was released from the witches' spell, and everything ended most happily.

The chief characters were as follows: – King Buonocora – Frank Dolman; Prince Florizel – May Linnell; Princess Zara – Grace Davies; Queen Butterfly – Christine Baker; Violetta – Elsie Allen; Grewsom – Dorothy Whitehall; Baron Locomo – Thomas Hanson; Camillo – Horace Sargent; Firenza – Marjorie Davis; Carina – Elsie Ward; Tortoiseshell – Edith Rose; Page – Walter Harding; Courtiers – John Roberts, Percy Stephens, Percy Dennett, Albert Heacock; Herald – Norman Hadley.

Besides these, other children played the parts of the chorus of Maids of Honour and Nobles, Butterfly Fairies, Witches, Vampires, Guards and Soldiers, etc. One and all performed their parts admirably, but, of course, there were bright particular stars. The King acted very well as did Baron Locomo, who was able to give a very graphic and amusing account of the way in which he had been boiled by the Princess. No less excellent were Prince Florizel, Princess Zara and Queen Butterfly, who each received a tribute of flowers at the close of the performances. The Page, a tiny, little boy, had only a small part, but performed it with great naivete and nonchalance. It only remains to be said that, in all respects, the whole performance was a great success.

1908

FRIDAY, JANUARY 31st

The new year had arrived and, with it, further bouts of illness. Sickness was prevalent in the District – measles, whooping cough and influenza being prominent. This situation lasted for nearly four months, during which time there were as many as 20% of the pupils away at any one time.

WEDNESDAY, APRIL 1st

The annual prize distribution took place this afternoon. In all 83 books were given out, 53 for attendance and 30 for efficiency and conduct. Below can be seen the inside of a book that was presented to Sidney Billings as a prize for never being absent or late during 1907.

Labor Omnia Vincit

County of Warwick Education Committee

Prize Awarded To

Sidney Billings

Slade Road Inft's School

Who was Never Absent or Never Late during the Year ending December 31st 1907

Chairman of Managers

STRANGE ADVENTURES

THRILLING STORIES AND ADVENTURES

BY

SHEILA BRAINE

AND

DR. GORDON STABLES

Book Prize, 1907.

SATURDAY, APRIL 11th

Slade Road's first football season came to a close, the team finishing eighth of the twelve schools participating in the Aston Schools' League.

FRIDAY, MAY 22nd

By the time that Empire Day rolled around again, everything was nearly back to normal, except that one of the Cottage Homes was closed due to an outbreak of scarlet fever. The

Top: Mixed School Class, c.1906. (Mr Page is to the left; Mr Phillips is to the right).
Bottom: Girls' School Class, c.1909. (Miss Butler is to the left).

teachers gave special lessons whilst the children subsequently performed songs and recitations. The school had already been tastefully decorated with flags, festoons of flowers and trailing ivy. First off, the young children of the Infant department, under the guidance of Miss Bryan, sang patriotic songs to the accompaniment of waving flags which they carried. It was quite touching to see young children saluting the engraving of His Majesty the King. Then followed a rendering of the National Anthem and three cheers for the King. The children of the upper department, meanwhile, had been staging their own choreographed programme. Songs included: *Hearts of Oak; Ye Mariners of England; Kipling's Recessional; Land of my Fathers; The March of the Men of Harlech; The Children's Empire Hymn.* There followed recitations – *Death of Wallace; The Revenge; England's Message to America; Children of the Empire; The Union Jack* – in the last of which the girls were adorned in the National costumes of England, Scotland and Ireland. Subsequently, the children assembled in the playground to witness the hoisting of the Union Jack, which was saluted in military style by the older boys. Yet again, the National Anthem and three cheers for the King rang out. After a speech from one of the managers, in which the children were counselled to love their parents, think well of their teachers, their school and their country, a brief rain shower interrupted the proceedings, before sixty boys and girls, trained by Miss Baum, gave a series of dances on the maypole. The music for the occasion was supplied by Mr Clegg on the fiddle and the whole ensemble won great applause from parents, children and visitors. In the afternoon, a holiday was given, and the day would live long in the memory of many of the children who took part.

FRIDAY, JUNE 5th to TUESDAY, JUNE 16th

Whitsun came and went and before long the school was breaking up for the midsummer vacation; but not before a large contingent of aesthetically-attired scholars, trained to perfection by Miss Baum, had given a charming display of maypole dancing and musical drill at the Erdington Charity Sports on Whitmonday, June 8th.

TUESDAY, AUGUST 25th

By this time the school year had been changed again and a new one started. Children were moved into higher standards and another year's work began.

FRIDAY, OCTOBER 9th

The school was still crowded, however, and children were transferred back to the Infants' department to relieve congestion. At this time, the Assistant Medical Officer of Health for the County made an inspection of selected children, though the results of his examinations are not known.

THURSDAY, OCTOBER 29th

An inspector from Warwickshire County Council called at the school today, where he inspected the Cookery Centre, finding the instruction proceeding in accordance with the timetable. Although the class was orderly and well conducted, one third of the girls had to work at the demonstration bench. Miss Merry was advised to obtain a third kitchen table. The inspector thought that the stove used for heating the hot pipes in the room caused considerable trouble by the dust it created. Furthermore, because the pipes became very hot, he felt they should be protected in some way, as the pupils were apt to come into contact with them as they moved about the room. The inspector also visited the Handicraft department, where he found the class enjoying the lesson provided by Mr H. H. Wilkes. Despite the newness of the school, the sash windows in the roof were defective, such that they had leaked so badly during the rains of the previous week that part of the room underneath could not be used!

MONDAY, NOVEMBER 9th
Attendance half-day holidays were still being given for good attendance and the children had a further holiday for the King's birthday today.

FRIDAY, DECEMBER 4th
It was recorded that Charles Wyatt, a sixth-standard boy, had been awarded a foundation scholarship to the Aston Grammar School, another fillip for the school.

FRIDAY, DECEMBER 11th
During the month, the school decided to have a collection for the *Poor Children's Christmas Treats.* This raised 9s.1½d.

FRIDAY, DECEMBER 18th
And to round the year off, the school was inspected and found to be performing satisfactorily. It was stated that continuing on the same path the school should produce the results desired. An early break for Christmas was occasioned by an outbreak of scarlet fever in the Erdington area, and the school duly broke up this afternoon.

1909

TUESDAY, JANUARY 12th
The school re-opened after the Christmas break to find that whooping cough was extremely prevalent.

FRIDAY, JANUARY 29th
The attendance was further affected by the severity of the cold weather which kept a number of children away.

SATURDAY, FEBRUARY 20th
A new caretaker took up residence today.

TUESDAY, FEBRUARY 23rd
The usual half-day's holiday was given for Shrove Tuesday.

FRIDAY, MARCH 5th to FRIDAY, MARCH 12th
It snowed heavily and, as a consequence, the attendance again took a nosedive.

FRIDAY, MARCH 19th

REPORT ON INFANTS' DEPARTMENT BY AN EDUCATION INSPECTOR FROM THE WARWICKSHIRE COUNTY COUNCIL.

Number on books 371 *Average attendance last quarter 328.6*

Teacher	*Rank*	*Class*	*No. in class*	*Allowed number*
MISS BRYAN	H.T.			50
MISS HILLIS	C.T.	STD. 1A	60	60
MISS BRINDLEY	S.T.	STD. 1B	44	30
MISS ATHERLEY	C.T.	CLASS 1	59	60
MISS JEFFERY	U.T.	CLASS 2	53	45
MISS WHEAVER	U.T.	CLASS 3	55	45
MISS A. SMITH	U.T.	CLASS 4	59	45
MISS ANDREWS	U.T.	BABIES	41	45
			371	380 (330 excl. H.T.)

It was unfortunate that my visit coincided with a half holiday at the school and I was unable to see the work of the school. But the Headmistress and the correspondent met me. As the committee is fully aware of the difficulties in regarding to overcrowding and sufficient staffing in this department, it is unnecessary for me to say anything about them. The pressure will be relieved when the Junior department of the school is built. At present, the classes are too large in four or five cases. With one exception, there are galleries in all the rooms. The headteacher is anxious to have one removed in the large room, but I do not recommend this. In the babies' room, there is a gallery which has been condemned by H.M.I. There are eight steps to the top of the gallery and, as about 45 babies are taught in this room, it can hardly be regarded as a suitable structure. It takes up room which is badly needed for other purposes and might with the greatest advantage be removed. The heating arrangements in this room are in need of serious attention. The temperature of the room during the cold weather of last week did not, I understand, reach 40°F. Today, the pipes were about cold in the early afternoon. There is evidently a serious loss of heat in the pipes on the way to the room and it is possible that the boiler is not adequate. This is a very bright and cheerful looking school. The rooms are well lighted.

During the inspector's visit, he called in to the Cookery Centre once more. Most of the cookery centres appeared to suffer from the former habit of admitting large numbers to a demonstration lesson. Hence, a great part of the room was occupied by a needlessly-large gallery of which only part was used. It was recommended that the front row of seats should be removed at an early stage. A third table had still not been added yet either. It would appear that the cookery stove was almost useless as far as the oven was concerned as it would not heat. Despite the fact that the fire had been going all day the oven was only comfortably warm to the hand; it had to be dealt with at an early date; a splasher was also needed at the back of the oven. Miss Merry was advised to requisition one.

THURSDAY, APRIL 8th to TUESDAY, APRIL 20th

Easter came and went.

SATURDAY, MAY 1st

Slade Road had now completed their second season in the Aston Schools' Football League.

Alongside is a copy of the final table for the 1908/1909 season.

	P	W	L	D	F	A	PTS
BURLINGTON STREET	24	20	2	2	106	12	42
THOMAS STREET	24	19	2	3	131	19	41
HIGHER ELEMENTARY	24	19	3	2	133	19	40
STATION ROAD	24	17	5	2	94	34	36
ASTON LANE	24	12	9	3	75	49	27
ST MARY'S	24	11	11	2	69	39	24
ALBERT ROAD	24	11	11	2	62	64	24
GOWER STREET	24	9	12	3	71	60	21
SLADE ROAD	24	8	12	4	47	82	20
OSBORNE ROAD	24	7	16	1	47	106	15
VICARAGE ROAD	24	6	17	1	34	103	13
LOZELLS STREET	24	4	20	0	28	189	8
ALMA STREET	24	0	23	1	14	118	1

Aston Schools' Football League, 1908/1909.

MONDAY, MAY 24th

The schoolchildren continued to keep their noses to the grindstone until, once again, Empire Day thrust itself onto the scene with a flourish. The teachers started the proceedings off by giving lessons on the growth and development of the Empire, the Headmaster supplementing the lessons by giving his own summation of the men who had made the Empire great. There followed a carefully-arranged programme, which included recitations and patriotic songs: *Dear Land of Hope; The Recessional; The Charge of the Light Brigade; Our Glorious Empire Day.* A short sketch entitled *Britannia's Birthday* was much appreciated. Children representing every British colony laid appropriate tributes at Britannia's feet. The taste shown in the choice of the subjects and the uniformly-high standard of excellence attained testified to the intelligence of the children and to the careful teaching of the school staff. At eleven o'clock, the boys and girls entered the playground, where were already assembled many parents and others of the general public who were interested in the celebrations. The boys saluted the flag as it was hoisted aloft by a Petty Officer of the Royal Navy Reserve. There then followed the singing of the National Anthem, after which Mr Page called for three cheers for the King, the Empire and the representative of the King's Navy. Boys and girls, superintended by Miss Baum, gave a very creditable display of maypole dances to the accompaniment of violin music supplied by Mr Clegg. The Reverend Anthony now addressed everyone present. He said that they were there to do honour to those old-time heroes – Nelson, Drake, Wellington among others – whose glorious deeds had done so much to make the Empire what it was. He went on to say that if its integrity were to be maintained a great deal would depend on those who were now at school. It was not by shouting and flag waving that the Empire would be held together. Rather should they look forward to the time when they would take their proper places as good and law-abiding citizens – good men and women prepared to follow the right, love, truth and do their duty. There had been great empires founded on slavery, selfishness and greed and, because of that, those empires had fallen. Let their watchword be responsibility, self-sacrifice, duty, sympathy and finally let them fear God, serve their country and honour the King. The proceedings terminated with the children giving the reverend gentleman three rousing cheers. A holiday was given in the afternoon.

WHIT MONDAY, MAY 31st
For the twelfth year in succession the Erdington Charity Sports were held on the grounds of the Sir Josiah Mason's Orphanage. This was the second year of the introduction again of the ½ mile Schools' Team Race, and, out of the 6 competing schools, that from Slade Road School were winners with 17 points, although St Thomas' ran well and were not very far behind. Pocket knives were presented to H. Taylor, H. Morris, R. Gardiner and L. Barnsley, who represented the school.

SATURDAY, JUNE 5th
The Public Library Committee of the Erdington District Council resolved that a box of books could be sent to the school for the use of the scholars; that the same be changed as required; and the number in use should never exceed 50 in number.

FRIDAY, JUNE 11th
One of the second standard boys, James Gardener, died during the holiday, the first such recorded event.

WEDNESDAY, JULY 7th
A holiday was given today, so that those children who wished could go into Birmingham to welcome their Majesties, the King and Queen, and Princess Victoria, who were visiting the city for the purpose of opening Birmingham University.

FRIDAY, OCTOBER 15th
The attendance suffered somewhat in consequence of a very severe storm, which started a half-hour before school began, and continued unabated for three quarters of an hour.

THURSDAY, NOVEMBER 4th

REPORT BY EDUCATION INSPECTOR FROM WARWICKSHIRE COUNTY COUNCIL REPORT NUMBER 61/11.

I visited this school to report on the managers' request for the recognition of Mr Clegg as first assistant at the school. I consider Mr Clegg to be well qualified for the post. His teaching is careful, his discipline is good and the specimen of written work submitted to me gave sufficient evidence of the good standard of work recorded in the highest class of the school which is under his charge. Mr Clegg has charge of a class of 66, a number far too large to permit of the best results. It speaks well for his powers as a teacher that the class reaches its present standard, but steps should be taken, if possible, to subdivide the class.

REPORT BY EDUCATION INSPECTOR FROM WARWICKSHIRE COUNTY COUNCIL REPORT NUMBER 62/11.

The managers of the school, having applied for the recognition of Miss Atherley as first assistant, I visited the school to report on her work. Notwithstanding that she is in charge of a class of between 60 and 70 of an average age between 6 and 7 years, she handles the class very well indeed and I have every reason to believe that the managers' recommendation, if adopted by the committee, will have beneficial results for the large department. It is hoped that the new building, when completed, will lead to a considerable reduction in the size of several of the classes in the school. They are too large to ensure the best educational results.

FRIDAY, NOVEMBER 12th
The annual King's Birthday holiday was given today.

1910
FRIDAY, JANUARY 21st
The school was closed as it was being used as a polling station for the General Election.

FRIDAY, SATURDAY and MONDAY evenings, MARCH 18th, 19th and 21st
The annual children's concert took place and excited great interest amongst parents and friends. Crowded audiences assembled on each evening, and some, who had not taken tickets beforehand, were regretfully turned away. The proceeds of the concert were devoted to augment a prize fund, which was used to decorate the schools with pictures and plants and to purchase extra things for the schools, which the Education Department did not provide. The entertainment started with the infants performing songs and National dances, whilst dressed in the appropriate costumes. Two historical games – *King Alfred and the Cakes* and *Bruce and the Spider* – were capitally carried out, whilst the songs of *The Little Soldiers* and *The Fairies* were vociferously applauded, the children being dressed in character. Those of *Teddy Bear* and *Froggies* were equally cleverly executed. During the interval on the Saturday evening, Councillor Batty, in the course of a few appropriate observations, said that there were over 1000 children in the schools and they were being enlarged to 1400. He went on to say that the teaching was most successful, several boys having been sent to Higher Grade schools and King Edward's, Aston, as well as Sutton Coldfield Grammar School. There were several shouts of "Hear! Hear!" He then went on to thank the parents and friends of the scholars for their co-operation in getting up the admirable entertainment, which reflected great credit on the teachers, and the children who had proved themselves such apt pupils. The audience applauded most loudly at this. After the interval, the older boys

and girls put on a cantata entitled *King Arthur*, the stage being tastefully decorated with evergreens and pictures, whilst the costumes had been provided by the parents under the direction and with the assistance of the teachers. Alfred Beesley starred as Arthur with Christine Baker, who had a very sweet voice, playing Elaine. Evelyn Pountney as Pompo the Jester and Clare Millichap as The Slut (A slave servant girl) were both very funny, particularly when they sang a duet, which was loudly applauded. Fanny Lane, who portrayed Endor the Witch, acted very finely in the closing scene, where she went mad, whilst Frank Goodall – The Robber King – made a fine show, despite suffering from an injured arm. All the performances were enthusiastically applauded and a net profit of £24.6s.5d. was made, which was equally divided between the three departments.

SATURDAY, APRIL 16th

Slade Road, owing to some feeling among the usual players – all of whom were dropped – placed an entirely-new football team against Higher Elementary, who won by 9 clear goals.

SATURDAY, APRIL 30th

The final matches in the Aston Schools' Football League were played a week earlier, resulting in the following table.

	P	W	L	D	F	A	PTS
THOMAS STREET	24	19	3	2	80	23	40
ALBERT ROAD	24	20	4	0	106	29	40
STATION ROAD	24	18	5	1	78	29	37
HIGHER ELEMENTARY	24	14	8	2	71	33	30
BURLINGTON STREET	24	11	9	4	60	33	26
GOWER STREET	24	10	10	4	68	62	24
ASTON LANE	24	10	10	4	60	58	24
ST MARY'S	24	7	9	8	35	50	22
OSBORNE ROAD	24	8	12	4	56	60	20
SLADE ROAD	24	8	15	1	49	84	17
VICARAGE ROAD	24	4	15	5	25	65	13
LOZELLS STREET	24	5	18	1	29	112	11
ALMA STREET	24	3	19	2	36	125	8

Aston Schools' Football League, 1909/1910.

TUESDAY, MAY 10th

A letter, received today from the Assistant Director of Education, responded to the matter of the large class sizes that had been raised with him by the school. He stated that reducing class sizes from 68 to 64 was not good enough, and that it was absolutely essential that they be reduced to 60 with immediate effect. The Board intended to be very strict in this matter, and would take serious action if the classes were not immediately brought into line. (What that action was was not stated.) Accordingly, Mr Page re-organised the classes by promoting boys to higher standards. One boy was removed from the school, having attained the age of fourteen, although it was in the middle of term!

WHITMONDAY, MAY 16th

At the Erdington Charity Sports, the school performed maypole dances, whilst gaily attired. Slade Road School was famous for its maypole dancing!

TUESDAY, MAY 24th

Empire Day was not celebrated in deference to the death of the King.

FRIDAY, MAY 27th

A number of Cottage Homes children were sent to Canada this week.

TUESDAY, JULY 12th

The school was closed as it was the occasion of the annual sports at the Cottage Homes.

MONDAY, AUGUST 22nd

The children returned after the month-long summer holiday to find that the school had been repainted. Not only that, but the new Boys' department, the plans for which had been submitted in February 1909, was ready for occupation.

THURSDAY, SEPTEMBER 1st

The boys moved into their new building today. It provided accommodation for 324, thus bringing that of the whole school to a total of 1300 children. Slade Road Council School now had the distinction of being, not only the largest school in Erdington, but in the whole of the administrative area of the Warwickshire County Council. Along one side of the new wing ran a verandah, modelled on the cloisters of older schools, in order to shelter children when they moved from class to class when it was raining. Furthermore, in the centre of the playground had been erected a new assembly room, which would be fitted up to be used as a drill hall. The school now embraced a manual centre, cookery kitchen, tennis court, two

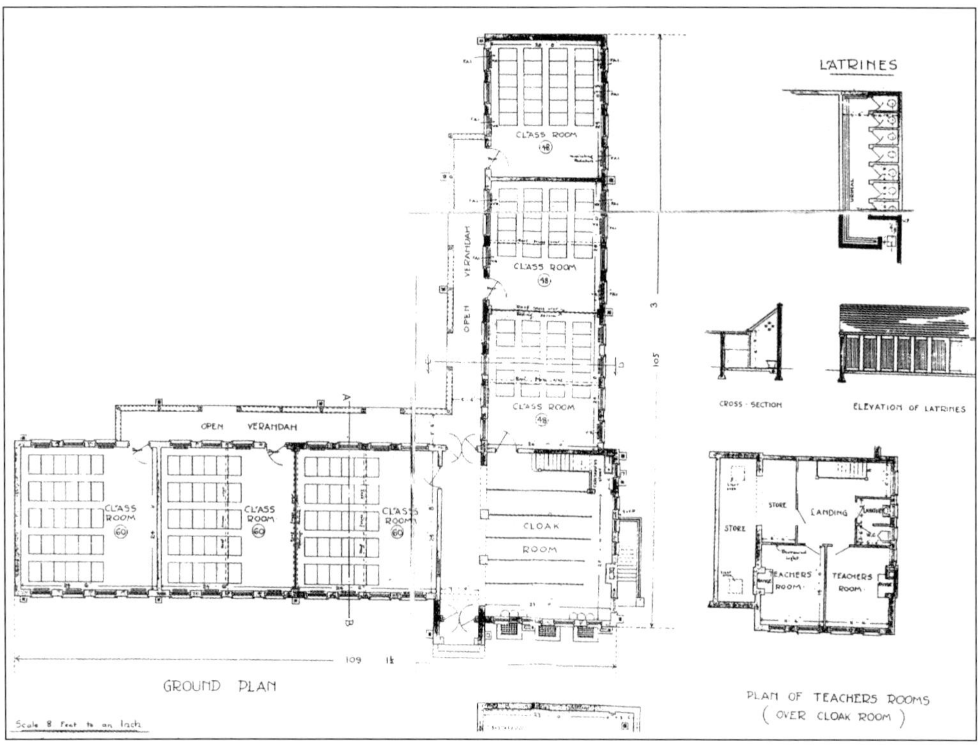

Ground floor plan of new Boys' School building.

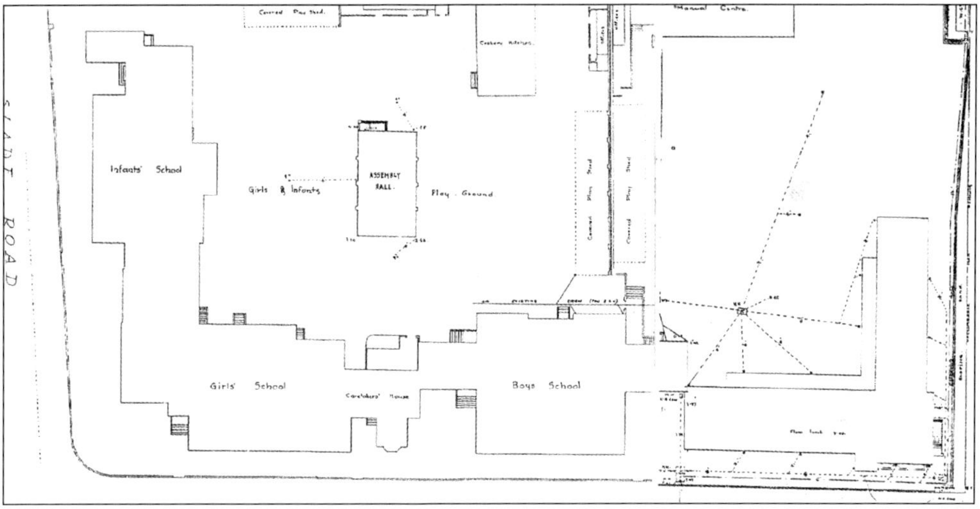

Outline plan of school as at September 1st, 1910.

maypoles and a large flag post, where the national emblem would be hoisted on notable anniversaries and occasions of public rejoicing. Everything had been done at the time to make the children as happy as possible, and to prepare them for their future responsibilities. There now, also, came into being a new Junior department which took over the premises recently vacated by the boys. There were now 1230 children on the roll.

SATURDAY, SEPTEMBER 24th

In the Aston Schools' Football League, Lozells Street were entertained by Slade Road when they paid a visit to Erdington, where the somewhat hilly ground militated against accurate passing and shots. Stringer, who kept goal for the home side, was the outstanding player on the field, as he repeatedly saved the day. One fast, low shot was heading for the corner of the net, when Stringer, from the other side of the goal, hurled himself across to stop it. An exciting mêlée took place before the ball was eventually scrambled away and the situation saved. Only Stringer's heroics were responsible for the school holding Lozells Street to a one-one draw.

TUESDAY, OCTOBER 4th

A medical inspection took place of 49 children who were leaving school during the year. Particular attention was paid to half a dozen 'special' cases. I wonder what was so special about them!

FRIDAY, OCTOBER 14th

Four 1st class, four 2nd class and one special mention certificates were awarded for work sent to the Leamington Exhibition.

MONDAY, DECEMBER 5th

Yet again, the school was informed that no class must exceed 60 under any circumstances whatsoever!

SATURDAY, DECEMBER 10th

Norman Stringer, vice captain of Slade Road School football team, came from Walsall, the training ground of so many fine footballers, at the age of 12. At first, it was thought he would make a left-wing forward, but his choice was goalkeeping and, during the past two seasons, he had undoubtedly proved himself the best custodian in the Aston Schools' League. Altogether, he took part in 36 league games for the school and, during the seasons 1909–10 and 1910–11, he played in representative games 10 times. His clever display at Wolverhampton on the previous Saturday was largely responsible for the division of honours with Wolverhampton Schools. Norman Stringer had now passed the age limit for the league, but would play for Aston as long as they were interested in the national competition that season.

Norman Stringer, 1910.

FRIDAY, DECEMBER 23rd

It was noted that two boys had each received a pair of boots from the Daily Mail Christmas tree fund.

1911

MONDAY, JANUARY 16th

Mr Oswald Dixon was appointed Manual Instructor and commenced his duties. He was to remain at the school for 39 years until his retirement on August 31st, 1950. He lived locally in Wheelwright Road.

WEDNESDAY, MARCH 29th

The Junior department closed for the remainder of the week, due to the boiler controlling the heating apparatus ceasing to function.

FRIDAY, MARCH 31st

There were now five Cottage Homes closed due to illness. The attendance at the school had fallen to 81.7% in consequence.

SATURDAY, APRIL 15th

In the final league match of the season, Albert Road visited Erdington, and though the home side scored first through Jennings, the visitors, when they had become accustomed

	P	W	L	D	F	A	PTS
ALBERT ROAD	22	19	1	2	134	17	40
THOMAS STREET	22	16	2	4	78	22	36
ST MARY'S	22	13	3	6	44	20	32
VICARAGE ROAD	22	12	6	4	43	19	28
HIGHER ELEMENTARY	22	11	6	4	43	38	26
SLADE ROAD	22	8	9	5	46	53	21
BURLINGTON STREET	22	8	9	5	32	32	21
ASTON LANE	22	8	10	4	47	40	20
GOWER STREET	22	5	12	5	28	50	15
STATION ROAD	22	5	15	1	18	49	11
DEYKIN AVENUE	22	2	15	2	20	77	6
LOZELLS STREET	22	1	19	2	15	113	4

Aston Schools' Football League, 1910/1911.

to the peculiar ground, enjoyed the bulk of the attack. The final score was 3–1 in favour of the champions of the Aston Schools' Football League, the final table for which is published above.

FRIDAY, MAY 12th

All the Cottage Homes were now open, so the attendance improved considerably. This was the first occasion since the beginning of February that this had been the case.

MONDAY, MAY 15th

The Boys' department was instructed to admit 52 children from the Infants' such that there were now 355 on the roll, 31 in excess of the accommodation.

WHIT MONDAY, JUNE 5th

At the Erdington Charity Sports, a team of four lads representing Slade Road School competed for the ½ mile Erdington Schools' Team Race against four other Erdington schools. The event aroused a great deal of interest amongst all the youngsters there. A special prize of a gold-centre medal was awarded to the first boy home, A. Heaton. Cricket bats were given to the three other members of the Slade Road winning team, N. Jennings, R. Gardiner and S. Mack.

WEDNESDAY, JUNE 21st

The infants were entertained today, so that they could be spared the crush of Coronation Day. The school had been gaily and appropriately decorated with little Union Jacks, which adorned the walls, the infants also being given their own miniature versions, all of them provided as a gift by Boots the chemists. They enjoyed games and maypole dancing, whilst toys were distributed amongst them. Afterwards, they were all provided with tea at a cost to the council of 4d for each child. During the afternoon specially designed Coronation mugs were presented to all the children. In total, 5500 were given out to the children at the various schools in Erdington. They were an aesthetic-yellowish-grey colour with handsome gold rims and Coronation embellishments. Made in England, they had cost 5d. wholesale.

THURSDAY, JUNE 22nd

The school was closed owing to the celebrations connected with the coronation of their Majesties, King George V and Queen Mary. The day was fine with a refreshing breeze blowing when the bulk of the older children marched to the Erdington Park by the nearest available route, in order to arrive at 2p.m., in time to witness the sports and entertainments that were to commence at 2.30p.m. There – having been given coupons entitling them to two buns, ¼lb cake and a pint of sterilized milk – they were dismissed by their teachers to thoroughly afford them the freedom of action as well as the thoughtful provisions provided. The teachers, together with other volunteers, were on duty in the refreshment tent to ensure the children obtained their provisions with due speed. The total cost to the council was estimated to be £235; buns had been supplied at ¾d. each; cakes at 4½d/lb; and 1000 pints of milk were purchased at a 1½d. per pint. During the afternoon and evening, the Erdington Athletic Club and the ladies of the Aston Villa Gymnasium gave displays of boxing, wrestling and other athletic pursuits. Around 20–30, 000 people turned up in total to watch the athletics, cycle racing, old English sports and championship races that were put on. The Erdington Early Morning School Band provided further entertainment. The following day was also given over as a holiday.

TUESDAY, JULY 18th

The occasion being the annual Cottage Homes sports day, the school closed for the afternoon.

FRIDAY, JULY 28th

The school closed for the summer vacation, not this time for four weeks, but five! An extra week's holiday had been granted as a special 'Coronation' holiday.

WEDNESDAY, SEPTEMBER 13th

The sanitary inspector called today, as a child had been in school the previous day with scarlet fever. The classroom and desks were, therefore, scrubbed thoroughly with disinfectant.

SATURDAY, SEPTEMBER 16th

Slade Road opened their Aston Schools' Football League campaign with a victory by two goals to one in their encounter with Higher Elementary. Always nippy in his movements, the school's speedy right-winger, Jennings, was forever dangerous, scoring one of the goals, the other coming from Eaton.

SATURDAY, OCTOBER 7th

Slade Road owed their victory over Station Road in the Aston Schools' Football League almost entirely to their right-winger, Jennings. Strong, speedy and clever and very deadly in his shooting, he was value for the four goals he scored, his second from fifteen yards range being a beauty. For the second year, he was sure of his place in the Aston Schools' representative team.

WEDNESDAY, NOVEMBER 1st
The school was closed for the Municipal Elections.

THURSDAY, NOVEMBER 9th
Erdington became amalgamated with Birmingham today. The school now came under the management of the City of Birmingham Education Committee.

SATURDAY, NOVEMBER 11th
The great difficulty which teachers meet with in their efforts to organise a school football team was brought home very vividly in the case of St. Mary's R. C. They turned up short of several players, the gaps being filled up with volunteers; and their apologies for boots, which most of them wore, were pitiful. Under the circumstances, Slade Road did pretty well as they liked and ought to have won by more than fourteen clear goals.

THURSDAY, NOVEMBER 16th
The outgoing managers expressed their high appreciation of the good work and loyal service that had characterised the history of Slade Road School.

FRIDAY, DECEMBER 1st
Mr Clegg terminated his engagement at the school today. He had been appointed Headmaster of a school at Stowmarket.

The Erdington Cottage Homes. (To the left is Fentham Road, and in the far top right-hand corner, Reservoir Road. The Birmingham to Lichfield railway line crisscrosses the photograph at the bottom, with the roofs of Fentham Road Council School just to be seen in the bottom left-hand corner. Highcroft Hall occupies the top part of the photograph.)

Looking across Slade Road towards the Girls' entrance, c.1911.

1912

SATURDAY, JANUARY 13th

The operation of the age limit was responsible for the appearance of many new faces in the teams that turned out today. Thomas Street, who had won all their previous matches, came a cropper against Slade Road, notwithstanding that the latter were below strength. Jennings was in top form and he was well supported by Dennett, Fell junior and Lord, the last named a very promising recruit. Gardiner also played a sterling game at right back. Slade Road won by four goals to one. The school was equally pleased to hear that Norman Jennings, captain of this year's Aston schools' team, had been honoured by being selected by the English Schools' Executive to play in the International Trial match at Newark on Trent.

THURSDAY, JANUARY 18th

In consequence of a heavy fall of snow, and only 47% of the children being present, they were sent home for the rest of the day.

FRIDAY, JANUARY 19th

The school was closed again because of the inclement weather.

SATURDAY, JANUARY 27th

Norman Jennings, 1912.

The weather didn't seem to have much of an effect on football matches, however! Today saw the commencement of the Aston Schools' Challenge Shield. It was unfortunate for Albert Road that three of their forwards failed to turn up on time for, while they were shorthanded, Slade Road scored the goal that won the match. The Fell brothers were prominent, with Yates the best forward, Jennings being too well watched to be troublesome on this occasion.

Few boys had had so long a football career at school as that of Jennings. This was the fifth year that he had played for the school, and the second year he had been in Aston's representative team. He commenced his career as an inside forward, but settled soon afterwards at outside right. Early in the previous season he had been moved to back, but it was quickly realised that in his case 'attack was the best means of defence' for he resumed his old position on the extreme right; and since then his goalscoring ability had been phenomenal. Quick to seize an opening, very clever in controlling the ball, and gifted with exceptional speed, he had won several prizes in sprint races at the Erdington Charity Sports. His flying down the wing and beautiful centres were always dangerous. Few, who had been present at the Molyneux ground, Wolverhampton when Aston were entertained in the National Schools' Shield the previous year, would have forgotten the thrilling run down the wing and grand goal that Jennings scored, that proved to be the turning point in a game that Aston unexpectedly won.

FRIDAY, FEBRUARY 9th

Thirty Cottage Homes children were granted permission to visit the Great Bostock Jungle during school hours.

SATURDAY, FEBRUARY 10th

Slade Road progressed to the semi-finals of the Aston Schools' Challenge Shield as a result of their six goals to nil victory over Aston Lane. The losers endeavoured to play the 'one back' game, but the intelligence of the Slade Road forwards – hanging behind the ball – resulted in Jennings scoring three times. Thus, for the second time, Slade Road were in the semi-finals. On the first occasion, the school had been narrowly beaten by one goal to nil by St. Mary's, Aston Brook in the 1908–1909 season.

TUESDAY, FEBRUARY 20th

The usual Shrove Tuesday half-day's holiday was given.

In the semi-finals of the Aston Schools' Challenge Shield, Burlington Street, who had won the trophy in 1906, entertained the school. It was evident early on that instructions had been given to watch Jennings, the most dangerous of Slade's forwards, very closely. The play in the first half was slightly in favour of Slade Road but, owing chiefly to the grand defence of Burlington Street, they failed to score. Early in the second half, Dennett at outside left scored with a good shot that proved to be the only goal of the match. The defence of T. Fell and Ketch had much to do with the victory.

TUESDAY, MARCH 5th

85 boys accompanied by their teachers visited 'The Jungle' this afternoon.

WEDNESDAY, MARCH 13th

Opinion in the crowd that witnessed the final of the Aston Schools' Challenge Shield was that Slade Road deserved their victory by three goals to nothing over Station Road. The forward play of the wingers, Dennett and Gardiner, followed by splendid centres and shots, kept the opposing defence always on the stretch. The trophy was afterwards presented by Alderman A. H. James who congratulated the school on going through the competition with a record of eleven goals for and none against.

MONDAY, MARCH 18th

An inspector from the Board of Education called today to inspect the school. He said that the work of the school was carefully directed by Mr Page and the scheme of instruction showed attention to modern methods of presenting the subjects to the children. In consequence a creditable level of attainment was being reached.

SATURDAY, APRIL 27th

The Aston schools' football season came to a conclusion today. Slade Road narrowly failed to complete the double by winning the league title as well as the shield.

	P	W	L	D	F	A	PTS
ALBERT ROAD	14	11	2	1	44	8	23
VICARAGE ROAD	14	10	1	3	32	15	23
SLADE ROAD	14	9	2	3	41	9	21
STATION ROAD	14	9	3	2	30	11	20
GOWER STREET	14	7	3	4	30	15	18
THOMAS STREET	14	8	5	1	38	21	17
ALMA STREET	14	6	4	4	25	11	16
ST MARY'S ASTON BROOK	14	6	4	4	23	11	16
HIGHER ELEMENTARY	14	7	6	1	33	25	15
BURLINGTON STREET	14	4	4	6	29	20	14
ASTON LANE	14	3	9	2	16	34	8
LOZELLS STREET	14	2	9	3	12	29	7
DEYKIN AVENUE	14	1	9	4	17	43	6
SACRED HEART	14	1	10	3	13	60	5
ST SILAS'	14	0	13	1	7	92	1

Aston Schools' Football League, 1911/1912.

FRIDAY, MAY 24th
Miss Mabel Whitehouse terminated her employment today. She had been appointed Headmistress at a school at Cannock.

FRIDAY, JULY 5th
The attendance was seriously affected by outbreaks of German measles, mumps and whooping cough.

THURSDAY, JULY 25th
The school was visited this afternoon by Alderman James, Councillor Swingler and Mr Paget Evans for the purpose of presenting the medals recently won by the football Team.

TUESDAY, NOVEMBER 26th
The attendance returns showed that the boys of the school had achieved the highest percentage of attendance (96.1%) in Birmingham during the five weeks ending November 8th. This was the second consecutive occasion on which they had had this distinction.

1913
SATURDAY, JANUARY 18th
After an interval extending from September 28th, during which the Aston playing field was not available, school football was recommenced in the district today. Of course, with so many weeks of the season wasted, it was found impossible to carry out the league programme as in former years. The sixteen schools in the competition had, therefore, been divided into four divisions and the four champions of their divisions would eventually meet for the possession of the shield and medals. Unfortunately, the school was unable to distinguish itself over the next two months, bowing out of the competition in the early stages.

WEDNESDAY, APRIL 23rd
The school was closed for the day as Her Royal Highness, Princess Louise, Duchess of Argyle, was visiting Birmingham for the purpose of laying the foundation stone of the new Children's Hospital, and to unveil a statue of the late King Edward VII.

FRIDAY, MAY 23rd
Empire Day was once again celebrated. Ordinary lessons were suspended at 2. 15p. m and a lesson on patriotism given throughout the school, followed by the National Hymn, songs, recitations and a dramatised history lesson of the Battle of Crecy. The afternoon concluded with the singing of the National Anthem and the saluting of the flag.

TUESDAY, JUNE 17th
During the afternoon, the girls gave a display of old English dances, maypole dancing and singing in the playground. The boys, in charge of their respective teachers, were allowed to witness this display!

JULY

A typical school report of the time, this one for Daisy Archer, aged 13, at the end of the summer term.

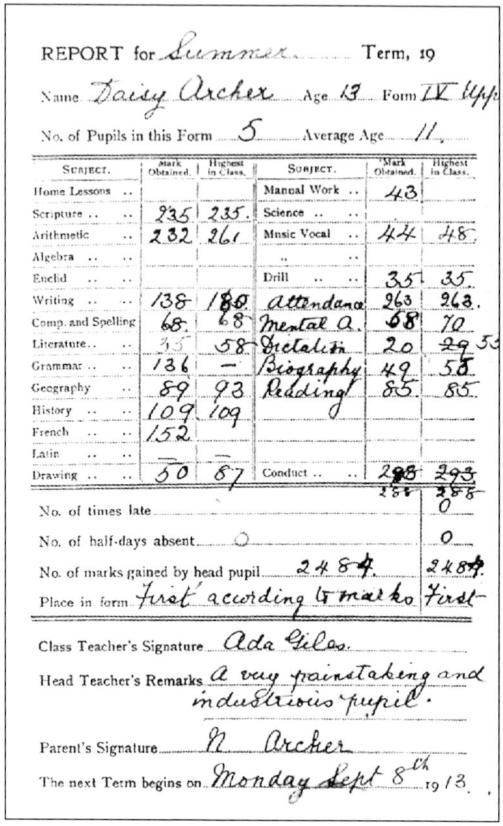
REPORT for Summer Term, 19

Name Daisy Archer Age 13 Form IV Upp.

No. of Pupils in this Form 5 Average Age 11.

Subject.	Mark Obtained.	Highest in Class.	Subject.	Mark Obtained.	Highest in Class.
Home Lessons ..			Manual Work ..	43	
Scripture	235	235.	Science		
Arithmetic ..	232	261	Music Vocal ..	44	48.
Algebra			.. ..		
Euclid			Drill	35	35.
Writing	138	180.	attendance	263	263.
Comp. and Spelling	68.	68	Mental A.	68	70
Literature	35	58	Dictation	20	29 53
Grammar	136	–	Biography	49	58
Geography ..	89	93	Reading	85.	85.
History	109	109			
French	152				
Latin	–	–			
Drawing	50	87	Conduct	288	288

No. of times late 0

No. of half-days absent 0 0

No. of marks gained by head pupil 2484. 2484.

Place in form First according to marks First

Class Teacher's Signature Ada Giles.

Head Teacher's Remarks A very painstaking and industrious pupil.

Parent's Signature N. Archer

The next Term begins on Monday Sept 8th 1913.

School Report, Summer 1913.

SATURDAY, AUGUST 23rd

The Erdington Swimming Club held their second annual sports at Brookvale Park open-air baths. The tit-bit of the afternoon was the Erdington schoolboys' championship. Boys from the National, Deykin Avenue, Moor End and Slade Road schools took part in the 2 lengths' race, which was won by Dennett of Slade Road. He was presented with a gold-centre medal for himself and the championship cup – Paget Evans cup – to be held by the school over the next twelve months. It was hoped at the time that his success would stimulate the boys of Erdington to much greater efforts in the useful art of swimming.

MONDAY, SEPTEMBER 8th

Slade Road Evening School opened for girls, women, youths and men to enrol.

MONDAY, SEPTEMBER 15th

On its first night, the Evening School admitted 90 males and 57 females. Initially, there was a technical course for males, a domestic course for females and a commercial course for both sexes. Eight staff were in attendance on that first night, but this was increased to eleven two nights later. Within a week, courses in English, Art, Cookery, Millinery and Domestic Economy had been added.

WEDNESDAY, NOVEMBER 5th

The average numbers attending classes at the Evening School during the week fell, because many of the younger students took the night off to celebrate Bonfire Night.

SATURDAY, NOVEMBER 29th

The time was when the school had a football team to be treated with respect but, this year, that teachers' bogey – casual labour – had played havoc with them. Burlington Street scored yet another four goals against them without reply and ought to have got more.

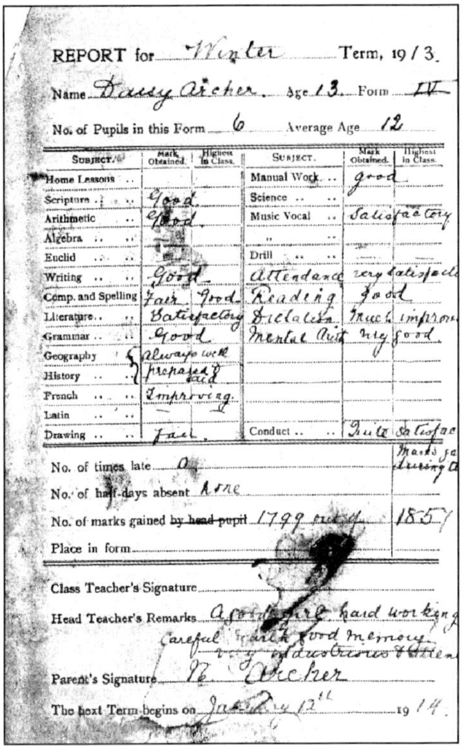

REPORT for Winter Term, 1913.

Name Daisy Archer. Age 13. Form IV

No. of Pupils in this Form 6 Average Age 12

Subject.	Mark Obtained.	Highest in Class.	Subject.	Mark Obtained.	Highest in Class.
Home Lessons			Manual Work	good	
Scripture	Good.		Science		
Arithmetic	Good.		Music Vocal	Satisfactory	
Algebra					
Euclid			Drill		
Writing	Good		Attendance	very satisfactory	
Comp. and Spelling	Fair	Good	Reading	good	
Literature	Satisfactory		Dictation	Much improved	
Grammar	Good		Mental Arit	very good.	
Geography	always well				
History	prepared				
French	Improving.				
Latin	—				
Drawing	Fair		Conduct	Quite Satisfac	

No. of times late 0

No. of half-days absent None

No. of marks gained ~~by head pupil~~ 1799 [illegible] 1857

Place in form

Class Teacher's Signature

Head Teacher's Remarks A good girl, hard working, careful with good memory. ~~very industrious & atten~~

Parent's Signature M. Archer

The next Term begins on January 12th 1914.

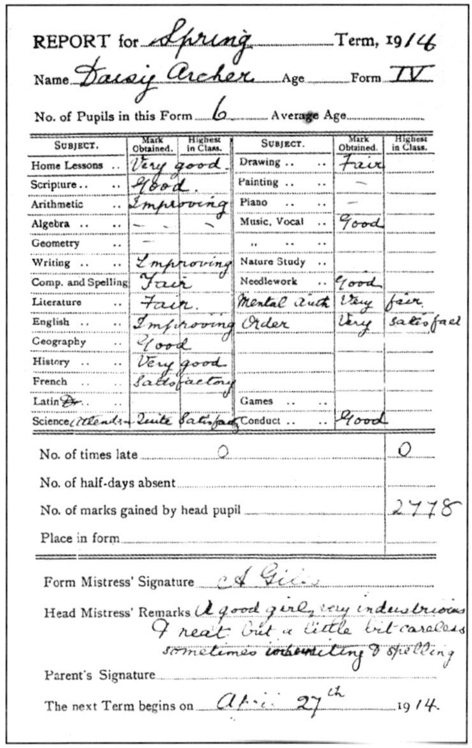

REPORT for Spring Term, 1914

Name Daisy Archer Age Form IV

No. of Pupils in this Form 6 Average Age

Subject.	Mark Obtained.	Highest in Class.	Subject.	Mark Obtained.	Highest in Class.
Home Lessons	Very good.		Drawing	Fair	
Scripture	Good.		Painting	—	
Arithmetic	Improving		Piano	—	
Algebra	—		Music, Vocal	Good	
Geometry	—				
Writing	Improving		Nature Study		
Comp. and Spelling	Fair		Needlework	Good	
Literature	Fair.		Mental Arith	Very fair.	
English	Improving		Order	Very satisfactory	
Geography	Good				
History	Very good.				
French	Satisfactory				
Latin			Games		
Science	Quite Satisfactory		Conduct	Good	

No. of times late 0 0

No. of half-days absent

No. of marks gained by head pupil 2778

Place in form

Form Mistress' Signature A Giles

Head Mistress' Remarks A good girl, very industrious & neat but a little bit careless sometimes [illegible] & spelling

Parent's Signature

The next Term begins on April 27th 1914.

Left: School Report, Winter 1913. Right: School Report, Spring 1914.

DECEMBER

Daisy Archer was still in Form IV, under the tutorship of Ada Giles, as we reached the end of the winter term.

1914

FRIDAY, JANUARY 30th

The appointment of Miss Alice Bertha Horne, who had been Headmistress of the Junior department since September 1st, 1910, terminated today. She left to become Headmistress of Osborne Road Girls' School.

TUESDAY, MARCH 24th to FRIDAY, MARCH 27th

In the Junior department, the acting Headmistress, Mrs Ward, examined all the children with regard to their Arithmetic, Transcription, Memory Dictation, Pencil Drawing, Reading as well as Pastel and Brushwork. The results were found to be very satisfactory.

FRIDAY, APRIL 10th

The end of the spring term, and another good report for Daisy Archer.

	P	W	L	D	F	A	PTS
GOWER STREET	13	11	1	1	51	8	23
ALBERT ROAD	13	10	2	1	28	8	21
ASTON LANE	13	9	2	2	26	10	20
DEYKIN AVENUE	13	8	2	3	21	8	19
HIGHER ELEMENTARY	13	8	4	1	30	17	17
STATION ROAD	13	6	4	3	38	12	15
BURLINGTON STREET	13	5	4	4	24	9	14
VICARAGE ROAD	13	5	4	4	21	19	14
THOMAS STREET	13	5	5	3	19	18	13
CANTERBURY ROAD	13	4	8	1	14	30	9
ALMA STREET	13	2	8	3	8	32	7
ST MARY'S ASTON BROOK	13	2	8	3	5	23	7
LOZELLS STREET	13	1	12	0	9	65	2
SLADE ROAD	13	0	12	1	2	47	1

Aston Schools' Football League, 1913/1914.

SATURDAY, APRIL 25th
Slade Road completed their worst football season to date. They finished bottom of the Aston Schools' League, securing only one point from their thirteen fixtures, in the process scoring just two goals, as can be seen from the table.

MONDAY, MAY 4th
In view of the suggested abolition of the Junior department, an inspector from the Board of Education visited the school today to inspect the premises.

SATURDAY, JUNE 6th
The school football team might have had a bad season, but not so the Slade Road Old Boys, who played in the second division of the Sutton Coldfield and Erdington Junior League. They won their division, totalling 18 points from their 11 games, all the players receiving silver medals in the process.

TUESDAY, JULY 14th
All the Cottage Homes boys were absent this afternoon, so that they could take part in their annual sports.

MONDAY, AUGUST 24th
In the Junior department, Kate Smith commenced duties as the temporary Headmistress. Mr Martin and Mr Mountford did not return to the Boys' department after the summer break as they had been called up for military service in connection with the war.

TUESDAY and THURSDAY, SEPTEMBER 8th and 10th
15 Cottage Homes boys were away from school as they were members of the Cottage Homes Band. They were assisting with the recruitment movement for the war.

MONDAY, SEPTEMBER 14th
The Junior department was overfull, having 347 children on the roll. No more scholars were being admitted for the time being.

THURSDAY, TUESDAY and THURSDAY, SEPTEMBER 17th, 22nd and 24th
The boys in the Cottage Homes Band were away again assisting with the war recruitment effort.

WEDNESDAY, SEPTEMBER 30th
Mr Wheatley terminated his engagement with the Boys' department today as he had joined the City Battalion.

FRIDAY, NOVEMBER 20th
The lessons in the Junior School were abandoned at 3.15p.m., so that prizegiving could be held. There were 51 prizes awarded.

Erdington Homes Prize Military Band.

1915

MONDAY, JANUARY 18th
An Education Inspector's report on the Boys' department was received today.

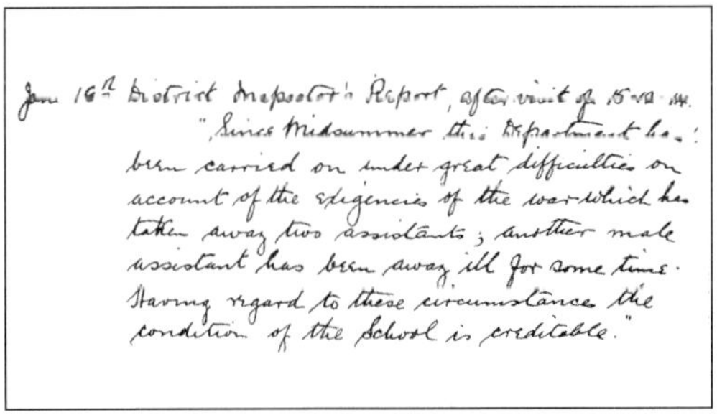

Jan 16th District Inspector's Report, after visit of 15-12-14.
"Since Midsummer this Department has been carried on under great difficulties on account of the exigencies of the war which has taken away two assistants; another male assistant has been away ill for some time. Having regard to these circumstance the condition of the School is creditable."

School Inspector's Report, 1915.

SATURDAY, JANUARY 23rd
A social evening was held at the school this evening. All the students attending the Evening School were invited along. Those that came considered it a great success. Many students, who had been working overtime during class evenings, turned up to join in the good musical programme that had been arranged by the students and their friends.

WEDNESDAY, FEBRUARY 10th
The lighting of the building was considerably reduced to meet the requirements of the Home Office.

WEDNESDAY, FEBRUARY 17th
Several parents withdrew their daughters from the classes at the Evening School due to the loneliness of the district.

SUNDAY, APRIL 11th

Mr Edmund. J. Dawes died today, having been absent through illness since November 9th, 1914. A keen and enthusiastic supporter of boys' sports, his optimism was so pronounced that, even immediately after a heavy football defeat, he could be seen encouraging the boys to greater efforts. The misfortune of losing was always softened by a cheery smile and hopeful words. He left two sons, of whose achievements he would have been proud. Reg became a teacher, eventually becoming Head Teacher of Slade Secondary Boys' School, whilst Sid was elected a councillor of the City, later becoming an alderman.

TUESDAY, JUNE 1st

A class of juniors was taken to Brookvale Park this afternoon for observation lessons.

FRIDAY, JUNE 11th

The Junior department ceased to exist today. In future, on leaving the Infants, children would move on to separate Boys' and Girls' departments, with Mr Page continuing to take charge of the boys and Miss Baum the girls.

SATURDAY, OCTOBER 16th

For the first time, girls had been invited to join the North Birmingham Schools' Sports Association. The final netball match of the season was played today between Slade Road and Canterbury Road. At full time, the result was thirteen all. Another five minutes were played, at which time the score was now fourteen each. The umpires decided to change sides and play a further five minutes. By now, excitement was running high amongst the spectators at Holford Drive, Witton. Play was watched keenly as first Slade Road and then Canterbury Road scored. At the end, Slade Road ran out winners by 18 goals to 16 and so became champions of the league, in the process winning all their matches. Other games had taken place against Alma Street, Westminster Road and Deykin Avenue. Miss Butler, the very capable and popular chief assistant, who had given a lot of time and thought to the training of the girls, coached the team, which was made up of Annie Garbett, Alice Hunt, Maud Price, Ethel Percival, Dora Short, Nellie Smith and Lois Whitby.

MONDAY, OCTOBER 18th

Owing to dense fog the attendance at the Evening School was below average. Obviously, Mr Lapwood, the teacher of Drawing, couldn't see what he was doing, as he inadvertently marked the register for Woodwork!

WEDNESDAY, NOVEMBER 24th

The falling off of numbers on the technical courses at the Evening School was due to the amount of overtime being worked by the students. The average Evening School attendance was only 102, although there were 191 students on the books.

Infant Class 2, c.1916.

FRIDAY, DECEMBER 10th
Mr J. H. Broscomb, a local Education Inspector, called into the school to say 'goodbye' on the occasion of his retirement.

1916
JANUARY
The School now had a capacity of 1324 children, consisting of 484 boys, 470 girls and 370 infants.

WEDNESDAY, FEBRUARY 16th
Owing to the fear of German Zeppelin raids, many students failed to put in an appearance during the week at the Evening School.

THURSDAY, FEBRUARY 24th
A heavy fall of snow took place on Wednesday night. In consequence, because only 40% of the children attended, the school closed down on Friday.

MONDAY, FEBRUARY 28th
Mr Emlyn Howell was called up for military service. However, as he was placed on reserve, he resumed his duties again on Wednesday.

TUESDAY, MARCH 7th

The police called at the school to complain that rays of light were escaping through the blinds and windows. Mr Shelton, the Headmaster of the Evening School, together with the caretaker, remedied the problem by hanging black charts across those windows. On the following evening, Mr Shelton carried out an inspection and considered himself satisfied that the light was now subdued.

MONDAY, MARCH 20th

The school was closed for the day due to a lack of fuel.

MONDAY, MARCH 27th

At Aston Police Court today the caretaker of the school was summoned for not having observed the blackout that was in force. He, not the school, was fined 10 shillings.

TUESDAY, MARCH 28th

Another heavy fall of snow resulted in only a quarter of the children turning up for school. In consequence, it was closed for the day.

TUESDAY, JULY 18th

All the Cottage Homes children were absent attending their annual sports.

FRIDAY, SEPTEMBER 8th

It was agreed that two classes, consisting of 25 boys each, would be sent to the Erdington Junior Technical School for practical Science on Tuesday and Wednesday afternoons respectively.

SATURDAY, SEPTEMBER 9th

The prospects for football in the Aston Schools' League, despite the unusual conditions, were considered bright. With the exception of Station Road, all of the previous season's teams had joined up. These were Alma Street; Aston Lane; Birchfield Road; Deykin Avenue; Burlington Street; Canterbury Road; Gower Street; Lozells Street; St. Mary's Aston Brook; Sacred Heart; Thomas Street; Vicarage Road and, of course, Slade Road.

TUESDAY, SEPTEMBER 12th

Albert Compton, who had left the school in July, started at King Edward's Grammar School, Aston today. A resident of the Erdington Cottage Homes, he eventually left the grammar school at the end of March 1920.

SATURDAY, SEPTEMBER 16th

At Holford Drive, in the Aston Schools' Football League, Slade Road reached top form and, by half-time, they had established a six goal lead. Seven more in the second brought the total to thirteen, while Fletcher scored Thomas Street's only point. Pritchett was in fine form and obtained no fewer than eight goals, whilst Sanders (2), Moore (2) and Newey got the rest.

SATURDAY, SEPTEMBER 30th
Out of sympathy with the munitions workers, many school football teams had a 'holiday' today, Slade School amongst them. The whole of the Aston Schools' League games were postponed.

WEDNESDAY, OCTOBER 11th
With the start of a new year on September 4th attendance at the Evening School was now running at an average of 150. However, some students were finding difficulty in attending owing to the irregularity of the trams.

SATURDAY, OCTOBER 14th
In the Aston Schools' Football League, Slade Road met Lozells Street at Holford Drive. After a fairly even first half in which Slade Road scored the only goal against the wind, they were rampant in the second, netting a further ten times. Pritchett scored ten of the goals.

Pritchett, 1917.

SATURDAY, OCTOBER 21st
Once again, the North Birmingham Shield for netball was won by the girls of Slade Road. The morning was bright, with just a touch of frost in the air, when play began in the final deciding match of the season at 10.45a.m. in Aston Park between Slade Road Girls and Fentham Road Girls. At half-time, the score was 9–5 in favour of Slade Road but, by full time, Fentham Road had levelled the score at ten goals apiece. There followed a period of extra time, during which Slade Road gained the upper hand once more, and eventually ran out winners by 14 goals to 12. The winning team was Lois Whitby, Edna Jones, Ivy Bishop, Dorothy Bayliss, Maud Dennett, Doris Nuttall and Winifred Harmer. Miss Butler, a chief assistant at the school, was once again in charge of coaching.

WEDNESDAY, NOVEMBER 15th
Mrs Hannah Cox, a teacher of dressmaking at the Evening School, was forced to resign. Her husband had joined the forces and, in consequence, she had taken over his district in the Eastern Counties as a traveller.

1917
When a boy began to play in a school's eleven at the age of nine, it was easily said that he was a born footballer. Such was the case with Pritchett, who, in 7 matches, had scored 26 goals out of a total of 42 for Slade Road School. It was no wonder that this demon goalgetter was the Aston XI's representative centre forward.

SATURDAY, JANUARY 27th

Today was recorded the untimely death of a child who attended the school. Percy Jasper died after having been ill for only a fortnight. He had contracted meningitis on top of influenza. He was described as having considerable artistic and scientific ability, as well as having high principles. All the boys in his class attended the funeral service which took place at Erdington Parish Church.

At Holford Drive, in the first round of the Aston Schools' Challenge Shield, Slade Road proved the better team throughout in their encounter with Canterbury Road. In the end, they were successful by the odd goal in three. Sanders and Pritchett were splendid in the forward line, the former being responsible for both the school's goals.

FRIDAY, FEBRUARY 16th

This morning, a party of children went to an exhibition of drawing at the Royal Society of Artists' rooms.

FRIDAY, FEBRUARY 23rd

The district inspector visited the school this morning. He said that the teachers were earnest, hardworking and anxious to put their best into their work. He expressed himself as being perfectly satisfied with what he had seen and heard.

SATURDAY, MARCH 17th

In the second round of the Aston Schools' Challenge Shield, Slade Road progressed to the next round, overwhelming Vicarage Road by five goals to nil.

SATURDAY, MARCH 24th

The semi-finals of the Aston Schools' Challenge Shield took place this morning at Holford Drive. St. Mary's went off with a rush and for the first ten minutes were the superior side. Three times in the first few minutes their forwards hit the posts but were unable to score. Then, Slade Road pulled themselves together and Pritchett, taking advantage of a miskick, scored the opening goal. A second goal from a corner kick followed before Wharton reduced the lead for St. Mary's. The second half went in favour of Slade Road who scored twice more, the goals coming from shots taken just outside the area. Thus, the school had reached the final of the Shield by a score of four to one.

SATURDAY, APRIL 21st

For the second time in their history, Slade Road were finalists in the Aston Schools' Challenge Shield. They started as favourites against Aston Lane, but soon found themselves one goal down. Pritchett, their top goalscorer, equalised, but Aston Lane again took the lead just before the interval. Although Slade Road pressed continuously in the second half, they were unable to push home their advantage and were beaten by two goals to one. However, to their consolation, they had already been crowned as champions of the Aston League.

TUESDAY, MAY 15th
The president, Alderman A. H. James, and the secretary, Mr Percy Evans, of the North Birmingham Schools' Sports Association visited the school for the purpose of presenting the trophy and medals won by the school football team.

THURSDAY, MAY 24th
Empire Day was celebrated in the afternoon.

FRIDAY, JULY 13th
In the Boys' department, 24 children went in for the Secondary and Grammar Schools' examinations. All eight boys who took the Suffolk Street Secondary School examination passed, but only two of them chose to go. It was a matter of expense!

TUESDAY, JULY 17th
All the Cottage Homes children were away from school during the afternoon as it was the occasion of their sports.

FRIDAY, JULY 27th
Richard Maddison was awarded third prize in the Fallows History Prize Competition.

MONDAY, AUGUST 27th
Mr Oswald Dixon, the manual instructor, was called to the colours.

SATURDAY, OCTOBER 6th
The Aston Schools' Football League was already well under way when Slade Road met Elkington Street. Although a strong wind rather spoilt play, the advantage in the first half was with Slade Road, who piled on the pressure to the effect that they were eight goals to the good when the sides changed ends. In the second half, the game was more even, although Slade Road scored again before Elkington Street got their orphan goal. Slade Road were much the speedier and cleverer act, Pritchett netting six times whilst Fell (2) and Jukes scored the other goals.

TUESDAY, OCTOBER 16th
The girls completed a hat-trick of championships when they won the North Birmingham Shield for netball for the third consecutive year. Today saw the final match of the season when they easily defeated Canterbury Road by 24 goals to 12.

FRIDAY, NOVEMBER 30th
Information was received that Mr Martin, who had been on military service since August of 1914, had received his commission as second lieutenant and been gazetted to the R. F. A.

1918

MONDAY, JANUARY 7th

The school re-opened after the Christmas break. In the interim, a new science room had been appointed. Although it now saved the boys having to go to the Technical School for their lessons, there was great difficulty in obtaining apparatus.

TUESDAY and THURSDAY, JANUARY 15th and 17th

Heavy snowstorms reduced attendances by 20%.

THURSDAY, FEBRUARY 7th

An address on hygiene and alcohol was given to the older boys today.

FRIDAY, MARCH 8th

In connection with the School's War Savings Association, 387 war savings certificates were sold during this, 'Dreadnought Week'. The certificates cost 15s 6d each, the aim being that Birmingham alone should contribute £2.5 million pounds towards the effort during the week, this being the cost of a Super-Dreadnought. By the following day, the people and businesses of Birmingham had exceeded this total by over £200,000.

SATURDAY, MARCH 9th

Slade Road had once again reached the semi-finals of the Aston Schools' Challenge Shield. The game with Thomas Street was evenly contested though the 'Toms' had the better of the midfield exchanges. Unfortunately, their shooting was rather erratic and the 'Slades' scored first through Pritchett. There was an awkward wind and the goalkeeper was rather surprised to find the ball roll between his legs and into the net. In the second half, the 'Toms' held their own and with a fine, long, dropping shot, Piggott equalised. In the concluding stages, the 'Slades' goal had some narrow escapes and with a little luck Thomas Street might have won.

SUNDAY, MARCH 10th

A Standard 4a boy, Edwin Johnson, died today.

WEDNESDAY, MARCH 13th

In the replayed semi-final of the Aston Schools' Challenge Shield, Thomas Street were unfortunate on having their team weakened by two or three of their best players having left the school. The defence of both sides was sound, but the 'Slades' forwards were bigger and faster than their opponents. Lingard, by persistent play, scored the first goal. Wood and Hunt were a fine pair of backs but Pritchett, with a splendid, long drive, added a second. Heath, Dodgson and Fry were too good for the Thomas Street forwards and kept them at bay while Pritchett, with another long drive, scored Slade Road's third to make the game safe and send the school into the final for the second year running.

SATURDAY, MARCH 16th

Another child, Howard Johnson of Standard 4b, died today.

Slade Road had reached the quarterfinal stage of another football competition, that of the H.M.S. Birmingham Shield. This trophy had been presented to the Birmingham Education Committee in November 1916 by three members of that ship, to be competed for by elementary schools in the City. It had been given in recognition of the interest shown by the citizens of Birmingham in the ship. Slade Road, who won the toss and kicked downhill, were meeting St Johns of Sparkhill. The Slade forwards attacked vigorously and kept the home defence busy. Nott, in goal, and Cashmore at full back repeatedly saved the situation for St. Johns. Keeping up the pressure, the 'Slades' gained the win through Tilyard, who gave Nott no chance with a well-placed shot. In the second half, the 'Slades' had most of the attacking, but failed to penetrate the St. Johns' goal again.

WEDNESDAY, MARCH 20th

Slade Road had reached the final of the Aston Schools' Challenge Shield where they met Vicarage Road. A keen struggle was anticipated between these two well-balanced teams, and expectations were fully realised. It was a splendid game, strongly contested and remarkably clean. The opening stages favoured the 'Slades' but Hoare was in rare form at back and his good play was applauded repeatedly. The 'Vics' next had a look in, but smart play by their forwards was spoilt by cramped work in front of goal. Halfway through the first half, Slade Road took the lead. Langham received a good pass from Fry, raced away, and got in a beautiful centre, Pritchett netting with a rasping shot. Just before the interval, however, Vicarage Road were back on level terms when they converted from the penalty spot. Immediately from the restart, a clumsy challenge resulted in a penalty being awarded to the 'Slades'. Pritchett scored from the spot, thus restoring the one goal advantage. Play swung from end to end, but there was no further scoring and Slade Road ran out winners by two goals to one. Having just failed to win the league by a single point, they had succeeded in having their name inscribed on the Challenge Shield for the second time in six years.

SATURDAY, APRIL 20th

Slade Road visited the Pickwick Club ground to play College Road in the semi final of the H.M.S. Birmingham Shield. College Road opened the scoring but, before half-time, Slade Road had obtained the lead through goals by Pritchett and Bradnock. The second half was all one-way traffic with the school running out victors by seven goals to one. They were now in the final.

TUESDAY, APRIL 30th

The members of the school football team were presented today with the challenge shield and their medals by Alderman James and Mr Paget Evans.

SATURDAY, MAY 4th

The final of the H.M.S. Birmingham Shield took place at Villa Park. Although the other finalists, Church Road, were a much heavier team, Slade Road were cleverer with the ball. Both goalkeepers were required to make some fine saves, the one that Wills tipped over the bar from Clarkson of Church Road being especially noteworthy. Pritchett made several magnificent runs down the wing but was unable to turn his fine work into goals. Jukes showed a fine turn of speed but was insufficiently fed. Fryer's powerful defensive work was a distinct feature of the game, although he would have been more effective if he had backed up his forwards, who were always a source of trouble to the Church Road defence. Wilkins scored twice for Church Road and was always dangerous in front of goal, though one of his goals really belonged to Clarkson, whose terrific shot cannoned off Wills and left him with an open net to shoot at. Langham netted a capital goal for Slade Road, who came close to equalising on a number of occasions, but eventually lost by the odd goal of three. The Shield and medals were presented on the ground at the close of the game.

FRIDAY, JULY 5th

The attendance had dropped to 80% in consequence of the influenza epidemic, which was prevalent all over the country.

WEDNESDAY, JULY 10th

Because of the influenza epidemic, the attendance had now fallen to 63%. In consequence, the school was closed until the following Wednesday.

SATURDAY, OCTOBER 5th

In the Aston Schools' Football League, the 'Slades' were all over the 'Marys' in the first half, during which Lingard (2), Langham and Hughes scored. The Saints fared worse in the second half, the 'Slades' scoring another nine times to run out victors by thirteen goals to nil, the scorers being Jukes (4), Langham (2), Handley, Dodgson and Lingard.

WEDNESDAY, OCTOBER 16th

The Evening School was now catering for 303 people.

SATURDAY, OCTOBER 19th

Slade Road met Lozells Street in the Aston Schools' Football League. Throughout the first half, the game was even and exciting, both sides netting twice. Towards the end of the match, Slade Road were able to overcome their opponents, running out winners by four goals to three. Both Hughes and Langham scored a brace.

FRIDAY, NOVEMBER 8th

Because of the ravages of the continuing influenza epidemic, the attendance during the first week back after the autumn holiday had fallen to 50%. Three boys, George Tomkins, Claude

Nicklin and James Read, had died of it during the holiday, so the school was once again closed for the whole of the following week.

MONDAY, NOVEMBER 11th
The Evening School decided not to open as only two students had turned in, welcome news of the Armistice having been received.

FRIDAY, DECEMBER 6th
Influenza was still having a major effect in running the school. At least a third of the children had not been in attendance during the previous week. Because the absence level was so high, it was decided to break up early for Christmas this afternoon and not re-open again until January 6th, 1919.

1919
SATURDAY, JANUARY 18th
In the Aston Schools' Football League, the defences were prominent on both sides in the game between Slade Road and Thomas Street. Slade Road were the heavier side although they were no smarter on the ball. They scored first through Langham, but Williams quickly equalised for Thomas Street. Further goals from Handley and Arkinstall restored the lead, before Berry, from a penalty, added one for Thomas Street. There was no further scoring so Slade Road came through by three goals to two.

MONDAY, JANUARY 27th
Mr Martin, who had been on military service since 1914, returned to his school duties.

SATURDAY, FEBRUARY 1st
Another match pitted Slade Road against Albert Road in the Aston Schools' Football League. With the wind in their favour, Slade Road pressed forward, scoring twice through Garbutt and Langham. In the second half, the 'Alberts' fared worse as Arkinstall (2), McLean and Langham added further goals.

SATURDAY, FEBRUARY 8th
Slade Road gave a fine exhibition of smart forward play when they faced Vicarage Road in a home game in the now renamed North Birmingham Schools' Football League. Although up against a strong defence Langham twice broke through to score in the first half. The same player added another couple in the second for Slade Road to run out winners by four goals to nil.

TUESDAY, MARCH 4th
A party of fifty children, with one teacher in charge, visited the Society of Artists' rooms this afternoon.

THURSDAY, MARCH 20th
A heavy snowstorm on Wednesday night adversely affected attendance, with one third of the children failing to put in an appearance.

TUESDAY, APRIL 1st
The girls attending the physical exercise class of the Evening School gave a display to which parents and friends were invited. It was a great success!

SATURDAY, APRIL 12th
In their final league match of the season in the North Birmingham Schools' Football League, Slade Road scored first against Canterbury Road, although the 'Lambs' soon equalised. The second half was heavily contested, but the defences of both sides held firm. The one-all draw was sufficient to give Slade Road the championship after what had been a hard-fought competition, with both Canterbury Road and Gower Street having made the fight interesting. Slade Road's title was considered a fitting conclusion to a splendid season's football, which reflected great credit on all those teachers who had so unselfishly given up so much of their leisure time for the benefit of schools' football.

THURSDAY, MAY 1st
The Junior children walked up to Erdington House with one of the maypoles in order to perform dances for the residents, this being May Day.

WEDNESDAY, MAY 21st
The school was closed today in connection with the visit to Birmingham of their Majesties the King and Queen. During the afternoon, a choir of 2000, including a few dozen from Slade Road School, who had been practising for the whole of the previous week, sang songs outside the Town Hall.

SATURDAY, MAY 31st
The cricket season had been underway for some weeks when Slade Road met Westminster Road in the North Birmingham Schools' Cricket League. Wheelwright with 16 and Handley with 11 held the school's batting together, enabling them to score 42 runs before they were all out. Westminster Road made a tough fight of it when it was their turn to take the crease, and managed to amass 34 runs before all their batsmen were back in the pavilion. Handley with 4 for 6 and Heywood with 4 for 7 did the damage.

FRIDAY, JUNE 27th
Owing to two Sunday School treats during the week, the attendances were pulled down.

SATURDAY, JUNE 28th
The school completed its first cricket season, participating in the South Division of the North Birmingham Schools' Cricket League. Handley and Heywood had been putting up good

NORTH DIVISION	P	W	L	PTS
LOZELLS STREET	6	5	1	10
VICARAGE ROAD	5	4	1	8
ST MARY'S ASTON BROOK	6	4	2	8
COWPER STREET	5	3	2	6
GOWER STREET	6	3	3	6
THOMAS STREET	6	1	5	2
ST MARY' R.C.	6	0	6	0
SOUTH DIVISION	**P**	**W**	**L**	**PTS**
CANTERBURY ROAD	6	6	0	12
SLADE ROAD	6	5	1	10
WESTMINSTER ROAD	6	4	2	8
STATION ROAD	6	3	3	6
BIRCHFIELD ROAD	6	2	4	4
ASTON LANE	5	0	5	0
ALBERT ROAD	5	0	5	0

North Birmingham Schools' Cricket League, 1919.

bowling deeds for the school. They had allowed Station Road to score just 21 and skittled Albert Road out for one fewer. Handley had got 9 batsmen out for 15 in those two matches, whilst his partner had taken 8 for 20. Slade Road, in the meantime, had annexed four points by scoring 30 and 31 respectively. They finished very creditable runners up, winning five of the six matches played. Their only loss came in the final encounter against Canterbury Road, who had also won all their fixtures. Canterbury Road went on to become champions beating the winners of the North Division, Vicarage Road, in the Championship Final.

THURSDAY, JULY 3rd

Councillor J. M. Swingler and Mr Paget Evans visited the school this afternoon to present the League Shield and medals won by the football team.

WEDNESDAY, JULY 9th

Another Sunday School treat!

FRIDAY, JULY 18th

This afternoon was given as a holiday in connection with the Peace Celebrations. The infants were treated to a special tea.

SATURDAY, JULY 19th

Arrangements had been in hand for some time for the peace celebrations in Erdington. The two principal items had been the entertainment of both the young and old. Those old, poor people had been given five shillings, or its coupon equivalent, to enable them to celebrate the memorable event. The principal part of the celebrations, however, was the entertainment of all the children attending the Public Elementary Schools in the district. The infants were all treated to games and tea on Friday afternoon. This afternoon, however, all the older children, in charge of their teachers, marched from their respective schools to Rookery Park, the numbers being as follows: Fentham Road Council School 266; Moor End Council School 405; Osborne Road

Council School 624; Ryland Road Council School 264; Church of England, High Street 321; Roman Catholic, Sutton Road 227 and, last but not least, Slade Road Council School 951, making a grand total of 3,058 children. The proceedings commenced at 2.30 with the singing of the Doxology and the saluting of the National Flag, after which there was a period of silence in memory of those who had fallen in the war. The children then sang *Land of Hope and Glory*; *Ye Mariners of England*; *Kipling's Children's Song* and the *National Anthem* before being entertained to various games and sports. Amusements provided included entertainment from Swinnerton's Band. Mr Howard Morris, a local greengrocer from Slade Road, threw pennies for the children of Slade School to fight over. At 4.30, at the sound of a bugle, all the children assembled in their several units in order to march back to their respective schools. On returning to school, a tea was laid on for everyone, before, doubtless worn out and happy, the children were handed over to their parents. Every child also received a Peace Medal.

MONDAY, SEPTEMBER 1st
The school re-opened today after the midsummer holiday. On top of the normal four weeks, an extra week had been granted in response to the express wish of His Majesty the King.

WEDNESDAY, SEPTEMBER 17th
Having passed the entrance examination, Louis Day, another Cottage Homer, who had been educated at Slade Road School for the previous four years, started at King Edward's Grammar School, Aston today.

SATURDAY, SEPTEMBER 20th
The North Birmingham Schools' Football League was due to make a start this morning. Sixteen teams had entered the league. These were Slade Road; Osborne Road; Albert Road; Station Road; Gower Street; Lozells Street; Aston Lane; Birchfield Road; Canterbury Road; Cowper Street; Deykin Avenue; Elkington Street; Thomas Street; Vicarage Road; St. Mary's and Westminster Road.

SATURDAY, OCTOBER 4th
Early in the football season and Slade Road had a decisive win over Vicarage Road, rattling in six without reply. The combination work amongst their forwards brought its rewards in goals from McLeod (2), Hughes, Bradnock, Arkinstall and Dodgson. The score would have been much greater but for the excellent goalkeeping of Scrivens.

SATURDAY, OCTOBER 11th
Generally speaking, the number of goals scored in the North Birmingham Schools' Football League today was rather moderate. There were only eighteen in the six games that were played. However, Slade Road proved to be the exception putting five past the 'keeper of Station Road without reply. They were considered fortunate in possessing players of more than average size. Handley (2), Heywood, Arkinstall and Marston were on target for the school.

SATURDAY, DECEMBER 13th

In the North Birmingham Schools' Football League, the Slade Road versus Thomas Street game was considered rather special, for it was a case of 'Greek meeting Greek'. Thomas Street, with the wind in their faces, had to act mainly on the defensive in the first half. In spite of good work by their full backs, Slade Road penetrated their defence twice through Marston and Hughes. Gallant attempts were made to reduce the lead, but the 'Slades' defence stood firm. After the interval, Thomas Street took up the attack, but were only able to score once. Dodgson for Slade Road put in sterling work at left back to hold them at bay.

1920

MONDAY and TUESDAY, JANUARY 19th and 20th

Mr William Shelton was away part of Monday afternoon and the whole of Tuesday at the new Handsworth Junior Technical School conducting an admission examination.

SATURDAY, JANUARY 24th

In the first round of the North Birmingham Schools' Challenge Shield, Slade Road, who were unbeaten in the league with 10 points, came up against Canterbury Road, who had likewise won all their five matches. Bradnock of Slade Road scored three goals in the first half and one in the second. The 'Lambs' were weak and couldn't shoot for 'nuts' and, in consequence, Slade Road won comfortably.

FRIDAY, JANUARY 30th

Two classes of boys, accompanied by their teachers, paid a visit to Bostock and Wombwells Menagerie at the junction of Aston Road and Lower Corporation Street this afternoon for a descriptive lecture, and performance by the highly-trained animals of Captain Wombwell, Professor Luck and Lieutenant Barnard. With elephants both large and small – 'Baby Tiny' was 2½ years old and 4½ feet tall, whilst 'Jenny' was 33 years of age and 11 feet – an almost-human ape, as well as a variety of other animals, the children were educated and entertained to an animal exhibition of extraordinary proportions.

SATURDAY, JANUARY 31st

Mr William Shelton's engagement officially terminated today, as he had been appointed Headmaster of the Handsworth Junior Technical School from February 1st. He had been employed in the Boys' department of Slade Road since February 1st, 1912. The boys presented him with a briefcase as a present. He was to remain at the Technical School until his retirement on May 1st, 1933, aged sixty two.

TUESDAY, FEBRUARY 3rd

The first four boys to pass the entrance examination for the Handsworth Junior Technical School attended there today. Frederick Cox, Arthur Izod, George Maddison and Charles Morris were all awarded free scholarships. This meant that they were entitled to a grant of fifteen shillings a term for a period of two years. They all successfully completed their courses.

Slade Road School Football Team 1919/1920 season.

SATURDAY, FEBRUARY 14th
Once again Bradnock wore his shooting boots, this time to the discomfiture of Birchfield Road. The final score in this North Birmingham Schools' League match was five goals to nil, Bradnock accounting for three of them.

SATURDAY, FEBRUARY 28th
St. Mary's had obviously profited from some good advice, for they were much smarter on the ball than they had been all season, when they met Slade Road in a North Birmingham Schools' League match. It was a close-run thing before the irrepressible Bradnock scored the solitary goal that gave Slade Road the win.

SATURDAY, MARCH 13th
There was a remarkable similarity in the North Birmingham Schools' Football League games between Slade Road and Osborne Road, and Westminster Road and Cowper Street. In both cases the weaker team led at the interval by a goal. However, in the second half, Slade Road netted six times as did Cowper Street.

MONDAY, MARCH 15th
In consequence of a heavy fall of snow, and the absence of a lot of children, the school closed down for the day.

SATURDAY, MARCH 20th
Slade Road and Aston Lane had fought their way into the final of the North Birmingham Schools' Football Challenge Shield by defeating Elkington Street and Cowper Street

respectively. Slade Road beat the 'Elks' by the odd goal in three while Aston Lane triumphed by three goals to one over the 'Cowboys'. It was a sad day for those two schools and their supporters who had had hopes of seeing the deadly rivals in the final. As it was, in the final a close and intense battle ensued, with the result in doubt until the final whistle – Aston Lane ran out winners by two goals to one.

THURSDAY, APRIL 15th
A swimming course was commenced this morning.

THURSDAY, APRIL 22nd
Councillor J. M. Swingler and Mr Paget Evans visited the school for the purpose of presenting the football team with their medals.

TUESDAY, JUNE 1st
Miss Baum lectured three girls in her office concerning their behaviour in the street. After school hours, she had observed them walking along laughing and enjoying themselves, and not even wearing their navy blue and yellow knitted hats either!

TUESDAY, JUNE 22nd
Another Sunday School treat resulted in many children being absent.

MONDAY, JUNE 28th
As Mr William Shelton, Headmaster of the Evening School, had been appointed Headmaster of the new Handsworth Junior Technical School from February 1st, the committee desired him to relinquish his post at Slade Road Evening School with immediate effect. Mr Valentine Thomas took up the vacant position from September 13th, eventually retiring from adult teaching on August 31st, 1942 at the age of 63.

WEDNESDAY, JULY 7th
A further Sunday School treat!

THURSDAY, JULY 8th
A party of 35 boys in charge of Mr Howell visited the Prince of Wales Theatre to see the matinee performance of *The Merchant of Venice*. Directed by Henry Baynton – he also played Shylock – it further starred Lilian Braithwaite as Portia. Part of a Shakespeare season, a different one of his plays was performed each day, with special terms being laid on for schools.

TUESDAY, JULY 13th
A representative of the Aston Labour Exchange attended the school today for the purpose of interviewing 'Leavers'. The parents of twelve of the boys also attended.

Competing in the North Birmingham Schools' Athletics Championships for the first time, the boys of the school won the sports shield.

NORTH DIVISION				
	P	W	L	PTS
STATION ROAD	8	7	1	14
ALBERT ROAD	8	6	2	12
BIRCHFIELD ROAD	8	6	2	12
CANTERBURY ROAD	8	6	2	12
SACRED HEART	8	4	4	8
ASTON LANE	8	3	5	6
SLADE ROAD	8	2	6	4
WESTMINSTER ROAD	8	2	6	4
DEYKIN AVENUE	8	0	8	0

SOUTH DIVISION					
	P	W	L	T	PTS
ST. MARY'S	7	7	0	0	14
VICARAGE ROAD	7	5	2	0	10
BURLINGTON STREET	7	4	3	0	8
LOZELLS STREET	7	4	3	0	8
GOWER STREET	7	3	3	1	7
THOMAS STREET	7	2	5	0	4
COWPER STREET	7	1	5	1	3
ELKINGTON STREET	7	1	6	0	2

North Birmingham Schools' Cricket League, 1920.

SATURDAY, JULY 17th
In their second season in the North Birmingham Schools' Cricket League, Slade Road did not fare so well. This time, competing in the North Division, they were only able to win two of their eight fixtures and consequently could only finish seventh.

SATURDAY, SEPTEMBER 11th
The Erdington Swimming Club held their championships at Brookvale Park open-air swimming baths. In the event for the Erdington Schools' championship, J. Law of Slade Road placed third.

FRIDAY, OCTOBER 8th
A schools' football league was formed embracing all the schools in Erdington. The Erdington Schools' Organised Games Association – of which the football league was one part – intended launching out in the direction of cricket in due season, hockey and netball for girls, and a general sports day for the schools of Erdington. The association's founding schools were Osborne Road; Ryland Road; Moor End Lane; the National; St. Thomas'; the Erdington Cottage Homes; Fentham Road and, of course, Slade Road.

THURSDAY, DECEMBER 2nd
A lesson was given to the older boys on temperance and hygiene.

SATURDAY, DECEMBER 11th
At Jaffray Road, in the second round of the Birmingham and District Schools' Shield, Erdington met Kings Norton. Yates of Osborne Road School, the captain, won the toss and

decided to kick with what little wind there was. Five representatives from Slade Road School played that day – Rawlings and Jackson at right and left half; Green on the right wing; Martin and Hayward at inside and outside left. Kings Norton took the lead early on, before a sizzling run by Green, who passed two defenders, ended with a centre that found Yates, who blasted the ball into the corner of the net, beating the goalkeeper all ends up. Thus the scores were tied. For most of the first half Kings Norton pressed strongly, but were unable to press home their advantage. Erdington went in at half-time a goal to the good, when Green yet again sped down the wing, his centre finding Yates, who put the ball home. Despite continued strong pressure from the boys of Kings Norton – they seemed permanently encamped in the Erdington half of the field – at last the ball came out to the left wing, where Hayward took it out of danger and passed to Yates, for the lad from Osborne Road to net his hat trick. In the dying minutes the desperate efforts of Kings Norton eventually paid off, although it was too little too late. Erdington had won by the odd goal in five.

Only four weeks earlier the same five lads had represented Erdington, when they had entertained Wolverhampton in the first round of the English Schools' Shield at the Cottage Homes grounds, Reservoir Road in front of 1500 wildly cheering spectators. On that occasion the crowd were treated to a goalscoring spectacular with Erdington running out winners by six goals to five.

1921

THURSDAY, FEBRUARY 24th

A party of 52 boys paid a visit to the Royal Society of Artists' rooms to view an exhibition of drawings from the elementary schools.

FRIDAY, MARCH 4th

The Headmaster, Mr Page, was taken ill.

SATURDAY, APRIL 9th

In the inaugural season of the Erdington Schools' Football League, Slade Road finished as runners up to Osborne Road.

There had been little to choose between the teams all through the season and, in the end, only one point separated them.

	P	W	L	D	F	A	PTS
OSBORNE ROAD	12	11	1	0	65	5	22
SLADE ROAD	12	10	1	1	46	8	21
NATIONAL	12	7	3	2	29	21	16
MOOR END	12	3	7	2	12	39	8
RYLAND ROAD	12	2	8	2	10	27	6
COTTAGE HOMES	12	1	7	4	12	37	6
ST.THOMAS'	12	2	9	1	10	47	5

Erdington Schools' Football League, 1920/1921.

FRIDAY, APRIL 15th

Joseph Ingles, aged 8, residing in the Cottage Homes, was knocked down in Slade Road whilst on the way home at midday. He had kicked a brick into the road and run after it in order to kick it again. Unfortunately, he did not see the delivery van as he ran behind a vehicle passing in the opposite direction and was struck. He died as a result of the accident.

SATURDAY, APRIL 16th

The Erdington Elementary Schools' football team met the Wednesbury boys in the semi-final of the Birmingham and District Schools' Shield. Slade Road were represented in the Erdington team by Russell, Tansley, Jackson and Hayward. Unfortunately, they were totally outclassed by the Wednesbury lads, who won by eleven goals to one.

MONDAY, APRIL 18th

At the Coroner's inquest into the death of Joseph Ingles, a verdict of accidental death was recorded. All the teachers in the school were asked to speak strongly to the children in their charge about street dangers.

THURSDAY, APRIL 28th

On the opening day of the Midland Competition Festival at the Town Hall, the Girls' School choir, conducted by Miss Ada Butler, won the cantata class for all Public Elementary Girls' School choirs in Birmingham. They were required to perform *Orpheus* by Rathbone.

FRIDAY, APRIL 29th

It was especially noted that, of seventeen boys leaving today, only two had situations fixed, whilst three were going on to the Junior Technical School, with seven having no prospect of employment at all.

TUESDAY, MAY 3rd

Another young schoolchild died today as a result of a road accident in Slade Road. Alice Mary Cluley, aged 5, living at 22 Slade Road, ran across in front of a tramcar and was knocked down by a motor vehicle that had overtaken it. The rear wheel passed over her head and she died instantly. The coroner returned a verdict of accidental death.

TUESDAY, MAY 10th

The Headmaster of the Boys' School, Mr Henry Page, died today after an illness lasting nine weeks. Heart disease, falling upon old-time rheumatism, was the serious source of trouble, with dropsy adding to the problem. He passed peaceably away in his 59th year, leaving a widow and three daughters to mourn his loss.

SATURDAY, MAY 14th

At Witton Cemetery, the funeral took place of the late Headmaster. A resident of Cecil Road, he was one of the best known and highly-respected dominoes of Erdington. His failing health had been a source of concern for some years, his friends being most desirous that he should leave to enjoy his superannuation allowance. Successive generations of boys, whose faculties he had trained and whose characters he had helped to form, learned not merely to respect him but to love and reverence one who had done so much, and on such admirable lines to prepare them for the future battle in life. Mr Page had taken a considerable interest in municipal affairs in Erdington in the days of the old District Council, and for some years acted as election agent to the successful candidate for the Short Heath Ward. On Saturday morning, at the interment in the family grave, a most impressive feature was the singing at the graveside of the hymn *O God our help in ages past* by twenty-five of the elder scholars of the Boys' School. Three members of the teaching staff were in attendance. There were a great number of floral wreaths and crosses, which included tributes from all three departments of the school as well as from the boys themselves. Children from the school used to refer to him affectionately as 'Pudgy Page'. On his arrival at school each morning, he would hurry up the playground to the gate that divided the Boys' department from the rest of the school. The children could not help but notice how out of breath he was, and how he had to lean on his rolled-up umbrella when he reached the gate before he could go any further. A sad loss!

FRIDAY, MAY 27th
Concern was being expressed about the dangerous condition of the playground.

Top Left: Girls' School class standard 2b, c.1920. Top Right: Girls' School class standard 2a, c.1921. Bottom Left: Boys' School class standard 8, c.1920. Bottom Right: Boys' School class standard 8, c.1921.

Top Left: Infant department, c.1920. Top Right: Infant department class 6, c.1922. Bottom Left: Infant department, c.1921. Bottom Right: Infant department class 5, c.1922.

TUESDAY, JUNE 14th
All the Cottage Homes children were away, as it was the occasion of their annual sports day this afternoon. It was known that at least 105 boys were involved.

WEDNESDAY and THURSDAY, JUNE 15th and 16th
The first Erdington Schools' Sports took place at the Cottage Homes grounds. The numerous heats were decided on the Wednesday evening, leaving the following evening free for the finals and the championships. As on the opening day, the weather was ideal for the purpose. A big crowd of freely-admitted boys and girls, together with a large gathering of parents, relatives and friends attended, besides other interested spectators. Altogether, there were 2, 182 entries, not including those for the schools' championships. The officials had a most arduous task, having to organise 177 heats with a dozen competitors in each and 40 finals and championship events. Championship shields were donated by Mr Wiggins-Davies and the famous prize band of the Cottage Homes, under the able and experienced conductorship of Mr Grainger, entertained the crowd with high-class and popular musical selections. Slade Road Boys' School not only won the tug of war, but took the overall Boys' Championship securing twice as many points as the runners up, Moor End Council School. The orderliness of the competitors largely contributed to the events getting off so expeditiously. It was favourably commented on and was a theme of universal

admiration. Many prizes were donated, notably two finger football tables by Mr Iles of the Daisy Vacuum Company. Mrs Gelling devoted almost the whole of a long Thursday evening distributing the prizes as they became due at the end of the various events. She had a kindly smile, often accompanied by an encouraging word for each of the recipients. Many dignitaries were in evidence besides those already mentioned, these including Councillor and Mrs Keatley; the Right Reverend Lord Abbot of Erdington, the Reverend Father Lambert Nolle; the Reverend A. R. Davies; and Councillor R. R. Gelling, who was chairman of the Parks Committee of Birmingham City Corporation.

Eric Russell with Wiggins-Davies Shield, 1921.

SATURDAY, JUNE 18th
It was considered a sad but illuminating commentary on the increasing street dangers of the times that there had been three fatal motor accidents involving children in Slade Road during the previous few weeks. Parents of the younger children were now becoming afraid to send them to school, and the seriousness of the situation can be realised by the fact that increased police supervision was being called for in the acknowledged danger zone by Councillor R. R. Gelling, the ward's representative.

TUESDAY, JUNE 21st
The newly-appointed Headmaster of the Boys' School, Mr Edmund Jones, paid a visit to the school today. He was fifty years of age, lived in Birchfield, and had been a schoolmaster in that area for twenty-five years. His starting salary was £489 per annum.

FRIDAY, JULY 1st
Mr Edmund Jones officially took up his duties as Headmaster of the Boys' School.

WEDNESDAY, JULY 13th
Another Sunday School treat seriously affected the attendance.

WEDNESDAY, JULY 20th
The new Headmaster of the Boys' School had noticed how prevalent unpunctuality was. On that day alone, 35 boys had been late in the morning, whilst over 50 had failed to make it back to school in time after lunch.

SATURDAY, AUGUST 27th
At the 10th annual Erdington Swimming Club's sports held at Brookvale Park open-air swimming baths, the boys of Slade Road Council School placed second in the Erdington Schools' championship, being narrowly beaten by Sir Josiah Mason's Orphanage.

THURSDAY, SEPTEMBER 1st
Whilst in the playground, a lad was struck by a stone on the lip, such that it had become swollen. The dangerous state of the playground was once again raised with the Chief Education Officer.

MONDAY, SEPTEMBER 19th
The Evening School re-opened after the summer vacation. For reasons of economy it had been considerably reduced in size. The Art section had, for the same reason, been closed down.

TUESDAY, SEPTEMBER 27th
A staff meeting was held this afternoon to discuss the prevalence of late coming, the smartening up of assemblies and the use and abuse of silent reading.

TUESDAY, OCTOBER 11th
A panoramic photograph of the pupils was taken by Panora this morning.

FRIDAY, NOVEMBER 11th
A special Remembrance Day assembly was held between 10.50a.m. and 11.15a.m. on this, Armistice Day, during which a two minutes' silence was observed and a short service held.

FRIDAY, DECEMBER 9th
Nine tickets for scholars' boots were received from the Daily Mail for distribution to suitable children.

WEDNESDAY, DECEMBER 21st
Mr N. J. Andrew left the school today as he had been appointed Headmaster of Kennington School in Kent.

1922

MONDAY, JANUARY 16th to TUESDAY, JANUARY 24th
A number of severe snowstorms raged, reducing the attendance at times by a third.

MONDAY, JANUARY 30th
Children being children, an accident occurred in the playground during morning break. Albert Pearson was playing the game 'Release' when he accidentally collided with the wall. He had to be taken to the General Hospital where it was found that he had broken his nose.

WEDNESDAY, FEBRUARY 1st
Five students from Springfield College, Moseley commenced a three-weeks' course of teaching practice at the school.

TUESDAY, FEBRUARY 28th
A holiday was granted today, this being the occasion of the marriage of Princess Mary.

SATURDAY, MARCH 11th
By defeating Osborne Road, the school football team won the Erdington Schools' championship. The Cottage Homes played 8 games in the competition before withdrawing when they were bottom, having lost all their games. Their results were annulled.

	P	W	L	D	F	A	PTS
SLADE ROAD	12	9	2	1	34	9	19
GREEN LANES	12	6	2	4	39	18	16
CHURCH OF ENGLAND	12	8	4	0	40	27	16
OSBORNE ROAD	12	7	5	0	41	33	14
MOOR END	12	5	6	1	47	44	11
RYLAND ROAD	12	3	8	1	21	31	7
ST.THOMAS'	12	0	11	1	7	62	1

Erdington Schools' Football League, 1921/1922.

THURSDAY, MARCH 16th
Mr Edmund Jones travelled to London to attend the annual meeting of the National League for Health, Maternity and Child Welfare, of which he was a member of the Executive Council.

MONDAY, MAY 1st
School having finished for the day, Slade Road opened their campaign for the Erdington Schools' Cricket League against the Cottage Homes on the Cottage Homes grounds. Batting first, they amassed 44 runs before their innings closed, Yardley taking 8 wickets for 20 runs whilst Horton prevented a higher score by his excellent fielding. The Cottage Homes were soon in trouble losing 9 wickets by the time that 14 runs were on the board. Tom Marks, Slade Road's captain, was responsible for the damage, finishing with 7 wickets for 12 runs, every chance being held.

Slade Road			*Cottage Homes*		
Harmer	b. Yardley	8	Haddon	b. Marks	0
Lissamer	b. Haddon	1	Horton	c. Godwin b. Marks	7
Marks	b. Yardley	0	Yardley	c. Godwin b. Marks	0
Godwin	b. Yardley	0	Pierce	c. Lissamer b. Marks	3
Brampton	b. Yardley	9	Moore	b. Harmer	0
Miller	b. Yardley	2	Ellis	c. Butler b. Harmer	1
Simmons	b. Yardley	13	Hands	b. Marks	1
Nicklin	b. Price	1	Drake	b. Marks	0
Butler	not out	0	Walker	run out	2
Smith	b. Yardley	6	Fisher	b. Marks	0
Raybon	c. Pierce b. Yardley	0	Smith	not out	8
	extras	4		extras	4
		44			26

TUESDAY, MAY 9th

At the Midland Competition Festival, the Girls' School, under the tuition of Miss Ethel Cope, placed first in the competition for Children's International Dances, open to competitors over 7 years of age and under 17 who were attending any school or class within the Midland Counties.

FRIDAY, MAY 12th

There was some excellent singing by the children's choirs at the Midland Competition Festival today. Slade Road Girls' School, conducted by Miss Ada Butler, achieved second place in the event for Public Elementary Girls' School choirs in Birmingham.

MONDAY, MAY 22nd

In the school's fourth match of the current cricket campaign they met Ryland Road at Short Heath Park. Considering that the ground was very slippery, many catches were well taken; Nicklin's work in the field was excellent. Marks with 6 for 10 caused major problems for Ryland Road, whilst Harmer with 2 for 11 and Brampton 1 for 3 took the other wickets.

Ryland Road			*Slade Road*		
W. Reynolds	b. Marks	0	T. Marks	c. Baldock b. Innes	1
R. Baldock	b. Marks	1	Harmer	b. Innes	7
E. Lewis	c. Nicklin b. Marks	0	Miller	c. Lewis b. Reynolds	1
A. Morgan	b. Harmer	3	Godwin	b. Innes	2
F. Bennett	c. Brampton b. Harmer	0	Smith	c. Innes b. Reynolds	0
R. Blackwell	c. Simmons b. Brampton	2	Simmons	c. Morgan b. Reynolds	9
J. Hudson	c. Harmer b. Marks	5	Brampton	b. Reynolds	3
L. Hill	run out	5	Lissamer	b. Reynolds	0
A. Innes	c. Nicklin b. Marks	4	Hodgetts	b. Hudson	8
A. Burr	c. Nicklin b. Harmer	0	Russell	c. Bennett b. Innes	5
H. Sims	not out	4	Nicklin	not out	6
Extras		2		Extras	0
		26			42

WEDNESDAY, MAY 24th

Parents and friends were invited to witness the work of the school in progress during the afternoon. A special timetable was arranged for them to meet and discuss the work of their own children with the respective teachers.

WEDNESDAY, JUNE 14th

Six students from Springfield College, Moseley commenced a three-weeks' teaching practice this morning.

TUESDAY and WEDNESDAY, JUNE 27th and 28th

The Erdington Schools' Athletics Sports were held on these evenings at the Cottage Homes grounds. Remembrance of the organisational triumph of the previous year attracted a large and enthusiastic crowd of spectators, whose behaviour provided the police on duty with a position of comparative sinecure. Each school that participated had obviously gone to a lot of trouble to making its champions as fast as possible, for each event was extremely closely contested. Throughout both evenings, the Cottage Homes Boys' Band played numerous selections and, despite the chilly weather, the refreshment stall did a roaring trade in ice cream. The programme was long and varied and included open events for which individual prizes were offered, and championship events for which points were awarded. This year, Slade Road failed to win one of the championships, narrowly being beaten by Osborne Road by one point for the girls' trophy. The boys could only muster fourth place out of the eight schools that participated in their competition.

WEDNESDAY, JULY 19th

Erdington Schools' Cricket League – Short Heath Park

Slade Road			*Moor End Lane*		
Nicklin	c. Mousley b. Darby	2	Jones	b. Marks	7
Butler	c. Spencer b. Darby	26	Wells	c. and b. Harmer	11
Miller	c. Spencer b. Langley	0	Sadler	run out	1
Russell	b. Darby	0	Mousley	run out	0
Simmons	b. Darby	2	Darby	b. Harmer	0
Brampton	c. Wells b. Langley	1	Langley	b. Marks	2
Smith	c. Sadler b. Langley	0	Thompson	c. Brampton b. Harmer	1
Harmer	b. Darby	8	Spencer	c. Simmons b. Marks	1
Marks	b. Langley	12	Baker	b. Harmer	3
Hodgetts	b. Darby	2	Madin	not out	2
Raybon	not out	5	May	run out	4
Extras		8	Extras		3
		66			35

Darby 6 for 17; Langley 4 for 28; Wells 0 for 13; Marks 3 for 16; Harmer 4 for 16

THURSDAY, JULY 20th

Slade Road played the final match of the cricket season against the National, and were soundly trounced by the Erdington League champions. In their first encounter on the tenth of June, the result had been much closer. In that match, Slade Road had scythed through the National's defences, dismissing them for only 16. They must have tasted victory, only to have it snatched from their grasp as no more than three of their players were able to score runs and they were all out for 14. The school could finish no better than fourth of the 8 competing schools after participating in 14 games. During the season, which had begun

	Played	Won	Lost	Drawn	Points
National	14	12	1	1	25
Osborne Road	14	12	2	0	24
Green Lanes	14	8	4	2	18
Slade Road	14	7	7	0	14
Moor End Lane	14	6	8	0	12
St Thomas'	14	5	8	1	11
Ryland Road	14	3	9	2	8
Cottage Homes	14	0	11	0	0

Erdington Schools' Cricket League, 1922.

back in May, both Tom Marks, the captain, and Harmer had performed heroic feats with the ball, but, unfortunately, the school's batting had not been as strong. Marks' bowling figures in six of the matches were 7 for 12; 6 for 27; 6 for 10; 6 for 19; 6 for 8 and 3 for 4. In 8 of the 14 matches, unfortunately, the school failed to put 30 runs on the scoreboard before they were all out. The remarkably keen spirit of all the boys that played in the Erdington Schools' Cricket League this season may be witnessed from the fact that three of the last nine fixtures that were played finished all square.

WEDNESDAY, JULY 26th
A typical leaving certificate of the time, this one from the Girls' School.

THURSDAY, AUGUST 31st
Miss Annie May Atherley, who had started in the Infants' department on its opening day as an uncertificated assistant, left the school today. She had achieved her certification on August 1st, 1906, being promoted three and a half years later to the position of chief assistant. Nearly 38 years of age, she had decided to go abroad and, although she intended to return, it would not be to Slade School.

SATURDAY, SEPTEMBER 16th
Saturday morning, and the weather did not look too promising, as the big ball, size number 4, used in all school leagues, was set in motion. The struggle for the Erdington

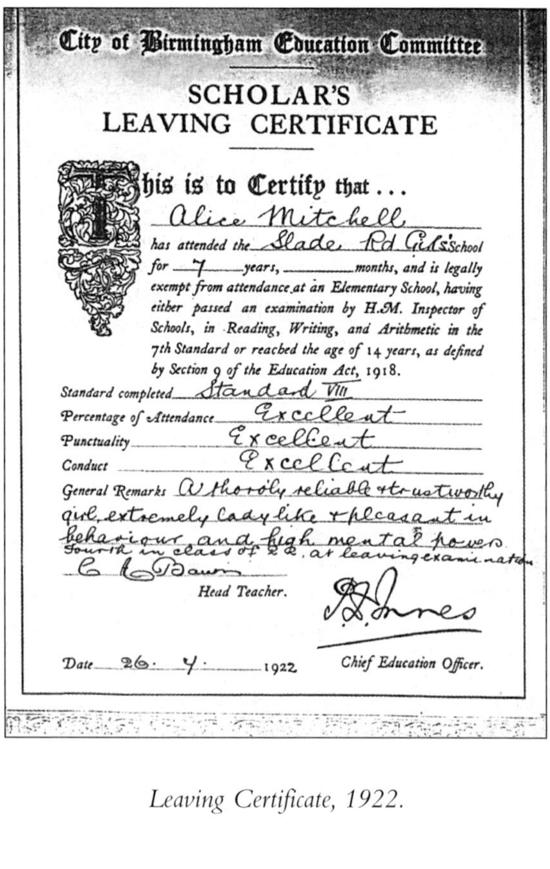

City of Birmingham Education Committee

SCHOLAR'S LEAVING CERTIFICATE

This is to Certify that . . . Alice Mitchell
has attended the Slade Rd Girls' School for 7 years, ______ months, and is legally exempt from attendance at an Elementary School, having either passed an examination by H.M. Inspector of Schools, in Reading, Writing, and Arithmetic in the 7th Standard or reached the age of 14 years, as defined by Section 9 of the Education Act, 1918.

Standard completed: Standard VIII
Percentage of Attendance: Excellent
Punctuality: Excellent
Conduct: Excellent
General Remarks: A thoroughly reliable & trustworthy girl, extremely ladylike & pleasant in behaviour and high mental powers. Fourth in class of 28 at leaving examination.

C. L. Bawn
Head Teacher.

[signature]
Chief Education Officer.

Date 26. 4. 1922

Leaving Certificate, 1922.

Schools' Football League honours had begun at Short Heath Park. There was a good muster of enthusiastic teachers and scholars from the various schools, and many new faces were seen in the different sides playing their first league games. Some of the boys, however, seemed to think that it was appropriate to stand and watch the game from behind the goalkeeper who had plenty of work to do. The goalkeeper had enough on his plate without being hampered by twenty boys around him! If they had wanted to stand in the goal, they should have gone and talked to the keeper who had nothing to do. He looked so lonely at times! Slade Road opened the new campaign against the National, who were wearing their new strip of blue and gold. As one little boy remarked, "Oh, arn't they pretty. "The result was 5–1 as the 'Slade' comfortably won the first match of the season in defence of their title against the 'Nats'. Godwin scored a hat trick, with Lissamer and Kirk adding the other two goals as 'Bubbles' at centre half kept his forwards moving well together.

SATURDAY, SEPTEMBER 23rd

The second set of fixtures were completed in ideal footballing weather. The air had a nip in it, but no wind to worry about. As was anticipated, Slade Road proved too strong for the Cottage Homes as the resounding 13–1 scoreline demonstrated. Godwin again found the mark registering six, whilst Kinning (4), Russell (2) and Raybon were the other marksmen for Slade Road.

SATURDAY, OCTOBER 7th

Considering the general state of the weather, the league was very fortunate to be able to complete the fourth set of football fixtures under ideal conditions. A brilliant sun was shining and a good crowd gathered to watch the struggles. St Thomas' started at a ferocious rate against Slade Road, who were soon a goal down before they realised what was happening. However, they settled down and a dingdong battle ensued, with neither side giving much away. Then, just before the interval, 'Bubbles' equalised. With the change of ends St Thomas' found it difficult to clear up the slope. Although they defended stubbornly they were eventually worn down with Lissamer and Kinning adding a goal each. The final score – Slade Road 3 St Thomas' 1.

SATURDAY, OCTOBER 21st

Another Saturday morning and another set of fixtures in the Erdington Schools' Football League. Ryland Road met Slade Road in what proved to be the titbit of the morning. The 'Rylanders' always rose to the occasion against the 'Slade' and today was no exception. They had never beaten them although they came close this morning. Ryland Road held the lead for the greater portion of the game before two slips in defence let in Godwin and Kinning to give Slade Road the victory.

FRIDAY, OCTOBER 27th

Special lessons on temperance were given to the older boys.

FRIDAY, NOVEMBER 10th

In response to the appeal of Earl Haig, poppies were sold in the school today.

SATURDAY, NOVEMBER 11th

Armistice Day dawned and a glorious morning it was too. During the first football matches of the morning in the Erdington Schools' Football League, the two minutes' silence occurred, which was observed most reverently by everyone. At 11a.m., the memorable hour, the whistle was blown and everyone stood bareheaded where they were. The silence was most perfect and impressive.

SATURDAY, NOVEMBER 18th

In the English Schools' football competition, Erdington met North Staffs. The Erdington team had been selected at trials that were held a month earlier and included two players from Slade Road, Simmons and Godwin. Their official colours were vertical stripes of black and white, similar to those of Moor End Lane.

THURSDAY, DECEMBER 7th

Six tickets were received for scholars' boots from the Daily Mail Xmas Tree Fund and were suitably distributed.

FRIDAY, DECEMBER 22nd

A sum of £14.7s.6d. was collected by the children and forwarded to the treasurer of the Children's Charities Fund of the N.U.T.

1923

SATURDAY, JANUARY 20th

With 4 games to go in the football campaign of the Erdington Schools' League, the table looked like this.

	played	won	lost	drawn	for	against	points
GREEN LANES	10	9	0	1	43	5	19
OSBORNE ROAD	10	8	1	1	54	9	17
SLADE ROAD	10	7	3	0	43	13	14
MOOR END LANE	10	5	5	0	22	29	10
RYLAND ROAD	10	3	5	2	15	23	8
NATIONAL	10	2	6	2	13	42	6
COTTAGE HOMES	10	1	7	2	7	58	4
ST. THOMAS'	10	1	9	0	16	34	2

Erdington Schools' Football League, 1922/1923.

Top and Centre: Maypole Dancing, c.1922.
Bottom: Maypole Dancing, c.1923.

MONDAY, FEBRUARY 19th
Painters and decorators were engaged at the school from today. The minimum of inconvenience appeared to be caused, such that the work of the children was not unduly interfered with over the next few weeks.

FRIDAY, MARCH 2nd
A film entitled *Hullo Mars*, amongst others, was shown at the school during the week by the Daily Mail (London). Prizes were offered for the best essays in a competition being run by the newspaper.

SATURDAY, MARCH 3rd
The Erdington Schools' football season had now concluded. Slade Road failed to win the championship for a second time, the title going to Green Lanes – a school incidentally that was in Sutton Coldfield, not Erdington – who remained unbeaten throughout.

THURSDAY, MARCH 15th
Prizes offered by the Daily Mail for the essay competition were awarded. Henry Doust, aged 10, won the first prize of a £1, whilst second and third prizes were presented of 10 shillings and 5 shillings each respectively.

TUESDAY, MARCH 20th
The painters and decorators completed their work today.

THURSDAY, APRIL 26th
The School was on holiday today due to the marriage of the Duke of York.

MONDAY, APRIL 30th
Mrs Mary Jane Ward officially retired from the Girls' School at the age of sixty. She had first started work as a teacher with the Aston School Board, leaving their service in 1891 when employed as Headmistress of Alma Street. It was not until March 1907 that she sought work as a teacher once again. As she was married, she must have lost her husband during the interim which allowed her to seek re-employment in the teaching profession. Married

women were not allowed to work as teachers. For the last 16 years, she had been at Slade Road School, serving in the Girls' department, except for a period of 4 years in the Junior department between 1911 and 1915. Her salary at retirement was £304p.a.

TUESDAY, MAY 1st

On the opening day at the Midland Musical Festival held in the Town Hall, in the competition for Children's International Dances, open to competitors over 7 years of age and under 17 attending a school or class in the Midland Counties, Miss Ethel Cope yet again guided her girls to first place with 90 marks out of 100.

At the meeting of Birmingham City Council, the Lord Mayor, Alderman David Davis, announced the receipt of a letter from Councillor Gelling offering, on behalf of a body of subscribers, a piece of freehold land with a frontage to Jaffray Road to be used for the purpose of organised games by children attending the Erdington Schools. Proposed and seconded on the conditions laid down by the donors, the resolution was carried with the proviso that the Education Committee provide such ground fixtures as were thought necessary. It was realised that this gift would enable the schools of Erdington to benefit much earlier in the matter of playing fields than others elsewhere.

WEDNESDAY, MAY 2nd

A choir of 40 boys competed at the Midland Musical Festival today, being awarded 150 marks out of 200. The test pieces were *County Guy* and *Hail to the Chief*, the former piece being accompanied whilst the latter wasn't.

Meanwhile, the Girls' choir, under the auspices of Miss Ada Butler, took first place and the Edgbaston Banner in the cantata class for choirs from any Public Elementary Girls' School in Birmingham.

Children travelled by tram to the Town Hall, where they had to sit on wooden benches up in the galleries until it became their turn to sing. They frequently didn't arrive back home until late in the evening.

WEDNESDAY, MAY 16th

Today, being Parents' Day, a large number of parents and friends visited the school during the morning to observe the ordinary work of the school in progress. During the afternoon, a special timetable, particularly suited for the occasion, was used. Both parents and teachers made good use of the opportunity by discussing the progress and capabilities of the children, and the day appeared to be appreciated very much by all concerned.

TUESDAY, MAY 29th

The school celebrated Empire Day, having returned after the Whitsun holiday one day earlier. The children, some of whom wore their father's medals to school, were given the opportunity to listen to a talk by the King and Queen given on the gramophone. Appropriate music was subsequently played. All around the school could be seen maps with large splotches of red on them indicating the British Empire.

TUESDAY, JUNE 12th

The School was closed today on account of the visit to Birmingham of His Royal Highness the Prince of Wales. Thirty boys and girls helped to form a choir of 2,000 children who welcomed him in Victoria Square. The remainder of the school assembled on a spacious verge at the side of the new Tyburn Road to greet him, where the Royal cortege slowed down especially for the purpose, so that the children had a splendid view. Amidst much waving of miniature Union Jacks, they cheered the Prince, who had just left Fort Dunlop, again and again with unbounded enthusiasm and received from His Royal Highness, who was evidently much pleased, a markedly gracious acknowledgement.

THURSDAY, JUNE 14th

At 3.30p.m., the whole school marched to a field, lent by the General Electric Company, for a sports day, which lasted until 5.30p.m.

THURSDAY, JUNE 21st

Temperance was once again the subject of a talk to the older boys by a representative of the United Kingdom Band of Hope Union.

WEDNESDAY and THURSDAY, JUNE 27th and 28th

The Erdington Schools' Athletics Sports were once again held at the Erdington Cottage Homes grounds. The heats took place on the Wednesday with the finals being decided on the following evening. There was a lengthy programme with as many as 100 entrants in each event, a commendable esprit de corps and determination being shown by the chosen champions, thus making the winning a greatly prized achievement and matter of much congratulation. The sports were splendidly organised and, although each event was participated in by such a multitude of children, they came off with clockwork punctuality according to the scheduled times. There was an enthusiastic attendance, particularly on the Thursday. Slade Road were once again to the fore, winning the Yenton trophy shield for girls, whilst the boys finished as runners up to St. Thomas'. The prizes were once again distributed by Mrs Gelling, her husband, Councillor R. R. Gelling, president of the association, presenting the shields.

THURSDAY, JULY 19th

Mr E. W. Jones and Mr V. W. G. Thomas, who were respectively the Headmasters of the Boys' and the Evening Schools, attended at the Victoria Law Courts today to oppose the granting of a licence for a Dancing Hall to be erected in Broomfield Road. Mr Henry Smithers was planning to build the hall on a site adjoining the picture house and opposite the school at a cost of £5000. He said that it would be a first-class establishment, which would not cater for jazz music. Mr Thomas stated that a dancing hall in that thoroughfare would result in distracting noise. In order to ensure efficient teaching it was necessary for both teachers and pupils to exercise all the concentration they were capable of; that concentration would be interfered with by outside attractions. The licensing justices duly refused the application.

MONDAY, JULY 23rd

The girls were not far behind the boys in matters of sport at this time, and the netball matches at Rookery Park had afforded much interest during the previous three months. The season ended today with Slade Road, as Champions of the League, playing in the annual match of Champions versus Erdington Girls. After the game, they were presented with the shield by Councillor and Mrs Gelling.

MONDAY, SEPTEMBER 10th

For the first time, children from the school attended the new playing field in Jaffray Road for organised games. The field was available for boys from the school on Monday afternoons and Thursday mornings.

TUESDAY, SEPTEMBER 11th

The Evening School had now become one of three, which included Edwards Road and Osborne Road, to be known as the Erdington Evening Institute. Edwards Road would cater for junior technical and commercial students up to the age of 17, whilst Osborne Road would be a general centre. Slade Road would be an adult and domestic centre. At this time, Slade Road held classes in the following: Woodwork; Metalwork; Machine Drawing; Mathematics; Book-keeping; Commercial subjects; Elocution; Literature; Singing; Millinery; Dressmaking; Cookery; Physical Exercises; Folk Dancing; English; Housewifery and Piano.

FRIDAY, SEPTEMBER 14th

Obviously, the injury that Albert Pearson suffered early in 1922 didn't cause any lasting damage, as it was learnt today that he had gained a free scholarship to the Handsworth Junior Technical School.

MONDAY, NOVEMBER 5th

The playground, which for a long time had been in a very bad state of repair, was now being asphalted at last!

FRIDAY, NOVEMBER 16th

The Headmaster, Mr E. W. Jones, had been appointed a member of the Burnham Committee and, as such, was attending a meeting of that body at the Board of Education in Whitehall.

FRIDAY, DECEMBER 21st

The installation of electric lighting commenced as the school broke for the Christmas holidays at midday.

1924

FRIDAY, JANUARY 11th

Mr E. W. Jones was away attending a meeting of the Burnham Committee in London.

THURSDAY, JANUARY 31st
Mr E. W. Jones was away again attending a meeting of the Burnham Committee at the Board of Education.

THURSDAY, MARCH 6th
The timetable was suspended for the afternoon in order that the older boys could perform scenes from plays by Shakespeare for the other classes. The scenes that they performed were from *Hamlet*, *Merchant of Venice* and *King Henry V111.*

FRIDAY and SATURDAY, MARCH 7th and 8th
A concert was given in the school on these two evenings in aid of the Lord Mayor's Unemployment Fund. The children performed songs and recitations as well as scenes from Shakespearian plays: *King Henry V111*; *Midsummer Night's Dream*, *Hamlet*. The concert raised £11.11s.0d.

FRIDAY, MARCH 21st
At a staff meeting held during the morning, discussion took place concerning the question of visits by the various members of the staff to each other's classrooms for the purpose of observing methods and progress.

TUESDAY, APRIL 1st
A meeting of head teachers in the Erdington district was held during the afternoon at Fentham Road School, in order to agree upon a suitable date for the proposed visit to the Empire Exhibition at Wembley. Two meetings had already been held during the previous few days – one at Suffolk Street Technical School and the other at the Education Office – to discuss plans for the children's visit. Thursday, June 17th was the date most favoured.

MONDAY, MAY 19th
Slade Road Girls' School competed at the Midland Musical Competition Festival. Today, the 'B' choir were judged equal first with St. Mary's R. C., being awarded 180 marks out of 200 with honours in the competition for Junior Choirs between 30 and 40 children under 11 years of age, in attendance at any Public Elementary School in Birmingham. However, the main competition of the day – that for the Harding Challenge Shield – was in every way an immensely encouraging experience. Nearly 50 choirs took part in it, but in coming through, not only first but with honours, the 'B' choir of Slade Road Girls' School gained high credit. Not one of the six schools to sing in the final test was a choir to win other than admiration, as were many among those who had to be omitted. As winners, Slade Road Girls' School Choir, tutored by Miss L. E. Bryan, were able to have their name inscribed on the Harding Challenge Shield for the first time.

TUESDAY, MAY 20th

It was a great night for children in the Midland Competition Festival, when the Girls' School, under the tutorship of Miss. A. Butler, took part in the cantata class for Elementary Schools' Choirs of not less than 25 and not more than 35 scholars in actual attendance at a Public Elementary School in Birmingham. They were awarded 92 marks out of 100 with an honours certificate and were presented with the Daily News Challenge Shield as winners of the competition.

WEDNESDAY, JUNE 4th

220

4.6.24. The attached report of H M I was received today.

18/6/24 Councillor Dr W. B. Featherstone, Visiting Manager, visited the school this afternoon.

CITY OF BIRMINGHAM EDUCATION COMMITTEE.

Copy of Report of H. M. Inspector, Mr. G. R. S. Loch, after visits paid on the 5th, 6th and 9th May, 1924.

Boys' Department: Head Master, Mr. E. W. Jones.

The numbers on the books exceeded the accommodation between the summer holidays and Christmas. Of the nine classes in the School seven have 53 or more boys on the registers.

A limited scheme of specialisation has been introduced with satisfactory results and History, Geography and Singing are carefully taught. In Mathematics the scope of the course is to be widened. Advantage might be taken of this opportunity to improve some of the methods in Arithmetic.

The Reading generally is very fair, but it is a matter for consideration whether the amount of class reading in certain classes might not be reduced with advantage and other methods adopted which would give the boys greater practice in word recognition.

Generally the work of the school is satisfactory.

In the last two years 60 boys have proceeded to Secondary and Junior Commercial Schools. [illegible signature] Chief Education Officer B. E. C. 10.6.24.

School Inspector's Report, 1924.

THURSDAY, JUNE 5th

For the last three months schools in the area had been discussing proposals for the visit of children to the British Empire Exhibition at Wembley. Today, those efforts culminated in 700 children, including many from Slade Road School – it is known that at least 70 boys went – making the journey. The school had in fact broken up for the Whitsuntide holiday on the previous evening especially so that the trip could take place. Assistance had been forthcoming from Messrs Cook's Tourist Agency, a train being laid on which collected children from both Erdington and Gravelly Hill stations. Arriving by eleven o'clock, the children had 8 hours in which to wander through the various halls, being allowed to take part in the amusements, as they were escorted around by their teachers in small groups. Returning home, the train steamed into the station at 10. 30 that night.

SATURDAY, JUNE 28th

The Erdington schools' cricket season was rapidly drawing to a close. A few matches still remained to be played before the winners would be crowned although, at the time, it looked like Ryland Road would probably take that honour. Unfortunately, the final results are lost to posterity, although it is known that Ryland Road did in fact win the championship remaining unbeaten all season. The above is the table as it stood on this day.

	P	W	D	L	PTS
RYLAND ROAD	8	8	0	0	16
CHURCH OF ENGLAND	10	7	1	2	15
GREEN LANES	11	5	0	6	10
SLADE ROAD	8	4	1	3	9
OSBORNE ROAD	10	4	1	5	9
MOOR END LANE	10	4	0	6	8
COTTAGE HOMES	9	2	2	5	6
ST.THOMAS'	10	1	1	8	3

Erdington Schools' Cricket League, 1924.

WEDNESDAY and FRIDAY, JULY 2nd and 4th

The annual Erdington Schools' sports were upon us once again. Due to a heavy downpour, the finals had to be postponed from the Thursday evening to the Friday. They took place once more on the grounds of the Erdington Cottage Homes and there were even more entries than in previous years. Many events had more than 200 entrants and, in consequence, a lengthy schedule was required to effect their completion. The public thoroughly appreciated the hard work that had gone in to making them a success, there being a large and enthusiastic audience. The Erdington Cottage Homes Band, under the conductorship of Mr H. Grainger, played a choice selection of music

Erdington Cottage Homes Band.

Above: Infants' Parents Day, 1924. Bottom Left: In the centre of the picture wearing a crown and ermine cloak is Theo (Ted) Allbeury, the celebrated spy novelist.

on each evening and added greatly to the gaiety of the gathering. Amidst much cheering, the prizes were distributed afterwards by Mrs Gelling, the Yenton trophy once again being won by the girls from Slade Road for the second year in succession.

FRIDAY, JULY 4th

A sum of 25 shillings was collected and sent to the Dartmouth Street Infants' Council School Annual Treat Fund by the Boys' School. A further collection for the Police Aided Association realised 10 shillings.

As the school had opened 20 years to this very day, the Infants' department celebrated with a special Parents' Day. The following photographs illustrate what the day must have been like for the children at the school at that time.

TUESDAY, SEPTEMBER 23rd

A violin class was formed under the direction of Mr Frank Cooper. The class consisted of 55 boys from Standards 4, 5 and 6, the violins being provided by the Maidstone School Orchestra Association.

FRIDAY, OCTOBER 3rd

The Headmaster of the Boys' School was becoming somewhat upset that stock, that had been ordered on June 30th, was still not to hand. He had written to the appropriate department in August; had twice sent a messenger to make enquiries, besides enquiring once more himself. He had now taken the matter up with the Midland Educational Company.

MONDAY, OCTOBER 6th

Good News! Most of the stock previously ordered had now arrived.

SATURDAY, DECEMBER 6th

A football match, which excited a good deal of local interest, especially amongst the juvenile portion of the community, took place this afternoon at Jaffray Road. The protagonists were boys, representative of the public elementary schools of Erdington and Aston. Large though the crowd was which was assembled to see this local 'Derby', it did not represent the thousands of penny tickets which, in connection with the fixture, had been sold for the

Left: Arriving for school 1924 style. Top Right: Boys' School Class Standard IV, c.1924. Bottom Right: Infant Class of 7 year olds, c.1924.

benefit of the British Legion Widows and Orphans Fund. Lieutenant Scott Goffe (chairman of the Erdington branch of the British Legion) acted as referee. Although Aston scored first, Erdington quickly equalised before going on to score twice more and run out 3–1 winners. Tea was provided afterwards at Fentham Road School. Commemoration medals were then presented to members of the winning team, the only representative from Slade Road being Armishaw, the Erdington goalkeeper.

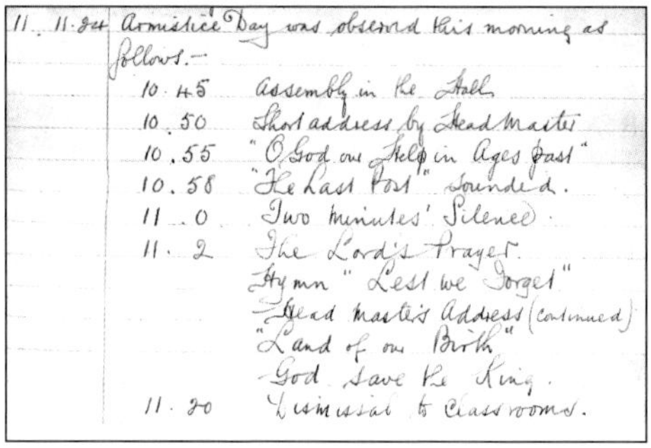
11. 11. 24 Armistice Day was observed this morning as follows.–
10. 45 Assembly in the Hall
10. 50 Short address by Head Master
10. 55 "O God our Help in Ages Past"
10. 58 "The Last Post" Sounded.
11. 0 Two minutes' Silence.
11. 2 The Lord's Prayer.
Hymn "Lest we Forget"
Head master's Address (continued)
"Land of our Birth"
God Save the King.
11. 20 Dismissal to Classrooms.

Top: Infant Class 6, 1924.
Bottom: Armistice Day Programme, 1924.

1925

SATURDAY, JANUARY 3rd

A congregational gathering took place at the school this evening. Known as the Parochial Christmas Party, it was organised by All Saints Church in George Road. Despite the unpleasant weather conditions that prevailed outside, it offered a veritable harbour of refuge in the seasonally decorated, brilliantly lit and pleasantly warm rooms. Over 150 people of all sexes and ages participated in the delightful social gathering, everything going right-merrily during the four hours that the well-arranged yet spontaneous programme lasted. There were games and dances, as well as a musical interlude given by the organist and choirmaster of the church with accompaniment on the violin. In addition, there were recitations and a variety of songs. A novel competition was held to see who could blow the biggest balloon, which excited keen interest and a vast amount of amusement. The evening finally concluded at 10.30p.m. with the singing of *Auld Lang Syne* amidst a carnival of coloured crackers, caps, balloons and streamers.

MONDAY, FEBRUARY 16th

The afternoon session opened at 1.30p.m. and closed at 3.45p.m., especially so that the boys could visit Bostock and Wombwells Menagerie at Holt Street, Gosta Green. Intrepid animal performances were put on at frequent intervals during the afternoon and evening, with special descriptive lectures and performances for schoolchildren. Admission to this zoological promenade of educated lions, tigers, leopards, polar bears, wolves, hyenas and elephants was one shilling for adults and sixpence for children. On the evening of the 10th, the Lord Mayor had paid a visit, the proceeds for the performance being donated to the Lord Mayor's Distress Fund. Baby lions and leopards, born only a few weeks earlier, had been handed round the audience.

THURSDAY, FRIDAY and SATURDAY, FEBRUARY 26th, 27th and 28th

The School Concert was held on these days. The first part consisted of miscellaneous selections. The school choir opened the proceedings with Beethoven's *Creation Hymn* which was followed by a recitation called *Ask Mamma* by Fred Morton. Once again, the school choir gave voice, this time to Mendelsohn's *Lift Thine Eyes* and Geibel's *The Oars are plashing lightly*, a recitation by Leslie Pitcher entitled *Ze Kick Ball* interposing between the two songs. After the interval, we came to part two, which was an operetta entitled *The Witch of the Wood*. To the accompaniment of Misses L. Bryan and E. G. Whitehall, there were solos, duets and choruses for the various characters. Programmes for the production were available for a penny each.

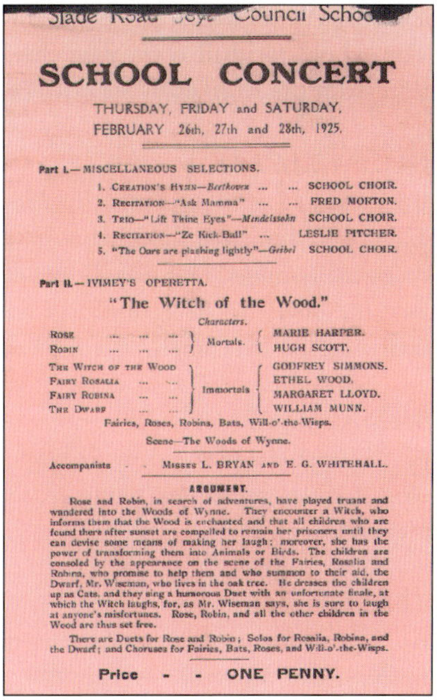

SCHOOL CONCERT

THURSDAY, FRIDAY and SATURDAY, FEBRUARY 26th, 27th and 28th, 1925.

Part I.—MISCELLANEOUS SELECTIONS.

1. Creation's Hymn—*Beethoven* ... ... SCHOOL CHOIR.
2. Recitation—"Ask Mamma" ... ... FRED MORTON.
3. Trio—"Lift Thine Eyes"—*Mendelssohn* SCHOOL CHOIR.
4. Recitation—"Ze Kick-Ball" ... LESLIE PITCHER.
5. "The Oars are plashing lightly"—*Geibel* SCHOOL CHOIR.

Part II.—IVIMEY'S OPERETTA.

"The Witch of the Wood."

Characters.

Rose	Mortals.	MARIE HARPER.
Robin		HUGH SCOTT.
The Witch of the Wood	Immortals	GODFREY SIMMONS.
Fairy Rosalia		ETHEL WOOD.
Fairy Robina		MARGARET LLOYD.
The Dwarf		WILLIAM MUNN.

Fairies, Roses, Robins, Bats, Will-o'-the-Wisps.

Scene—The Woods of Wynne.

Accompanists - - Misses L. BRYAN and E. G. WHITEHALL.

ARGUMENT.

Rose and Robin, in search of adventures, have played truant and wandered into the Woods of Wynne. They encounter a Witch, who informs them that the Wood is enchanted and that all children who are found there after sunset are compelled to remain her prisoners until they can devise some means of making her laugh; moreover, she has the power of transforming them into Animals or Birds. The children are consoled by the appearance on the scene of the Fairies, Rosalia and Robina, who promise to help them and who summon to their aid, the Dwarf, Mr. Wiseman, who lives in the oak tree. He dresses the children up as Cats, and they sing a humorous Duet with an unfortunate finale, at which the Witch laughs, for, as Mr. Wiseman says, she is sure to laugh at anyone's misfortunes. Rose, Robin, and all the other children in the Wood are thus set free.

There are Duets for Rose and Robin; Solos for Rosalia, Robina, and the Dwarf; and Choruses for Fairies, Bats, Roses, and Will-o'-the-Wisps.

Price - - ONE PENNY.

Concert Programme, 1925.

TUESDAY, MARCH 31st

Chief Assistant, Mr Francis Nokes, left to take up the position of Headmaster of Bishop Ryder's Church of England School.

WEDNESDAY, APRIL 1st

As from today, all teachers had their salaries reduced until further notice by 5%.

FRIDAY, APRIL 3rd

The Headmaster was absent during the afternoon in order to attend an educational conference with representatives of the Farmers' Union in London.

THURSDAY, FRIDAY and SATURDAY, APRIL 2nd, 3rd and 4th

An entertainment was given by the children of the Infants' department on each of these three evenings. Large audiences, principally consisting of parents, family and friends of the youngsters participating, assembled to do honour to the occasion; and to enjoy themselves, which they did in no unsustained measure. The programme consisted of seventeen items – songs, dances, rhythmic plays, fantasies and games – which were gone through with marked finish and precision and reflected great credit on the young children, as well as the teachers, who had spent so much time and bestowed so much painstaking care on its preparation. There were songs like *Little Soldiers* and *Ride a Cock Horse* and plays about fairies and nature. The make-up of the fairies, springtime flowers, rats and sea nymphs was very ingenious and praiseworthy. The children were full of life and enjoyment and all their cleverly executed items were loudly applauded.

TUESDAY, APRIL 7th

The school football team won the Erdington Schools' Football Shield, whilst the Junior team won the Erdington Schools' Football Cup.

FRIDAY, MAY 1st

Boys and girls went to Erdington House today to perform maypole dancing for the inmates. They wore blue and gold boleros and jackets made from sateen at school, as well as similar coloured bonnets. The play *Who killed Cock Robin* was also performed. Mourning for her love, the dove should have said, "I will be the chief mourner." To roars of laughter from the audience, she exclaimed, "I will be the chief parson."

WEDNESDAY, MAY 6th

At the opening of the new Erdington Swimming Baths in Mason Road, George Garbett won a silver medal by being placed second in the schoolboys' event. The school also placed fourth.

TUESDAY, MAY 12th

At the Midland Musical Festival held at the Town Hall, the Girls' School, under the tutorship of Miss Doris Handley, finished as runners up, gaining 100 marks and an honours certificate, in the competition for International Dances for teams of no fewer than four children aged 12 to 16, who were in regular attendance at a school within the Midland Counties.

THURSDAY, MAY 14th

Under the tuition of Miss Ada Butler, the Girls' School choir achieved a first class certificate with 88 marks in the cantata class, finishing as runners up in the competition confined to Birmingham Elementary Schools held at the Midland Musical Festival.

FRIDAY, MAY 15th

The Boys' School choir, under the conductorship of Mr Cooper, competed at the Music Festival at the Town Hall. By gaining 170 marks out of 200, they were awarded a first class certificate.

Meanwhile, the Junior Girls' choir, with 176 marks, won their event under the conductorship of Miss Chamberlain. This was for children under the age of 11 in attendance at any Birmingham Elementary School.

TUESDAY and WEDNESDAY, JUNE 16th and 17th

The Erdington Schools' Sports were held at the Cottage Homes grounds in Reservoir Road. No fewer than 1320 children entered for the events of which 770 were girls. On this occasion, the girls could only manage to finish as runners up to Fentham Road. During the two evenings, the Boys Military Prize Band of the Erdington Cottage Homes entertained the crowds with selections of music.

TUESDAY, JUNE 30th

A staff meeting was held this morning to discuss certain relevant issues. It was considered that there needed to be a prompter attention paid to the marking of registers to avoid irregularities, greater variety should be introduced into drawing lessons and there should be an avoidance of extravagance in the replenishment of stock. The tidying up of classrooms was equally extolled.

WEDNESDAY, JULY 8th

During the afternoon, the school was opened for Parents' Day and many friends as well as parents chose to attend.

A programme of music was organised, which commenced at 2.20p.m., concluding nearly two hours later.

SATURDAY, JULY 18th

Ethel Wood was awarded a £50 scholarship, being the first prize in a competition organised by the British Commercial Gas Association. This was augmented by Birmingham Education Committee to the extent of a further £20. The 12 year old received her prize for an essay on 'The gas meter and household economy'.

MONDAY, JULY 20th

The Headmaster, Mr Jones, seemed to get around a bit, for today he was attending a World Conference on Education in Edinburgh.

FRIDAY, JULY 24th

The school closed for the summer holidays.

MONDAY, AUGUST 24th

Only four weeks later and the children returned to school.

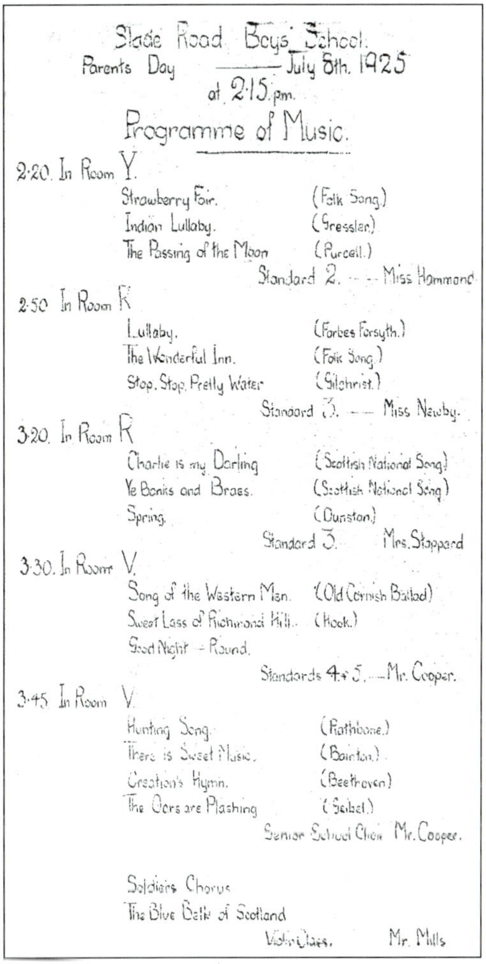

Slade Road Boys' School.
Parents Day ——— July 8th. 1925
at 2.15.pm.
Programme of Music.

2.20. In Room Y.
Strawberry Fair. (Folk Song.)
Indian Lullaby. (Gressler.)
The Passing of the Moon (Purcell.)
Standard 2. — Miss Hammond

2.50 In Room R
Lullaby. (Forbes Forsyth.)
The Wonderful Inn. (Folk Song.)
Stop, Stop, Pretty Water (Gilchrist.)
Standard 3. — Miss Newby.

3.20. In Room R
Charlie is my Darling (Scottish National Song)
Ye Banks and Braes. (Scottish National Song)
Spring. (Dunston.)
Standard 3. Mrs. Stoppard

3.30. In Room V.
Song of the Western Men. (Old Cornish Ballad)
Sweet Lass of Richmond Hill. (Hook.)
Good Night – Round.
Standards 4 & 5. — Mr. Cooper.

3.45 In Room V.
Hunting Song. (Rathbone.)
There is Sweet Music. (Bainton.)
Creation's Hymn. (Beethoven)
The Oars are Plashing (Seibel.)
Senior School Choir Mr. Cooper.

Soldiers Chorus
The Blue Bells of Scotland
Violin Class. Mr. Mills

Top: Parents Day Programme, 1925.
Bottom: Girls' School Class
(taken in the Boys' playground) c.1925.

Boys' School Class c.1925. Mr Jones, the Headmaster, is at the back of the class.

TUESDAY, SEPTEMBER 1st
Safety First was the issue today. Mr Jones addressed the boys at morning assembly on this important topic. Unbelievably, at midday, on going home for lunch, Alfred Anderson was knocked down by a car whilst crossing Slade Road. The result was that he was taken to hospital, but fortunately was not badly hurt and consequently was not detained.

THURSDAY, OCTOBER 15th
The attendance officer, Mr Ridge, was transferred to another district. The school was extremely sorry to lose the services of such a thoroughly efficient and courteous officer, who had been involved with the school since March 1912. He wore a trilby hat and, when he came to your door, you were always filled with trepidation.

THURSDAY, OCTOBER 29th
A day best forgotten! Four boys – Major Dunkley; Hugh Scott; Leonard Davies; Sidney Morbey – were punished for cigarette smoking in the playground, letters being sent to their parents acquainting them of the facts. Hugh Scott was a star of school concerts, performing in both *The Witch of the Wood* and *The Pay of the Pied Piper.* Two other boys were punished for bad conduct in the streets, a matter about which the Headmaster spoke to the assembled Boys' School.

FRIDAY, NOVEMBER 27th
A special service and address to the assembled school took place, the occasion being the funeral of Queen Alexandra.

FRIDAY, DECEMBER 11th
A gramophone was purchased with monies from the School Fund.

WEDNESDAY, DECEMBER 23rd
Major Dunkley left the school today having passed the entrance examination for the Handsworth Junior Technical School, where he started the following year on January 12th.

He successfully completed his course and left the technical school on December 20th, 1927 to take up work as an apprentice travelling salesman.

THURSDAY, DECEMBER 31st

Mr Cooper terminated his engagement at the school, as he had been appointed headmaster at a school near Bedford. Thirty-two years of age, he had been on the staff of the Boys' School for just over two years.

1926

MONDAY, JANUARY 11th

The funeral took place today of Alfred Thomas Upton, aged 8 years 10 months, of 1A Copeley Hill, who had met with a fatal accident during the Christmas break. Whilst playing on his scooter in Slade Road, he had hit the kerb whilst trying to pass on the inside of a coal lorry, with which he had then collided. The result was that he was thrown under the wagon resulting in his accidental death as adjudged by the coroner.

THURSDAY and SATURDAY,
FEBRUARY 25th and 27th

The annual children's concert by the boys of the school took place at the All Saints Parochial Hall on these evenings. The piece selected for presentation – involving the display of both histrionic and verbal gifts – was *The Pay of the Pied Piper*. A well selected cast brought out the humour to the best possible advantage in a fitting environment of musical melody. The acting was clever and the singing bright, all the boys being in excellent voice throughout. William Munn as the Burgomaster was the undoubted 'star' and around him, as in a brilliant constellation, the other principals gathered. Councillor Dixon chaired the proceedings on Thursday, whilst Councillor Smith performed the duties on Saturday. During the intermission, the Councillors spoke to the assembled audiences of the successes achieved in passing scholars into higher education. Equal emphasis was placed on the prowess of the school in field sports, particularly football. Mr Jones, in reply, referred to the great devotion of the teachers, all of whom had taken a very active part in the preparation for the opera, the brunt of the work in training for the choruses, dialogues, etc. falling upon Mr Emlyn Howell, the chief assistant. He, also, acknowledged with gratitude the interest of the parents in the making of the costumes for their children who took part in the programme. The proceeds were devoted to the School Fund, which provided for its sports and other amenities.

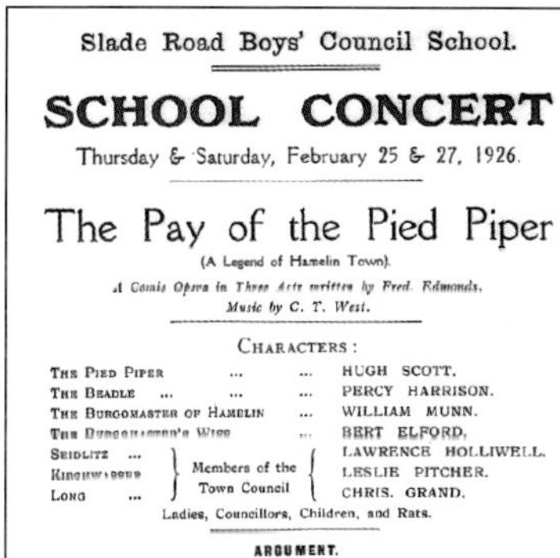

Slade Road Boys' Council School.

SCHOOL CONCERT

Thursday & Saturday, February 25 & 27, 1926.

The Pay of the Pied Piper

(A Legend of Hamelin Town).

A Comic Opera in Three Acts written by Fred. Edmonds.
Music by C. T. West.

CHARACTERS:

The Pied Piper	HUGH SCOTT.
The Beadle	PERCY HARRISON.
The Burgomaster of Hamelin ...	WILLIAM MUNN.
The Burgomaster's Wife ...	BERT ELFORD.
Seidlitz ... (Members of the Town Council)	LAWRENCE HOLLIWELL.
[illegible] ... (Members of the Town Council)	LESLIE PITCHER.
Long ... (Members of the Town Council)	CHRIS. GRAND.

Ladies, Councillors, Children, and Rats.

ARGUMENT.

Act 1. SCENE: Council Chamber at Hamelin.

Hamelin Town is besieged with rats. The Councillors of Hamelin are endeavouring to solve the problem of the rats. During their session a deputation of ladies is ushered in. They demand a voice in the settlement of the rat question, and insist that the Council should take drastic measures. The rats invade the Council Chamber to the consternation of ladies and councillors. This incident brings matters to a crisis, and the Council unanimously [illegible] to advertise for a "cure."

Act 2. SCENE: Council Chamber of Hamelin after an interval of three days.

The Pied Piper answers the advertisement. He demonstrates the wonderful charm of his pipe before the Beadle by making the official respond to it in a very undignified manner. The Council are the next to "have a sample" of the power of the magic pipe. They are completely mesmerised by the Piper who charms them into a conflicting series of moods. Upon recovering, they immediately engage the Piper to rid them of the rats. This he does to the satisfaction of everyone, but when the question of payment arises the Council fail to honour their obligations, whereupon the Piper lures the children of Hamelin through the meadows towards Koppelberg Hill.

Act 3. A Meadow near Hamelin.

Realising their mistake the Council implore the Piper to return with the children, and beseech him to accept his fee. He does so, and the children are returned to their parents.

– ALL'S WELL THAT ENDS WELL. –

Chairman (Thursday) - - COUNCILLOR S. J. DIXON.

Price – ONE PENNY.

Concert Programme, 1926.

WEDNESDAY, MARCH 17th

It was the time of the year for the Oxford versus Cambridge boat race. In the Boys' department of Slade Road, they wore a light or dark blue ribbon, purchased from Bon Marche, to indicate their favourite. They even supported their teams further by playing football matches in the playground. Coincidentally, it may also have been possible that the house teams at the Cottage Homes – they were called Oxford and Cambridge – might have rubbed off on the school.

THURSDAY, APRIL 15th

Another funeral was held today. This time, Joseph Hill, a scholar in Standard 8, had met an untimely death during the Easter holidays.

TUESDAY, APRIL 27th

During the week, term examinations were held in Reading, Writing and Arithmetic.

WEDNESDAY, APRIL 28th

At the Midland Competition Festival, once again the Girls' School had to be content with the position of runners up with 80 marks in the cantata class for choirs of not less than 25 and more than 35 scholars in actual attendance at a Public Elementary Day School in Birmingham.

Boys' School Concert – Pay of the Pied Piper, 1926.

MONDAY, MAY 10th

As an experiment, all the teachers were given charge of children in different standards for a whole week.

MONDAY, MAY 17th

Travelling from Snow Hill, approximately 100 girls, with their respective teachers, went by train to Liverpool. They explored warehouses and took a ride on the overhead railway, arriving back in Birmingham after the trams had stopped running. Their parents met them, and they all walked home together.

WEDNESDAY, JUNE 16th

The postponed Erdington Schools' Sports were concluded today at Jaffray Road. A total of nine schools competed, Slade Road being narrowly beaten into second place in both the boys' and girls' events. Green Lanes took the Wiggins-Davies Shield by one point, whilst Fentham Road gained a narrower victory by the margin of ½ point.

JULY
The boys had something to celebrate this month as they had won the Erdington Schools' Junior Cricket Championship, losing only one match in the process to Ryland Road; they had won the inaugural competition the previous year. The team was Albert Birkenhead, Sidney Ingram (Captain), Kenny Vale, Alf Anderson, Jack Bromley, Tommy Nash, Freddy McComb, Billy Bullock, Ronnie Wright, Freddie Guest and a lad called Sketchley.

FRIDAY, SEPTEMBER 3rd
Two boys truanted today. Their parents were summoned by the Headmaster and seriously spoken to about the offence. The one lad who had told many untruths in connection with the matter, received one stroke of the cane on each hand.

TUESDAY, SEPTEMBER 7th
Despite having made an application to the Education Office on August 26th for a supply teacher, it wasn't until this morning that one commenced duty.

FRIDAY, SEPTEMBER 24th
A joint swimming gala was held at the Erdington Baths in Mason Road this evening between the Boldmere Swimming Club and the Erdington Athletic Club. Many events were specially staged to give encouragement to the children who attended the Erdington Elementary Schools and, in the four lengths' relay race for the Erdington Girls' Championship, a prize of four silver medals was awarded to the winning team from Slade Road.

Swimming certificate, 1926.

MONDAY, NOVEMBER 8th
School re-opened after the mid-term break. In the Boys' School, not only were all the teachers present but 476 out of the 494 boys on the roll.

THURSDAY, NOVEMBER 11th
Armistice Day was observed by a short service and address, followed by the two minutes' silence.

FRIDAY, DECEMBER 10th
Despite the fact that some science materials had been ordered in July, these were still not to hand. Enquiries had been made at the Education Office regarding the long delay, only to be

met with astonishment as they were under the mistaken impression that the boys attended a separate Science Centre, so they hadn't bothered to action the request. This, despite the fact that the school had had its own Science Room since January 1918!

Infant Class, c.1926.

SATURDAY and MONDAY, DECEMBER 18th and 20th

The annual School Concert given by the Boys' School was held on these evenings at the All Saints Parochial Hall, both performances being most successful and much appreciated by the large audiences. On the Saturday, Councillor Gelling, accompanied by his wife, and Councillor Dixon were present. At the second performance on the Monday, Councillor Featherstone presided. The first part of the programme consisted of an excerpt from *The Pied Piper of Hamelin*. Following the intermission, the second half was devoted to the presentation of a comic opera in three acts entitled *Ali Ba-Ba and the Forty Black Sheep*. The story from the Arabian Nights' Entertainments was retold, including new and amusing features such as Mrs Cassim's Girls' School, the girls at the end pairing off with the thieves, who are chloroformed, not killed by Morgiana. At the first performance, Councillor Gelling said that one of the objects of the School Concert was to raise money for the School Sports Fund, but he felt that there was a second more important object, that of educating the boys, and he was sure that everyone present would agree that the performance could not fail to do much for those taking part. He went on to compliment the school on their sports record, and thought that the opera that they were presenting so excellently reflected great credit on the principal organiser, Mr Emlyn Howell, the chief assistant at the school. Councillor Dixon then went on to congratulate the school on their scholarship successes in 1926, reading out a total of twenty-six boys names. The Headmaster, Mr Jones, tendered, on his own behalf and that of the staff, children and audience, very sincere thanks to the Councillors for their presence. He went on to say how grateful he was to Mr Howell and the rest of the staff for their hearty co-operation and to the boys themselves for the amount of spare time that they had given. He finally concluded by saying that the concert had been produced without interfering with the general work of the school.

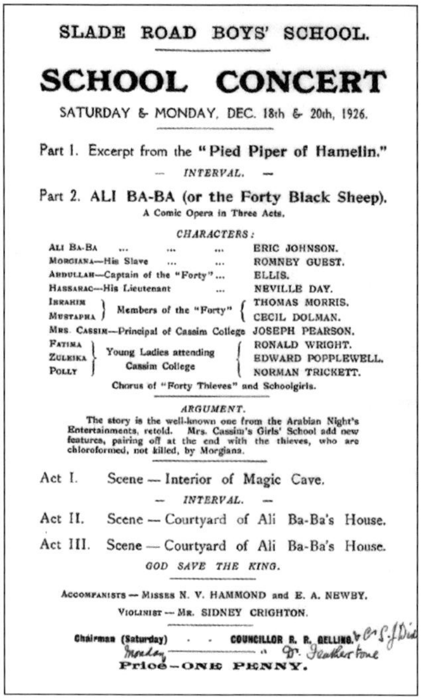

SLADE ROAD BOYS' SCHOOL.

SCHOOL CONCERT

SATURDAY & MONDAY, DEC. 18th & 20th, 1926.

Part 1. Excerpt from the "Pied Piper of Hamelin."

— INTERVAL. —

Part 2. ALI BA-BA (or the Forty Black Sheep).

A Comic Opera in Three Acts.

CHARACTERS:

ALI BA-BA	ERIC JOHNSON.
MORGIANA—His Slave	ROMNEY GUEST.
ABDULLAH—Captain of the "Forty" ...	ELLIS.
HASSARAC—His Lieutenant ...	NEVILLE DAY.
IBRAHIM — Members of the "Forty"	THOMAS MORRIS.
MUSTAPHA — Members of the "Forty"	CECIL DOLMAN.
MRS. CASSIM—Principal of Cassim College	JOSEPH PEARSON.
FATIMA — Young Ladies attending Cassim College	RONALD WRIGHT.
ZULEIKA — Young Ladies attending Cassim College	EDWARD POPPLEWELL.
POLLY — Young Ladies attending Cassim College	NORMAN TRICKETT.

Chorus of "Forty Thieves" and Schoolgirls.

ARGUMENT.

The story is the well-known one from the Arabian Night's Entertainments, retold. Mrs. Cassim's Girls' School add new features, pairing off at the end with the thieves, who are chloroformed, not killed, by Morgiana.

Act I. Scene — Interior of Magic Cave.

— INTERVAL. —

Act II. Scene — Courtyard of Ali Ba-Ba's House.

Act III. Scene — Courtyard of Ali Ba-Ba's House.

GOD SAVE THE KING.

ACCOMPANISTS — MISSES N. V. HAMMOND and E. A. NEWBY.

VIOLINIST — MR. SIDNEY CRIGHTON.

Chairman (Saturday) - - COUNCILLOR R. R. GELLING. & Cr. S. J. Dix[illegible]

Monday —— " Dr. Featherstone

Price—ONE PENNY.

Concert Programme, 1926.

1927

SATURDAY, FEBRUARY 12th

Another 5½ acres of land, adjoining the 3½ acres already being used as a playing field, was purchased by the Education Committee as an additional playing field for the Erdington Schools at what was considered then, the very reasonable price of 1s.8d. per square yard. This followed the continued efforts of several prominent men in the district who had secured the first 3½ acres as a playing field for the Erdington Elementary Schools in perpetuity in October 1922. Originally, there had been a hugely successful draw accompanied by the slogan, 'Piano for a Tanner'.

TUESDAY, FEBRUARY 15th

The majority of the items specified in the requisition for Science equipment of July 1926 were finally delivered today. Mr Jones had already written a number of letters to the Education Department this year. It had taken a personal visit on February 11th to see the official concerned before his requisition was finally actioned.

TUESDAY, MARCH 1st

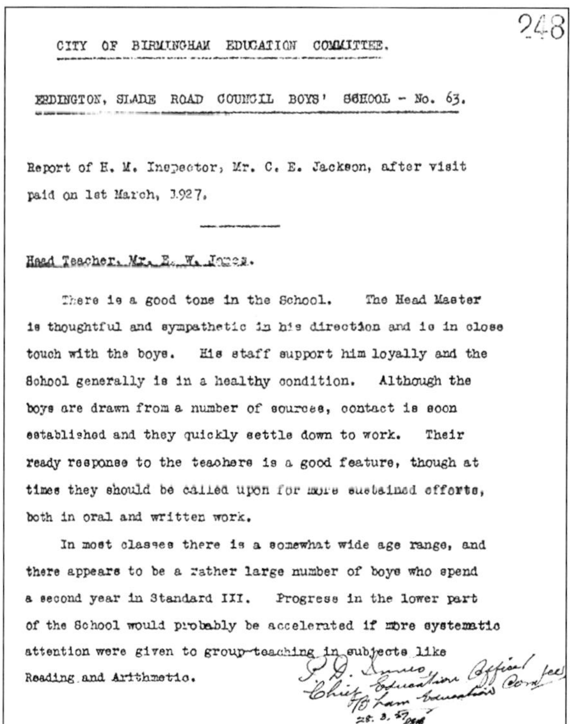

248

CITY OF BIRMINGHAM EDUCATION COMMITTEE.

ERDINGTON, SLADE ROAD COUNCIL BOYS' SCHOOL - No. 63.

Report of H. M. Inspector, Mr. C. E. Jackson, after visit paid on 1st March, 1927.

Head Teacher, Mr. E. W. Jones.

There is a good tone in the School. The Head Master is thoughtful and sympathetic in his direction and is in close touch with the boys. His staff support him loyally and the School generally is in a healthy condition. Although the boys are drawn from a number of sources, contact is soon established and they quickly settle down to work. Their ready response to the teachers is a good feature, though at times they should be called upon for more sustained efforts, both in oral and written work.

In most classes there is a somewhat wide age range, and there appears to be a rather large number of boys who spend a second year in Standard III. Progress in the lower part of the School would probably be accelerated if more systematic attention were given to group-teaching in subjects like Reading and Arithmetic.

School Inspector's Report, 1927.

League 1

	Played	Won	Drawn	Lost	Goals For	Goals Agst.	Pts.
SLADE ROAD	12	9	0	3	48	29	18
GREEN LANES	12	6	4	2	44	32	16
St.THOMAS'	12	5	5	2	35	28	15
OSBORNE ROAD	12	4	5	3	33	29	13
RYLAND ROAD	12	4	3	5	24	24	11
MOOR END LANE	12	2	2	8	26	52	6
NATIONAL C.of E.	12	2	1	9	28	44	5

League 2

	Played	Won	Drawn	Lost	Goals For	Goals Agst.	Pts.
SLADE ROAD	12	9	2	1	56	17	20
St.THOMAS'	12	8	1	3	56	27	17
GREEN LANES	12	6	1	5	42	27	13
OSBORNE ROAD	12	5	3	4	29	24	13
NATIONAL C.of E.	12	3	3	6	19	46	9
RYLAND ROAD	12	3	2	7	21	41	8
MOOR END LANE	12	1	2	9	17	58	4

Erdington Schools' Football League, 1926/1927.

SATURDAY, MARCH 12th

Today saw the close of the Erdington Schools' Football League season. In Division 1, there had been a keen struggle between Slade Road and Green Lanes, resulting in Slade Road winning the championship for the third time by only two points.

FRIDAY, MARCH 25th

A large number of workmen were present on the premises, engaged in re-decorating the school. This naturally required some re-organisation of classes.

TUESDAY, APRIL 12th

A lady from the Education Department of the Gramophone Company Limited spoke to the higher standards on the subject of Musical Appreciation.

THURSDAY, MAY 12th

At the Midland Musical Festival held at the Town Hall, the Girls' School choir won the Stockwell Banner, having finished first amongst all Girls' Elementary Schools in the Midland Counties.

FRIDAY, MAY 13th

At the Midland Musical Festival, in the cantata class for girls', boys' and mixed choirs in any Birmingham Elementary School, the Girls' School choir had to be content with the position of runners up for the Daily News Challenge Shield accumulating 86 marks, although they were awarded the Edgbaston Banner for their performances.

Meanwhile, in the competition for the Harding Shield, awarded to the best junior choir under the age of 11 in attendance at any Birmingham Elementary School, the Girls' School also had to be content with the position of runners up, although they did win the Arden Banner as the top Junior Girls' choir with 171 marks. The test pieces were *The Summer Winds* and *The Two Musicians*.

TUESDAY, MAY 24th

The upper standards were addressed during the morning by a lady from the League of Nations Union on the League's work.

TUESDAY and WEDNESDAY, JUNE 28th and 29th

The Erdington Schools' Sports were held at the Cottage Homes grounds in Reservoir Road. The girls of Slade Road could only finish as runners up to Fentham Road, although they won four of the seven events contested. They were unable to fill the minor placings. However, they did take first and third places in the Old Girls' open race. Mr Grainger, the chairman of the association, paid tribute to the fine spirit which had prevailed throughout. He said that there had not been a single unpleasant incident and such spirit spoke well for Erdington boys and girls. Councillor and Mrs Gelling, who presented the trophies and prizes, heartily congratulated the winners and all the competitors on the results of the sports, which they looked forward to more than any other event.

WEDNESDAY, JULY 13th

A large number of parents and friends visited the school during the afternoon for Parents' Day. They were treated to an exhibition of music, recitation and physical exercises, as well as being able to observe the children at work.

MONDAY, AUGUST 22nd

The school re-opened following the four week summer holiday. All members of the staff were present with the exception of Mr Jones, the Headmaster, and Miss Hammond, who had not yet returned from Canada, where they had been attending the Biennial Congress of the World Federation of Educational Associations in Toronto.

Left: Girls' School class with Miss Doris Handley, c.1927.
Right: Part of Girls' School Class with Miss Baum, c.1927.

2 Girls' School classes, c.1927.

WEDNESDAY, AUGUST 31st
Mr Valentine Thomas was appointed to the full-time post as Headmaster of the Evening Schools in Erdington as from today. He had been at the school since July 2nd, 1915. Mr Jones considered that he had rendered long, faithful and excellent service to the school since his original appointment. To the boys that he taught he was known as 'Felix' for his habit of prowling up and down the gangways during lessons.

SATURDAY, SEPTEMBER 17th
A party of 44 boys were taken to London. During the day, they visited Whitehall, the Houses of Parliament, Westminster Abbey, the Tower of London and the Zoo. They appear to have had a most enjoyable day, even though it was rather cool and cloudy with rain at times.

MONDAY, SEPTEMBER 26th
The Headmaster was away again, this time until October 1st. He was attending the Jubilee Conference of the Library Association at Edinburgh as a representative of the National Union of Teachers.

MONDAY, OCTOBER 3rd
A new teacher, Mr Hobday, who was later known to the boys as 'Pop', was appointed from today so that all the boys in the three top classes might have a full course of science in the laboratory attached to the school. He was placed in charge of Standard 3, whilst Mr Simpson took charge of the science room.

THURSDAY, OCTOBER 13th
The whole of Standard 8 of the Boys' School went to the Theatre Royal to see the matinee performance – it started at 2p.m. – of *Julius Caesar*, performed by the Bensonians, under the leadership of Sir Frank Benson and Gerald Lawrence.

THURSDAY, NOVEMBER 10th
A gentleman from the Royal Institution for the Blind addressed the school this morning on the work of the society.

Boys' School class c.1927 with the Headmaster.

FRIDAY, NOVEMBER 11th
Armistice Day was observed, during which a short address was given together with the two minutes' silence.

1928
THURSDAY, FEBRUARY 23rd
The whole school marched to Tyburn Road at 2p.m. in order to see their Majesties, the King and Queen, pass by on their way to the British Industries Fair at Castle Bromwich. Although they were sat in an enclosed car, they were clearly visible to all the children. They had driven from the City Centre along Aston Road North and Lichfield Road until they reached Salford Bridge, whereupon they had turned into Tyburn Road.

MONDAY, MARCH 19th
For the first time, the children were supplied with ⅓ pint bottles of milk. The cost, ½d. a bottle, had to be paid on the opening day of the week. The children were supplied with a straw with which to drink it.

MONDAY, MAY 7th
In the competition held at the Midland Musical Festival for National Dances other than English Folk Dances, for teams of not less than 6 children aged 11 to 13, who were in attendance at a school within the Midland Counties, the Girls' School, under the tutorship of Miss Doris Handley, finished as runners up with 185 marks.

Infant class c.1928.

THURSDAY, MAY 10th
In the competition held at the Midland Musical Festival for the Stockwell Banner, awarded to the best choir from a Girls' Council School, Slade Road finished as runners up with 162 marks under the guidance of Miss Elsie Badcock.

FRIDAY, MAY 11th
Once again, Miss Ada Butler and the Girls' School choir, competing in the cantata class at the Midland Musical Festival, had to be content with the position as runners up with 86 marks. However, the school did enjoy some well-deserved success, for the choir under the tutorship of Miss Chamberlain won the Harding Shield, awarded to any Junior Elementary School choir in Birmingham, with 163 marks, with a rendering that was considered both charming and natural. Not only that, but the school's other choir tutored by Miss Badcock finished as runners up with 161 marks.

FRIDAY, MAY 18th
During the morning session, boys from the top standards – 150 of them – went to the Gravelly Hill Picture House to see an educational film dealing with the History of the League of Nations. The film was entitled *The World War and After.*

SATURDAY, MAY 19th
50 boys, in charge of Mr Howell, assisted by Miss Newby and Messrs. Bosker, King and Simpson, went to Liverpool, travelling by train from Snow Hill. It must have been difficult for Mr King as he had a wooden leg, the result of his experiences during the war. Also, I wonder whether Mr Bosker and Miss Newby were able to totally concentrate on the boys in their charge as they were shortly to marry and must have had eyes for each other. They visited the Docks, the Cunarder Corinthia – they were actually allowed to go over it – the Cathedral, the Royal Liver Building, New Brighton and other places of interest. Whilst there, they had a ride on the overhead railway and were taken round the warehouses, where they saw leather and wool in storage. The outing was considered to have been a most enjoyable and instructive one. The cost five shillings.

THURSDAY, MAY 24th
Empire Day was suitably observed, during which time special lessons were given. Subsequently, there was a parade in the playground, where the boys saluted the flag. In conclusion, there then followed the singing of the National Anthem.

TUESDAY and WEDNESDAY, JUNE 12th and 13th
The eighth annual athletics sports of the Erdington Elementary Schools were held under A. A. A. rules at the Erdington Cottage Homes grounds. Slade Road was victorious, winning both the Girls' and Boys' Championships. In the Girls' Championship, the school won five out of the eight events contested, whilst in the Boys' Championship, they recorded three wins in the ten events. The president of the association, Councillor R. R. Gelling, addressed

the large gathering, speaking in congratulatory terms of the splendid arrangements made by all the officials of the sports, and of the fine spirit in which they had been entered into by all the competitors. The Yenton and Wiggins-Davies Trophies were then presented to the winning teams that had represented the school.

WEDNESDAY, JULY 11th

A very successful and well-attended Parents' Day was held at the Boys' School during the afternoon. Councillor W. B. Featherstone, who was the chairman of the Erdington Education Committee, attended, and spoke to the assembled gathering of the boys' recent Higher Education examination successes, which numbered 53. He went on to speak of the educational changes that were forecast, where primary education would cease at the age of eleven, and all children of eleven and over would go on to some form of advanced education. Children would receive an education to suit their capacity, their special needs and aptitudes. In reply, Mr Jones thanked the Councillor for being present and went on to speak of the success of the boys with regard to sport. He expressed thanks to the parents for their co-operation, which had always been most helpful, securing as it did the punctuality and general orderliness of the boys. Excellent exhibitions of work were on view in all the classrooms and visitors were able to see the boys at work in their ordinary class routines, hear them at dramatisation and singing and witness very smart displays of physical exercises in the playground. In the science laboratory, the boys were at work and specimens of their work were on view, as was also the case in the manual room. The proceedings concluded at 4.30p.m.

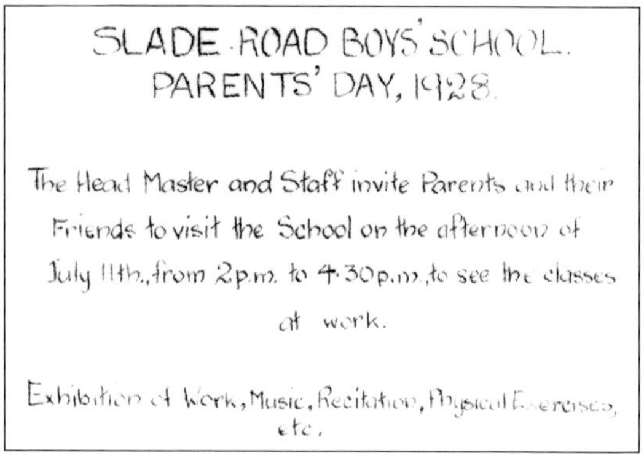
SLADE ROAD BOYS' SCHOOL.
PARENTS' DAY, 1928.

The Head Master and Staff invite Parents and their Friends to visit the School on the afternoon of July 11th., from 2p.m. to 4.30p.m., to see the classes at work.

Exhibition of Work, Music, Recitation, Physical Exercises, etc.

Parents' Day Invitation, 1928.

WEDNESDAY, JULY 18th

For the second year in succession, the boys won the Erdington Schools' Cricket Shield. John Whelan of Standard 7, who passed the entrance examination for Handsworth Junior Technical School, was awarded the 'Jackson' Exhibition by that school. This was worth £10 per annum for two years.

THURSDAY, JULY 26th

Miss Newby, who had commenced at the school on August 23rd, 1920, terminated her employment on this, the last day of term, on account of her forthcoming marriage to Mr Bosker on August 2nd. Mr Bosker was a widower, his wife having passed away in July of 1922.

MONDAY, SEPTEMBER 3rd

An exchange teacher from Australia, Miss Gillett, who was on the supply staff, came to assist at the school for a period of four weeks. Her visit was thoroughly enjoyed by both scholars and staff. She eventually returned to Australia via Genoa, Basle, Bremen, Rio De Janeiro, New York and San Francisco.

MONDAY, SEPTEMBER 10th

Mr George Ridge resumed duties as the Attendance Officer for the district. His son, Frank, had attended the school until the end of 1924, when he had passed for the Handsworth Junior Technical School. He successfully completed his course and went on to work at the G.E.C. in Witton.

TUESDAY, OCTOBER 2nd

The first annual Championship Swimming Gala of the Erdington Elementary Schools' Athletics Association took place at Mason Road Baths. Although the school only won one of the events, that being in the boys' novelty race, the girls finished as runners up in their competition to Moor End Lane, achieving four second place finishes. At the conclusion of the evening, the cups were presented to the winning schools by Councillor W. B. Featherstone.

FRIDAY, OCTOBER 12th

A successful meeting of parents and old scholars was held this evening under the chairmanship of Councillor Featherstone. The discussion centred on the idea that education did not cease the moment that the children left school. After good early training, it was now appreciated that there should be a linking up between school and work, as well as other social organisations. Great advantages were, therefore, accruing for the Evening Institutes, who currently had 1200 to 1300 students on their books. Talks were given by an organiser of the Juvenile Employment and Welfare Department and an inspector of the Evening Institutes. During the intermission, delightful singing by the City Ladies Choir – it had started out as an Old Scholars' Club – was greatly appreciated and added considerably to the enjoyment of the evening.

FRIDAY, NOVEMBER 23rd

The boys of the school subscribed £1.7s.0d. to the Birmingham Royal Institution for the Blind.

WEDNESDAY, DECEMBER 5th

The boys of the school, by buying poppies, collected £3.7s.3d. for Remembrance Day. This was today acknowledged by Earl Jellicoe.

FRIDAY, DECEMBER 14th

The collection for the Children's Charities amounted to £18.14s.3d., this being sent to the Treasurer of the Fund

Christmas bookmark photographs were all the rage in the Infants.

1929

FRIDAY, FEBRUARY 1st

Over the previous few weeks, there had been a tremendous amount of sickness in the school. By today, the absentee rate had reached its highest level of 30%!

MONDAY, APRIL 1st

During the Easter holidays, Mr and Mrs Morgan, the newly-appointed caretakers, commenced their duties.

FRIDAY, APRIL 26th

End of Term examinations were given in all classes during the week.

THURSDAY, MAY 2nd

Standard 6b visited Fort Dunlop. During the interesting and instructive visit, the whole process from the growth of the rubber tree to the manufactured articles was explained and demonstrated as far as possible.

FRIDAY, MAY 3rd

The Girls' School had two successes at the Midland Musical Festival today. Under the tutorship of Miss Ada Butler, they won the cantata class with 86 marks, whilst Miss

Chamberlain saw her choir through to victory in the competition for Girls' Council School choirs with 174 marks.

THURSDAY, JUNE 13th
A party of 50 boys visited the Royal Society of Artists' rooms in New Street to view an exhibition of drawings which had been done in Elementary Schools.

WEDNESDAY, JUNE 19th
A party of boys from Standard 5 visited Aston Hall as part of the History period, in which they were studying the Tudors.

FRIDAY, JUNE 21st
83 boys from Standards 5, 6, 7 and 8 attended an evening performance – beginning at 7.15p.m. – of *Twelfth Night* at the Prince of Wales Theatre. This was one of numerous plays being performed over a period of a fortnight by the Stratford upon Avon Shakespeare Theatre Company under the direction of Mr Bridges Adams.

SATURDAY, JUNE 29th
Nine members of staff accompanied 34 boys on a visit to Llangollen. After ascending 1, 900 feet of Moel Gamelin, they returned via the Horseshoe Pass and Vale Crucis Abbey. There were many opportunities for geographical observation en route. Much was learnt of the work of rivers, the gradation of pastures from valley to summit, the birth of a canal, and of mountain and river vegetation.

WEDNESDAY and THURSDAY, JULY 3rd and 4th
The ninth annual sports of the Erdington Elementary Schools' Athletic Association were held at the Cottage Homes grounds in Reservoir Road. There were 1,600 entries for the sports and, besides Slade School, the following were represented: Osborne Road; Church of England; Moor End Lane; Paget Road; Sir Josiah Mason's; St. Thomas' R. C.; Fentham Road; Ryland Road; Green Lanes and Hastings Road. Over 2,000 people saw the finals of the events, which were contested on Thursday night. As in previous years, the organisation of the sports was excellent, reflecting great credit on all the officers concerned. The events were keenly contested and the usual fine spirit of good sportsmanship prevailed. The prizes were once again distributed by Mrs Gelling, her husband being the president of the association. Slade School distinguished themselves well, finishing as runners up in both the Girls' and Boys' Championships. They won five of the events contested, namely the Senior Girls' 100 yards, 100 yards skipping and relay, whilst taking first place in the Senior Boys' tug of war and throwing the cricket ball.

WEDNESDAY, JULY 24th
A visit to the studios of the British Broadcasting Association was organised today for a party of 35 boys from Standards 6 and 8.

THURSDAY, JULY 25th

The Headmaster, Mr Jones, was absent as he was attending the Conference of the World Federation of Educational Associations in Geneva.

MONDAY, AUGUST 26th

The school re-opened after the summer holiday. Nearly ten percent of the children were still away on holidays. There was a gradual trickle back over the next three weeks.

FRIDAY, SEPTEMBER 20th

Harvest Festival was celebrated today. The fruit and vegetables that were collected were sent as gifts to the children of Dartmouth Street Infants' School, Staniforth Street and St. Mary's Aston Brook Schools.

MONDAY, SEPTEMBER 30th

The District Inspector gave permission to increase the size of classes from 50 to 55.

THURSDAY, OCTOBER 17th

Following a visit from a gentleman, representing the Royal Institution for the Blind, the boys of the school collected £1.4s.3d.

FRIDAY, OCTOBER 18th

In a flurry of excitement, all the children were allowed out of their classrooms this morning, so that they could stand in the playground and witness the R101 Airship pass over the school. It had left Cardington at 8.12a.m. and was performing turning trials over Birmingham at 1,500 feet at about eleven o'clock in the morning.

R101, 1928.

MONDAY, NOVEMBER 11th

The assembled school listened to the Armistice Service from 10.45a.m. until 11.15a.m., which was being broadcast from the Cenotaph in Whitehall.

THURSDAY, DECEMBER 5th

A party of 50 boys was taken on a visit of Lucas's in Great King Street.

1930

MONDAY, FEBRUARY 17th

100 boys from Standards 3 and 4, under the supervision of two teachers, travelled by train to Lichfield. The visit was of an historical nature for they were conducted over the Cathedral by the chief verger, whose descriptions were very interesting and educational.

FRIDAY, FEBRUARY 28th

An epidemic of whooping cough saw the attendance levels slip to 90%.

WEDNESDAY, MARCH 12th

For one week *Peter Pan* was put on at the Prince of Wales Theatre. Although there were special prices for schools at evening performances, the girls of Standard 8 – mainly 14 year olds – went to see a matinee performance today, provided they could afford it; that is except for a few who had been lucky enough to have won a ticket at school. The production was said to have run on well-trod, effective lines and was calculated to give as great a delight as ever to children of every age. Lionel Gadsden played Hook, Judy Hallett – Wendy, whilst the height of excellence was struck by Sheila Maloney – a well-nigh perfect little Peter, who had the youth, the wistfulness, the reserve, the mischievous spirit and all the other qualities essential to the successful characteristics of the boy who would not grow up. The girls were taken there and back by Miss Chamberlain on the tram.

THURSDAY, APRIL 10th

Another trip out, but this time for the boys of Standard 5, who, accompanied by two teachers, went to look around Tamworth Castle.

MONDAY, APRIL 28th

School re-opened this morning after the Easter holidays. Although a new school had opened today at Marsh Hill for boys and girls up to the age of 9, it had only affected Slade School slightly, a few children having left to attend the new school.

APRIL

On the next page can be found the final tables for the Erdington Schools' Football League for the season 1929/1930.

THURSDAY, MAY 8th to SATURDAY, MAY 10th
A short course of five lectures was arranged for all head teachers and chief assistants at the Midland Institute by the Local Education Authority. The new prospect for schools was outlined by H.M.I., Mr C. E. Jackson, who was assisted by H.M.I., Mr C. A. Richardson. The curriculum, tests, examinations and the psychological considerations of organisation and classification were all thoroughly discussed. The object was to explain how old methods and subjects would work in a new setting with a new outlook. Subsequently, the following week, the subject matter was outlined to all members of staff and discussed.

LEAGUE 1

	P	W	D	L	F	A	PTS
GREEN LANES	16	13	1	2	68	31	27
OSBORNE ROAD	16	10	1	5	51	23	21
SLADE ROAD	16	8	4	4	50	35	20
NATIONAL	16	7	4	5	47	30	18
MOOR END LANE	16	8	2	6	38	34	18
PERRY COMMON	16	5	2	9	38	47	12
ST THOMAS'	16	4	2	10	37	72	10
PAGET ROAD	16	4	2	10	22	55	10
RYLAND ROAD	16	3	2	11	32	58	8

LEAGUE 2

	P	W	D	L	F	A	PTS
PERRY COMMON	16	14	1	1	106	17	29
GREEN LANES	16	13	2	1	105	19	28
OSBORNE ROAD	16	10	1	5	57	27	21
SLADE ROAD	16	9	1	6	54	41	19
RYLAND ROAD	16	8	1	7	60	43	17
PAGET ROAD	16	6	0	10	33	65	12
MOOR END LANE	16	5	2	9	27	87	12
ST THOMAS'	16	2	2	12	23	77	6
NATIONAL	16	0	0	16	6	89	0

Top: Erdington Schools' Football League, 1929/1930. Bottom: Infant Class 1 with Miss Blake c.1930.

WEDNESDAY, MAY 14th
At the Midland Musical Festival, in the competition for the Laura Sharpe Banner, which was awarded for National Dances and other English Folk Dances for teams of not less than 6 children aged 11 to 13 from a school in the Midland Counties, Miss Doris Handley guided her troupe to finish as runners up with 178 marks.

FRIDAY, MAY 16th
At the Midland Musical Festival, in the competition for the Stockwell Banner, awarded to a girls' choir from any Public Elementary School in the Midland Counties, the Girls' School, under the guidance of Miss Elsie Badcock, finished as runners up with 174 marks.

SATURDAY, MAY 24th
The Headmaster, together with six teachers, accompanied 95 boys by train to spend a most interesting and enjoyable day out at Windsor Castle and Runneymede, especially so they could see where King John signed the Magna Carta.

THURSDAY, JULY 3rd
A visit for 24 boys of Standards 4 and 5 was arranged today, in order to visit Kenilworth Castle.

WEDNESDAY, JULY 9th

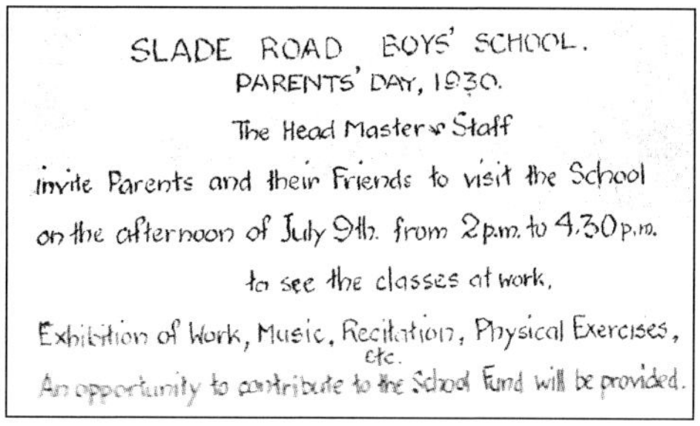
SLADE ROAD BOYS' SCHOOL.
PARENTS' DAY, 1930.
The Head Master & Staff
invite Parents and their Friends to visit the School
on the afternoon of July 9th. from 2p.m. to 4.30p.m.
to see the classes at work.
Exhibition of Work, Music, Recitation, Physical Exercises, etc.
An opportunity to contribute to the School Fund will be provided.

Parents' Day Invitation, 1930.

MONDAY, AUGUST 25th
The school re-opened after the summer break. In view of the impending re-organisation in line with the 'Hadow Report', the scheme of instruction in standards was suspended. In its place, classification now took place by age. However, each class was divided into groups according to attainment and records kept by each teacher to show the work that each group was performing during the week.

WEDNESDAY, SEPTEMBER 17th
A Harvest Festival was once again held at the school. Large quantities of vegetables and other produce were brought in and later distributed amongst the poor children of Nechells, Aston Brook and Aston Lane Schools.

FRIDAY, OCTOBER 3rd
The third annual Swimming Gala of the Erdington Elementary Schools' Athletic Association was held at Mason Road baths in the presence of a large audience. In the Boys' Championship, Slade Road and Green Lanes tied for first place, each with 10 points out of a possible 15, and shared the trophy, which was presented by Mr W. J. Davies.

FRIDAY, OCTOBER 24th
The engagement of the chief assistant, Mr Emlyn Howell, terminated today. He had been recognised as a certificated teacher since 1915 and, in fact, joined Slade Road in August of that year. He left to take up the Headship of Shepshed Council School in Leicestershire. On the wall of his classroom he kept a certificate, on which were a pair of boxing gloves with money pouring out of them.

TUESDAY, NOVEMBER 11th
Today being Armistice Day, a short service was held for the assembled school between 10.50a.m. and 11.15a.m. The programme consisted of a short address followed by the Last Post. After the two minutes' silence, the children sang *O God, our help in ages past* before

reciting the Lord's Prayer. With the sound of reveille still echoing in the hall, they concluded the service with the singing of the National Anthem, before retiring to their classrooms. The sum of £3.17s.0d. was raised by the boys from the sale of Flanders Poppies.

MONDAY, NOVEMBER 17th
Forty boys went to the Camp School at Bell Heath, Belbroughton, where they spent two weeks before returning to school on December 1st. They all looked very well and appeared to have thoroughly enjoyed themselves.

DECEMBER
A blackboard appeared outside the Star Picture House, by the first house in Broomfield Road, opposite the school, which most of the children must have seen. It begged people to sign a petition for the reprieve of Herbert Charles Ridley, who was due to hang for the murder of William Thomas Andrews. At Taylors in Potters Hill, Mr Andrews had been killed during the course of a robbery of the firm's takings of £908. Ridley's partner in crime, Victor Edward Betts, was hung on January 3rd, 1931 because he had been responsible for striking the fatal blow, but Ridley's sentence was commuted to life imprisonment. His petition for clemency was, therefore, successful.

TUESDAY, DECEMBER 16th
An amount of £17.10s.6d. was collected for the Children's Charities Fund, which was forwarded on to the Treasurer.

1931

FRIDAY, FEBRUARY 13th
Mr Jones, the Headmaster, was absent today attending meetings of the executive of the National Union of Teachers in London, regarding the War Aid Fund.

WEDNESDAY and THURSDAY, MARCH 18th and 19th
The school was closed on the mornings of both these days, in order that it might be used as an overflow centre in connection with the examination for admission to secondary schools. A total of 236 boys sat the examination which was supervised by members of the staff.

SUNDAY, APRIL 12th
Because of the impending changes, Miss Ada Butler decided to leave the Girls' School and became chief assistant at Rubery. She had started at Slade Road on the opening day in 1904 and it must have been something of a wrench, at the age of 50, to leave the school after 27 years of service. She drove an Austin 7 with flapping windows – not glass.

TUESDAY, MAY 5th
A party of 40 boys was taken by motor coach to a camp school at Headington, near Oxford, where they remained until May 26th. During the time that they spent there, they enjoyed

good weather and paid a number of educational visits to places of interest, including most of the Oxford Colleges.

SUNDAY, MAY 31st
Another departure, this time of the Headmistress of the Girls' School, Miss Clara Amelia Baum. She had started at the school as chief assistant on its opening day, becoming Headmistress of the Girls' School on September 1st, 1906 at the time of the school's first re-organisation. She would be remembered as an extremely elegant and stately lady, her hair done up on top of her head, who always wore a white blouse and long black skirt. Hanging from a chain around her neck would be a gold fob watch, which would be tucked into the waistband of her skirt, around which was a belt with a golden buckle. Each morning, as the girls filed into assembly, she would check that their shoes were polished and their hands clean. In class, you knew you were in trouble when you heard a clicking sound coming from the object she carried around with her in her hand. After nearly 25 years as head, she moved to become the Headmistress at Nansen Road Senior Girls' School, where she remained until she retired in 1940 at the age of 60.

MONDAY, JUNE 8th
Miss Mackintosh, the district inspector, came to the school to interview all the staff concerning their desires in view of the re-organisation which was to take place after the summer holidays.

WEDNESDAY and THURSDAY, JUNE 17th and 18th
The 11th annual sports of the Erdington Elementary Schools took place at the Erdington Cottage Homes grounds. This would be the last time that the senior girls challenged for the Yenton Trophy, as from July 22nd they would no longer be able to attend the school. On this occasion, the school failed to gain any success.

WEDNESDAY, JULY 22nd
Miss Harriet Ransford Dupen had been on the Domestic Subjects staff since 1909. Her work with the girls of Slade Road ceased today as all girls over the age of 11would now be taught at Fentham Road.

THURSDAY, JULY 23rd
The school having broken up for the summer vacation, the staff presented themselves in order to re-organise everything in preparation for the changes taking place at the start of the new term. This required the removal of items from the junior classrooms of the Boys' School to the junior classrooms of the Girls' School and from the senior classrooms of the Girls' School to the senior classrooms of the Boys' School.

MONDAY, AUGUST 24th
The new term commenced. The school was now divided into Infants, Juniors and Senior Boys. As such, this resulted in a number of staff changes. Miss Griffiths-Jones, Miss Benwell

and Mrs Stoppard moved from the Boys' School to the Junior School, whilst the Boys' School employed four newly-qualified teachers as well as a transferee from Osborne Road. Mr Fox, Mr Neville, Mr T. A. Jones and Mr Kennedy were all newly-qualified, the latter two taking up lodgings with Mr Macken, who himself had been at the school for only six months. Mr John Oldroyd moved from Osborne Road, where he had spent the previous 18 years. Miss Kay, Miss Badcock and Mrs Tarling chose to continue to work with senior girls and so moved to Fentham Road Girls' School. No girls over the age of 11 were now taught at the school and 193 boys, under the age of 11, were transferred to the Junior School. From Osborne Road, 103 boys were admitted to the Senior Boys' School. The school now catered for 360 Senior Boys, 450 Junior Mixed and 300 Infants. Incidentally, the Senior Boys' School was now staffed completely by men. With the introduction of the newly-formed Junior School, it was found necessary to employ a new Head Teacher. Mr C. Gooding Clarke took up his duties today.

TUESDAY, AUGUST 25th
One day after the resumption of school and the playground was being re-topped with asphalt! It wasn't completed until the second week of September.

FRIDAY, NOVEMBER 6th
The caretakers, Mr and Mrs Morgan, were moved to another school. Mr and Mrs Lester were appointed in their stead.

SATURDAY, NOVEMBER 28th
All the ordinary fixtures in the Erdington Schools' Football League were suspended in order to receive a visit from Shepshed Council School in Leicestershire, where Mr Emlyn Howell had taken up the post of Headmaster. In dull weather, two games were played, both ending in victories for the Erdington representative sides by scores of 5-1. After the game, 70 were entertained to tea at the Yenton Masonic Lodge, the evening being spent at the Cattle show.

The Erdington Cottage Homes Boys' Band taken at the back of cottage number 16 on the bank of the sports field in the early thirties.

Left: At 11.40 on one morning late in 1931, Form 3A display the results of their woodworking skills in the manual room of the school. The teachers are Mr Wedd (left) and Mr Dixon (right). Right: A greetings photograph from the Senior Boys' School Christmas 1931.

THURSDAY, DECEMBER 31st
Miss Nellie Matilda Bryan retired at the age of 60. She had been the Headmistress of the Infants' department for 27 years since the school opened in 1904. She was a strict, white haired, little lady who wore pince-nez. Many children were frightened of her for she would smack them for the slightest reason. Every day they had to show their hands were clean. Their handkerchieves – even if they were only pieces of old rag – had to be used to wipe their noses. Woe betide them if they wiped them on their sleeves and as for sniffing…!

1932
JANUARY
Miss G. M. Freeling became Headmistress of the Infants' department.

MONDAY, FEBRUARY 29th
The sum of £8.11s.3d. was collected by the Boys' School in aid of the Children's Charities Fund.

WEDNESDAY and THURSDAY, MARCH 9th and 10th
The Boys' School was closed today, so that it might be used as an overflow centre in connection with the examination for admission to secondary schools. The staff acted as invigilators and 185 boys took the examination.

SATURDAY, APRIL 2nd
It was noted that Mr Edmund Jones, the Headmaster of the Senior Boys' School, had been re-elected to the executive of the National Union of Teachers. He had been honorary

Senior Boys' School Class 3b with Mr Fox, c.1931.
Senior Boys' School Class 1c with Mr Neville, c.1933.

secretary of the Birmingham Association since 1920 and was well known throughout Birmingham as an expert on educational matters. He had now completed 17 years membership of the executive.

SENIOR A	P	W	D	L	F	A	PTS
PERRY COMMON	14	14	0	0	74	10	28
PAGET ROAD	14	9	2	3	51	42	20
GREEN LANES	14	8	2	4	36	29	18
RYLAND ROAD	14	5	2	7	42	48	12
NATIONAL	14	5	2	7	31	34	12
JOSIAH MASON'S	14	3	2	9	36	59	8
MOOR END	14	3	2	9	22	52	8
SLADE ROAD	14	2	2	10	26	48	6

SENIOR B	P	W	D	L	F	A	PTS
PERRY COMMON	14	14	0	0	86	13	28
RYLAND ROAD	14	8	2	4	48	31	18
SLADE ROAD	14	7	3	4	58	30	17
NATIONAL	14	4	4	6	37	47	12
GREEN LANES	14	4	4	6	31	50	12
PAGET ROAD	14	4	3	7	28	43	11
MOOR END	14	3	2	9	23	50	8
JOSIAH MASON'S	14	2	2	10	18	61	6

JUNIOR	P	W	D	L	F	A	PTS
GUNTER ROAD	7	6	0	1	25	5	12
PAGET ROAD	7	6	0	1	27	9	12
OSBORNE ROAD	7	4	0	3	25	9	8
SLADE ROAD	7	4	0	3	14	7	8
RYLAND ROAD	7	4	0	3	18	15	8
NATIONAL	7	3	0	4	18	17	6
BIRCHES GREEN	7	1	0	6	6	20	2
TEDBURY CRESCENT	7	0	0	7	3	57	0

Final Tables Erdington Schools' Football League 1931/1932 Season.

THURSDAY, APRIL 7th
Some disruption was being caused to the ordinary work of the school as a number of workmen, including painters, were engaged there.

MONDAY, APRIL 11th
The newly-appointed science room in the Senior Boys' School was used for the first time this week.

THURSDAY, APRIL 21st
A party of 20 boys visited the Science Exhibition at Acocks Green Council School during the afternoon.

SATURDAY, APRIL 30th
In the Junior Cup Final of the Erdington Schools' Football League, Slade Road met Paget Road. There was a keen ding-dong struggle and, early on, Paget Road took the lead through Landell. Birbeck put Slade Road back on level terms and the game appeared to be heading for extra time when Landell broke through to register the winning goal for Paget Road.

Losing finalists, Erdington Schools' Junior Football Cup, Slade Road Junior Football Team.

TUESDAY, JUNE 14th
During the afternoon, 50 boys attended an exhibition of Elementary Schools' drawings at the Royal Society of Artists in New Street.

WEDNESDAY, JULY 13th
Today was Parents' Day, and a large number visited the school together with many friends. Inspecting the literacy efforts at the exhibition of school work, parents must have been amused by the composition of one small fellow from the second form. He had expressed a desire, in the first sentence, that he might change his identity and said, that if this was possible, he would rather be Larry Gains, the famous coloured boxer, than anyone else. He was obviously a fan, asserting that Gains was at the height of his career, having defeated the Italian boxer, Carnera. If this young writer's ambition had come true, he would certainly have commanded the respect from his schoolfellows! Miss Mackintosh, the district inspector, and Mr Jones, the Headmaster, later addressed the large gathering of parents. It was said that efforts were being made at the school to give attention to character training as well as physical and academic education. It was considered that, more than ever before, the authorities needed the co-operation of parents and their frank criticism. Changes had been made at the school with the erection of a new science laboratory and increased accommodation in the handicrafts room. The exhibition of work on view gave an idea of the standard that might be expected two or three years into the future when the school had passed the experimental stages of the changes that had then only recently occurred. Examination successes were also highlighted, these taking the form of 42 passes for secondary schools, which included 16 scholarships for King Edward's, Aston.

SATURDAY, JULY 23rd
The cricket season had now concluded, Slade Road finishing as runners up in the Erdington Schools' Senior Cricket League to Paget Road. At this time, Lesley Croom, son of the Warwickshire opening batsman, A. J. W. Croom, was attending the school. Naturally, he

SENIOR				
	P	W	L	PTS
PAGET ROAD	5	5	0	10
SLADE ROAD	6	4	2	8
RYLAND ROAD	6	4	2	8
HASTINGS ROAD	6	3	3	6
NATIONAL	5	2	3	4
MOOR END	6	1	5	2
GREEN LANES	6	1	5	2

JUNIOR				
	P	W	L	PTS
PAGET ROAD	6	5	1	10
RYLAND ROAD	6	5	1	10
GUNTER ROAD	6	4	2	8
SLADE ROAD	6	3	3	6
BIRCHES GREEN	6	2	4	4
OSBORNE ROAD	6	1	5	2
MOOR END	6	1	5	2

Final Tables Erdington Schools' Cricket League.

played cricket for Slade Road, as well as football, until he left for Handsworth Technical School in 1934. He later represented Warwickshire in 1949, although he only scored 73 runs in 8 innings.

MONDAY, AUGUST 22nd

Returning after the summer holidays, expecting to find a full-time teacher of handicrafts, the Headmaster, Mr Jones, was greeted by the arrival of a letter from the chief education officer to the effect that this service would now only be provided on a part-time basis. This, coming out of the blue, completely upset the plans that had been made in the organisation of the classes. It now necessitated the preparation of a totally new timetable!

SEPTEMBER

During this month, Mr Jones appears to have had his hands full with two problems. Firstly, there appeared to be some controversy as to whether visits to school camps were regarded as educational or not. A number of meetings took place before he received a telephone call from the Education Office telling him that he could send boys to a camp that had been previously arranged. The other ongoing matter seemed to have been resolved when he received a letter from the chief education officer informing him that the placement of a teacher of handicrafts was now once again full time. However, there still appeared to be one small matter to be ironed out for the handicrafts room had not been equipped for metalwork.

TUESDAY, SEPTEMBER 27th

Today, 40 boys in charge of one teacher, Mr Macken, went to a school camp at St. Ebba's Priory, near Oxford, for three weeks.

MONDAY, OCTOBER 3rd
Good reports were received concerning the health, conduct and attendance of those boys at the school camp.

TUESDAY, OCTOBER 18th
23 more boys were taken to the camp school at St. Ebba's Priory by Mr T. A. Jones, who returned with 34 of the original 40. The remaining 6 stayed on for a further three weeks, together with the later arrivals, under the direction of Mr Macken.

THURSDAY, OCTOBER 20th
The situation regarding the teaching of Handicrafts would simply not go away. The services of the appointed teacher were now required at Hastings Road School with immediate effect! A supply teacher was despatched to the school to cover the seven days left until the autumn holiday commenced. It was also felt by the Education Office that the scheme for the teaching of metalwork at the school should be abandoned and the manual room used for the teaching of woodwork only.

MONDAY, NOVEMBER 7th
The school re-opened after the break with the manual room being used by 40 boys for the first time. Deykin Avenue, apparently, would continue to use the facilities on Tuesday afternoons and all day on Thursdays as they had previously done. The teacher sent to Hastings Road now returned. Equally returning were the second lot of boys who had been to camp.

FRIDAY, NOVEMBER 11th
Remembrance Day was suitably observed with appropriate hymns, prayers and an address between 10.50a.m. and 11.15a.m. A sum of £2.14s.6d. was collected for the ex-servicemen of Birmingham and their dependants.

SATURDAY, DECEMBER 10th
A second football clash between an Erdington representative team and a team from Shepshed Council School was arranged. The only player selected from Slade School was Horsman. Unfortunately, the result is not known.

1933

MONDAY, JANUARY 23rd
Examinations were given during the week in connection with half-yearly promotions.

WEDNESDAY, JANUARY 24th
The Boys' School, together with all the members of the staff, visited a Telephone Exhibition at Suffolk Street.

FRIDAY, FEBRUARY 3rd

14 boys left school today having attained the leaving age. Altogether, 83 new scholars were admitted to the Boys' School, including 47 from the Junior School, 8 from Osborne Road Junior School and 25 from the Erdington Cottage Homes.

THURSDAY, FEBRUARY 16th

The subject of the hygiene of food and drink was once again raised with the boys this morning by the Midland Band of Hope Union.

SATURDAY, APRIL 29th

Slade Road reached the final of the Intermediate Knock Out Cup in the Erdington Schools' Football League. Having previously beaten Hastings Road by three goals to two in the semi-final, they came up against Paget Road, who had been equally successful by a similar margin in their tie with Ryland Road. In a close fought game, they lost out to Paget Road by two goals to one, their only tally coming from Croom.

SATURDAY, MAY 13th

Everything was set for the 13th season of the Erdington Schools' Cricket League. Arrangements had been made for two divisions – one Junior and one Senior – as well as an Intermediate knock out competition. Fixture cards were on sale in all the schools priced one penny.

SENIOR A

	P	W	D	L	F	A	PTS
HASTINGS ROAD	14	10	3	1	31	13	23
PAGET ROAD	14	10	1	3	67	19	21
JOSIAH MASON'S	14	6	5	3	39	21	17
GREEN LANES	14	7	2	5	37	28	16
SLADE ROAD	14	6	1	7	38	32	13
RYLAND ROAD	14	6	1	7	27	44	13
NATIONAL	14	1	3	10	22	54	5
MOOR END	14	0	4	10	18	78	4

SENIOR B

	P	W	D	L	F	A	PTS
HASTINGS ROAD	14	14	0	0	123	10	28
NATIONAL	14	10	2	2	53	33	22
PAGET ROAD	14	8	2	4	71	41	18
SLADE ROAD	14	5	1	8	35	57	11
RYLAND ROAD	14	4	2	8	34	42	10
GREEN LANES	14	4	1	9	32	79	9
JOSIAH MASON'S	14	3	1	10	24	72	7
MOOR END	14	3	1	10	19	57	7

JUNIOR

	P	W	D	L	F	A	PTS
GUNTER ROAD	16	11	3	2	42	17	25
PAGET ROAD	16	9	3	4	47	19	21
SLADE ROAD	16	8	5	3	32	15	21
OSBORNE ROAD	16	6	5	5	31	25	17
RYLAND ROAD	16	7	3	6	27	28	17
MOOR END	16	5	5	6	22	30	15
NATIONAL	16	4	4	8	15	35	12
BIRCHES GREEN	16	3	4	9	15	35	10
GREEN LANES	16	2	2	12	6	40	6

Final League Tables Erdington Schools' Football League 1932/1933 Season.

WEDNESDAY, MAY 24th

The results of the Secondary Schools' admission examination were to hand and 32 boys from the school had passed.

TUESDAY and WEDNESDAY, JUNE 27th and 28th

Good weather favoured the 13th annual Erdington Elementary Schools' Athletic Association sports, which were held on these two days at the sports ground in Reservoir Road. Attendance on the Tuesday, when the heats and semi-finals were run off, showed the keen interest taken in the sports. Again, on the Wednesday, the attendance did not belie the occasion, when some fine running was seen. Slade Road, the holders, once again won the

Junior Girls' Shield, whilst the boys were equally successful in their junior competition. In the girls' events, wins were obtained in the relay, and the 80 yards for girls under the age of ten. The junior boys took first place in the 100 yards, and the 80 yards for boys under the age of ten. In the Senior Boys' competition, the school's only success came in throwing the cricket ball. Afterwards, Councillor R. R. Gelling, the president of the association, presented the prizes for the open events, whilst Mr R. H. Bryan, superintendent of the Erdington Cottage Homes, presented the championship shields.

SATURDAY, JULY 29th

SENIOR

	P	W	L	PTS
PAGET ROAD	6	5	1	10
NATIONAL	6	5	1	10
MOOR END	6	4	2	8
HASTINGS ROAD	6	2	4	4
SLADE ROAD	6	2	4	4
GREEN LANES	6	2	4	4
RYLAND ROAD	6	1	5	2

Championship Decider
Paget Road 39 for 4 National 7

JUNIOR

	P	W	L	PTS
MOOR END	5	5	0	10
GUNTER ROAD	5	4	1	8
BIRCHES GREEN	5	3	2	6
SLADE ROAD	5	2	3	4
RYLAND ROAD	5	1	4	2
OSBORNE ROAD	5	0	5	0

All the matches played by Paget Road in the junior section were expunged from the records due to a 'mistake' !

Top Left: Final Erdington Schools' Cricket League Tables. Top Right: Miss Handley and Junior Class 10, c.1931/2. Bottom: Infant class, c.1933.

Infant class, c.1933.

LATE AUGUST

First day at school for these five-year-old infants.

Sword Dance, 1933.

THURSDAY, AUGUST 31st

Mrs Adeline Stoppard officially retired from the Junior School, shortly before her sixty-second birthday. She had commenced there in September 1910, transferring to the Boys' School in 1915 when the Junior School was closed down. When another re-organisation took place on August 23rd, 1931, she returned to the Junior School for her last two years of service. Kind but fierce looking, she was remembered from her earlier years as having a son, who was in one of the higher standards. She would send for him to look after her class whenever she was called away. As married female teachers could not be employed at the time, her husband must have died. In fact, she appears to have left teaching for twelve years between 1893 and 1905.

TUESDAY, OCTOBER 3rd

The sixth annual Championship Gala of the Erdington Elementary Schools was held at Mason Road baths. New shields had been presented to the association by the headmaster and staff of Green Lanes Boys' School in Wylde Green. In the Junior Girls' Championship, Slade Road tied for first place with Sir Josiah Mason's, whilst the boys finished as runners up to Green Lanes in the Junior Boys' Championship. The school placed first in both of the events for two widths for girls and boys.

SATURDAY, DECEMBER 9th

Once again, an Erdington representative football team met an eleven from Shepshed Council School. Selected to play from Slade Road were Hines and Parkes, both scoring twice in a ten to nothing drubbing of the visitors. Harry Parkes, born in January, 1920, was later to find fame and fortune playing at right back for Aston Villa for ten years.

WEDNESDAY, DECEMBER 20th

The boys of the Cottage Homes Boys' Band brought their instruments to school, in order to go around the different classes playing carols.

1934

MONDAY, FEBRUARY 19th

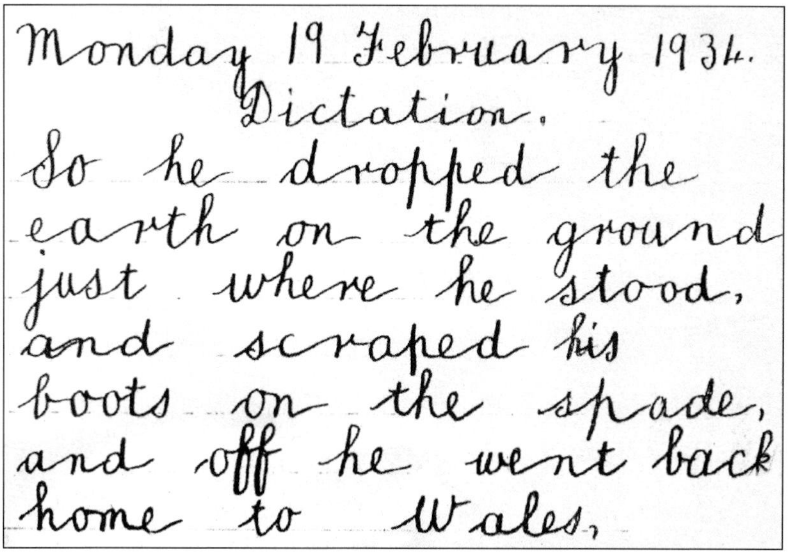

Monday 19 February 1934.
Dictation.
So he dropped the earth on the ground just where he stood, and scraped his boots on the spade, and off he went back home to Wales,

An example of work from a nine year old in the Juniors.

THURSDAY, FEBRUARY 22nd

At assembly this morning, Mr Jones addressed the senior boys regarding an unacceptable incident that had taken place. He asked the culprits to own up immediately, but no one chose to do so. In consequence, all the boys from the Cottage Homes were told to remain where they were, whilst the other boys were dismissed to their classes. He, then, repeated his question to them obtaining no response, whereupon he levied each with one stroke of the cane across each hand. This was a not uncommon practice by someone who was considered to be at the forefront of educational practice in Birmingham.

SATURDAY, MARCH 10th

In the Junior Knock Out Cup of the Erdington Schools' Football League, Slade Road met Moor End in the semi-final. After an even first half, during which both sides scored early on, the game settled into a terse struggle to decide the winner. In the end, just when a draw seemed the most likely result, Boon popped up to score his second goal and reward Slade Road with a place in the final against Green Lanes.

SATURDAY, MARCH 17th

Slade Road played Green Lanes in the final of the Junior Knock Out Cup, the first half being a pretty even affair. After the interval, Slade Road slowly got the better of the 'Lanes' and Ingram scored two capital goals to give Slade Road the victory and the cup.

THURSDAY, MARCH 22nd

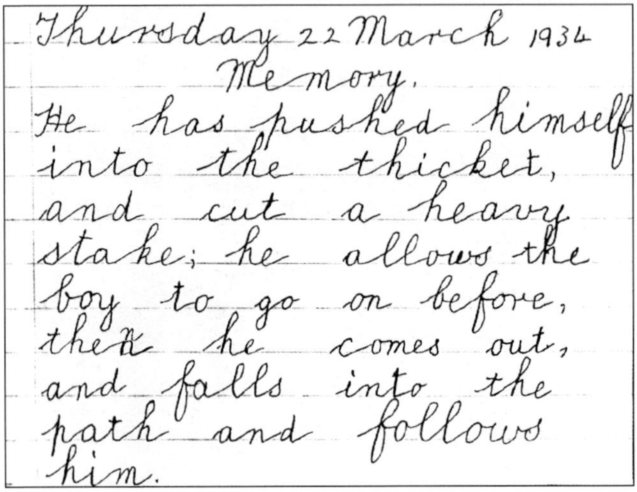

Thursday 22 March 1934
Memory.
He has pushed himself
into the thicket,
and cut a heavy
stake; he allows the
boy to go on before,
then he comes out,
and falls into the
path and follows
him.

Another example of work from a nine year old.

WEDNESDAY, MARCH 28th

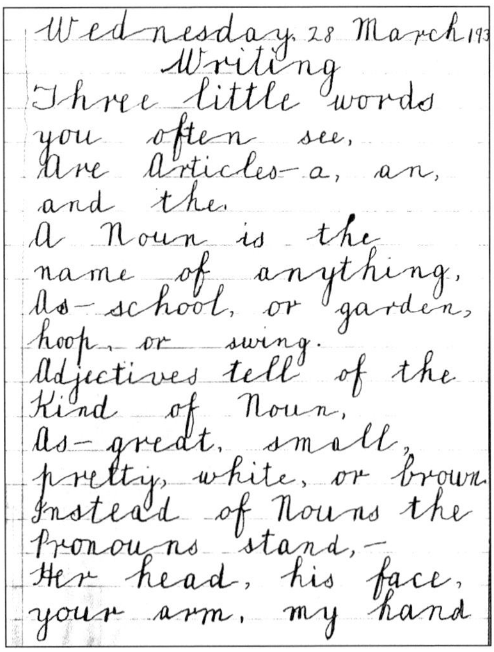

Wednesday 28 March 193
Writing
Three little words
you often see,
Are Articles — a, an,
and the.
A Noun is the
name of anything,
As — school, or garden,
hoop, or swing.
Adjectives tell of the
Kind of Noun,
As — great, small,
pretty, white, or brown.
Instead of Nouns the
Pronouns stand, —
Her head, his face,
your arm, my hand

Yet another example of the same child's work illustrated a week earlier.

SATURDAY, MARCH 31st

SENIOR	P	W	D	L	F	A	PTS
RYLAND ROAD	14	10	2	2	50	19	22
GREEN LANES	14	9	3	2	52	23	21
PAGET ROAD	14	8	2	4	51	23	18
HASTINGS ROAD	14	9	0	5	49	41	18
NATIONAL	14	7	2	5	32	27	16
SLADE ROAD	14	6	0	8	37	40	12
JOSIAH MASON'S	14	2	0	12	19	52	4
MOOR END	14	0	1	13	13	80	1

RESERVE	P	W	D	L	F	A	PTS
HASTINGS ROAD	14	13	1	0	97	13	27
PAGET ROAD	14	7	6	1	50	32	20
RYLAND ROAD	14	7	4	3	54	26	18
SLADE ROAD	14	6	4	4	36	49	16
NATIONAL	14	4	6	4	42	35	14
MOOR END	14	4	2	8	19	40	10
JOSIAH MASON'S	14	1	2	11	16	66	4
GREEN LANES	14	0	3	11	17	70	3

JUNIOR	P	W	D	L	F	A	PTS
PAGET ROAD	12	11	0	1	97	13	22
OSBORNE ROAD	12	6	4	2	27	11	16
MOOR END	12	5	1	6	17	18	11
GREEN LANES	12	5	0	7	12	31	10
BIRCHES GREEN	12	4	1	7	15	26	9
SLADE ROAD	12	4	1	7	12	23	9
RYLAND ROAD	12	3	1	8	20	33	7

Final Tables Erdington Schools' Football League 1933/1934 Season.

SATURDAY, APRIL 7th

Yet again we saw an arranged football match between Erdington and Shepshed, the only representative for Slade Road being Lewis. No result is known.

SATURDAY, JULY 21st

At Birches Green, the staff of Paget Road entertained the staff of Slade Road to a cricket match, which the former won by 83 runs to 74. For Slade Road, Mr Fox took 2 for 11 and Mr Airdrie 2 for 4, whilst Mr Hockaday scored an admirable 24 and Mr Evans 19.

SATURDAY, JULY 28th

A return cricket fixture was arranged between the staffs of Paget Road and Slade Road. This time, Slade Road batted first and, thanks to 23 runs from Mr Ross, assembled a reasonably respectable score. However, Paget Road put on 69 for the first wicket and passed the total with two wickets to spare.

TUESDAY, DECEMBER 18th

At the Parochial Hall in Broomfield Road the Junior School gave a repeat performance of their ballet and folk dance concert.

SENIOR	P	W	D	L	F	A	PTS
PAGET ROAD	6	5	0	1	253	150	10
SLADE ROAD	6	4	0	2	361	229	8
MOOR END	6	3	1	2	297	203	7
HASTINGS ROAD	6	3	1	2	178	203	7
RYLAND ROAD	6	3	0	3	228	203	6
NATIONAL	6	2	0	4	173	236	4
GREEN LANES	6	0	0	6	140	405	0

JUNIOR	P	W	D	L	F	A	PTS
BIRCHES GREEN	7	6	0	1	281	241	12
SLADE ROAD	7	5	0	2	345	249	10
GUNTER ROAD	7	4	1	2	287	204	9
PAGET ROAD	7	4	0	3	262	233	8
OSBORNE ROAD	7	3	0	4	265	281	6
NATIONAL	7	2	0	5	277	347	4
RYLAND ROAD	7	1	2	4	180	273	4
MOOR END	7	1	1	5	194	259	3

Final Tables Erdington Schools' Cricket League.

1935

THURSDAY, JANUARY 10th

Francis Aldridge and Eric Robinson commenced at Handsworth Junior Technical School, having passed the entrance examination and received the Jackson Exhibition. They had left Slade School just before Christmas.

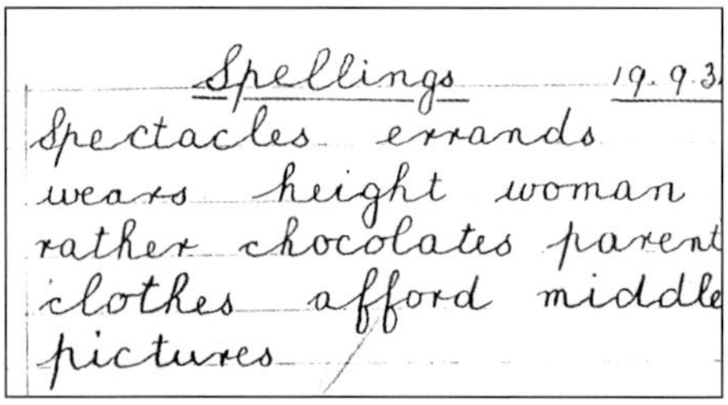

Spellings 19.9.3

Spectacles errands
wears height woman
rather chocolates parent
clothes afford middle
pictures

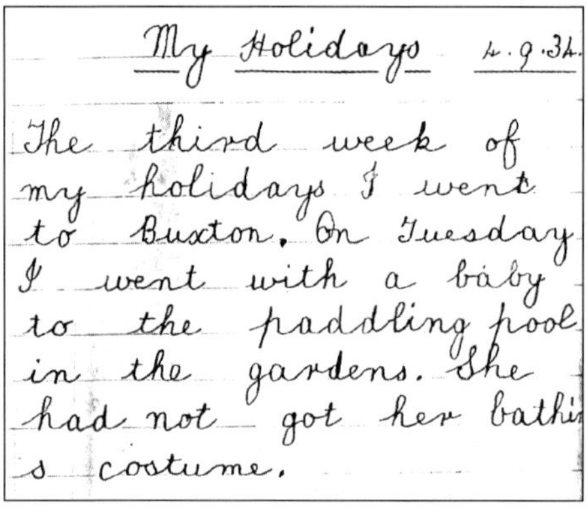

My Holidays 4.9.34.

The third week of
my holidays I went
to Buxton. On Tuesday
I went with a baby
to the paddling pool
in the gardens. She
had not got her bathi
s costume.

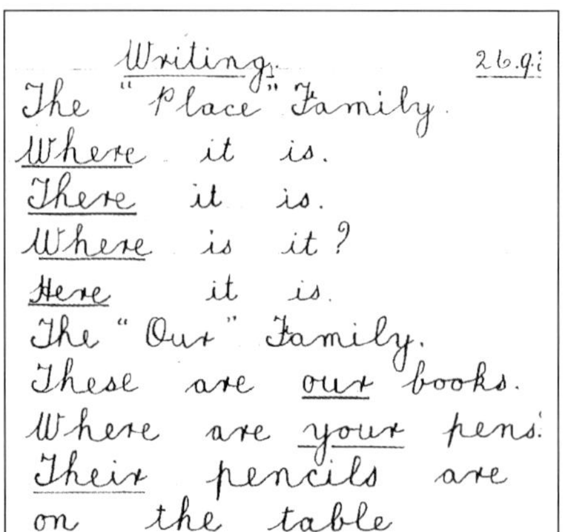

Writing 26.9.

The "Place" Family.
Where it is.
There it is.
Where is it?
Here it is.
The "Our" Family.
These are our books.
Where are your pens.
Their pencils are
on the table

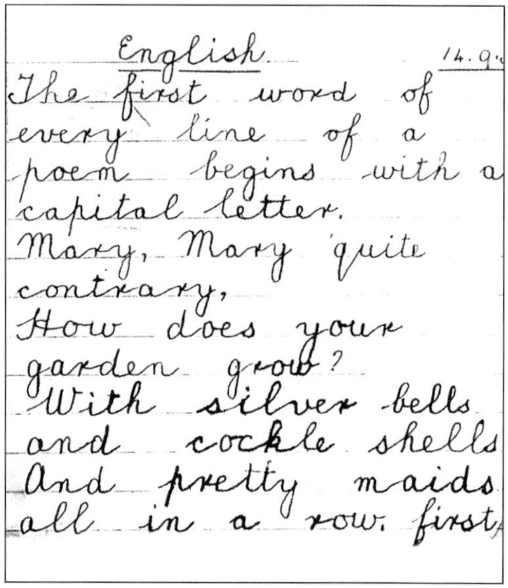

English. 14.9.

The first word of
every line of a
poem begins with a
capital letter.
Mary, Mary quite
contrary,
How does your
garden grow?
With silver bells
and cockle shells
And pretty maids
all in a row. first

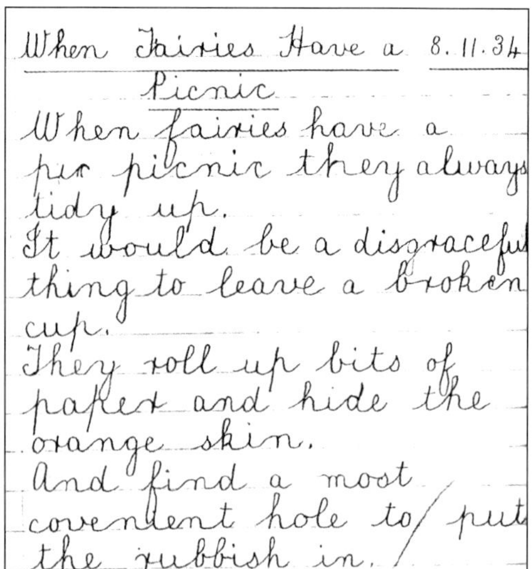

When Fairies Have a 8.11.34
Picnic

When fairies have a
pic picnic they always
tidy up.
It would be a disgraceful
thing to leave a broken
cup.
They roll up bits of
paper and hide the
orange skin.
And find a most
covenient hole to put
the rubbish in.

Examples of the same young girl's work seen earlier, now aged 10.

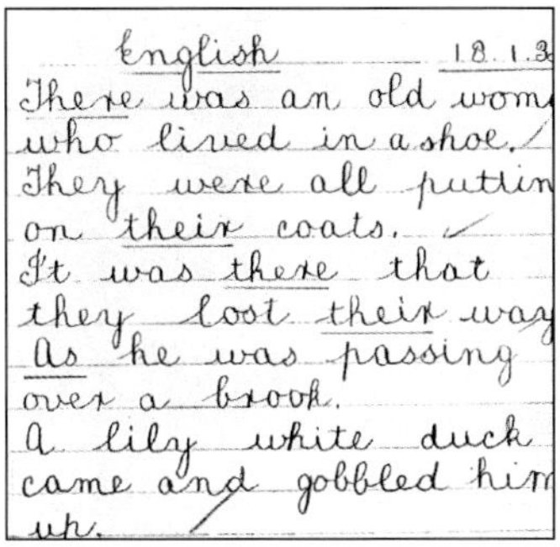
English 18.1.3
There was an old wom
who lived in a shoe.
They were all puttin
on their coats.
It was there that
they lost their way
As he was passing
over a brook.
A lily white duck
came and gobbled him
up.

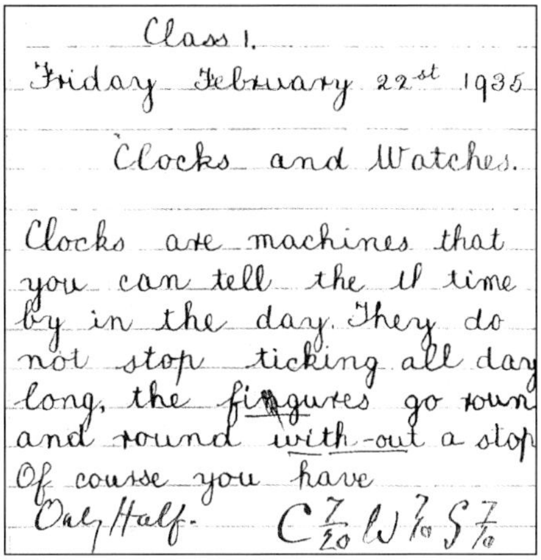
Class 1.
Friday February 22st 1935
Clocks and Watches.
Clocks are machines that
you can tell the time
by in the day. They do
not stop ticking all day
long, the figures go roun
and round with-out a stop
Of course you have
Only Half. C 7/20 W 7/10 S 7/10

Monday March 18th 1935.
Plan of Composition
Spring cleani
Preparations
The start clearing the room
and thoroughly cleaning.
Carpets and furniture.
Staircases landings and
hall
Curtains and windows
Finishing Touches

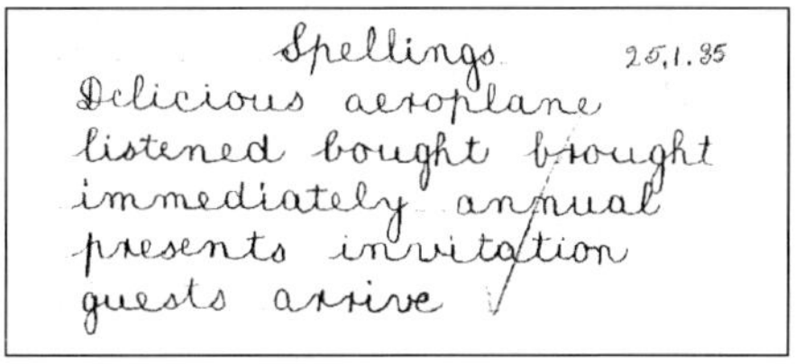
Spellings 25.1.35
Delicious aeroplane
listened bought brought
immediately annual
presents invitation
guests arrive

Further examples of the young girl's work, now just eleven.

THURSDAY, MAY 2nd

Another recipient of the Jackson Exhibition from Handsworth Junior Technical School. This time, Raymond Wilde had passed the entrance examination, leaving Slade School before Easter to start his first day at Handsworth today.

SATURDAY, MAY 4th

SENIOR	P	W	D	L	F	A	PTS
PAGET ROAD	16	14	2	0	70	7	30
NATIONAL	16	13	2	1	87	15	28
HASTINGS ROAD	16	10	1	5	67	30	21
RYLAND ROAD	16	8	1	7	52	33	17
MOOR END	16	7	1	8	43	55	15
JOSIAH MASON'S	16	6	2	8	31	30	14
SLADE ROAD	16	6	0	10	42	50	12
ST. THOMAS'	16	2	0	14	11	122	4
GREEN LANES	16	1	1	14	14	75	3

JUNIOR	P	W	D	L	F	A	PTS
NATIONAL	18	12	3	3	38	12	27
RYLAND ROAD	18	10	6	2	52	33	26
PAGET ROAD	18	10	5	3	41	15	25
OSBORNE ROAD	18	11	2	5	43	21	24
MOOR END	18	7	4	7	24	26	18
GUNTER ROAD	18	7	4	7	21	25	18
BIRCHES GREEN	18	5	3	10	22	40	13
SLADE ROAD	18	4	2	12	16	38	10
GREEN LANES	18	4	2	12	13	33	10
ST. THOMAS'	18	2	5	11	17	55	9

RESERVE	P	W	D	L	F	A	PTS
PAGET ROAD	14	13	1	0	113	10	27
HASTINGS ROAD	14	11	0	3	64	17	22
SLADE ROAD	14	8	2	4	44	40	18
NATIONAL	14	6	3	5	42	40	15
RYLAND ROAD	14	4	4	6	44	34	12
MOOR END	14	4	2	8	43	53	10
GREEN LANES	14	2	3	9	18	80	7
JOSIAH MASON'S	14	0	1	13	6	100	1

Final Tables Erdington Schools' Football League 1934/1935 Season.

MONDAY, MAY 6th
A gentleman, attired in topi and shorts, describing himself as an African explorer, gave a lecture at the Boys' School on his exploits. There was a charge of three pence to attend.

Silver Jubilee, 1935.

MAY
A special pageant was held at the school to celebrate the Silver Jubilee of King George V and Queen Mary. All the children were presented with bars of Cadburys chocolate inside special presentation tins.

MONDAY, JULY 1st
The deductions of 5% of teachers' salaries, that had been taking place for 10 years, ceased as from today. Salaries were restored to those of April 1st, 1925.

THURSDAY, JULY 4th
The Erdington Elementary Schools' Athletic Association held their annual sports at Fentham Road. There were the usual championship events as well as several open races. For the second year in succession, Slade Road won the Junior Mixed trophy.

SATURDAY, JULY 27th
The Erdington Schools' cricket season had come to a close but, unfortunately, for Slade Road, it was not a very successful one.

SENIOR	P	W	D	L	PTS
PAGET ROAD	7	6	0	1	12
HASTINGS ROAD	7	6	0	1	12
MOOR END	7	4	1	2	9
RYLAND ROAD	7	4	1	2	9
SLADE ROAD	7	3	0	4	6
ST.THOMAS'	7	2	0	5	4
GREEN LANES	7	1	0	6	2
NATIONAL	7	1	0	6	2

JUNIOR	P	W	D	L	PTS
BIRCHES GREEN	7	6	0	1	12
NATIONAL	7	5	0	2	10
OSBORNE ROAD	7	4	0	3	8
GUNTER ROAD	7	4	0	3	8
MOOR END	7	3	0	4	6
PAGET ROAD	6	2	0	4	4
RYLAND ROAD	6	2	0	4	4
SLADE ROAD	7	1	0	6	2

Erdington Schools' Cricket League, 1935.

TUESDAY, OCTOBER 1st
Keen juvenile swimming was to be seen at Mason Road Baths when the Erdington Elementary Schools' Athletics Association held its eighth annual swimming gala. Slade School emerged head and shoulders above the other competing schools, achieving a praiseworthy 'double' by winning both the Senior Boys' and Junior Girls' Trophies. In the senior events, Slade Road came away with three first places, the junior girls being equal to the task, also notching up three victories. At the end of the proceedings, Alderman Gelling, as president of the association, was on hand to distribute the prizes and trophies.

Top: "Living Pictures" – A striking tableau, recalling the days of elegance and deportment as given by the children of the Junior School at the Parochial Hall in the Christmas Concert for 1935. Bottom: Safety certificate, 1935.

DECEMBER

Collection boxes were placed in the hall, so that letters might be posted to each other, relative to Christmas. These were then sorted through and delivered round to each classroom in the afternoons.

A copy of a certificate awarded to Alan Cantrill by the Birmingham Safety First Council for his proficiency in a Schools' Essay Competition.

1936

TUESDAY, JANUARY 21st

King George V died at five minutes to midnight on the evening of January 20th. In consequence, a number of the boys in the Senior School, who delivered newspapers, were late due to the late delivery of the papers to the newsagents. They had had to be reprinted. In normal circumstances, they would have been punished for their tardiness. On this occasion, however, they were let off with a simple warning!

SATURDAY, FEBRUARY 15th

Mr Edmund Jones, the Headmaster of the Boys' School, was chosen to be the new president of the Birmingham Association of the National Union of Teachers. Although Welsh by birth, Mr Jones had spent most of his life in Birmingham, where he had worked for the benefit of Birmingham Education all his scholastic life.

SATURDAY, MARCH 28th

In the first round of the Erdington Schools' Junior Football Knockout Cup, Slade Road went through courtesy of a two goals to one win over Green Lanes.

SATURDAY, APRIL 4th

The second round of the Junior Football Knockout Cup, Slade Road advancing with an easy seven nil victory over the National. Goals from Bushell(3), Waterson(2), Chappell and Turner sealed the win.

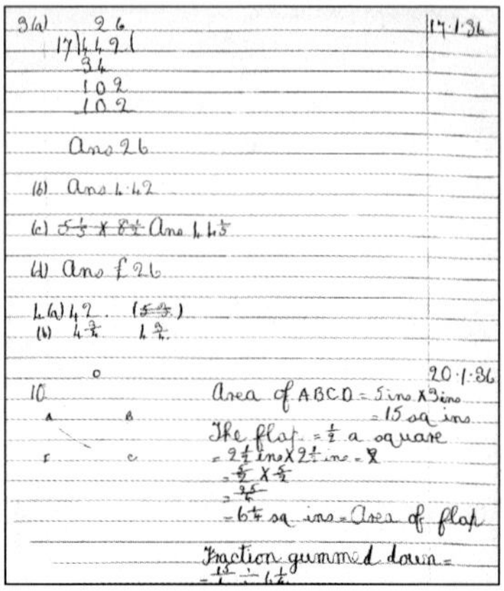

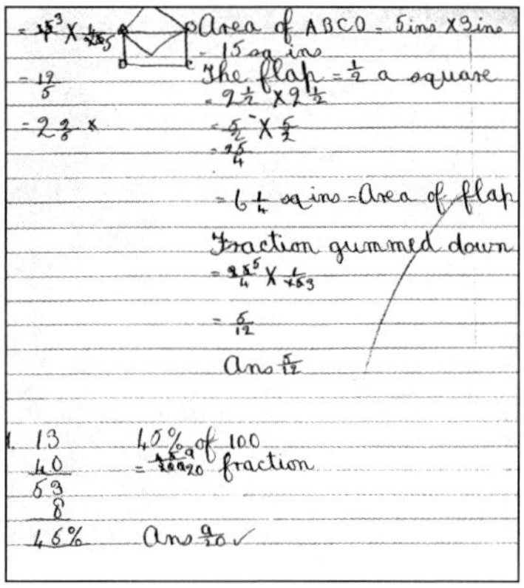

An example of the Mathematics set for eleven year olds.

SATURDAY, APRIL 11th

It was the conclusion of the Erdington Schools' Football League season. In the final of the Junior Knockout Cup, Slade Road met Birches Green. Slade Road Juniors had had a poor season thus far, whilst Birches Green had claimed the runners up spot in the League, only narrowly being beaten to the title by Paget Road. The final was a very close affair in which Slade Road scored through Wilde in the very first minute of the game. During the rest of the match, neither side looked likely to score again, so Slade Road emerged as winners with a piece of silverware to display in their trophy cabinet. Meanwhile, in the final of the Intermediate Knock Out Cup, a keenly contested game was played between Ryland Road and Slade Road. Atkins gave Ryland Road the lead, but Chappell forced the goalkeeper to carry over his own line to put the scores level. In the second half, Atkins registered his second goal for Ryland Road, so giving them the cup for the first time.

SATURDAY, APRIL 18th

SENIOR	P	W	D	L	F	A	PTS
PAGET ROAD	14	11	1	2	71	15	23
SLADE ROAD	14	10	1	3	45	21	21
HASTINGS ROAD	14	10	0	4	53	21	20
MOOR END	14	6	3	5	42	25	15
RYLAND ROAD	14	6	2	6	35	39	14
ST.THOMAS'	14	5	2	7	30	48	12
GREEN LANES	14	2	0	12	16	77	4
JOSIAH MASON'S	14	1	1	12	22	68	3
RESERVE	P	W	D	L	F	A	PTS
PAGET ROAD	14	13	0	1	136	6	26
HASTINGS ROAD	14	10	1	3	71	27	21
SLADE ROAD	14	9	0	5	69	26	18
GREEN LANES	14	7	1	6	39	48	15
MOOR END	14	6	3	5	32	53	15
RYLAND ROAD	14	5	2	7	30	67	12
JOSIAH MASON'S	14	1	1	12	9	104	3
ST.THOMAS'	14	1	0	13	18	73	2
JUNIOR	P	W	D	L	F	A	PTS
PAGET ROAD	16	13	1	2	48	8	27
BIRCHES GREEN	16	12	1	3	33	12	25
GREEN LANES	16	9	3	4	44	21	21
GUNTER ROAD	16	7	3	6	21	16	17
OSBORNE ROAD	16	7	1	8	23	33	15
SLADE ROAD	16	5	4	7	20	24	14
RYLAND ROAD	16	5	4	7	16	25	14
MOOR END	16	2	4	10	12	35	8
NATIONAL	16	0	3	13	8	51	3

Final Tables Erdington Schools' Football League 1935/1936 Season.

SATURDAY, MAY 16th

The stage was set for the 16th season of the Erdington Schools' Cricket League under the chairmanship of Mr Claydon of the National School. John Oldroyd of Slade Road Senior Boys' School took over the duties of secretary. Due to re-organisation, the National School disappeared from the list of senior schools.

THURSDAY, MAY 21st

Mr Edmund William Jones, Headmaster of the Senior Boys' School, retired today, aged 65. Born on the 22nd of May, 1871, he had held many positions, having initially qualified as a teacher in 1896. After 15 months as Headmaster at Dartmouth Street, he arrived at Slade School on July 1st, 1921, where he spent the final 15 years of his teaching career. He was a portly, balding man, who wore pince-nez and was generally respected by the pupils in his charge. As has been stated earlier, he was extremely prominent in Trades Union matters.

FRIDAY, JUNE 19th

At Sutton Coldfield Court today, Ernest Bosker, who was a teacher in the Senior Boys' School, was brought before the bench. Apparently, he had been driving his motor car along

Chester Road in the direction of Brownhills at a speed exceeding 30 miles per hour. On observing him overtaking a stream of traffic, a police patrol car pulled out and commenced to check his speed. He was seen to be doing 40 miles an hour for three tenths of a mile and 35 miles an hour for two tenths of a mile. Mr Bosker, seeing the car in his mirror, had signalled with his outstretched hand for the vehicle to overtake him. He was most astonished to see that the car, on pulling in front of him, contained two police officers. When stopped, he expressed surprise, stating that it was very difficult to keep down to thirty unless you were looking at your speedometer. He put out his hand, had it well and truly caned by the magistrates, and was fined ten shillings.

WEDNESDAY and THURSDAY, JUNE 24th and 25th
The annual athletic sports of the Erdington Elementary Schools were once again held at the Erdington Homes grounds in Fentham Road. This time, Slade Road were successful in the Senior Boys' Championship, winning half the events contested, and thus securing the Wiggins-Davies Shield for a year. The Junior Boys claimed the runners up spot to Green Lanes in their competition, winning one of their events, the 80 yard sprint.

MONDAY, JULY 13th
At an inquest at the Coroner's Court in Birmingham, a verdict of accidental death was recorded in the case of a 9-year-old boy, who had drowned in a brook swollen by floodwater on the previous Friday. Apparently, Ralph Walters and his friend, Albert Clarrie, had been making their way back to Slade School after lunch and had decided to cross the tip from George Road. They had scrambled down a 30 foot slope and climbed under some railings so that they could paddle in a brook that they had visited before. On this occasion, unfortunately, Ralph, who could not swim, had taken all his clothes off and said he was going to try. The current was so fierce that it carried him away. Subsequently, a police inspector, who plunged into the water, found Ralph's body lying against the grid that covered the culvert. Except for that, he would have been drawn underground. It was considered to have been a silly thing for an adult to have tried let alone a young lad. As it was, Ralph didn't stand a chance. A sad tale of misadventure! The following day, a special assembly was held to enforce on the children the dangers of such practices.

SATURDAY, JULY 18th
The 16th season of the Erdington Schools' Cricket League was rapidly drawing to a close. Slade Road had finished as runners up to Paget Road who were invincible in the senior division, winning all their 12 matches. However, the final of the Intermediate Knock Out Cup Competition had still to be decided. This was played at the Cottage Homes grounds and the contestants were Slade Road and Paget Road. Slade Road batted first, but were only able to amass 21 runs before they were all back in the pavilion. However, Paget Road equally found runs difficult to come by and 5 men were out before they eventually passed Slade Road's total. They had now won the competition for five straight seasons.

SATURDAY, JULY 25th

SENIOR	P	W	D	L	PTS
PAGET ROAD	12	12	0	0	24
SLADE ROAD	12	7	0	5	14
MOOR END	12	6	0	6	12
HASTINGS ROAD	12	5	2	5	12
ST.THOMAS'	12	5	0	7	10
GREEN LANES	12	3	0	9	6
RYLAND ROAD	12	2	2	8	6
JUNIOR	**P**	**W**	**D**	**L**	**PTS**
PAGET ROAD	7	7	0	0	14
BIRCHES GREEN	7	5	0	2	10
GUNTER ROAD	7	5	0	2	10
OSBORNE ROAD	7	4	0	3	8
MOOR END	7	3	0	4	6
NATIONAL	7	2	0	5	4
RYLAND ROAD	7	1	0	6	2
SLADE ROAD	7	1	0	6	2

Final Tables Erdington Schools' Cricket League.

MONDAY, AUGUST 24th
The new Headmaster of the Senior Boys' School, Mr Harold Caddick, aged 48, commenced his duties. He had been a headmaster for the previous nine years, five of them at Holy Trinity, Handsworth and the last four at Hope Street. He was a resident of Holly Lane, Erdington. Amazingly, his salary appeared to have reduced as he started at Slade School on £474 per annum, whereas one year earlier it had been £510!

SEPTEMBER
Tall and baldheaded, Mr Blackie could be found in the science room making drinking chocolate or cocoa, which the children would queue up to buy at halfpenny a cup at break. He, also, had a seismograph installed which was used to measure the vibrations from lorries going up and down Broomfield Road. It was around this time that he bought himself a Riley Pathfinder motor car as well. Incidentally, outside the science room at one time actually stood the chassis of an old car, which the boys found useful to work on, whilst inside the room – instead of diagrams – there were actual items to be explored like telephones and bells.

FRIDAY, OCTOBER 16th
Miss Lee from The Drive ran a Brownie pack in the Drill Hall at the school on Friday evenings. The pack belonged to All Saints Church.

1937

THURSDAY, JANUARY 14th
Another sad event to be recorded, this time in respect of the Infants' department. At lunch time, Rita Lance, aged 5, was knocked down and killed by a motor van, which mounted

the pavement after a collision with a runaway horse. Her schoolmate, Iris Eggington, was also struck, but she was luckier receiving only a fractured arm. The runaway horse, which was attached to a coal cart, had been standing in Broomfield Road when it bolted. Galloping down the slope, it had careered across Slade Road and into a motor van which was travelling citywards. The two children were then knocked down by the van as it mounted the pavement. The horse escaped with just a few slight cuts. Another sad tragedy that touched the school!

MAY

Celebrations were held at the school in recognition of the Coronation of King George VI that was to take place on May 12th. In honour of the occasion, a special commemorative mug was presented to each child. The children, all dressed in British National costumes, performed dances for parents and friends. Other children wore uniforms denoting the various armed services, whilst songs consisting of *Banks and Braes*, *The Ashgrove* and *The Minstrel Boy* were performed.

Coronation, 1937.

SATURDAY, JUNE 12th

A school outing to London was arranged for the Senior Boys' School. A booklet, containing everything they needed to know for the trip, was given to every lad. Whilst they were there, they had rides on the elephants and the camels. All in all, the fifty to sixty lads that went had a marvellous though tiring day.

School Trip Booklet, 1937.

WEDNESDAY and THURSDAY, JUNE 16th and 17th

The 17th annual Erdington Elementary Schools' sports took place at the Erdington Cottage Homes grounds in Fentham Road. A total of 16 schools competed and the trophies and shields were presented by Alderman R. R. Gelling at the conclusion of the events. Slade Road finished as runners up to Hastings Road in the Junior Girls' competition.

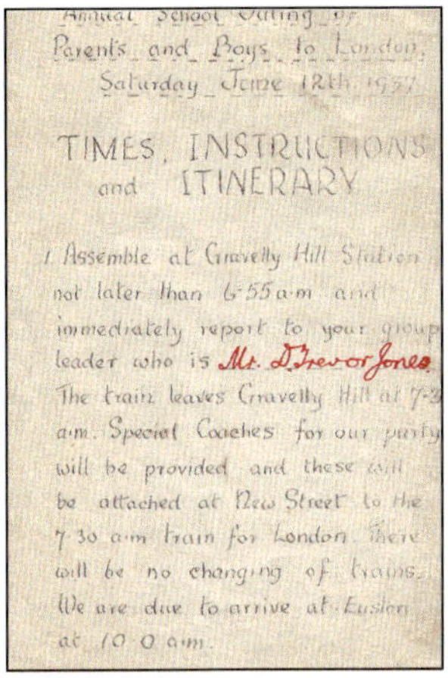
Annual School Outing of Parents and Boys to London, Saturday June 12th 1937

TIMES, INSTRUCTIONS and ITINERARY

1. Assemble at Gravelly Hill Station not later than 6·55 a.m and immediately report to your group leader who is Mr. D. Trevor Jones. The train leaves Gravelly Hill at 7-2 a.m. Special Coaches for our party will be provided and these will be attached at New Street to the 7·30 a.m train for London. There will be no changing of trains. We are due to arrive at Euston at 10·0 a.m.

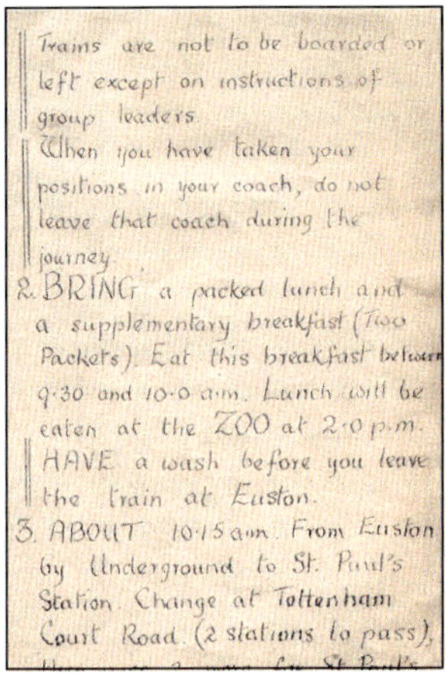
Trains are not to be boarded or left except on instructions of group leaders. When you have taken your positions in your coach, do not leave that coach during the journey.

2. BRING a packed lunch and a supplementary breakfast (Two Packets). Eat this breakfast between 9·30 and 10·0 a.m. Lunch will be eaten at the ZOO at 2·0 p.m. HAVE a wash before you leave the train at Euston.

3. ABOUT 10·15 a.m. From Euston by Underground to St. Paul's Station. Change at Tottenham Court Road (2 stations to pass).

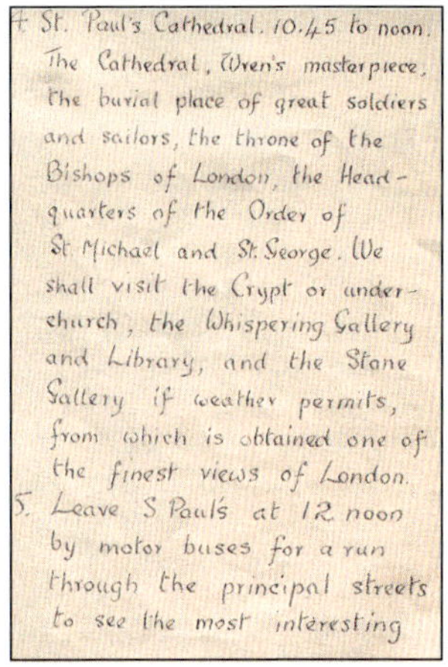
4. St. Paul's Cathedral. 10.45 to noon. The Cathedral, Wren's masterpiece, the burial place of great soldiers and sailors, the throne of the Bishops of London, the Head-quarters of the Order of St Michael and St George. We shall visit the Crypt or under-church, the Whispering Gallery and Library, and the Stone Gallery if weather permits, from which is obtained one of the finest views of London.

5. Leave S Paul's at 12 noon by motor buses for a run through the principal streets to see the most interesting

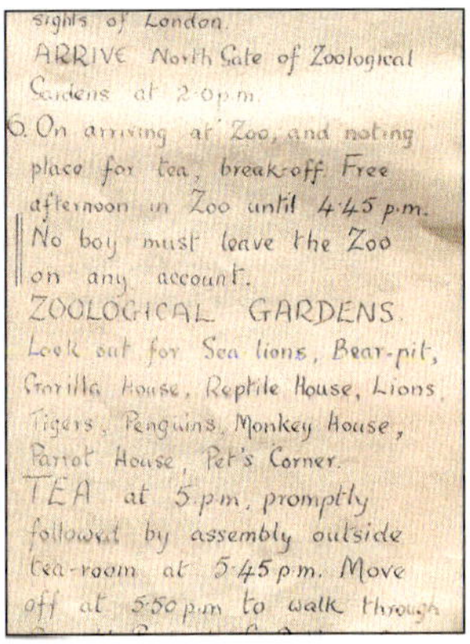
sights of London. ARRIVE North Gate of Zoological Gardens at 2·0 p.m.

6. On arriving at Zoo, and noting place for tea, break-off. Free afternoon in Zoo until 4·45 p.m. No boy must leave the Zoo on any account.

ZOOLOGICAL GARDENS. Look out for Sea lions, Bear-pit, Gorilla House, Reptile House, Lions, Tigers, Penguins, Monkey House, Parrot House, Pet's Corner.

TEA at 5 p.m. promptly followed by assembly outside tea-room at 5·45 p.m. Move off at 5·50 p.m to walk through

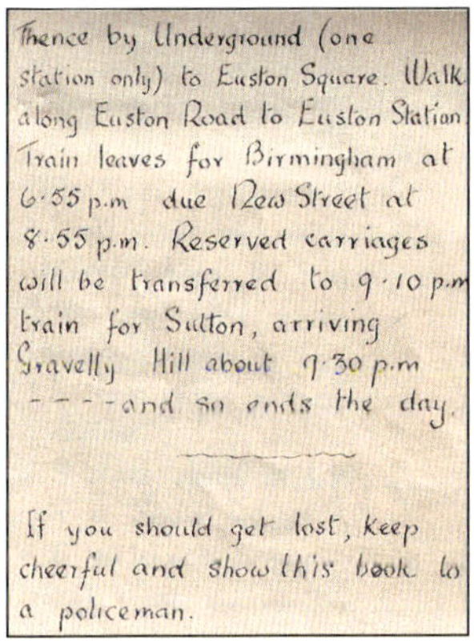
Thence by Underground (one station only) to Euston Square. Walk along Euston Road to Euston Station. Train leaves for Birmingham at 6·55 p.m due New Street at 8·55 p.m. Reserved carriages will be transferred to 9·10 p.m train for Sutton, arriving Gravelly Hill about 9·30 p.m ----and so ends the day.

If you should get lost, keep cheerful and show this book to a policeman.

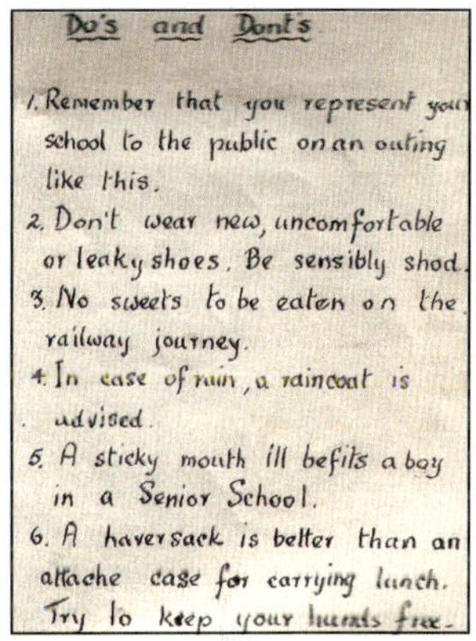
Do's and Dont's

1. Remember that you represent your school to the public on an outing like this.
2. Don't wear new, uncomfortable or leaky shoes. Be sensibly shod.
3. No sweets to be eaten on the railway journey.
4. In case of rain, a raincoat is advised.
5. A sticky mouth ill befits a boy in a Senior School.
6. A haversack is better than an attache case for carrying lunch. Try to keep your hands free.

School Trip Booklet, 1937.

SATURDAY, JULY 3rd

Chief interest was given over to the Intermediate Cricket Knock Out Cup of the Erdington Elementary Schools. The boys had to be under 13 years of age on May 1st. Slade Road had reached the final yet again, which was played on the Erdington Cottage Homes grounds against Ryland Road. Slade Road batted first and quickly found themselves 8 wickets down with only 5 runs on the board. A small recovery enabled them to reach 18 before they were all out. Ryland Road passed the total for the loss of only four wickets and, thus, Slade Road lost out yet again.

SATURDAY, JULY 24th

The 17th season of the Erdington Schools' Cricket League was now concluded. Games had been played at Jaffray Road on Tuesdays, Wednesdays and Thursdays, whilst those at Spring Lane took place on Mondays, Wednesdays and Thursdays. The third venue was at

Short Heath where games were played on Tuesdays and Thursdays. All games were played on evenings only. The final tables can be found alongside:

SENIOR	P	W	L	PTS
HASTINGS ROAD	10	10	0	20
MOOR END	10	7	3	14
SLADE ROAD	10	6	4	12
RYLAND ROAD	10	5	5	10
ST.THOMAS'	10	2	8	4
GREEN LANES	10	0	10	0
JUNIOR	**P**	**W**	**L**	**PTS**
GUNTER ROAD	6	5	1	10
MOOR END	6	4	2	8
OSBORNE ROAD	6	4	2	8
SLADE ROAD	6	4	2	8
NATIONAL	6	3	3	6
BIRCHES GREEN	6	1	5	2
RYLAND ROAD	6	0	6	0

Erdington Schools' Cricket League, 1937.

THURSDAY, OCTOBER 21st

Mr Williams' new car sustained damage whilst it was parked outside the school today. He had always parked it at the bottom of Broomfield Road, opposite the Star Picture House. Unfortunately, the brakes of a lorry, which was being driven out of the garage next to the cinema, failed, and it crunched into the side of his car. One of the boys, who came to tell him about the accident, had his ears boxed for his trouble! The lads tended to torment 'Toddles' – that was their nickname for him – by telling him that something had happened to his car until, in the end, he didn't believe them anymore. After that incident, he used to park his car in the playground, where the girls would clean it for him. He was a busy, little man with really short legs, who could be rather sarcastic at times. His brother was a surgeon at the Eye Hospital.

Christmas in the Junior School.

1938

SATURDAY, MARCH 5th

Slade Road reached the final of the Erdington Schools' Junior Knock Out Cup, where they met Gunter Road, the previous year's winners. Although they defended stubbornly, Gunter Road eventually wore them down to score twice and so win the cup for the second successive season.

Meanwhile, in the semi-final of the Intermediate Cup, Ryland Road were the opponents. Slade Road had the better of the opening exchanges, Cook scoring twice. Ryland Road fought back to level before Hayes gave Slade Road the lead again. Once more, Ryland Road fought back to equalise, the whistle going with the scores all tied up at three apiece. Extra time was played and, with the last kick of the game, Hook centred. The ball bounced about three yards in front of the goalkeeper, who expected it to bounce over the bar. It didn't and Slade Road were in the final.

SATURDAY, MARCH 19th

In the Intermediate Knock Out Cup Final, Slade Road met Sir Josiah Mason's, who had finished bottom of both the Senior and Reserve Leagues. Despite this a tight tussle developed, although Slade Road gradually gained the upper hand to win by three goals to one.

SATURDAY, MARCH 26th

SENIOR	P	W	L	D	F	A	PTS
HASTINGS ROAD	10	7	3	0	46	16	14
MOOR END	10	6	4	0	40	22	12
SLADE ROAD	10	6	4	0	43	25	12
ST.THOMAS'	10	5	5	0	28	26	10
RYLAND ROAD	10	5	5	0	34	41	10
JOSIAH MASON'S	10	1	9	0	3	70	2
RESERVE (according to recorded results)	P	W	L	D	F	A	PTS
SLADE ROAD	10	9	1	0	72	9	18
HASTINGS ROAD	10	8	1	1	95	14	17
MOOR END	10	5	4	1	75	42	11
RYLAND ROAD	10	4	5	1	28	45	9
ST.THOMAS'	10	2	7	1	14	80	5
JOSIAH MASON'S	10	0	10	0	1	91	0
JUNIOR (according to recorded results)	P	W	L	D	F	A	PTS
RYLAND ROAD	14	12	1	1	41	8	25
MOOR END	14	9	4	1	23	18	19
GUNTER ROAD	14	8	4	2	34	9	18
NATIONAL	14	5	6	3	23	19	13
OSBORNE ROAD	14	4	5	5	15	13	13
SLADE ROAD	14	3	7	4	21	30	10
BIRCHES GREEN	14	2	6	6	7	23	10
GREEN LANES	14	1	11	2	8	51	4

Final Tables Erdington Schools' Football League 1937/1938 Season.

SUNDAY, JUNE 19th

Sunday School Festivals were all the rage. Latest was that of All Saints Church where the children's choir – many of whom would have attended Slade School – sang in the morning. At 3p.m. a United Sunday Schools' procession left the church, proceeding via Slade Road, Mere Road, Doidge Road and George Road to Brookvale Park, where a short service commenced half an hour later.

SATURDAY, JULY 23rd

The cricket season concluded with Slade Road playing Ryland Road once again in the final of the Intermediate Knock Out Cup. In late June, they had already defeated the favourites, Hastings Road, by 6 wickets, Millington taking 7 for 15, so they felt quietly confident. However, having batted first, they only registered 33 runs, of which Cousins contributed 14. Millington with 5 for 16 and Hook with 4 for 15 had Ryland Road reeling when their turn came to take the crease. They

SENIOR	P	W	L	D	PTS
HASTINGS ROAD	8	7	1	0	14
RYLAND ROAD	8	6	2	0	12
MOOR END	8	5	3	0	10
SLADE ROAD	8	1	6	1	3
ST.THOMAS'	8	0	7	1	1

JUNIOR	P	W	L	PTS
GUNTER ROAD	6	6	0	12
MOOR END	6	4	2	8
BIRCHES GREEN	6	3	3	6
NATIONAL	6	3	3	6
RYLAND ROAD	6	3	3	6
SLADE ROAD	6	2	4	4
OSBORNE ROAD	6	0	6	0

Final Tables Erdington Schools' Cricket League.

Junior School Athletics, 1938.

lost their ninth wicket with 30 runs on the board in what was a very close game. Their last man came in and a run was attempted. The fielder unfortunately overthrew and, as a result, Ryland Road scored a further three runs and won the match and the cup.

SUNDAY, JULY 31st

Miss Effie May Loescher officially left the school today. She had trained for two years at Cheltenham St. Mary's, where she gained her teaching certificate in 1909. Her first appointment was with Slade Road Junior School, which she joined on October 1st, 1909. When the Junior School was phased out in favour of Boys' and Girls' Schools in 1915, she moved onto the staff of the Girls' School; in the later re-organisation in 1931, she transferred back to the Junior School again. She had been at the school for nearly 29 years, her family owning a farm at Stockland Green, where the Stockland Public House was built in 1924. She was always well-dressed albeit in an old-fashioned way. In earlier days, girls knew that they were favoured if they were invited to have tea at the farm.

MONDAY, OCTOBER 31st

Another teacher left the school today after a lengthy period of service. Born on June 9th, 1878, Miss Florian Mary Hobson came to the Junior School on November 1st, 1912 from Nechells. After a spell in the Girls' establishment from 1915 until 1931, she returned to the newly-formed Junior School. At the age of 60, she decided to retire, having spent 26 years with the school.

1939
FEBRUARY

United Kingdom Band of Hope Union.
PRESIDENT:
ANGUS WATSON, ESQ., J.P.
Certificate of Merit
awarded to
ALAN CANTRILL
for Excellence in Reporting a Lecture
on the
Hygiene of Food & Drink.
U.K.B.OF.H.U. FIRST YEAR
OFFICES OF THE UNION, 59 & 60, OLD BAILEY, E.C.4
PRESIDENT
DATE FEB.1939.

In the final year of school, aged 14, and a certificate awarded for writing up a lecture.

MARCH

SENIOR FINAL TABLE

	P	W	L	D	F	A	PTS
RYLAND ROAD	10	8	0	2	48	8	18
SLADE ROAD	10	6	2	2	37	24	14
HASTINGS ROAD	10	5	5	0			10
JOSIAH MASON'S	10	3	6	1	16	40	7
MOOR END	10	3	7	0			6
ST.THOMAS'	10	2	7	1			5

RESERVE FINAL TABLE

	P	W	L	D	F	A	PTS
RYLAND ROAD	10	8	1	1	58	20	17
HASTINGS ROAD	10	7	2	1	36	13	15
MOOR END	10	6	3	1	38	21	13
SLADE ROAD	10	5	4	1	50	20	11
JOSIAH MASON'S	10	1	8	1	7	69	3
ST.THOMAS'	10	0	9	1	9	56	1

Final Tables Erdington Schools' Football League 1938/1939 Season.

In the Junior League, Slade Road could only finish sixth out of the seven competing schools, recording seven points from their twelve games. Gunter Road won the championship.

SATURDAY, JUNE 24th
In the first round proper of the Docker Shield, Slade Road met Deykin Avenue. The latter batted first and, despite Hook taking 7 for 30 bowling a good length, Deykin Avenue amassed 96 for the loss of 8 wickets. Slade Road set about their target and 30 runs were on the board before the first wicket fell. The score gradually mounted, Hayes making 35, Rosser adding 22 and Evans 19. When the last man went in, only 4 runs were required to win, but the final wicket went down when Slade Road were just one run short of their target. They had made a most valiant effort, but Deykin Avenue went through to the next round.

THURSDAY, JULY 6th
The Erdington Elementary Schools' Sports were concluded today. Slade Road Senior Boys' School finished as runners up to Ryland Road for the Wiggins-Davies Shield, losing out by two points. However, the same two schools could not be separated in the fight for the Junior Boys' Shield, ending up sharing the title.

SATURDAY, JULY 29th
As Slade Road and Hastings Road had tied for first place in the senior division of the Erdington Schools' Cricket League, a further game to decide the championship was required. In their first meeting of the season – way back in May – Hastings Road had dismissed Slade Road for 13 runs, hitting off the total for the loss of three wickets. They met again in June in a preliminary round of the Docker Shield. On this occasion, the tables were turned with Hastings Road being bowled out for 13 whilst Slade Road lost five wickets in passing the total. A few days later, the schools met again in what they believed to be their last encounter of the season. Slade Road batted first and scored 28 runs. Hastings Road looked set to win with their score at 27 for 5, but their last five men were all out for just one run, the game ending all square. So, we came to the end of the season, and what proved to be the last event that took place in the Erdington Schools' Sports Association before the outbreak of World War Two. In the deciding match, Hastings Road batted first, but to their chagrin were only able to amass 19 runs before their innings closed. Slade Road passed the total with five wickets to spare and were declared champions for 1939.

SENIOR	P	W	L	D	PTS
HASTINGS ROAD	6	4	1	1	9
SLADE ROAD	6	4	1	1	9
RYLAND ROAD	6	2	4	0	4
MOOR END	6	1	5	0	2
JUNIOR	P	W	L	D	PTS
NATIONAL	7	6	1	0	12
GUNTER ROAD	7	5	2	0	10
RYLAND ROAD	7	5	2	0	10
MOOR END	7	4	3	0	8
BIRCHES GREEN	7	3	4	0	6
PAGET ROAD	7	3	4	0	6
SLADE ROAD	7	1	6	0	2
OSBORNE ROAD	7	1	6	0	2

Final Tables Erdington Schools' Cricket League.

JULY

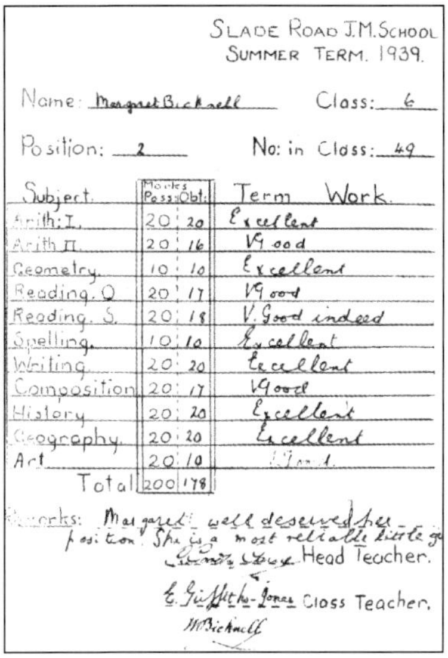

SLADE ROAD J.M. SCHOOL
SUMMER TERM. 1939.

Name: Margaret Bicknell Class: 6

Position: 2 No: in Class: 49

Subject.	Marks Poss:	Marks Obt:	Term Work.
Arith: I.	20	20	Excellent
Arith II.	20	16	V Good
Geometry.	10	10	Excellent
Reading. O.	20	17	V Good
Reading. S.	20	18	V. Good indeed
Spelling.	10	10	Excellent
Writing.	20	20	Excellent
Composition	20	17	V Good
History	20	20	Excellent
Geography.	20	20	Excellent
Art	20	10	[illegible]
Total	200	178	

Remarks: Margaret well deserved her position. She is a most reliable little girl

Head Teacher.

E. Griffiths-Jones Class Teacher.

M. Bicknell

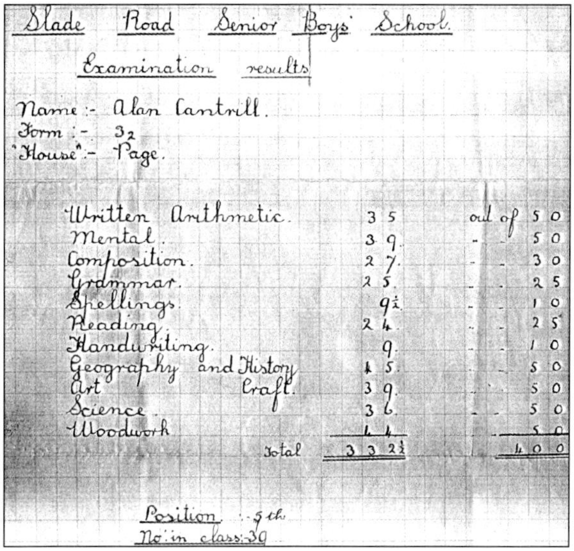

Slade Road Senior Boys' School.

Examination results

Name :- Alan Cantrill.
Form :- 3₂
"House" :- Page.

Written Arithmetic.	35	out of 50
Mental.	39	50
Composition.	27	30
Grammar.	25	25
Spellings.	9½	10
Reading.	24	25
Handwriting.	9	10
Geography and History	45	50
Art Craft.	39	50
Science.	36	50
Woodwork	44	50
Total	332½	400

Position :- 5th.
No: in class: 30

Left: A Junior School report for the Summer term of 1939. War was to break out less than two months later. Right: The Senior Boys' School and the final examination before the outbreak of war.

AUGUST

The Infants' department of the school was taken over for the purposes of being used as a First Aid Post in case of gas attacks, which were expected to happen with the outbreak of the Second World War. In consequence, the school had to be re-organised. The infants and juniors would still continue to attend, but some classes in the Senior Boys' School would need to share facilities with the senior girls at Fentham Road Girls' School on alternate mornings and afternoons. The Infants' department, fronting Slade Road, was now dark and shuttered. It had a musty smell, with blankets lying all around; whilst showers had been installed.

TUESDAY, AUGUST 29th

Schools were instructed that they were to open until further notice. As the space available at Slade Road School was now severely limited, the senior boys had to attend Fentham Road Girls' School. On this, the opening day of the new school year, the girls started back at 8.30a.m. and would work until 12.30, whilst the boys of Slade Road would commence at 1.30p.m. and finish at 5.30p.m.

MONDAY, SEPTEMBER 4th

As Britain had entered the War from Sunday, all the schools in Birmingham were instructed to remain closed from today, owing to the lack of air-raid cover that existed. It was some time before surface brick shelters were built in the playgrounds.

FRIDAY, SEPTEMBER 8th

Instructions were still being issued from the Council that schools in neutral areas were not to open until provisions were made for air-raid cover.

FRIDAY, SEPTEMBER 29th

At last, it was announced that a decision had been taken that certain secondary schools could open on a voluntary basis, provided that they supplied first-aid equipment and sand for each classroom. The nearest A.R.P. Wardens Post had to be known to the headteacher and all staff; and one member of the staff appointed to act as a messenger between the school and post. All children were also required to take their respirators to school, where an air-raid rehearsal had to take place each day, 15 minutes before the close of the school day. Quite a number of secondary schools in Erdington were to be allowed to open including those at Fentham Road and Paget Road.

THURSDAY, OCTOBER 5th

Fentham Road Girls' School opened today on a voluntary basis, the girls there attending between the hours of 8.30a.m. and 12.30p.m. The senior boys of Slade Road attended for four hours starting at 1.30p.m.

FRIDAY, OCTOBER 13th

Permission was now given to hold meetings of parents at all junior schools in neutral areas of the city as to whether they wished them to open on a voluntary basis, even though air-raid cover was still not necessarily available. Brown paper was stuck across all the windows in Slade Road School in the form of a cross so as to prevent injury in case of breaking glass due to bomb damage. Black drape-like cloths hung down from the windows to ensure that light could not escape, as well as over the lights. Sand bags were placed all around the school, particularly in corridors. Even in the early morning, the lights were never on, presumably to save on fuel. The children had to bring their gas masks to school with them and place them in the corner of the classroom, as they would not fit into their desks.

TUESDAY and WEDNESDAY, OCTOBER 17th and 18th

Junior Schools were now open.

FRIDAY, OCTOBER 27th

All Schools in Birmingham, excepting those in evacuation areas, were now open, as it had finally been decided that infant schools could follow the way of junior and secondary schools.

MONDAY, OCTOBER 30th

It was all change at Fentham Road Girls' School, as the boys and girls now assumed the times of the other.

MONDAY, DECEMBER 4th
The girls of Fentham Road reverted to their previously scheduled hours of 8. 30 to 12. 30. The boys, meanwhile, had to finish at 4p.m. or 4.15p.m. according to how light it remained.

1940

MONDAY, JANUARY 8th
Following the Christmas holiday, a new term began. The Education Committee had now issued instructions that made it compulsory for schools to open. The senior boys of Slade Road started this morning at Fentham Road at 8.30a.m. whilst the girls would return to school in the afternoon.

MONDAY, FEBRUARY 5th
At Fentham Road, the boys and girls swapped their attendance times around once more.

MONDAY, FEBRUARY 12th
As from today, the boys of Slade Road and the girls of Fentham Road would now alternate their attendance on a weekly basis. The afternoon session was changed so that it started at 1p.m. and finished at 5p.m.

TUESDAY, MAY 14th
Children had to attend school today as the authorities had officially cancelled the Whit Tuesday holiday.

FRIDAY, JULY 5th
The Fentham Road Senior Girls' School and the Slade Road Senior Boys' School had recently embarked on a scheme for the collection of scrap metal, etc. in the Erdington District. The result was that £18 was raised, which was used as a contribution towards the fund for the purchase of an ambulance.

FRIDAY, JULY 12th
The girls of Fentham Road attended at school this morning especially so that they could give a performance of their annual Rose Festival – Patricia Stone had been officially crowned Queen only three days earlier – to the senior boys of Slade Road School.

SUNDAY, JULY 14th
A tragic day for the school, as two teachers passed away within hours of each other in the same hospital. Firstly, Mr John Richard Oldroyd, who was seven weeks short of his fifty-second birthday, died. He had worked at the Senior Boys' School, teaching Mathematics, which included Calculus, Trigonometry and Logarithms, since the re-organisation of August 24th, 1931 and lived in Erdington at Douay Road. He had previously been employed at Osborne Road for 18 years, and for a long time had been involved with the District's school sports. He was the founder and secretary of the Erdington Schools' Football League. An

accurate thrower of chalk, the other teacher, Mr William Frederick Wedd, had been the chief assistant master at the Senior Boys' School since February 6th, 1931. He had died suddenly following an operation. He was 57 years of age.

SATURDAY, JULY 27th
The interment of Mr Wedd at St. Michaels Church in Boldmere was reported today. There were numerous family mourners, seven members of the staff of the Senior Boys' School, as well as ladies and gentlemen representing the various education committees, unions and associations. Altogether there were about 75 floral tributes. The six bearers were made up of a representative of each of the following: Birmingham Evening Institute; Erdington Schools' Athletic Association; Slade Road School; Aston Villa Charity Cup Competition; Goldieslie Bowling Club and an old college friend. The reverence in which he was held cannot simply be drawn from the illustrious list of mourners, but from the fact that a number of boys from the Senior Boys' School attended and formed a Guard of Honour at the west entrance to the church. Mr Wedd, a native of Tutbury, was educated at Saltley College. He had been a keen supporter of Birmingham City Football Club and a former playing member. In 1914, he had joined the army and been mentioned in despatches. He was vice-president of the Birmingham Branch of the National Union of Teachers and president of the Birmingham Continuative Teachers' Association. He left a widow, a daughter and a son.

FRIDAY, SEPTEMBER 6th
A crowd of children, who were waiting to board a stationary tram outside the school, were scattered when they were startled by a youth who, when opposite the school, rang his bell whilst pedalling furiously along. A police officer caught up to him and arrested him. He later emerged from Aston Police Court having had his bell rung to the tune of five shillings. His explanation was that he didn't see the kids as he was in a hurry.

FRIDAY, SEPTEMBER 27th
This afternoon the senior boys held their Harvest Festival in the hall of Fentham Road Girls' School. Miss Ward and class 32 of the Girls' School had arranged an exhibition of produce, contributions of which had come from both the boys and girls. The service was conducted by Mr Caddick, the Headmaster of Slade Road Senior Boys' School, whilst the address was read by the Reverend May. Miss L. A. Vaughan, Headmistress, and Miss Forster, chief assistant, of Fentham Road Girls' School were also present. The fruit and vegetables were later forwarded on to the Jaffray Hospital and Erdington House.

MONDAY, NOVEMBER 11th
An alert sounded at midday lasting for 27 minutes. A further air-raid warning came at 3.15p.m., 40 minutes elapsing until the all-clear was given. When the sirens went off to warn of an air raid, a bell would be rung. The children would then leave their classrooms and march in twos to the shelters. These were pitch black inside as they were not lighted. The children would have to hold onto the coat tails of the one in front of them in order to find

One of only two air-raid shelters still standing, this one in the Nursery, which was formerly the Boys' School.

their way. To pass the time, whilst sitting on the hard wooden benches, they would either sing or repeat their multiplication tables, until the all clear sounded.

WEDNESDAY, NOVEMBER 13th
At 12.48p.m. the air-raid sirens sounded, the all-clear not coming until 26 minutes past two. Less than two hours later they went off again at three minutes past four. It wasn't until 52 minutes had gone by that it was possible to leave the shelters. During today's daylight raids the Austin aero factory was hit killing 6 people.

FRIDAY, NOVEMBER 15th
Another air-raid warning! This time the sirens sounded just before four o'clock in the afternoon, the all-clear coming at 4.35.

THURSDAY, NOVEMBER 21st
Yet again the alarm was given, this time at ten past ten in the morning. Twenty minutes later it was considered safe to return to the classrooms.

SUNDAY, NOVEMBER 24th
During the nights of the 22nd and 23rd the bombing had been that fierce that many parts of Birmingham found themselves without any water supply. All headteachers in the designated areas, which included Erdington, were summoned to the Education Office this morning for a discussion on how to deal with the matter.

A favourite pastime amongst the lads at this time was to collect shrapnel, with swaps at school. However, should they be seen by someone from the A.F.S. exploring a bombed-out building, they were warned off. Well, there might be body parts lying around to be recovered!

DECEMBER

The children in the Junior School had their photographs taken especially for Christmas. They were then attached to the inside of a Christmas Card to be given to their parents.

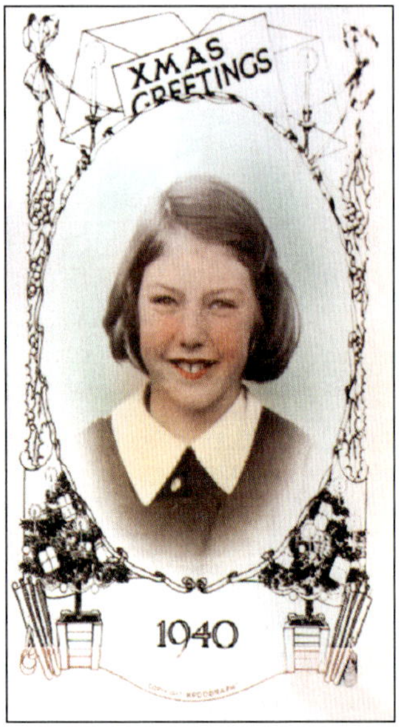

Junior School Christmas, 1940.

FRIDAY, DECEMBER 20th

During the morning session, the girls of class 3 of Fentham Road Girls' School attended especially, so that they could perform their Nativity play for the benefit of the senior boys of Slade Road.

1941

THURSDAY, JANUARY 30th

The senior boys and girls of Slade Road and Fentham Road Schools had combined over the previous three weeks to make a collection for the Children's Charities Fund, the accumulated amount being handed over today.

MONDAY, MAY 5th

The Junior and the Infant departments came together as one school under the Headship of Mr Charley Gooding Clarke.

TUESDAY, SEPTEMBER 30th

This afternoon, a special Harvest Festival service was held at Fentham Road Girls' School. It had been arranged by Miss Ward, the male staff of Slade Road, together with boys and girls from the two schools. Two sisters from the Jaffray Hospital attended the service which was taken by the Reverend Dickson Black of the Baptist Church, Six Ways, Erdington. It commenced at 12.30p.m., the girls and staff of the Girls' School staying behind after their morning session, whilst the senior boys of Slade Road came in early. After appropriate hymns had been sung, a reading from the Old Testament was given by George Rose, one of the boys. Subsequently, Winnie Brammer, the Fentham Road Rose Queen for 1941/2, gave a reading from the New Testament. The flowers, fruit and vegetables were later shared equally between the Jaffray Hospital and Erdington House, both of whom greatly appreciated the gifts. A feature was the joint effort of the two schools in assembling at the main entrance of Fentham Road Girls' School a large table, laden with produce from the boys' and girls' school gardens, which they had started that summer in response to the 'Dig for Victory' campaign.

OCTOBER
Mr Clarke caned a number of children on each hand. Three times to be exact. The young lads had been doing papier mâché in the classroom, became bored, and started flicking it about. Nearing the start of the afternoon session, they had rapidly cleared up the mess; or so they thought! The Headmaster walked into the classroom, noticed that there were three pieces stuck to the clock, and asked who had put them there. As no one owned up, he promptly enquired who had been doing the papier mâché. Having established that, they were marched to his office and given six of the best across the palms of the hand.

1942
FRIDAY, MAY 1st
At last, the senior boys could return to their normal school premises as there was now sufficient room, once again, to accommodate them. Desks, books and cupboards, that had been taken up to Fentham Road Girls' School, were brought back to their original homes today. After 2 years and 8 months of half-time schooling, both schools could now get back to normal working; if you could call the Second World War normal!

WEDNESDAY, JULY 8th
The top class of the Senior Boys' School was invited to attend Fentham Road Girls' School this afternoon, together with parents from that school, in order to see the annual Rose Festival. Chosen as Rose Queen for 1942/3 was Margaret Williams, who had been crowned the previous day.

TUESDAY, AUGUST 25th
Once again this afternoon the boys of Slade Road Senior Boys' School were back at Fentham Road Girls' School. This time they were taken to see an Edinburgh safety-first film, which the girls of Fentham Road had already seen that morning.

FRIDAY, SEPTEMBER 25th
The Senior Boys' School held their annual Harvest Festival at 9.15a.m. As the girls of Fentham Road had made a considerable contribution of their own, their Headmistress, Miss Vaughan, together with the captain and vice-captain of the school, attended the service. Once again, the produce was donated to the same two just causes.

1943
SEPTEMBER
Mr Weedon took the boys of the Senior School to a plot of land at the rear of the Parochial Hall to grow vegetables in aid of the war effort. This was a weekly lesson in the 'Dig for Victory' campaign. They grew potatoes, cabbages, peas and cauliflowers, which were distributed to deserving local people.

1944

MONDAY, JUNE 26th

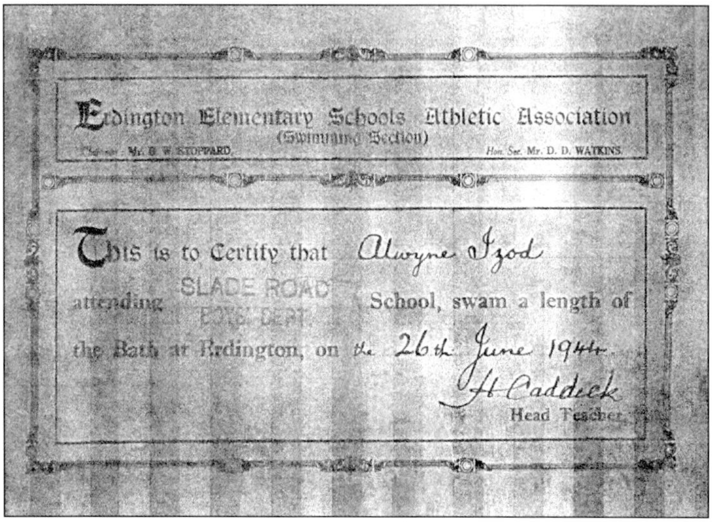

1945

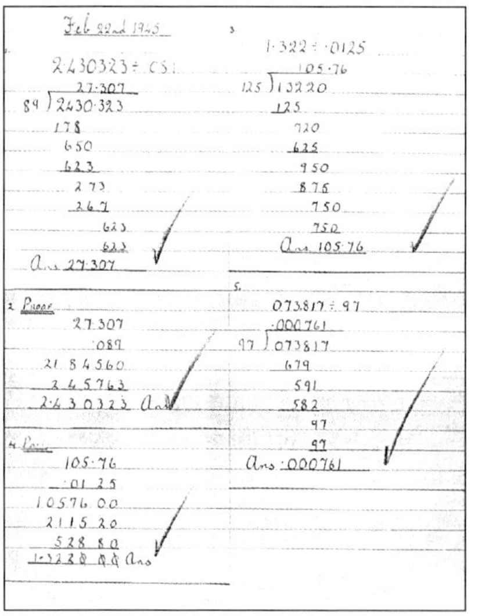

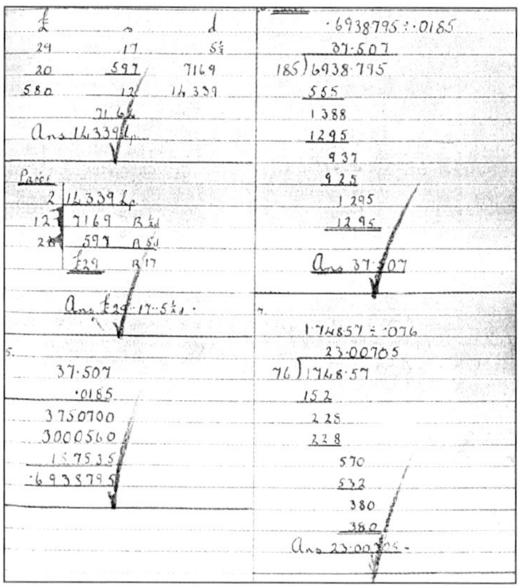

Top Left: A swimming certificate issued today by the Erdington Elementary Schools' Athletic Association. Top Right: Slade Road School was amongst a list of 30 establishments throughout Birmingham that was used as a Local Distribution Centre for the issue of ration books. The only other one in Erdington was at the Fire Station in Orphanage Road. Bottom: Examples of Mathematics by a 14 year old in the Boys' School.

How the People lived. June 26th
The enclosures of the land for sheep farms, the closing of the monastries and gilds and the bad coinage, caused great suffering in England. Armies of beggars about the land, and were a danger to the countryside. Laws were past to punish the lazy, and to help the old, so that the danger was removed.
Farming was the chief work of the people, but woollen goods were made in the cottages, and houses of the villages and towns. Yorkshire, Norfolk, Gloucestershire and Cornwall were the chief seats of the woollen trade.
Coal was used in London, and a few other towns. Iron was smelted in Sussex, Kent, Gloucestershire Worcestershire, Warwickshire and Staffordshire.
Fine houses of red brick were built instead of the gloomy castles of the middle ages.
This period is famous for its writers, especially those who wrote poetry: Spensor, Sidney and Shakespeare are the three of them

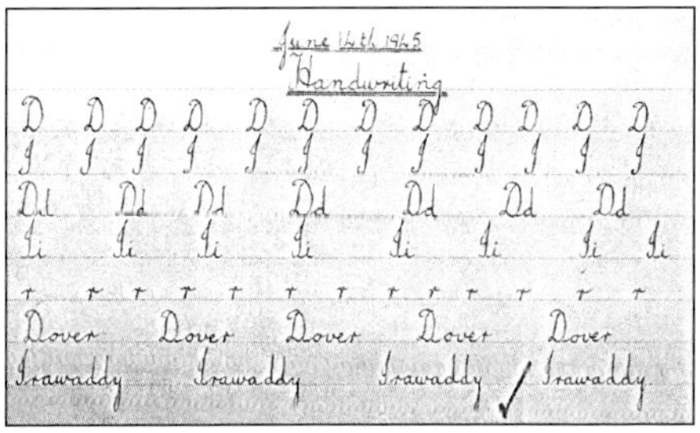

June 14th 1945
Handwriting
D D D D D D D D D D D D
J J J J J J J J J J J J
Dd Dd Dd Dd Dd Dd Dd
Ji Ji Ji Ji Ji Ji Ji Ji
r r r r r r r r r r r r r r
Dover Dover Dover Dover Dover
Irawaddy Irawaddy Irawaddy Irawaddy

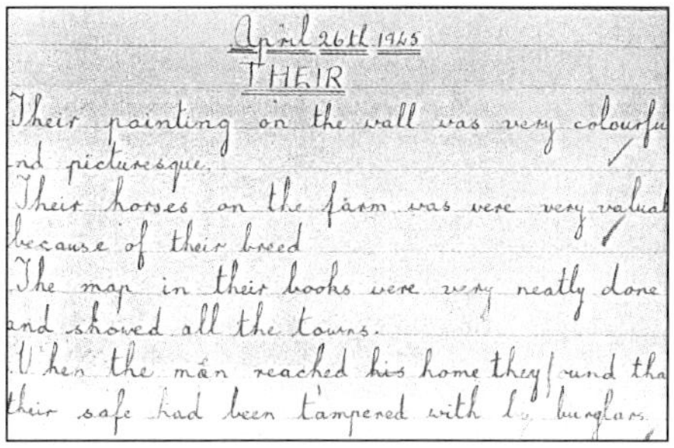

April 26th 1945
THEIR
Their painting on the wall was very colourful and picturesque.
Their horses on the farm was were very valuable because of their breed
The map in their books were very neatly done and showed all the towns.
When the man reached his home they found that their safe had been tampered with by burglars.

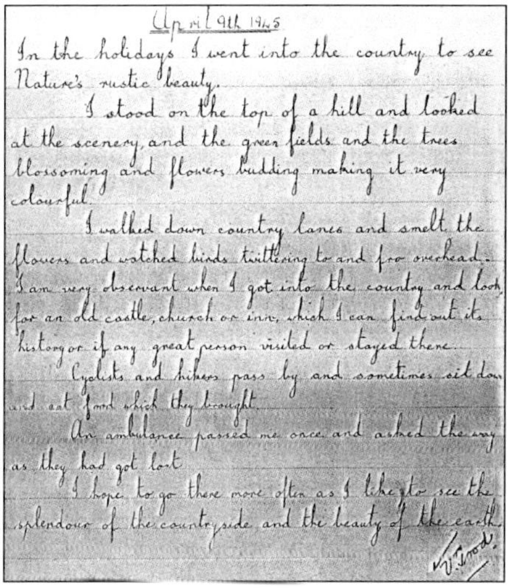

April 9th 1945
In the holidays I went into the country to see Nature's rustic beauty.
I stood on the top of a hill and looked at the scenery, and the green fields and the trees blossoming and flowers budding making it very colourful.
I walked down country lanes and smelt the flowers and watched birds twittering to and fro overhead. I am very observant when I got into the country and look for an old castle, church or inn, which I can find out its history or if any great person visited or stayed there.
Cyclists and hikers pass by and sometimes sit down and eat food which they brought.
An ambulance passed me once and asked the way as they had got lost
I hope to go there more often as I like to see the splendour of the countryside and the beauty of the earth.
V. Good.

Examples of English and History by the same 14 year old in the Boys' School.

SEPTEMBER
The Senior Boys' School became a totally separate school to be known as the Slade Boys' County Modern School. The Infants and Juniors, meanwhile, for a time used two classrooms in the senior school.

FRIDAY, SEPTEMBER 28th
The Boys' School held their annual Harvest Festival service at nine o'clock this morning. Invited were the Headmistress of Fentham Road Senior Girls' School, Miss Vaughan, as well as the school's Rose Queen for 1945/6, Brenda Guy, and her deputy. The produce continued to be shared between the Jaffray Hospital and Highcroft Hall.

SUNDAY, SEPTEMBER 30th
Miss May Beatrice Jeffery officially retired at the age of 60 after 40 years service in the Infants' department of the school. She was an uncertificated assistant, who had first come to the school

on September 1st, 1905, her only previous appointment being for seven months at Upper Thomas Street. She would be fondly remembered by many children who passed through her care as the first teacher that they came to know – just the sort of teacher you wanted on your first day to mother you. She was a gentle lady who wore her hair tied up in a bun.

MONDAY to FRIDAY, OCTOBER 22nd to 26th
The whole of the Senior Boys' School visited the Palace Cinema over a period of a week in order to see the film *King Henry V* starring Lawrence Olivier. Matinees were at 2p.m. and it was anticipated that the film, which was in colour, would please everyone who enjoyed spectacle.

WEDNESDAY, NOVEMBER 7th
The King and Queen paid an official visit to Birmingham today. All the schoolchildren in the city were granted a day off, many of them taking the opportunity to go and see them as they toured the inner city at noon.

1946

TUESDAY, APRIL 30th
Two lads from the Erdington Cottage Homes – Ronald Reeves and Glyn Williams – along with six other former pupils of Slade Road commenced at the Handsworth Junior Technical School today, having passed the entrance examination some months earlier.

WEDNESDAY, JULY 3rd
For the first time since 1939 the Erdington Elementary Schools' Athletic Association held their championship meeting, this time on Jaffray Road playing fields. Every event was well supported and the ground arrangements were excellent. The weather was kind and several thousand spectators wildly cheered every winner. A total of fourteen schools participated, Slade Road finishing as runners up to Paget Road in the fight for the Senior Boys' Championship Shield, although they could take some consolation from the fact that the junior girls tied for first place with Moor End Lane in their competition.

SATURDAY, OCTOBER 19th
A new football season had begun and the junior team from Slade Road was a particularly fine one. Their first match in the H.M.S. Birmingham Shield was against Sir Josiah Mason's who they convincingly beat 3–0. Walker scored a hat trick.

SATURDAY, NOVEMBER 9th
Walker scored again as Slade Road narrowly defeated Turfpits Lane by the only goal in the next round of the H.M.S. Birmingham Shield.

SATURDAY, NOVEMBER 16th
In the English Schools' Shield, Erdington Boys, who were much lighter than their opponents, were soundly beaten by South Birmingham Boys by a score of five goals to two.

At back for Erdington that day – the only representative from Slade Road – was Graham Sissons, later to find fame with Birmingham City.

1947

SATURDAY, JANUARY 11th

Slade Road progressed further in the H.M.S. Birmingham Shield, this time to the chagrin of Upper Thomas Street.

THURSDAY, JANUARY 23rd

Mr Harold Caddick, Headmaster of Slade Boys' County Modern School, was presented with a message of appreciation – in album form – at the annual meeting of the Birmingham Local Board of the Benevolent and Orphan Fund of the National Union of Teachers at the Birmingham Council House. He had been its treasurer for 21 years and at the meeting was elected chairman. His wife was given a new handbag.

SATURDAY, JANUARY 25th

In the Erdington Schools' Junior Football League, Slade Road showed no more sympathy for their opponents than in the Shield competition. They finally met Moor End Lane who were, like themselves, unbeaten, not having conceded a goal all season. Slade Road crushed them by six goals to nil, Walker bagging five of them.

MONDAY, FEBRUARY 17th

Miss Frances Ann Marsh, who had worked in the Infants' since January 1st, 1914 – her first post since qualifying in August, 1913 – left today after 33 years to take up a position at Moor End Junior and Infants' School. She eventually retired from there on December 31st, 1953. Between August 17th, 1942 and October 31st, 1946, she had been promoted to temporary chief assistant.

TUESDAY, APRIL 1st

As from today, children were now required to stay at school until the age of fifteen. In the Secondary Modern Boys' School, the only way that they could accommodate this was to place the additional year of children in the Parochial Hall. The lads were put into separate graded rows, all under the stewardship of Tom Jones, a five foot ten teacher with a stiff leg.

WEDNESDAY, APRIL 30th

Mr Ernest Albert Bosker retired today aged 65. He had qualified as a certificated teacher in 1903 and had worked for many schools in Aston before joining Slade Road as a chief assistant on October 1st, 1921. He had struck up a relationship with an assistant mistress at the school, Miss Newby, 18 years his junior, and they had been married on August 2nd, 1928. He was remembered as an affable man, but very strict.

SATURDAY, MAY 3rd

In the semifinals of the H.M.S. Birmingham Shield, Slade Road met Severne Road, who led twice, each time Slade Road levelling through Walker. Slade Road finally overcame their opponents, Robertson scoring the winning goal in the last minute of play.

SATURDAY, MAY 10th

For the first time since 1918 Slade Road had reached the final of the H.M.S. Birmingham Shield. The competition was open to all junior schools in Birmingham; and there was a record entry of 51. Amazingly, the other finalists were also from Erdington, setting up a unique confrontation with Gunter Road. In the first half, played at Jaffray Road playing fields, Slade Road had the greater part of the play, Ellen, the goalkeeper for Gunter Road, needing to make some fine saves, although he had no chance with the effort of Walker, who sent Slade Road in at half time a goal to the good. After the resumption, it was a ding-dong affair with both goalkeepers having anxious moments. A feature of the game was the heading and the good, clean play; the Slade Road forward line in particular showing some flashes of fine combination work. Each side scored once in the second half, Nicholls netting the winner for Slade Road, who thus won the H.M.S. Birmingham Shield for the first time by a score of two goals to one. At the conclusion of the match, the Shield was presented by Mr H. Wise, treasurer of the Birmingham Schools' Federation. The boys were later paraded on stage at the Plaza Cinema. To add to their joy, they had also been crowned as champions of the Erdington Schools' Junior Football League, remaining unbeaten all season. The Senior Boys finished as runners up to Paget Road in the Erdington Schools' Football League A and B competitions.

Senior 'A'							
PAGET ROAD	6	6	0	0	32	8	12
SLADE ROAD	6	4	0	2	16	12	8
RYLAND ROAD	6	3	0	3	14	16	6
MOOR END LANE	6	3	0	3	9	16	6
SIR JOSIAH MASON'S	6	2	1	3	11	8	5
BOLDMERE	6	1	1	4	11	17	3
St.THOMAS'	6	1	0	5	4	21	2

Final Table Senior League 1946/7 Season.

WEDNESDAY, JUNE 25th

The Erdington Schools' Athletic Association held its annual sports at Jaffray Road playing fields this evening. Amongst the spectators were many local councillors, Mr R. R. Gelling J. P., the president, presenting the trophies after the conclusion of the meeting. Twenty schools took part, Paget Road carrying off three of the four trophies. Slade Road were able to finish as runners up in the Junior Girls' competition, losing out by a single point.

AUGUST

During the summer holidays, extra pocket money could be earned by the boys in the secondary school. They put their names down on a list so that they could be chosen to go potato picking at Minworth.

FRIDAY, OCTOBER 3rd

More than 150 competitors from 16 schools took part in the first post-war swimming gala of the Erdington Schools' Athletic Association at Erdington baths this evening. Major F. T. Monk M. C. subsequently presented the trophies to the winning schools. Slade Road were able to finish level on points with Osborne Road in the Junior Girls' competition, thus sharing that trophy for the next twelve months.

THURSDAY, NOVEMBER 20th

The school was closed for the day as it was the occasion of the marriage of Princess Elizabeth to Prince Philip.

WEDNESDAY, DECEMBER 17th

The headmistress of Fentham Road Girls' School was invited to the senior boys' Christmas carol service.

1948

SATURDAY, MAY 8th

A new trophy was donated to the Erdington Schools' Football League to be known as the Oldroyd-Wedd Trophy, in recognition of the two teachers from Slade Road School who had both died on the same day in 1940. Mrs Wedd presented the trophy to the first winners who were Paget Road. It was competed for by senior boys' football teams in the form of a knockout cup competition.

Senior 'A'	Played	W	D	L	F	A	PTS
PAGET ROAD	10	8	1	1	50	14	17
RYLAND ROAD	10	6	2	2	36	9	14
MOOR END LANE	10	7	0	3	34	19	14
SLADE ROAD	10	3	2	5	16	19	8
BOLDMERE	10	2	1	7	13	46	5
St.THOMAS'	10	0	2	8	8	50	2
Senior 'B'							
PAGET ROAD	10	7	1	2	30	9	16
MOOR END LANE	10	7	1	2	46	15	15
SLADE ROAD	10	6	2	2	31	15	14
RYLAND ROAD	10	4	3	3	27	26	11
BOLDMERE	10	2	1	7	18	42	5
St.THOMAS'	10	0	0	10	5	55	0

Final Tables Erdington Schools' Football League Senior Divisions 1947/8 Season.

WEDNESDAY, JUNE 30th

The Erdington Schools' Athletic Association sports rolled round once again. Between 1,500 and 2,000 spectators attended the annual event which took place between 26 schools at the Jaffray Road playing fields. The boys of Slade Road Junior School were able to gain some success for the school, comfortably winning the Junior Boys' Championship Shield, which was presented afterwards by Major F. Monk M. C., senior vice president.

JULY

Mr C. J. Fox started his teaching career at Slade Road Senior Boys' School in 1931. He was an all-round sportsman, who had an appreciation of good music. During the Second World War, he had spent 4 years in the Royal Navy as both a Lieutenant Commander and Commander, before returning to the school after the war. Leaving this month, he took up positions with the National, Erdington; Dudley Road and All Saints, Hockley before joining

Cockerham Church of England School in Lancaster in September 1954 as Headmaster. His daughter, Gillian, attended Slade Road Infants' during the early fifties, her portrait being painted, when she was six, by a local artist for submission to the Royal Academy.

SATURDAY, JULY 17th

Visitors to the 13th annual swimming gala of the Erdington Schools' Athletic Association included two vice presidents, Mr Julius Silverman M.P. and Major F. Monk M. C., the latter presenting the trophies to the winning teams. Yet again Slade Road came away with a championship shield winning the Secondary Modern Boys' competition. During the events, an excellent demonstration of life saving was put on.

SATURDAY, JULY 24th

The Erdington schools' cricket season ended with Slade Road finishing as runners up in the Intermediate League. The last game against Paget Road was a cracker! Goodenough with 7 for 5 and Robertson with 3 for 2 were responsible for Paget Road being dismissed for the season's lowest total of 7 runs. However, in the Junior League, which comprised 12 schools, they tied for first place with Osborne Road, despite beating them in their only encounter of the season, when having bowled them all out for 31 runs, they had passed the total with 4 wickets to spare.

Senior	Played	W	L	PTS
PAGET ROAD	5	5	0	10
BOLDMERE	5	3	2	6
RYLAND ROAD	5	3	2	6
SLADE ROAD	5	2	3	4
MOOR END LANE	5	1	4	2
St.THOMAS'	5	1	4	2
Intermediate				
MOOR END LANE	5	5	0	10
SLADE ROAD	5	4	1	8
PAGET ROAD	5	3	2	6
BOLDMERE	5	2	3	4
RYLAND ROAD	5	1	4	2
St.THOMAS'	5	0	5	0
Junior				
SLADE ROAD	11	8	3	16
OSBORNE ROAD	11	8	3	16
BIRCHES GREEN	11	7	4	14
GUNTER ROAD	11	7	4	14
NATIONAL	11	6	5	12
PAGET ROAD	11	6	5	12
RYLAND ROAD	11	6	5	12
SIR JOSIAH MASON'S	11	5	6	10
MOOR END LANE	11	4	7	8
MARSH HILL	11	4	7	8
TEDBURY CRESCENT	11	3	8	6
TURFPITS LANE	11	2	9	4

Final Tables Erdington Schools' Cricket League.

SEPTEMBER

In the Boys' School, if two of the lads were caught fighting, the school had an easy solution to the matter. Mr Blackie kept boxing gloves in the science room, and the antagonists would be invited to settle their differences in a ring which would be assembled in the hall. Whilst on the subject of boxing, Johnny Prescott – well known in the sixties as one of the golden boys of heavyweight boxing – attended the school, whilst a resident of the Erdington Cottage Homes.

FRIDAY, OCTOBER 1st

Mr Tom Jones of the Secondary Boys' School left to take up an appointment at Axminster. He had been an enthusiastic worker for the Erdington Schools' Sports Association for 17 years, being chairman of the football section as well as secretary of the athletics sports. Naturally, he was in charge of sport at the Boys' School.

FINAL JUNIOR LEAGUE TABLE	P	W	L	D	F	A	PTS
GUNTER ROAD	12	12	0	0	56	2	24
TURFPITS LANE	12	6	3	3	28	10	15
NATIONAL	12	7	4	1	24	16	15
RYLAND ROAD	12	6	3	3	19	17	15
BIRCHES GREEN	12	7	4	1	16	18	15
TEDBURY CRESCENT	12	7	5	0	27	20	14
HAWTHORN ROAD	12	6	5	1	23	16	13
PAGET ROAD	12	4	5	3	13	16	11
SLADE ROAD	12	4	5	3	17	22	11
BOLDMERE	12	2	4	6	11	14	10
OSBORNE ROAD	12	2	6	4	10	21	8
MOOR END LANE	12	1	9	2	6	20	4
SIR JOSIAH MASON'S	12	0	11	1	2	51	1

Erdington Schools' Football League, 1948/1949.

1949

SATURDAY, FEBRUARY 26th

In the first round of the Erdington Junior Football Cup, Slade Road disposed of Ryland Road by an only goal scored by Yates.

SATURDAY, MARCH 5th

The Erdington Junior Football League was now concluded resulting in the final table above.

SATURDAY, MARCH 19th

In the second round of the Erdington Junior Football Cup, Slade Road comfortably defeated Tedbury Crescent by four goals to one, Rhodes and Kilburn netting a brace apiece.

SATURDAY, APRIL 2nd

The semifinals of the Junior Football Cup were now concluded, Slade Road getting the best of Birches Green by the odd goal in five.

SATURDAY, APRIL 9th

A large crowd saw defences on top in the final of the Erdington Junior Football Cup, which took place between Slade Road and the National. Neither team was able to score, even after extra time, so a replay was required.

SATURDAY, APRIL 16th

In the replayed Junior Cup Final, yet again the teams remained deadlocked after extra time, neither being able to put the ball past the opposition's goalkeeper. As a result, it was decided that the two teams should hold the trophy jointly.

Junior School Football Team, 1948/9.

Senior							
PAGET ROAD	12	11	0	1	66	7	23
RYLAND ROAD	12	10	2	0	43	10	20
SLADE ROAD	12	6	5	1	30	18	13
Intermediate							
PAGET ROAD	12	11	1	0	81	5	22
BOLDMERE	12	9	3	0	31	14	18
MOOR END LANE	12	7	4	1	24	22	15

Final leading positions Erdington Schools' Football League Senior Divisions.

SATURDAY, JULY 9th

The girls of Slade Road Junior School were successful in capturing two trophies this week. They won both the athletics and the swimming shields of the Erdington Schools' Sports Association.

SATURDAY, JULY 16th

Slade Road Boys' School completed the cricket season in the Erdington Schools' Cricket League going undefeated in the senior division, thus winning the championship. The Junior eleven remained unbeaten until the final encounter of the season when they met Boldmere. A narrow defeat left them as runners up in the northern section of the league, Boldmere taking the championship when they defeated the southern section winners, the National, in the final.

SEPTEMBER

A policeman would stand on point duty outside the school to ensure the children were able to cross Slade Road safely.

	P	W	L	Pts
SLADE ROAD	6	6	0	12
PAGET ROAD	6	5	1	10
MOOR END LANE	6	4	2	8
BOLDMERE	6	3	3	6
RYLAND ROAD	5	1	4	2
VICTORIA ROAD	5	1	4	2
ST THOMAS'	6	0	6	0

Erdington Schools' Cricket League Senior Division.

1950

SATURDAY, JANUARY 14th

At this point in the football season, it was hoped that schools would be able to complete their junior league fixtures before they were disorganised by promotions to secondary schools, which were due to take place the first week in February. They would then commence their knockout cup games.

FRIDAY, FEBRUARY 3rd

Miss Edith Emily Griffiths-Jones decided that, at the age of 63, it was time for her to leave. She had worked at the school since September 1st, 1910. For five years, until the re-organisation of 1915, she had worked in the Junior department. During the next 16 years she taught in the Boys' School, until changes took place there in 1931, whereupon she transferred back into the Junior department once again. During her younger years, she rode a sit-up and beg bicycle with a dress bar at the back. She was remembered as a rather plump lady, who carried all before her.

JUNIOR							
Gunter Road	12	12	0	0	62	5	24
Birches Green	13	11	2	0	42	9	22
Tedbury Crescent	13	10	2	1	53	12	21
Hawthorn Road	13	8	3	2	24	15	18
Slade Road	12	8	4	0	42	13	16
Boldmere	13	5	5	3	21	17	13
National	13	5	5	3	18	18	13
Turfpits Lane	13	5	5	3	14	27	13
Paget Road	12	3	4	5	22	17	11
Sir Josiah Mason's	13	4	7	2	15	24	10
Abbey	13	2	8	3	4	36	7
Moor End Lane	13	2	10	1	5	63	5
Osborne Road	13	2	11	0	10	50	4
Ryland Road	12	0	11	1	0	36	1

Erdington Schools' Football League, Junior Division.

SATURDAY, MARCH 4th
The league fixtures were now concluded in the Junior Division of the Erdington Schools' Football League, resulting in the table above.

SATURDAY, MAY 6th
In the Senior and Intermediate competitions of the Erdington Schools' Football League, Slade Road and Paget Road were the teams to beat. Slade Road finished as runners up to Paget Road in the Intermediate League, whilst in the Senior League they won the championship, losing only one game back in October of 1949. The two Knockout Trophy finals were to be decided today, and yet again the protagonists were to be Slade Road and Paget Road. In the Intermediate Cup Final, Paget Road ran out convincing winners by four goals to nil. Now, it was the turn of the senior sides. Slade Road took the lead early in the first half when Burlace, the right back, netted with a thirty yard drive. They held onto this lead until the dying moments of the game when Paget Road were awarded a penalty, Liggins converting the spot kick, the score thus being tied up at one apiece. Extra time was played during which Slade Road were awarded a penalty of their own when Davies gave them the lead once more. Evans quickly equalised for Paget Road, but further goals by Mason and Walker made the issue safe for Slade Road. They were, therefore, able at last to put their name onto the Oldroyd-Wedd

Senior

	P	W	L	D	F	A	PTS
SLADE ROAD	12	11	1	0	55	13	22
PAGET ROAD	12	9	3	0	39	19	18
MOOR END LANE	12	8	3	1	37	19	17
BOLDMERE	12	6	5	1	36	29	13
St.THOMAS'	12	4	8	0	33	23	8
RYLAND ROAD	12	2	10	0	16	38	4
VICTORIA ROAD	12	1	11	0	10	75	2

Intermediate

	P	W	L	D	F	A	Pts
PAGET ROAD	10	9	0	1	45	8	18
SLADE ROAD	10	7	2	1	22	14	15
BOLDMERE	10	6	4	0	30	21	12
RYLAND ROAD	10	3	5	2	29	21	8
VICTORIA ROAD	10	1	7	2	11	29	4
St.THOMAS'	10	0	8	2	9	53	2

Erdington Schools' Football League Season 1949/1950.

Trophy for the first time. During the season, Davies, Bettley, Fulford and Machin had all been chosen to represent Erdington Schools. The final league tables appear on the previous page.

TUESDAY, MAY 16th
Slade Road, together with Ryland Road, Moor End Lane and Osborne Road, sent choirs to compete in the annual North Birmingham Junior Schools' Musical Festival at the Town Hall in Birmingham. Twenty schools took part, and the combined choirs totalled 500 voices. In addition, each school entertained the audience in its own unique way. Moor End Lane mimed the cries of London, whilst dressed in Stuart period costumes; Ryland Road gave choral speaking; Osborne Road gave a display of country dances and Slade Road chose to perform National dances in costume.

THURSDAY, JUNE 22nd
Rain just failed to spoil the first annual sports day of Slade Road Primary School, which took place at Jaffray Road playing fields. The event had had to be postponed from the previous afternoon because of rain, and the children could barely have reached their homes, or the shelter of the school, after the completion of the sports when there was a torrential downpour. About 400 competitors took part in the 40 events that had been provided for them. Mr E. Roberts, an ex-navy man, who had organised the sports, made a mahogany shield for presentation to the class winners each year; Class 1 recording the most points on this occasion. Events included 60 and 80 yards running; skipping; high jump; three-legged; potato and spoon; sack and relay races. Mr Roberts' wife, together with another lady, served up refreshments for the benefit of the children.

THURSDAY, JUNE 29th
One week later, and it was time for the annual Erdington schools' sports. About 200 competitors from 28 schools took part at Jaffray Road playing fields. The fine weather attracted around 3,000 spectators who thoroughly enjoyed themselves. This year, the girls of Slade Road Primary School had to be satisfied with being runners up to Tedbury Crescent. However, the boys rose to the occasion and captured the Junior Boys' Shield, edging out perennial rivals, Paget Road, by half a point. Major F. Monk, the president of the association, presented the prizes.

SATURDAY, JULY 1st
A good standard of swimming was seen when the Erdington Schools' Sports Association held its 15th annual swimming gala at Erdington baths. Excitement ran high when some of the races were evenly contested between the 200 competitors representing the 22 schools that took part. The Headmaster of Slade Secondary Boys' School, Mr Caddick, presided as chairman of the swimming committee, whilst Mr Julius Silverman, M.P. for Erdington, presented the prizes. Unfortunately, the school was unable to record any success on this occasion.

TUESDAY, JULY 18th

About one hundred parents, mostly consisting of mothers, took advantage of the opportunity to visit Slade Road Secondary Modern Boys' School on Parents' Day to see the boys at work, talk to the teachers and discuss careers. The latter part of the afternoon was devoted to plays and singing. There were two plays, *The Reckoning* and *Thread of Scarlet*, both of which were produced by Mr Wilson; whilst the choir, trained and conducted by Trevor Jones, rendered songs and rounds. Mr Harold Caddick, who was retiring as Head of the School within a few days, expressed his thanks to all concerned for their efforts. The new Headmaster, Mr Griffin, who would be taking up his duties at the start of the new term, came over from Ilmington Secondary Modern Boys' School in Weoley Castle, where he was the headmaster, to lend his weight to the proceedings.

SATURDAY, JULY 22nd

All the matches had now been played in the Erdington Schools' Cricket League. In the Intermediate League, Slade Road finished as runners up losing only one game, but that was to the eventual, unbeaten winners, Paget Road. As far as the Senior League was concerned, this was an extremely close affair with only two points separating the top five schools. Three schools tied for first place, so the championship had to be shared between them.

SENIOR	P	W	L	PTS
SLADE ROAD	6	4	2	8
MOOR END LANE	6	4	2	8
PAGET ROAD	6	4	2	8
BOLDMERE	6	3	3	6
St.THOMAS'	6	3	3	6
VICTORIA ROAD	6	2	4	4
RYLAND ROAD	6	1	5	2

INTERMEDIATE				
PAGET ROAD	5	5	0	10
SLADE ROAD	5	4	1	8
BOLDMERE	5	2	3	4
MOOR END LANE	5	2	3	4
VICTORIA ROAD	5	2	3	4
St.THOMAS'	5	0	5	0

JUNIOR NORTH				
MARSH HILL	7	7	0	14
BOLDMERE	7	6	1	12
SLADE ROAD	7	4	3	8
HAWTHORN ROAD	7	3	4	6
SIR JOSIAH MASON'S	7	0	4	6
TEDBURY CRESCENT	7	3	4	6
ELIOT STREET	7	2	5	4
TURFPITS LANE	7	0	7	0

JUNIOR SOUTH	P	W	L	T	PTS
NATIONAL	7	6	0	1	13
PAGET ROAD	7	6	1	0	12
BIRCHES GREEN	7	5	1	1	1[illegible]
GUNTER ROAD	7	3	4	0	6
OSBORNE ROAD	7	2	5	0	4

Left: Erdington Schools' Cricket League Final Tables. Right Top: Primary School Cricket Eleven. Right Bottom: Primary School class c.1950.

SATURDAY, JULY 29th

A certificate awarded to Pamela Ashton of the Junior School for accident prevention.

Oswald George Pearce Dixon, 5' 7" with light brown hair, had been recognised as a teacher of handicrafts since June lst, 1907. He first came to work at Slade Road School on January 11th, 1911. During the Second World War – from June 17th until July 25th, 1940 – he carried out munitions work at a technical college. Then, again, between May and October of 1943, he was seconded as a handicraft supply teacher. Except for those few months, he spent 39 years working with the senior boys of Slade Road School, before reaching his 65th birthday on June 21st of 1950, such that he had now reached retirement age. Officially, he retired on August 31st. Mr Dixon, who generally took woodwork, always wore plus-fours, a feature for which he stood out at the time. Over the years, he was well known by the boys as being a good teacher, but strict. Woe betide you if you weren't paying attention, for he had a habit of throwing pieces of wood at you across the classroom to attract it! This generally caused the children who weren't involved to snigger helplessly. It also seemed to encourage Mr Dixon to do it even more! He suffered from a nervous twitching of his head and, so the story went, this was because someone had thrown a mallet at it! Leaving on the last day of term as well was Mr Harold Caddick, the Headmaster of the Secondary Modern Boys' School, who had decided to take his retirement at the age of 62. At a 'Thank You' party that he gave at the Yenton Masonic Hall, he paid high tribute to the 'Hearty spirit of co-operation that existed between the Education Committee, its administrative offices and the teaching profession'. He commented that he had spent 14 good years as headmaster at Slade School due to the loyalty, co-operation and friendship of the staff. He was sure that great days still lay ahead under the leadership of Mr Griffin, the new Head Teacher. He was only retiring as an active teacher, who had worked in the profession for 46 years; all his other work would go on; and he would be taking up a part-time masonic post. More than 100 people attended the function including Sir Wilfred Martineau (chairman of the Birmingham Education Committee); Mr Byng Kenrick (former chairman of the B. E. C.); Mr A. Gooch (senior inspector for the Birmingham district); Mr F. E. Dyke (H.M.I.); Mr R. E. Cousens (assistant education officer); Mr J. P. Carter (president of the Birmingham Branch of the National Union of Teachers); Mr S. Ogden (national chairman of the Benevolent and Orphans Fund); Mr L. G. Brandon (Headmaster of King Edward's, Aston) and Canon W. S. Power. Also in attendance was Mrs M. J. Ward, Slade Road's oldest, former teacher at the time, who had retired 27 years earlier. Three familiar faces would also be missing from the staff of Slade Road Primary School. Miss E. Wakeham, who had been the Deputy Head Teacher for the previous 3½ years, was leaving to become Head Teacher at Redcross Street Primary Infants' School in Wolverhampton. Miss Barson was moving to a Home Office School near Nottingham after three years at Slade Road, whilst Miss G. Heppenstall was leaving after 5 years to get married.

FRIDAY, SEPTEMBER 1st

After only seven months away, Miss Griffiths-Jones returned to the fray in the Junior and Infants' department. With the loss of three teachers she was obviously needed to take the strain.

Top: Mr Griffin (3rd from left, front row) with prefects, September 1950.
Bottom: Secondary Boys' School Class, 1950.

OCTOBER

SLADE ROAD SECONDARY MODERN BOYS' SCHOOL.

SESSION 1960 1961

This Certificate has been awarded to

JOHN GREENWOOD

for

HARVEST POSTER COMPETITION.

The Secondary Modern Boys' School ran a Harvest poster competition, a certificate for which can be seen above.

DECEMBER

Another example of photographs being taken at Christmas.

1951

SATURDAY, MARCH 3rd

The Erdington Schools' Football League were delighted to learn that a new trophy had been presented to them as a Junior Cup. This cup was donated by Mr Frank Riego, the manager of the Plaza Cinema in Stockland Green; and would be presented to the season's winners of the Junior Knockout Cup. He had also promised to give medals to the winning team. The new trophy was to be known as the Plaza Cup.

SATURDAY, MARCH 17th

An award for an ex-pupil came to light today. It was a great surprise to Firewoman Miss Dorothy Hood to learn that she had been awarded a medal by the French Government for helping to fight forest fires in France in August 1949. She was the only woman amongst 11 other British volunteers. She was educated at Slade Road until, at the age of eleven, she went to Fentham Road Senior Girls' School. She joined the National Fire Brigade in Birmingham in 1942, transferring to the Kent Fire Brigade in 1947. The medals were handed over by the French Consul General, Monsieur Xavier Gauthier, at a Maidstone Hotel.

SATURDAY, APRIL 28th

In the final of the Intermediate Knock Out Cup, Slade Road, winners of the Intermediate League, comfortably beat St. Thomas' by three clear goals.

Boys' School Intermediate Team, 1951.

WEDNESDAY, JUNE 13th

About 380 children took part in the annual sports of the Primary School, which were held in fine weather in front of 400 spectators at Jaffray Road playing fields. Mr Edwin Sullivan Roberts once again organised the sports, the prizes being distributed by the Headmaster's wife, Mrs C. G. Clarke. This year, it was the turn of Class 5 to win the shield. Prizes were also given to the best boy, George Luker; and girl, Eileen Rose and Margaret Johnson tying for the honour. There were a total of 48 events which took on the same form as the previous year with refreshments being provided for the thirsty children.

WEDNESDAY, JUNE 20th

160 boys and 28 adults and staff of the Secondary Modern Boys' School visited the South Bank Exhibition today. Groups of 20 equipped with school-printed timetables and guides had a long, glorious, exciting and instructive day, during which they took in the Dome of Discovery, Homes and Gardens and the Health Hall. The watchword of the day was 'hasten slowly'.

The thoughtfulness of the boys was shown in their presents. Souvenir ties, penknives, 5-shilling crown pieces, brooches for mum and humble woodbines for dad were the order of the day. The verdict of the boys: 'May we have another visit soon?'

THURSDAY, JUNE 28th

5, 000 spectators turned up at Jaffray Road playing fields to watch the annual sports of the Erdington Schools' Athletic Association. Altogether, there were about 300 competitors representing 29 schools. This year, Slade School was able to come first in only one event and, in consequence, failed to put their name on any of the trophies. The best that they could achieve was to finish as runners up to Boldmere for the Senior Boys' Trophy, the Wiggins-Davies Shield. On presenting the prizes at the end of the event, Major F. Monk M. C., the president of the association, commented that it was the school that mattered. He urged the losers not to be discouraged, but to still continue training hard for the following year. A good loser was just as important as a good winner. As everyone made their way home afterwards, the roads around the playing fields were awash with throngs of children, teachers, parents and friends.

THURSDAY, JULY 5th

Now it was the turn of the Secondary Modern Boys' School to hold their annual sports, which took place at the Erdington Cottage Homes sports ground. Though rain had threatened during the morning, conditions were ideal in the afternoon. About 200 boys took part in the events, where children from each year competed against each other, everyone representing their own House team. The running events consisted of sprints of 80 yards to 220 yards according to age, with relays later on. There were also sack and three-legged races. The other two competitions consisted of the high jump and throwing the cricket ball. The Houses were named after birds; the Falcons (Blue) easily defeating the Eagles (Yellow), Kestrels (Green) and Seagulls (Red), who finished in that order.

SATURDAY, JULY 7th

Slade Road had reached the quarterfinal stage of the Docker Shield. In May they had defeated old adversaries Paget Road by 38 runs to 18. In the next round they faced Eliot Street, who were bowled out for 38, Morris taking 6 wickets for 10 runs, whilst his partner, Robinson, had disposed of the other four Eliot Street batsmen for 23 runs. Robinson had then scored 21 as Slade Road easily passed the Eliot Street total, recording 41 for the loss of 1 wicket. A fortnight later, and they met St Joseph's. Morris was yet again a major factor, when he took 7 for 12. The final scores – Slade Road 32 St Joseph's 29. Now, they were up against Osler Street. Although Morris yet again performed heroics with the ball, dismissing five Osler Street batsmen for 13 runs, there was to be no more glory. Osler Street scored 51 runs, whilst Slade Road could only put together 21.

1952

SATURDAY, APRIL 26th

Slade Road nearly won five football trophies in the 1951/1952 season. In both the Senior and Intermediate Divisions of the Erdington Schools' Football League, they finished as runners up to Paget Road, failing by just two points in both competitions and losing just one game in the process. They reached the final of the Oldroyd-Wedd Trophy, but were beaten 3–1 by Boldmere. In the Intermediate Knock Out final, they lost 2–1 to Paget Road, whilst Gunter Road despatched them by 4–2 in the Plaza Cup final.

Senior

	P	W	L	D	F	A	PTS
PAGET ROAD	12	9	0	3	51	8	21
SLADE ROAD	12	8	1	3	46	12	19
BOLDMERE	12	7	4	1	33	23	15
RYLAND ROAD	12	5	5	2	26	13	12
RILAND-BEDFORD	12	3	8	1	15	38	7
St.THOMAS'	12	2	9	1	13	42	5
MOOR END LANE	12	2	9	1	11	53	5

Leading Scorers for Slade Road were Powell and Winsper.

Intermediate

	P	W	L	D	F	A	PTS
PAGET ROAD	12	11	0	1	75	5	23
SLADE ROAD	12	10	1	1	69	10	21
BOLDMERE	12	8	4	0	26	22	16
RILAND-BEDFORD	12	3	6	3	16	42	9
RYLAND ROAD	12	2	8	2	12	43	6
St.THOMAS'	12	2	9	1	10	38	5
MOOR END LANE	12	2	10	0	3	55	4

Junior

	P	W	L	D	F	A	PTS
PAGET ROAD	14	12	1	1	90	9	25
TEDBURY CRESCENT	14	12	1	1	49	16	25
HAWTHORN ROAD	14	12	2	0	50	8	24
GUNTER ROAD	14	12	2	0	78	14	24
SLADE ROAD	14	8	4	2	38	10	18
CHESTER ROAD	14	8	4	2	32	16	18
BIRCHES GREEN	14	8	6	0	36	21	16
TURFPITS LANE	14	7	6	1	42	21	15
OSBORNE ROAD	14	5	8	1	21	29	11
NATIONAL	14	4	9	1	27	41	9
St.MARY & St.JOHN	14	2	11	1	8	108	5
MOOR END LANE	12	2	9	1	11	53	5

Final Tables Erdington Schools' Football League 1951/1952 Season.

SATURDAY, MAY 10th

At the Plaza Cinema in Stockland Green, Mr Frank Riego presented the cup and medals to Gunter Road and Slade Road before the beginning of the afternoon show. The two teams were brought up on stage to receive the congratulations of the audience. The Plaza Cup was intended to foster junior football in the Erdington district.

The Slade Road team were: G. Lapsley; E. Oakley; S. Lewis; J. Lapsley; M. Nichols; E. Burch; J. Robertson; R. Baker; R. Fitton; B. Kilburn; J. Webster with B. Brierwood as reserve.

Top: Secondary Boys' School Class, 1951. Bottom: Secondary Boys' School Class, 1952.

(Mr Ralph Corden, far left, born in 1914, was an ex-pupil of the school, who had attended between 1921 and 1925. He passed the entrance examination for King Edward's Grammar School, Aston, which he attended for a period of seven years, eventually leaving five weeks after attaining his eighteenth birthday. He was awarded an initial Birmingham maintenance allowance of £3p.a. increasing to £15p.a. in 1928. During the 1950s many of the boys in his charge were liable to encounter his size 12 slipper, which he used with a vengeance to maintain discipline.)

TUESDAY, MAY 27th

A meeting of 300 local residents was held at the school this evening, which was presided over by the Headmaster of the Primary School, Mr Clarke. Parents were threatening to keep their children away from school and approach the Education Committee for alternative schooling, unless Birmingham City Council provided a safe passage for pedestrians under the railway bridge in Slade Road. The road under the bridge was considered to be a 'Death Trap' because the footpaths on either side were too narrow. Mud and filth were splashed up by inconsiderate motorists travelling at high speed under the bridge on wet days. The bridge had been considered adequate when Slade Road was Slade Lane. You could even pat a horse passing by, but who would want to pat a tin horse travelling at 30 to 40 M.P.H! Mr Clarke's view was that this was a dangerous spot, which would become more so with the ever-increasing volume of traffic, and the advent of buses in place of trams. The path on the one side was so narrow that no mother could push a pram with any degree of safety; and the protection offered by the guard on the other side, that had only been installed one year earlier, was more apparent than real. It would appear that proposals had been made to build a pedestrian tunnel, but Ministry sanction had been refused owing to financial stringency. A petition containing 800 signatures had already been presented six months earlier and now parents were becoming seriously concerned about their children's welfare and safety. On hearing that the Ministry had turned down a request for finances to be provided, members of the audience were outraged! They shouted back that money could be provided for Salford Park track; and that they would rather have the bridge made safe than have tulips in Victoria Square! The cost of the tunnel was estimated to be £15,000 or, alternatively, it was considered that the roadway under the bridge could be turned into a one-way thoroughfare with traffic signals at a cost of £5,000. At the conclusion of the meeting, it was agreed to send a resolution to the Ministry of Transport urging reconsideration of the matter. If this failed, it was intended to send a deputation. As one can now see, a pedestrian tunnel was eventually cut. It didn't open, though, until October 29th, 1957; and some elements of society treat it rather badly!

Slade Road railway bridge on the 25th of April 1953 – The tunnel is not yet built.

THURSDAY, JUNE 19th

The Primary School sports were once again organised by Mr Roberts and held at Jaffray Road playing fields. Mr Clarke's wife distributed the prizes to the winners of the 49 events.

THURSDAY, JUNE 26th

Yet again the Erdington Schools' Athletic Association held their annual sports at the Jaffray Road playing fields in front of an extremely large crowd of approximately 5, 000 spectators. Many thousands of enthusiastic youngsters, parents and friends cheered their favourites on. Altogether there were 300 entries from 26 schools. Major F. Monk M. C. again distributed the prizes, but Slade Road was not amongst them this year. They only won one event, that of throwing the cricket ball.

SATURDAY, JULY 5th

At Woodcock Street baths the 17th annual swimming gala of the Erdington Schools' Athletic Association was held. Approximately 100 competitors from 11 Junior Schools and 9 Secondary Schools took part, Mr Julius Silverman, M.P. for Erdington, honouring them by presenting the trophies. Slade Road were a ½ point out in runners up spot in the Senior Boys' competition, but the Junior Boys did the school proud by winning their trophy.

TUESDAY, JULY 8th

Rubber from Malaya, coconuts from the tropics and material from Japan attracted the attention of 120 boys, aged 12 and 13, of the Secondary Modern Boys' School, when they visited Liverpool Docks on the way to New Brighton for a day's coach trip. Travelling along the overhead railway, which ran parallel with the Docks, they saw many great ships being unloaded. They later took a steamer from New Brighton along the Mersey and saw the Ark Royal being completed. Much excitement was also caused by the Empress of Canada as she left her moorings. On top of all this activity, the children also found time to visit Liverpool Cathedral and the Mersey Tunnel. Assistant master, Mr John Roberts, organised the trip, and the Assistant Headmaster, Mr Parker, was amongst the staff that accompanied the party. It's not surprising to learn that they started out as early as 6.30a.m. and didn't arrive back until 10.00p.m.

TUESDAY, JULY 22nd

There was exceptionally keen competition between the houses at the annual sports of the Secondary Modern Boys' School, which were held once again at the Erdington Cottage Homes grounds. Twenty-five events were organised, six for each year group, with an extra 220 yards sprint thrown in for the fourth years. The competition was so intense that the Eagles and Seagulls tied for first place with 145 points. Only two points behind came the Falcons, the Kestrels languishing in fourth place. There were nineteen officials.

SATURDAY, JULY 26th

The Erdington schools' cricket season had drawn to a conclusion with Slade Road failing to enjoy any success this year. The final tables follow:

	P	W	L	D	PTS
SENIOR					
RILAND-BEDFORD	6	5	1	0	10
PAGET ROAD	6	4	2	0	8
RYLAND ROAD	6	3	2	1	7
SLADE ROAD	6	3	2	1	7
St.THOMAS'	6	3	3	0	6
BOLDMERE	6	1	3	2	4
MOOR END LANE	6	0	6	0	0
INTERMEDIATE					
St.THOMAS'	6	5	1	0	10
PAGET ROAD	6	5	1	0	10
RILAND-BEDFORD	6	3	3	0	6
BOLDMERE	6	3	3	0	6
MOOR END LANE	6	2	4	0	4
SLADE ROAD	6	2	4	0	4
RYLAND ROAD	6	0	6	0	0
JUNIOR LEAGUE NORTH					
MARSH HILL	7	6	0	1	13
TEDBURY CRESCENT	7	5	2	0	10
CHESTER ROAD	7	5	2	0	10
SLADE ROAD	6	4	2	0	8
HAWTHORN ROAD	7	3	4	0	6
ELIOT STREET	7	2	5	0	4
BOLDMERE	7	1	5	1	3
St.MARY & St.JOHN	6	0	6	0	0
JUNIOR LEAGUE SOUTH					
GUNTER ROAD	7	6	0	1	13
PAGET ROAD	7	6	1	0	12
BIRCHES GREEN	7	5	1	1	11
ABBEY	7	3	4	0	6
NATIONAL	7	3	4	0	6
OSBORNE ROAD	7	3	4	0	6
RYLAND ROAD	7	1	6	0	2
MOOR END LANE	7	0	7	0	0

JUNIOR CHAMPIONSHIP
MARSH HILL 64
GUNTER ROAD 40

Erdington Schools' Cricket League, 1953.

1953

Senior Football team.

FRIDAY, MAY 29th

The week had been one of high activity at the Primary School, with sports day, parents day and displays all being well attended. On sports day, a total of 540 children took part in the preliminary heats with 48 finals being held later. Miss Hazel Clarke, daughter of the Headmaster, distributed the prizes, her father being unable to attend. They were organised once more by Mr Roberts – his wife again took charge of the refreshments – and assisted on the day by Mr Griffin, Headmaster of the Boys' School. Parents' Day arrived and about 450 parents attended. After inspecting the children's work, they saw a display of physical training by the pupils of Mr Reakes; an exhibition of National and Maypole dancing by those pupils of Miss Handley; and a display of marching by the pupils trained by Mr Roberts. The parents showed great interest in the school, their chief concern being whether their children were progressing sufficiently to pass the Grammar Schools' entrance examination. To close out the week of activity, there was community singing of National songs followed by maypole dancing. Coronation mugs and spoons were then presented and the Queen's health was drunk.

WEDNESDAY, JUNE 24th

The annual sports of the Erdington Schools' Athletic Association were once more upon us. For the first time they were held at Salford Park Stadium. The president of the association, Major F. Monk M. C., presented the trophies again but, unfortunately, the best that Slade Road could do on this occasion was to finish third in the Junior Boys' and Senior Boys' competitions respectively. The under 10 year olds, however, did succeed in winning both of the events especially organised for their age group – the girls' and boys' 80 yards.

FRIDAY, JULY 17th

Nearly all the 297 pupils of the Boys' School took part in the third annual house championships that were held at the Jaffray Road playing fields. The only remaining house

Junior School Class, c. 1953.

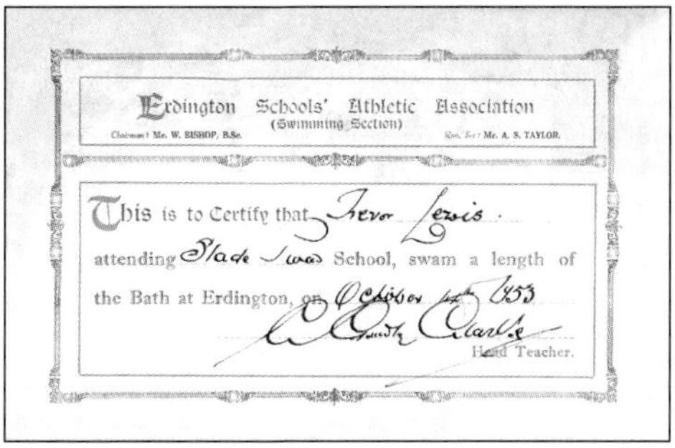
Erdington Schools' Athletic Association
(Swimming Section)
Chairman: Mr. W. BISHOP, B.Sc. Hon. Sec: Mr. A. S. TAYLOR.

This is to Certify that Trevor Lewis
attending Slade Road School, swam a length of
the Bath at Erdington, on [illegible]
Head Teacher.

Swimming Certificate.

not to have won the championship was the Kestrels, who had finished at the bottom of the pile in 1952. This year, their fortunes were in for they placed first, 4½ points ahead of the Seagulls, who had to be content with second place. Falcons came in third with Eagles holding up the rest. The number of events had increased to 37, although the format was virtually the same.

SATURDAY, AUGUST 1st

SENIOR	P	W	L	D	PTS
PAGET ROAD	6	6	0	0	12
MOOR END LANE	6	4	2	0	8
BOLDMERE	6	3	3	0	6
SLADE ROAD	6	3	3	0	6
St.THOMAS'	6	3	3	0	6
RII AND-BEDFORD	6	2	4	0	4
RYLAND ROAD	6	0	6	0	0
INTERMEDIATE	**P**	**W**	**L**	**D**	**PTS**
MOOR END LANE	6	5	1	0	10
BOLDMERE	6	3	2	1	7
SLADE ROAD	6	3	3	0	6
PAGET ROAD	6	3	3	0	6
St.THOMAS'	6	2	4	0	4
RILAND-BEDFORD	6	2	4	0	4
RYLAND ROAD	6	1	4	1	3
JUNIOR NORTH	**P**	**W**	**L**	**D**	**PTS**
MARSH HILL	7	5	2	0	10
BOLDMERE	7	5	2	0	10
HAWTHORN ROAD	7	4	3	0	8
CHESTER ROAD	7	4	3	0	8
ELIOT STREET	6	3	3	0	6
TEDBURY CRESCENT	7	3	4	0	6
SLADE ROAD	6	2	4	0	4
St.MARY & St.JOHN	5	0	5	0	0
JUNIOR SOUTH	**P**	**W**	**L**	**D**	**PTS**
BIRCHES GREEN	7	7	0	0	14
OSBORNE ROAD	7	5	2	0	10
GUNTER ROAD	4	3	1	0	6
ABBEY	5	2	3	0	4
RYLAND ROAD	5	2	3	0	4
MOOR END LANE	7	2	5	0	4
NATIONAL	7	2	5	0	4
PAGET ROAD	6	1	5	0	2

Final Tables Erdington Schools' Cricket League.

MONDAY, AUGUST 31st

Miss Griffiths-Jones retired for the second time. She was now 66 years of age and would have left at the end of July when the school closed for the summer holiday.

WEDNESDAY, SEPTEMBER 23rd

Another sad day for the school! Christine Wright, aged only six, was knocked down and killed by a lorry in Slade Road, near to the junction with George Road, as she was going home from school this afternoon. At the inquest, five weeks later, a verdict of accidental death was recorded by the coroner. The Headmaster, Mr Clarke, attended the inquest, making an impassioned plea for a halt sign to be placed on the down gradient. He said that, unless some sign could be put across the road, he feared that there would be a recurrence, as the road had become increasingly dangerous since he had first come to the school 22 years earlier.

TUESDAY and WEDNESDAY, DECEMBER 15th and 16th

The pantomime season started merrily, not in the commercial theatre, but with the Junior School's production of *Robin Hood* at the Parochial Hall in Broomfield Road. The two nightly performances were warmly received by packed audiences. The scenes had been ingeniously painted and took the audience into the minstrel's headquarters; through the forest to Robin's camp; and on to Nottingham Fair. The opening chorus, and the charming ballet in the best pantomime tradition, were preceded by the minstrel reader, excellently played by Sally Moore. There was some riotous 'funny business' and laughter at the antics of the horse – the front legs were played by David Smith and the back legs by Douglas Corfield. Romantic complications of the plot were revealed in Robin's camp, where Jeannette Brannigan made a sweet Maid Marion to John Griffith's Robin Hood. At Nottingham Fair, the 'Footballer's Ballet' was excruciatingly funny – the boys were dressed as ballerinas in tutus and football boots – whilst the 'male' voice choir leader, John Evans, made the song hit of the evening. Boys chosen to be ballerinas were selected on account of their lack of singing ability! – they growled – and wore hats made out of crepe paper. Whilst dancing, they sang a song entitled *When Slade Road play football* to the tune, *The Swedish Rhapsody*. The tumblers added to the gaiety and a puppet show

Scenes from the Junior School pantomime Robin Hood.

was very amusing. The arrows were made in the workshop, the points being sharpened with chisels, whilst the flights were of cardboard. Mr Roberts produced the show from a book by Messrs. Roberts and Darby, whilst various members of staff supplied musical numbers.

1954

FRIDAY, JUNE 25th

The annual sports of the Boys' School were toned down somewhat with only 16 events taking place this year at the Jaffray Road playing fields. On this occasion, the third and fourth years competed against each other in the same events. The House Shield was won by Eagles, followed by Kestrels, Falcons and Seagulls in that order. Altogether, about 200 boys took part.

SATURDAY, JULY 3rd

The Erdington Schools' Sports Association held their annual swimming gala this evening with 20 schools taking part. Mr Julius Silverman, the local Member of Parliament, distributed the prizes. In the competition for the Secondary Modern Boys' Championship, there was a triple tie for first place between St. Thomas', Boldmere and Slade Road.

WEDNESDAY, JULY 7th

At Salford Park Stadium, the annual sports of the Erdington Schools' Sports Association were held. The best that Slade Road could do was to finish as runners up in the Junior Girls' competition, in which they won both of the individual sprints. However, it wasn't sufficient for they were pipped by Boldmere by just one point.

Winners Erdington Senior Football League (Bottom row far left: Mike Kenning Aston Villa & Norwich) (Centre with trophy: Ray Bird Birmingham City & Cardiff).

SEPTEMBER
Mr W. Barnett took over as Headmaster of the Secondary Modern Boys' School from Mr Griffin, who had had the shortest tenure of any headmaster at the school yet – four years.

FRIDAY, SEPTEMBER 17th
First games of the new season in all three of the Erdington Schools' Football Leagues were due to be played on the following morning. In the Senior League, Slade Road were undefeated since October 1951, although they had a less than happy record in cup competitions. There would be eight schools participating in the Senior and Intermediate leagues, whilst the Juniors would comprise fifteen. For the first few weeks it was envisaged that evening as well as Saturday morning fixtures would be arranged.

THURSDAY, SEPTEMBER 30th
This evening, Paget Road wrote 'finis' to the unbeaten record of Slade Road in the Senior Football League. Their last defeat in the league had been against Boldmere on October 10th, 1951. Since that time, Slade senior sides had scored 210 goals while conceding a mere 38. Paget Road, who had last defeated Slade Road on September 26th, 1950, won the encounter by the slimmest of margins – 3 goals to 2.

SATURDAY, OCTOBER 15th
The senior team to represent Erdington Schools was chosen. It included three lads from Slade Road – Reynolds, Broadfield and Bird.

1955

FRIDAY, APRIL 15th
The end of the Erdington schools' football season. The best that the school could do was to finish as runners up to Paget Road, who were runaway winners of the Senior League.

Top: Canoe making in the Secondary Modern Boys' School (Mr Jenns can be seen in the top picture instructing the boys), 1954/1955. Bottom: Carrying 'Battle' one of the Boys' School's canoes across the playground. Note the large thermometer hanging on the wall of the building in the background.

MONDAY, MAY 23rd

The Primary School held its annual sports day at Jaffray Road playing fields. Around 350 parents turned up to witness the athletic prowess of the youngsters, who were divided into four categories – 8, 9, 10 and 11 year olds – with 12 events in each. These consisted of sprint, potato, sack, three-legged and relay races for the 8 to 10 year olds, with separate races for both boys and girls. The girls then had their own skipping race, whilst the boys had an obstacle race instead. Meanwhile, the 11 year olds dropped the potato race from their schedule of events having a high jump in its place.

TUESDAY, MAY 24th

Now, it was the turn of the Boys' School to hold their sports day, which also took place at Jaffray Road. The third and fourth years continued to participate against each other, whilst the number of events had been increased from the previous year to 29. Those added were the relay, high jump, long jump and throwing the cricket ball. The result of the House Championship was another close-run thing with the Eagles and Falcons tying for first place, whilst the Kestrels and Seagulls had to be content with the minor positions. Around 250 boys took part.

THURSDAY, JUNE 30th

Jaffray Road playing fields once again hosted the Erdington schools' athletics, the attendance being in the order of 4,000. Yet again, the school was unable to win a championship trophy, their best position being as runners up to Boldmere in the Junior Girls' Championship.

SENIOR	P	W	D	L	F	A	PTS
PAGET ROAD	14	13	1	0	91	14	27
SLADE ROAD	14	8	2	4	60	33	18
RILAND-BEDFORD	14	9	0	5	68	49	18
ELIOT STREET	14	8	0	6	52	36	16
RYLAND ROAD	14	5	1	8	38	57	11
St.THOMAS'	14	4	1	9	26	64	9
BOLDMERE	14	3	1	10	27	56	7
MOOR END LANE	14	3	0	11	29	82	6

Erdington Schools' Football League, 1954/1955.

A canoe trip to the River Leam for boys from the Senior School, 1955.

Class 1/1, c.1955.

THURSDAY, OCTOBER 6th

A Harvest Festival service was celebrated by the teachers and pupils of the Boys' School, this being the twentieth that the school had organised. The service was held in All Saints Church in George Road, Reverend C. B. Chute, the vicar, giving the address, whilst the lesson, 'The Parable of the Sower', was read by Frank Pepper. Subsequently, the produce – consisting of fruit, flowers and vegetables collected by the boys – was sent to the Cowley Home for the Blind and the Raymond Priestley Home for Old People.

SATURDAY, OCTOBER 22nd

Talk of the Erdington Schools' Junior Football League these days was the goalkeeping of Williams, the Slade Road 'keeper. Since he had been 'accidentally' played in goal the school hadn't lost a match! Against Hawthorn he put up a wonderful display making many seemingly impossible saves. It was little wonder that he was given a rousing cheer by players and spectators alike as he left the field. The result: Hawthorn 0 Slade Road 1.

THURSDAY, DECEMBER 15th

A Christmas musical of tremendous proportions was put on at the Parochial Hall in Broomfield Road by the boys of the Secondary Modern School. The Headmaster, Mr Barnett, was in charge of the production of *The King of Sherwood*. The show had been

Secondary Boys' School Christmas Concert – King of Sherwood, 1955.

designed on spectacular lines with a cast of 60 boys – the ages ranging from 11 to 15 – representing all the classes of the school. There were 25 songs in the show and, in order that the boys had as much time as possible in which to make sure that they knew all the words, rehearsals had started on the music as far back as the summer when the temperatures were in the 70s. At that stage of production, the boys had to do all the work on the play during their own time. There was no room on the school timetable to allow them to rehearse in class time. When it became necessary to consider making the scenery, many of the boys volunteered to help Mr C. H. Jenns and Mr J. Humphrey, the two masters who were in charge of its construction. They were soon hammering and painting. The musical director of the show was Mr D. T. Jones who was busy rehearsing the boys, his fellow teachers marshalling the resources building scenery. Whilst all of this was going on, there was one other person who was hard at work. This was Mrs Barnett, the wife of the headmaster, who was busy producing most of the costumes needed for the play, which she did within six weeks. In the show itself, 22 boys set out to hoodwink the audience into thinking they were girls. Unfortunately, everybody was in the know, including the large number of parents and friends that came to see it. All in all, it was considered a pretty good show, carrying on in the English stage tradition of casting boys in feminine roles as Shakespeare did. Mr Barnett later said that the boys had worked wonderfully well and been surprisingly enthusiastic about the whole thing.

1956

FRIDAY, JANUARY 20th

An opportunity to see the musical *King of Sherwood* was given to the nearly 100 residents at the Home for Old People at Witton Hall. The cast of the production – including three lads who had left at Christmas to start work – made their way to Witton Hall especially to put the production on for one last time.

SATURDAY, MARCH 31st

SENIOR	P	W	L	D	F	A	PTS
PAGET ROAD	14	11	1	2	83	21	24
St. THOMAS'	14	9	1	4	62	31	22
BOLDMERE	14	7	4	3	42	37	17
SLADE ROAD	14	6	6	2	43	57	14
RILAND-BEDFORD	14	5	8	1	35	47	11
MOOR END LANE	14	4	8	2	41	55	10
ERDINGTON HALL	14	3	9	2	35	57	8
NECHELLS	14	3	11	0	31	71	6
INTERMEDIATE							
MOOR END LANE	14	11	2	1	80	27	23
NECHELLS	14	11	2	1	62	24	23
St.THOMAS'	14	9	2	3	62	35	21
RILAND-BEDFORD	14	9	5	0	48	38	18
SLADE ROAD	14	3	8	3	42	60	9
PAGET ROAD	14	4	10	0	36	71	8
BOLDMERE	14	3	10	1	41	60	7
ERDINGTON HALL	14	1	12	1	29	85	3
JUNIOR							
PAGET ROAD	15	14	0	1	63	6	29
TEDBURY CRESCENT	15	11	2	2	56	11	24
HAWTHORN ROAD	15	10	2	3	65	16	23
HASTINGS ROAD	15	10	4	1	42	16	21
SLADE ROAD	15	10	5	0	47	16	20
NECHELLS	15	10	5	0	61	26	20
BIRCHES GREEN	15	9	4	2	39	26	20
YENTON	15	8	4	3	40	16	19
RYLAND ROAD	15	8	5	2	42	35	18
St. MARY & St.JOHN	15	5	9	1	26	42	11
TURFPITS LANE	15	3	8	4	26	41	10
GUNTER ROAD	15	4	10	1	24	61	9
ASTON HALL	15	3	12	0	15	64	6
OSBORNE ROAD	15	2	11	2	15	58	6
NATIONAL	15	2	11	2	14	56	6
ABBEY	15	0	15	0	5	87	0

Final Tables Erdington Schools' Football League 1955/1956 Season.
(The leading goalscorer for Slade Road in the Senior League was Allen with 18 goals).
(In the juniors, Cooper, Taylor and Kenning all represented the district).

FRIDAY, JUNE 29th

Two Erdington children were winners of a literary competition organised by the Erdington Rotary Club. One of these was Reginald Vernon, aged 14, who attended Slade Road Secondary Modern School for Boys and was a resident of the Erdington Cottage Homes. Both children, accompanied by their head teachers, were presented with silver cups and 5 National Savings Certificates each by the Deputy Education Officer of Birmingham. No apology is made for producing Reginald's 500 word essay here in full, for it was considered to be of lasting interest, as well as providing something for those critics of our educational system. It was entitled:

THE MOST USEFUL JOB IN SOCIETY

The most useful job in society is being a good citizen. This is because everybody, regardless of race, religion, colour, creed or occupation can be a good citizen. You need not be a bank manager or a businessman. You can be a dustman or a street sweep and still be a good citizen. Good citizenship includes keeping the Ten Commandments, obeying the law of the land, and being kind, helpful, generous and sympathetic, ensuring that others obey the law and generally speaking, "loving one's neighbour as one's self."

The origin of citizenship is in the home and school and a great deal depends upon the way we, the citizens of tomorrow, are brought up in the homes and schools of today. A modern teacher's instruction and discipline is helpful and, indeed, important to a child in that it encourages road sense, courtesy, cleanliness and gives a sense of right and wrong. Our parents also play an important part in the encouragement of good citizenship among us. It is largely because of the need for closer co-operation between parents and teachers that Parent-Teacher organisations have been formed. There are various social organisations at work which do a great job in the encouragement of good citizenship among schoolchildren and young workers. Typical of these are the Youth Hostellers' Association, the Young Men's Christian Association, National Association of Boys' Clubs and Boy Scouts.

BAD CITIZENSHIP

The origin of bad citizenship is in the home and rarely in school. Insufficient food, unclean surroundings, unsympathetic parents and lack of understanding shown by adults are among the main causes of bad citizenship nowadays. The conditions just mentioned encourage a young child to be a bad citizen because they give him or her a grudge against society. In general, the instruction given by school teachers and others in charge of youth helps to counteract the bad effects of home life in the child, but lack of understanding can help to ruin a child's future life. The effects are noticed early in the child's life. Among the main signs are unruliness, cruelty, spite and bad behaviour in home, school and outdoors. These, if inclined, will gradually grow into contempt for the law and for the efficiency of the police force. Once having reached this stage, the child will be spending most of its life in remand homes, children's homes and as he or she grows, prisons.

PREVENTION BEST

Many children need never have been sent to remand homes had it not been for the lack of understanding and sympathy shown by certain adults. People have said in the past and I am sure will say in the future that 'prevention is better than cure'. They should have encouraged those who have been trying to help such children as have been walking along the wrong road through life up till now. A little extra understanding and sympathy shown by adults would help a lot and go a long way to help possible juvenile delinquents to become again normal and healthy young citizens of tomorrow. To the people who will read this in the future, may I just say that the future peace and prosperity of this world rests upon the way you educate in the home, in the school and in the factory us, the young citizens of tomorrow.

FRIDAY, JULY 13th

The boys in the senior school had been growing vegetables all year long on the allotment behind All Saints Church. This took place on one afternoon a week. Previously, the gardening section had used the allotments at Stockland Green, until Stockland Green Secondary School was built. Arriving there today, they found to their horror that someone had been round the previous night and dug up the lot! They were utterly horrified to discover what had happened as they had been very proud of what they had grown.

Left: Class 2/1, c.1956. Right: Mr W. Barnett.

SEPTEMBER

Mr R. Dawes took over as Head of the Boys' School, as Mr Barnett had been appointed to the Headship at the new Stockland Green Secondary Boys' School at Marsh Hill. Mr Dawes was the son of a previous teacher at the school, Mr Edmund J. Dawes, who had passed away on April 11th, 1915. His brother, Sid, was a long-time Birmingham City Councillor and Alderman, both of them having attended the school for a time as children.

A certificate awarded to Ann Skelding for accident prevention.

FRIDAY, DECEMBER 14th

It was an atomic-age pantomime at the Junior School this week. Eighty children, between the ages of 7 and 11, appeared in a production of *Snow White and the Seven Dwarfs*. Mind you, this was a production with a difference! The Queen in the story didn't have a mirror – she had a magic television set. As a reward for killing Snow White, the Queen promised Dishonest Fred that he could look at her wonderful television. The result was an hilarious making of 'What's My Line'. There was no such excuse for the Old Time Music Hall sequences, but that wasn't important, as it gave the children the opportunity to sing the old songs from before the First World War. Mr J. M. Darby wrote and produced the show, besides being responsible for the new lyrics set to a number of well-known titles. Mr B. S. Reakes directed the 'What's My Line' scene. For the first time, the pantomime was actually held on school premises – for many years they had been held in the Parochial Hall. Members of the staff worked late at night for some time before the show to rig up the stage, fix the lights, paint the scenery and generally get everything ready, so that a successful show could be put on.

With an amazed chorus of little ladies in the background, David Hicks serenades another 10 year old, Mary Trenbirth, with the song Daisy, Daisy, give me your answer do in the Junior School pantomime Snow White.

1957

FRIDAY, MARCH 8th

Decorators commenced work in the Primary department. It was expected to take about a month to complete. In the meanwhile, the school had to make do the best that it could!

MARCH

SENIOR

	P	W	L	D	F	A	PTS
NECHELLS	14	11	1	2	68	32	24
PAGET ROAD	14	9	3	2	85	36	20
RILAND-BEDFORD	14	8	4	2	57	49	18
BOLDMERE	14	5	4	5	45	39	15
ABBEY	14	7	6	1	46	40	15
ERDINGTON HALL	14	5	8	1	45	56	11
MOOR END LANE	14	3	8	3	30	47	9
SLADE ROAD	14	0	14	0	16	95	0

INTERMEDIATE

	P	W	L	D	F	A	PTS
NECHELLS	16	14	1	1	63	19	29
MOOR END LANE	16	11	4	1	54	25	23
RILAND-BEDFORD	16	9	6	1	50	27	19
SLADE ROAD	16	8	6	2	58	36	18
PAGET ROAD	16	6	7	3	33	36	15
STOCKLAND GREEN	16	6	8	2	47	43	14
ABBEY	16	4	9	3	24	49	11
BOLDMERE	16	3	11	2	28	78	8
ERDINGTON HALL	16	3	12	1	27	71	7

JUNIOR (LEADING POSITIONS)

	P	W	L	D	F	A	PTS
COURT FARM	16	15	1	0	74	4	30
ERDINGTON HALL	16	15	1	0	72	18	30
NECHELLS	16	13	2	1	66	9	27
PAGET ROAD	16	13	3	0	53	8	26
HAWTHORN ROAD	16	12	3	1	42	18	25
YENTON	16	12	4	0	53	19	24
St.MARY & St.JOHN	16	9	7	0	37	31	18

Final Tables Erdington Schools' Football League 1956/1957 Season.

WEDNESDAY, APRIL 10th
The decorators finished their work just in time for the school to break up for Easter!

THURSDAY, MAY 9th
The school was closed for the Municipal Elections.

WEDNESDAY, JUNE 5th
The Junior School was closed for the afternoon in order for their sports to take place. There was a very good attendance by parents, medals donated by Mr Darby being much appreciated.

FRIDAY, JULY 5th
Today was the annual outing of the Junior School. Around 200 went off to enjoy themselves at Cheddar and Weston-Super-Mare, travelling by train from Snow Hill Station, whilst the rest of the school remained in session.

FRIDAY, JULY 19th
At the annual Erdington schools' sports, the Boys' School won the Wiggins-Davies Trophy, bolstered by victories in the long jump and the discus. Moor End and Paget Road finished as runners up.

WEDNESDAY, JULY 24th
Staff and scholars' presentations were made to Mrs Moore and Miss Baker on their retirement from teaching. Miss Baker was 60, whilst Mrs Kate Moore had attained the age of 70. Mrs Moore had started out as an uncertificated teacher way back on January 1st, 1906 in Rowley Regis, but it wasn't until November 4th, 1947 that she came to work at Slade Junior and Infant School, when she was already 60 years of age.

WEDNESDAY, AUGUST 28th
Miss Ethel Derrett, a teacher of long-standing at the school, died today at the age of 63. She had become a certificated teacher on August 1st, 1915, joining the Infant department nine months later on May 1st, 1916. She had given 41 years of service to the school.

FRIDAY, SEPTEMBER 27th
Heavy absences resulted due to the influenza epidemic. Around 30% of the children were away during the week.

MONDAY, SEPTEMBER 30th
One class in the Junior School had been experiencing difficulties all term due to the lack of a teacher. The class was being taught by two teachers with the headmaster taking three afternoon sessions. He regarded it as essential that the class should have one permanent teacher only, as they were a particularly retarded unit!

Intermediate Football Team.

FRIDAY, NOVEMBER 15th
Rehearsals commenced for the Junior School Christmas Pantomime.

MONDAY to FRIDAY,
DECEMBER 9th to 13th
The annual Junior School Pantomime was performed each evening during the week to 'Sold Out' audiences. The presentation was a topical treat entitled *The Interplanetary Peter Pan.* That's not to say that we didn't have the usual list of characters with Christine Yates playing Peter to Jean Penn's Wendy. Meanwhile, Margaret Hughes and Florence Muir crewed a menacing crocodile! The pirates certainly felt threatened whilst the Red Indians showed their inborn wisdom by keeping away from the business end! (photographs of the production follow).

Top Left: Wendy tells a story to her friends. To the left of her is Peter Pan. Top Right: The crocodile threatens the pirates. Bottom: The chorus and dancers with some of the cast.

MONDAY, DECEMBER 23rd

There's much work behind the scenes in a school play. The production of *Treasure Island* by the Boys' School was an absolute masterpiece of improvisation in every aspect. When one considered the wealth of talent that lay hidden amongst the staff, who could seemingly put their hand to carpentry, painting, designing, music and electrics, this had to be recognised. The array of talent was welded successfully together by the producer, Haydn Jones. There were five settings, admirably built by Messrs Jenns and Francis, whilst the costumes, which were ingenious, attractive and a real labour of love, were the work of Mrs Dawes, the wife of the headmaster. From time to time, in the background, could be heard the singing of sea shanties, which had previously been recorded by the boys. One lad, Graham Smith, should be congratulated for putting on such a good performance, because he had only been given a week to learn his part as one of the main characters, Dr Livesey. Peter Blenkinsopp and Keith Newman played Jim and Silver, whilst Douglas Corfield had a fine appraisal of his part as Captain Smollett. Despite the occasional hiccups, all in all an enjoyable evening was had by the audience. The production was subsequently put on at Highcroft Hospital. (photographs follow).

Top Left: Yo! Ho! Ho! and a bottle of rum. A group of pirates take in a bottle of Dutch courage. Top Right: Benjamin shows his gun to the rest of the bold, bad pirates. Bottom Left: The good (or bad?) ship, Hispaniola, is underway with the helmsman keeping a weather eye open. Bottom Right: Captain Smollett and members of his crew.

1958

WEDNESDAY, FEBRUARY 26th

60 children from the Junior School, accompanied by 4 members of staff, visited the Wildfowl Trust at Slimbridge. Despite the poor weather conditions, everyone had an interesting and most enjoyable day, during which the school adopted a pink-footed goose.

THURSDAY, MARCH 27th

The second and final inoculation against polio was administered during the morning session for those juniors and infants who had previously been treated.

MARCH

SENIOR	P	W	L	D	F	A	PTS
NECHELLS	16	12	1	3	88	23	25
RILAND-BEDFORD	16	10	3	3	58	27	23
BOLDMERE	16	9	3	4	63	29	22
PAGET ROAD	16	9	5	2	54	32	20
ABBEY	16	8	6	2	36	49	18
SLADE ROAD	16	6	8	2	42	49	14
ERDINGTON HALL	16	5	9	2	40	53	12
MOOR END LANE	16	3	13	0	29	70	6
STOCKLAND GREEN	16	1	15	0	15	92	2

INTERMEDIATE	P	W	L	D	F	A	PTS
PAGET ROAD	16	12	2	2	56	15	26
RILAND-BEDFORD	16	11	3	2	82	18	24
STOCKLAND GREEN	16	9	4	3	73	27	21
SLADE ROAD	16	8	5	3	43	28	19
NECHELLS	16	8	6	2	51	43	18
ABBEY	16	7	6	3	45	27	17
ERDINGTON HALL	16	6	8	2	48	36	14
MOOR END LANE	16	1	14	1	16	116	3
BOLDMERE	16	1	15	0	13	126	2

Final Tables Erdington Schools' Football League 1957/1958 Season.

THURSDAY, APRIL 24th

Mr Reakes took 30 children from the Junior School to Birkenhead. The purpose was to visit 'Our Ship' M. V. Welch City. The children were entertained on board, where food was provided for them; and a most interesting and instructive time was had by everyone.

SATURDAY, MAY 10th

C.Q.M.S. Jack Lawton, aged 31, and a pupil of Slade Road School until 1941, was chosen to drive the Queen Mother at the great Territorial Army Jubilee Revue in Northern Ireland in front of 14,000 ticketholding spectators.

TUESDAY, MAY 20th

The string section of the City of Birmingham Orchestra played at the school today.

Top: A class from the Secondary Modern Boys' School, c.1958.
Bottom: Another class from the Secondary Modern Boys' School, c.1958.

TUESDAY, JUNE 10th
The Junior School sent a dancing team to perform at the North Birmingham District Festival, which was held at the Town Hall.

FRIDAY, JULY 4th
Today was the Junior School's annual outing to Rhyl. Around 160 children and parents went on the trip whilst the school remained open for everyone else.

SATURDAY, NOVEMBER 1st

The best Erdington Junior representative side for many a long year was the opinion of everybody who saw them trounce Aston Juniors 6–3. Moving the ball about with great purpose they frequently had the Aston defence in trouble. Woolaston scored one of his side's goals, whilst the other player from Slade, Sanders, had an excellent game in defence.

SATURDAY, NOVEMBER 8th

Pupils from the Senior Boys' School paid a visit to the canoe exhibition at the Friends' Institute in Moseley Road as they had an exhibit in the show. Not only that, but they were the only school in the Midlands to have one. Over the previous four years the canoeing club had built up a fleet of ten boats, of which nine had been made in the school's workshops by the boys under the supervision of Mr Jenns. The boats were built on Friday nights when the club met for two hours between 6 and 8 o'clock. Some were made of canvas and some of wood, but the school had also pioneered the do-it-yourself construction of fibreglass boats; Slade was believed to be the only school in the Midlands to have built its own fibreglass boat from scratch. Qualification for membership of the club was the ability to swim ten lengths of the local swimming baths. The boats had been used to take the club on annual 90 mile trips each Whitsun down the river Wye, since the first one had been undertaken in 1956. It had taken six months of negotiation with the Education Department before that first trip had been allowed to take place. Lloyds of London had to insure the boys

A crib was built by some of the pupils of the Secondary Boys' School for All Saints Parish Church, whose vicar, the Reverend Richard L. Coote, paid visits to the school for religious quizzes. The pottery figures were made under the supervision of the master in charge of pottery, Mr C. B. Francis, pictured right. Building the crib was under the watchful eye of Mr C. Jenns.

– and to quote the policy – against "adventurers and peril, rovers and pirates, men o' war, thieves, jettisons and takings at sea." Most of the boats accommodated two boys, although there were one or two solo canoeists. The camping equipment was carried, well-wrapped, in tiny cramped compartments. The boys camped on the river banks, cooked their own food and, during the day, steered their flimsy craft through the rapids and the deeps of the Wye. Before going on each trip, all the boys concerned had been taken to the pools at Sutton Park, where they had spent an afternoon deliberately capsizing the boats, as it was considered that forewarned was forearmed. The point of the trips was to build teamwork and this was certainly achieved. At the outset, there had been sixteen individuals, but after two days they were all pulling together.

1959

SATURDAY, JANUARY 31st

At long last Paget School had lost their unbeaten Erdington Junior Schools' football record. Their first defeat was recorded against Slade School in the final qualifying round of the H.M.S. Birmingham Shield. Though Paget played the better football they came unstuck in the penalty area. They opened the scoring through Hill, but goals by Blunden and Pountney for Slade took them through to the first round proper after what was considered the best match seen in Erdington so far that season.

THURSDAY, FEBRUARY 5th

Further polio injections were given.

THURSDAY, FEBRUARY 12th

Attendance had dropped rapidly over the previous week owing to the influenza epidemic, with as many as a quarter of the children absent. However, at the end of the afternoon session, the school closed for the half-term, re-opening five days later.

FRIDAY, FEBRUARY 27th

With a number of teachers being absent in the Junior School for one reason or another, Mr Clarke found it necessary to comment, "We manage somehow!"

FRIDAY, MARCH 13th

A party of twenty junior children – 10 boys and 10 girls – accompanied by two teachers, left for London, where they spent the weekend, not returning until the following Monday night. They were accommodated at the Earls Court Hotel.

SATURDAY, MARCH 14th

Slade School had reached the quarterfinal stage of the H.M.S. Birmingham Shield. In the first round proper they had led two goals to nil four minutes from time only for Kings Rise to equalise in the final minute. In the replay a single goal by Woolaston was sufficient to put them through. Pountney was the hero for Slade School in round two, converting twice in a two goals to one win over Wattville. Now came the match against Hillstone, but unfortunately there was to be no more glory, for the school were narrowly defeated by the odd goal in three.

MONDAY, MARCH 16th
Another trip, and this time it was a return visit to see 'Our Ship' although it was now docked at Tilbury. Thirty-four children, together with two teachers, made the journey by coach. They were warmly greeted and received the most excellent hospitality, souvenirs from foreign ports being presented to the school by the captain.

WEDNESDAY, MARCH 18th
Mr Dawes gave an instructional talk to the senior boys at assembly this morning on what to do in the event of a fire. His talk was so useful that he was indirectly responsible for the prompt attention of firecrews at a fire in Aston that lunchtime. When John Meddings, aged 13, went home for lunch, he saw smoke and flames in the region of Vyse Street. Because of the talk, he was able to run confidently and without panic to the nearest telephone box and summon firemen to the scene. His prompt action was praised by a senior fire officer, who stated that the damage would have been infinitely greater but for his immediate response.

SATURDAY, APRIL 18th
The Junior School football team had reached the final of the Plaza Cup, where they met old adversaries, Gunter Road. In a hard-fought match, the result was a draw, one goal apiece. In the replay, Gunter Road were the comfortable winners by the score of four goals to nil. Gunter Road also won the Erdington Junior League for the 1958/9 season, whilst Slade Road finished in third place. Representing Slade Road were: – Cutler; Anderson; Rushton; Penn; Lord; Blunden; Woolaston; Sanders; Pountney; Smith and Holton, while the reserves were Thompson; Picton and Mogg.

The Senior Boys' Intermediate football team played superbly all season losing just one match, thus winning their division in the Erdington Schools' Football League.

SENIOR	P	W	L	D	F	A	PTS
NECHELLS	16	13	2	1	70	16	27
RILAND-BEDFORD	16	12	3	1	42	18	25
PAGET	16	9	5	2	62	23	20
STOCKLAND GREEN	16	9	5	2	56	40	20
ERDINGTON HALL	16	8	7	1	39	42	17
SLADE	16	6	8	2	38	50	14
BOLDMERE	16	4	9	3	30	59	11
MOOR END LANE	16	4	11	1	32	50	9
ABBEY	16	0	15	1	11	83	1
INTERMEDIATE	**P**	**W**	**L**	**D**	**F**	**A**	**PTS**
SLADE	16	14	1	1	84	16	29
ERDINGTON HALL	16	13	2	1	82	20	27
NECHELLS	16	13	3	0	77	17	26
MOOR END LANE	16	7	7	2	24	39	16
PAGET	10	7	0	0	66	47	14
RILAND-BEDFORD	16	6	9	1	38	57	13
STOCKLAND GREEN	16	4	10	1	25	60	9
ABBEY	16	2	13	1	21	64	5
BOLDMERE	16	1	14	1	18	104	3
JUNIOR A	**P**	**W**	**L**	**D**	**F**	**A**	**PTS**
GUNTER	16	12	2	2	63	14	26
YENTON	16	11	3	2	51	21	24
SLADE	16	9	3	4	45	19	22
TURFPITS	16	8	3	5	54	20	21
NECHELLS	16	9	4	3	40	10	21
OSBORNE	16	6	6	4	39	35	16
ERDINGTON HALL	16	3	11	2	17	66	8
COURT FARM	16	2	12	2	20	42	6
NATIONAL	16	0	16	0	1	102	0
JUNIOR B (LEADING POSITIONS)	**P**	**W**	**L**	**D**	**F**	**A**	**PTS**
MARSH HILL	14	11	2	1	64	8	23
PAGET	14	11	3	0	53	11	22
ASTON HALL	14	10	2	2	39	13	22
JUNIOR RESERVES (LEADING POSITIONS)	**P**	**W**	**L**	**D**	**F**	**A**	**PTS**
YENTON SECONDS	16	13	0	3	72	2	29
SLADE SECONDS	16	13	3	0	50	17	26
NECHELLS SECONDS	16	11	3	2	63	10	24

Final Tables Erdington Schools' Football League 1958/1959 Season.

THURSDAY, MAY 7th
The school was closed for the local elections.

Above is the victorious Erdington Schools' Football Association's junior team that won the B.S.S.F. Trophy at its first attempt. Three players from Slade Road were represented in the team: Back Row second from left – P. Sanders fourth from left – C. Rushton Front Row fourth from left – R. Woolaston.

WEDNESDAY, JULY 1st

The Senior Boys' School produced its first edition of a new annual magazine entitled 'Fanfare' which ran to 60 pages and was edited by Mr Haydn Jones. Approximately 8in. by 4in., it ran for many years, being published at this time once a year. It included sections on photography, model making, popular music, sport and a teachers' section. Bound in a hard cover with a boot-like fastening, it was produced – one copy at a time – on a gestetner machine with someone turning the handle. Copies were free.

FRIDAY, JULY 3rd

It was that time of year again when 200 children, with 30 parents in attendance, went on the annual Junior School outing to Rhyl.

THURSDAY, JULY 23rd

The Headmaster of the Junior and Infant School, Mr Charley Gooding Clarke – he was a very tall gentleman, well over six feet, bespectacled with angular features – retired at the age of 65. He had served the school for 28 years having previously been Headmaster at Osborne Road Boys' School for 5 years.

TUESDAY, SEPTEMBER 8th

School resumed today after the summer holidays. Mr G. N. Conduct had joined the Junior and Infant School as its new Headmaster, having been appointed from his previous position as Headmaster of Birches Green School.

Secondary Boys' School Class with Mr McLeod, c.1959.

FRIDAY, SEPTEMBER 18th
Talks were given by the police to all classes in the school on the subject of road safety.

FRIDAY, OCTOBER 2nd
Mr Conduct was absent in London, being one of a deputation of teachers complaining about the chronic shortage of teachers in Birmingham.

TUESDAY, OCTOBER 6th
The Senior Boys' School held a mock election, as part of the lessons being taught on how to become a Member of Parliament. Three candidates, representing the three main political parties, had already been chosen by each class, the boys standing for various districts in Birmingham. The mock election had involved the boys in gallup polls and, on October 5th, there had been an eve-of-election hustings, at which the three candidates had addressed the whole school, putting forward their party's policies in a last attempt to sway the floating voters. Ballot papers were distributed to every pupil and, during the voting which took place in school hours, a boy, dressed in the uniform of a police officer, kept an eye on the polling booths. Mr Dawes commented that the election was not a political lesson, but merely a way of teaching the boys something of the English Parliamentary system in the most interesting and practical way.

Voting gets underway at the polling booths.

MONDAY, DECEMBER 14th
The string section of the City of Birmingham Orchestra gave a concert this afternoon to the children of the Junior School.

WEDNESDAY, DECEMBER 16th
What a busy week of activity! The Junior School held not only a carol service today, but the older juniors had an evening party, whilst the infants held an open day. Meanwhile, the Senior Boys' School had been rather ambitious, putting on a production of George Bernard Shaw's *Androcles and the Lion*. Although it was an extremely difficult play for the boys to embark on, they rallied round and worked very hard at it. M. Horrocks, who played the Captain, gave an outstanding performance during the first act, which was set on the road to Rome. S. Gould as the Emperor was well suited to the part, whilst D. Hubbocks made a gallant effort in portraying Lavinia. Mr Haydn Jones was not only the producer, but make-up artist and official photographer, making a quite professional job of all his undertakings. Mr Francis and Mr Jenns had produced the sets and lighting. At the end of the show Mr Dawes commended the boys on the wonderful performance of all concerned.

Androcles and the Lion. Top Left: Androcles. Top Right: Lavinia. Bottom Left: The Captain. Bottom Right: A Christian.

1960
JANUARY
Boxing matches were still being arranged in the Secondary Boys' School – in a ring which would be installed in the hall – provided both boys were in agreement that they wished to settle their dispute in this way. If nothing else, it allowed them to let off their pent-up aggression, whilst they were being closely supervised.

TUESDAY, FEBRUARY 9th
82 children sat the first part of the Junior Schools' leaving examination today.

TUESDAY, FEBRUARY 16th

The second part of the Junior Schools' leaving examination took place.

WEDNESDAY, THURSDAY and FRIDAY, APRIL 27th, 28th and 29th

Each morning the Junior School choir rehearsed at the Town Hall under the direction of Miss Doris Handley and Miss Taylor in order to perform at the North Birmingham District Festival. This took place on both the morning and evening of Tuesday, May 3rd.

FRIDAY, MAY 6th

The school was closed today for the wedding of Princess Margaret.

MONDAY, MAY 30th

The woodwind section of the City of Birmingham Symphony Orchestra gave a concert to the children of the Junior School this morning.

SATURDAY, JUNE 4th

Another extremely sad day for the school! A man was questioned by police this afternoon after a seven-year-old boy was found with severe head injuries in Slade Road, near Hunton Hill. Brian Cross, who was a pupil at the school, later died in hospital. The man, who had been a voluntary patient at Highcroft Hall Mental Hospital for four months, was exercising in the grounds under the stewardship of a male nurse, when he disappeared; later to be seen climbing over the hospital gates. Half an hour later, Brian Cross, who was on his way to visit a friend, was seen by a number of people being grabbed by the man, who struck him several blows to the head with a piece of scaffolding, fracturing his head in numerous places. Jamaican, Aldrick Rockhead, aged 26, was subsequently charged with his murder. At the next session of the Birmingham Assizes, he was found unfit to plead and ordered to be kept in custody until Her Majesty's pleasure was known. The only person to be called was a doctor who attested to the fact that he was a schizophrenic with homicidal tendencies. Although the hospital knew, from personal experience, that he was violent, they gave him less restraint – not more! The result was a call to the Minister of Health for changes to be made to the Mental Health Act, as well as an investigation into practices at Highcroft Hospital.

MONDAY, JUNE 13th

Mr Conduct, the Head, and Mrs Harkin, the Deputy Head, attended the funeral of Brian Cross today, having some days earlier visited his parents to pay condolences on their tragic loss.

TUESDAY, JUNE 14th

At an Erdington Rotary Club luncheon, a presentation was made to two Erdington schoolchildren for winning the annual essay competition sponsored by the club. David Looney of Slade Road School was one of the recipients for his essay on the subject of teenagers.

MONDAY, JUNE 20th
Four Junior School classes paid a visit to Dudley Zoo.

FRIDAY, JULY 1st
The annual excursion to Rhyl took place.

THURSDAY, SEPTEMBER 15th
Once again we saw a headteacher from the school being involved in the politics of teaching. This time, Mr Conduct was part of a deputation seeking a dependants' pension scheme for teachers.

THURSDAY, SEPTEMBER 22nd
The police were at the school showing road safety films to all the children.

THURSDAY, OCTOBER 13th
Mr Conduct was again involved with a deputation, this time over the development of swimming for children in Birmingham.

THURSDAY, OCTOBER 20th
Once more Mr Conduct was back at the Education Department, this time to discuss the lack of stability in school staffing.

Junior School Class with Mr Massingham, c.1960.

TUESDAY, OCTOBER 25th
One class, accompanied by Mr Reakes, paid a visit to the school's adopted ship, 'Welch City', at Woolwich Docks.

MONDAY to FRIDAY, DECEMBER 12th to 16th
Over the course of the week there were four parties held in the afternoons, one for each year group. On the fourteenth the juniors held their carol service, whilst the infants had an open day. Then, on the evening of December 16th, the fourth year juniors had a party to which 30 children from Bishop Ryder's School were invited as guests.

MONDAY, DECEMBER 19th
This afternoon the Junior School choir sang carols at the Raymond Priestley Home for Aged People.

1961
TUESDAY, JANUARY 31st
Miss Doris Handley took two teams of dancers for a demonstration at Anthony Road Schools this evening.

SUNDAY to THURSDAY, MARCH 26th to 30th
On each of the five nights the Secondary Boys' School staged a performance of *A Midsummer Night's Dream* by William Shakespeare. They performed a shortened version of the play retaining the complete fairy and mechanical plots. The production was brash and businesslike; and came to a triumphant and hilarious conclusion in the "Interlude before the Duke on his wedding day and night." Mr Jenns, who did the sets and props, also directed the lighting, which was varied and suitably atmospheric.

Secondary Boys' School Concert – Midsummer Night's Dream, 1961.

FRIDAY, APRIL 7th
Thirty-four boys from the Secondary School left for a tour of Germany's Golden Rhine, accompanied by Mr Dawes, the Headmaster, and two other teachers. They travelled to Southend Airport where they dined before taking off for Rotterdam at seven o'clock in the evening. Having arrived there two hours later, they caught a coach for Nijmegen, where at

11.30p.m. they boarded the motor vessel Machiel VI – and so to bed. After breakfast they spent the day sightseeing in Nijmegen, paying particular attention to the battle that took place there towards the end of the Second World War. Then, they were on to Germany via the River Waal – which eventually became the Rhine – sailing through the industrial Rhineland until they reached Dusseldorf. After that, it was onto Cologne to Konigswinter for a trip by funicular railway up the Drachenfel mountains. Coblenz and further beauty spots further upstream followed before they turned about north for the cruise back; and a return to school by the route that they had taken on their outward journey. Each boy was given an informative and artistic book to carry. This contained the itinerary, information about customs and so on, descriptions of places of interest, pictures, maps, valuable hints and even a few German phrases with phonetic keys. A photographic competition was also run in conjunction with the trip. The introduction in the booklet stated: "The reputation of your school and of your country is in your hands. We hope that you will have a happy holiday but please remember, wherever you are and whatever you are doing, to ask yourself this question: Am I making myself a nuisance to anyone else? If the answer is Yes, please put matters right immediately." The party travelled about 1,500 miles in various forms of transport and it was hoped that the lads would retain the booklet as a souvenir of their holiday.

FRIDAY, JUNE 2nd
The choir and dancers of the Junior School attended the North District Music Festival, which was held during the morning and evening.

FRIDAY, JULY 7th
It was that time of year again for the Junior School's annual outing to Rhyl. Six members of staff and four other adults accompanied 140 children on the day out.

FRIDAY, JULY 14th
The Secondary Boys' School raised £26 in one week to help the Erdington Old Age Pensioners' Association provide money for their building fund. An appeal had been sent out to twelve schools and the boys of Slade Road had responded immediately. The school's own printing club had produced the collecting cards on the school press; and every boy in the school had been asked to help by collecting money from his friends and relatives. Every boy in the school did something towards raising the amount that was collected.

WEDNESDAY, JULY 19th
The Junior and Infant School held an open day during the evening. An exhibition of work was on display and around 350 parents found the time to attend.

WEDNESDAY, SEPTEMBER 20th
Because of a strike organised by the National Association of Schoolmasters, all the children were sent home for the day.

THURSDAY, OCTOBER 12th
The police gave all of the classes in the Junior and Infant School lessons in road safety.

FRIDAY, OCTOBER 13th
Harvest Festival services were held today. The Junior School raised £6.10s.0d. by means of a sale and a collection, the proceeds being given to the Church of England Children's Society.

FRIDAY, NOVEMBER 10th
The Theatre for Youth came along to the school to give two performances of Pinocchio during the morning.

FRIDAY, DECEMBER 1st
Despite cuts considered necessary in the education services of the City, the local authority had endeavoured to institute modern facilities in the older schools to bring them more in line with their newer contemporaries. The school had used All Saints Parochial Hall for many years, particularly to put on plays. However, the venue had been condemned for use some time ago and the school was faced with the dilemma of where to hold their productions. The education authorities were approached and they responded by converting two classrooms in the Boys' School into a small hall, as well as supplying a portable stage.

TUESDAY to SATURDAY, DECEMBER 12th to 16th
The new hall and stage were put to use with immediate effect when the boys of the Secondary School presented their Christmas show entitled *Lively Venture* a three-act play of E. Price Jones. The play centred around Tom Johnson, a smuggler and famous pilot of the Napoleonic era. It lasted 2¼ hours and could have been cut down with profit. However, the play had all the necessary ingredients: a murder, a pistol fire, a cutlass duel (staged by Errol Stennet and Graham Lord with commendable realism) and well-defined players were well

Tom Johnson, Janet, Sir Hector.

to the fore. The colourful costumes were made by the wife of the headmaster. The four leading roles were exceptionally well-taken. Graham Lord as Tom Johnson – a long part involving three disguises and a great deal of straight acting – was outstanding. Derek Foar played the bluff squire, Sir Hector Brandon, with fine attack and consistent characterisation – altogether an excellent performance. Michael Leach as Silas sparkled throughout the play. He had a great deal of natural acting ability and a fine sense of timing. Errol Stennet played the villain, Pike, with distinction. He had a good voice, a telling stage presence, and a quality of relaxation. Of the female characters, Jeffrey Barnsley as Janet and Anthony Showell as Sally were most convincing, the parts suffering nothing from being played by boys. Among the minor roles, Dennis Turner as Roper, the blacksmith, made 'the most of a fine part'. The set – an inn interior – and the lighting used with point throughout, were the responsibility of Mr C. Jenns. The play was produced by Messrs. T. Dutton and H. Jones and provided a most entertaining evening to anyone with the good fortune to have seen it.

1962

TUESDAY, FEBRUARY 6th and TUESDAY, FEBRUARY 13th

The first and second parts of the Junior Schools' leaving examination took place on these days. A total of 88 children sat the examination, the school employing three invigilators for the purpose.

MARCH

SENIOR

	P	W	L	D	F	A	PTS
HODGE HILL	20	17	2	1	85	9	35
RILAND-BEDFORD	19	13	3	3	87	26	29
MARSH HILL TECH	18	13	3	2	132	19	28
PAGET	18	11	5	2	108	44	24
MOOR END	18	10	4	4	69	30	24
STOCKLAND GREEN	19	10	6	3	68	45	23
NECHELLS	18	8	9	1	65	58	17
BOLDMERE	19	6	12	1	41	80	13
ERDINGTON HALL	19	3	15	1	26	117	7
ABBEY	20	2	18	0	25	186	4
SLADE	19	1	16	2	24	100	4

INTERMEDIATE

	P	W	L	D	F	A	PTS
PAGET	18	17	0	1	89	16	35
HODGE HILL	20	17	3	0	95	32	34
MARSH HILL TECH	20	13	4	3	92	36	29
MOOR END	19	13	4	2	66	36	28
STOCKLAND GREEN	19	7	6	6	46	44	20
SLADE	20	8	9	3	59	47	19
RILAND-BEDFORD	19	7	8	4	27	44	18
ABBEY	19	5	14	0	47	88	10
BOLDMERE	18	4	13	1	37	66	9
ERDINGTON HALL	17	3	14	0	18	86	6
NECHELLS	18	1	17	0	27	98	2

JUNIOR A

	P	W	L	D	PTS
YENTON	16	13	1	2	28
NECHELLS	16	12	1	3	27
OSBORNE	16	11	2	3	25
MARSH HILL	16	9	7	0	18
ASTON HALL	16	6	9	1	13
BIRCHES GREEN	16	6	10	0	12
COURT FARM	16	4	8	4	12
GUNTER	16	4	11	1	9
TURFPITS	16	0	16	0	0

JUNIOR B

	P	W	L	D	PTS
SLADE	16	15	0	1	31
PAGET	16	13	3	0	26
HAWTHORN	16	10	5	1	21
MANOR PARK	16	10	5	1	21
LYNDHURST	16	8	6	2	18
ABBEY	16	5	9	2	12
ERDINGTON HALL	16	5	11	0	10
ST.MARY & ST.JOHN	16	2	13	1	5
NATIONAL	16	0	16	0	0

JUNIOR RESERVE

	P	W	L	D	PTS
NECHELLS THIRDS	16	13	1	2	28
ST.MARY'S	16	9	3	4	22
NECHELLS SECONDS	16	9	5	2	20
YENTON THIRDS	16	7	4	5	19
SLADE SECONDS	16	7	7	2	16
ABBEY SECONDS	16	7	8	1	15
YENTON SECONDS	16	6	8	2	14
MANOR PARK SECONDS	16	3	13	0	6
ST.PETER'S	16	1	13	2	4

SENIOR CUP
HODGE HILL 1 RILAND-BEDFORD 0

INTERMEDIATE CUP
PAGET 2 HODGE HILL 1

UNDER 14 CUP
MARSH HILL TECH AND PAGET JOINT HOLDERS

UNDER 12 CUP
WINNERS HODGE HILL RUNNERS UP PAGET

PLAZA CUP
WINNERS YENTON RUNNERS UP MARSH HILL

JUNIOR RESERVE CUP
WINNERS ST.MARY'S RUNNERS UP YENTON

7-a-side LEAGUE A TROPHY
WINNERS OSBORNE RUNNERS UP NECHELLS

7-a-side LEAGUE B TROPHY
WINNERS PAGET RUNNERS UP SLADE

Final Tables Erdington Schools' Football League 1961/1962 Season.

MONDAY, MARCH 26th
There seems to have been a great deal of illness amongst the teaching staff. On this day alone six, including the deputy head, were away sick in the Junior School. The Headmaster, Mr Conduct, was also absent at a funeral. Since the start of the year at least sixty days had already been lost through illness. Mr Conduct expressed gratitude for the fact that, where teachers were absent, students on school practice came in very useful for taking classes!

WEDNESDAY, MARCH 28th
Two of Her Majesty's Inspectors were in school today to discuss the teaching of science and mathematics to junior children.

WEDNESDAY, APRIL 4th
The University of Birmingham presented the school with a grant of £20 to assist in the work of primary school science.

MONDAY, MAY 7th
One of the classes in the Junior School visited the Lichfield cattle market this morning.

MONDAY, MAY 21st
Absence levels amongst the staff still appeared to be on the high side. Two teachers in the Junior School had been away for a total of 81 working days alone so far during the year with illness.

Secondary boys' school trip – Lake Lugano.

FRIDAY, JUNE 15th
At the Erdington Rotary Club exhibition, the first prize in the photography section was awarded to Roger Everton, a pupil in the Secondary Boys' School.

THURSDAY, JUNE 21st
The Junior Schools' exhibition at the Co-operative Hall in High Street, Birmingham opened. Classes from the school attended and gave demonstrations in Dancing, Woodwork, Arithmetic and Science.

WEDNESDAY, JULY 4th
65 children from the junior part of the school spent an enjoyable day at Dudley Zoo.

FRIDAY, JULY 6th
It was that time of the year again for the annual Junior School outing. This time, the older children spent the day at New Brighton. Meanwhile, in the Secondary Boys' School, Friday afternoons were given over to general knowledge quizzes, which lasted until a quarter to five.

WEDNESDAY, JULY 11th
Open Day at the Junior and Infant School and 350 people attended the exhibition that was laid on for them.

THURSDAY, JULY 12th
Mr Brunton, a driver with British Railways, addressed the school concerning the dangers of playing on the railways.

FRIDAY, SEPTEMBER 14th
A collection for the Persian earthquake relief fund took place, which realised £10.10s., this amount being sent to the British Red Cross.

FRIDAY, NOVEMBER 23rd
Sergeant Turner of the Birmingham City Police gave road safety talks to the children during the morning.

THURSDAY, NOVEMBER 29th
In school this morning were the Theatre for Youth. They gave two performances of *Alice in Wonderland*.

FRIDAY, DECEMBER 14th
Pirates, buried treasure, a witch doctor, a conjuring show and cross-talk comedy all provided the ingredients for the play *The Singing Dolphin* put on by the Secondary Boys' School. Judging by the audience's reaction, the resulting omelette was obviously to their taste. Two backdrops were used – a seascape and a jungle river scene – both of a vivid formalised design

The Witch Doctor, Captain Lasher, The Ship's Cook, The Bosun.

by Mr C. Jenns, who also stage-managed and did the tricky lighting effects. The costumes, which were extremely colourful, were once again made by the headmaster's wife, Mrs Dawes. The singing, chorus and solos by T. Ireson were most effective, the music being arranged by Mr D.T. Jones. Although the play opened slowly, the pace soon quickened much to the audience's appreciation. Unquestionably, the acting honours went to Michael Leach as Captain Lasher, whilst he was admirably supported by Graham Lord as Mr Wilkinson, the ship's cook, and Roger Morris who played the bosun, Nosey Morgan. Both tribesmen and pirates moved with impressive rapidity around the pocket-handkerchief stage. The play was produced by Messrs. Dutton and Jones.

FRIDAY, DECEMBER 21st

Miss Doris Handley retired today, having been on the staff of Slade Road School for 39 years. Her own class, other children, and the staff all combined to give her presents on the occasion. She had first set foot in the school in 1907 when she attended as an infant at the age of five. In her younger days, she was thought of by many of the girls as pretty beyond belief with big brown eyes. In the late twenties, she gave personal presents – such as a comb in a leather case – to the twelve children, who placed highest in her class examinations. Both with the Girls' School and, later, the Junior School, she produced excellent dancing troupes.

1963

MONDAY, JANUARY 7th

School commenced today after the Christmas break with all members of the staff present.

WEDNESDAY, JANUARY 23rd

The school was closed during the afternoon as there had been a complete freeze up. By 4p.m. the caretaker and the head teacher had restored the situation enough to let the school re-open the following day.

TUESDAY, JANUARY 29th

Following a talk to the Junior School on the work of the Blind Society by one of its representatives, a collection was held which raised £65.

TUESDAY, FEBRUARY 5th and 12th

The first and second parts of the Junior Schools' leaving examination were held on these days, a total of 6l children taking the tests.

THURSDAY, FEBRUARY 21st

The school broke up for the half-term with a tragedy! Diane Thomas, a junior pupil in Class 1, was killed on her way home from school. Mr Conduct and Mr Whittall later attended her funeral which took place on March 1st.

FRIDAY, MARCH 1st

Pupils and staff at the Boys' School were anxiously looking forward to the day when their school would be rebuilt on another site. At this time, a location had been recommended in Marsh Lane but the scheme had already been on the Education Authority building-authorisation programme for five years with no sign of work going ahead. The Ministry of Education only allocated so much money annually for building programmes and Slade School had still not been included. Mr Dawes, the Headmaster, was naturally disappointed as he did not believe that there was enough space for the wide range of subjects and activities that took place at the school. The school was catering for 250 boys with the benefit of 11 teachers, the curriculum including Mathematics, English, History, Geography, Woodwork, Science, Music, Metalwork, Art, Technical Drawing, Social Studies, Physical Education and Religious Educational Knowledge. The older boys took Metalwork at the Gem Street centre. In the academic field, the fourth-year pupils took

Left: The Secondary Boys' School Library. Right: 16 second-year boys in the Secondary Boys' School sing along enthusiastically as Mr D. T. Jones, Deputy Headmaster, who had been with the school for the previous 31 years, accompanies them on the piano.

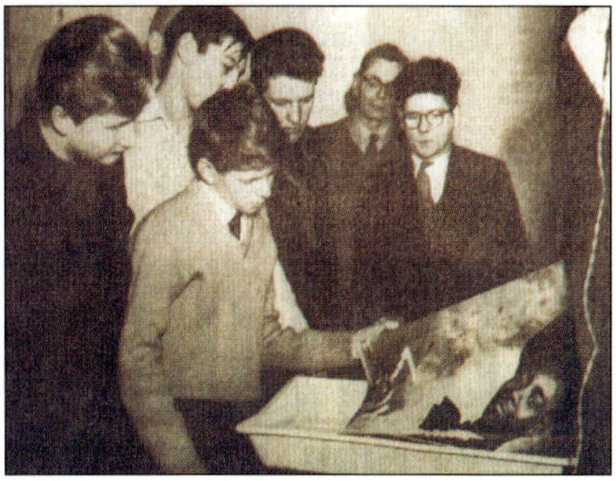

Left: Members of the Secondary Boys' School's canoeing club, of which 18 were going on a cruise down the river Wye at Whitsun. They had eight double and six single canoes, all built by the boys themselves under the guidance of Mr Charles Jenns. To qualify for membership, a boy had to be able to swim at least 10 lengths. Right: The Secondary Boys' School's photography club, which met on a Wednesday evening, had 16 members.

the U.E.I. Technical Grade A examination, whilst the fifth-year boys undertook the Secondary School Certificate. There were 9 after-school activity clubs, which embraced canoeing, modelling, chess, printing, records, drama, table tennis and photography, which the boys attended at lunch times and various nights of the week. However, the photography club had to meet in a disused air-raid shelter, which had been improvised as a dark room, conditions being very cold as there was no heating. A school library had been developed out of an old staff room and, besides housing books, had to be used for visual aids and medical inspections. Mr Dawes' own study was not really private as it was called into service for the purpose of conducting interviews when the youth employment officer came, as there was nowhere else. It was also noted at the time that parties of boys were regularly being taken on educational trips, which included the Royal Shakespeare Theatre and the Birmingham Repertory Theatre. As many as 36 would go to see the plays at one time. Speaking of plays, the boys were now presenting two big plays each year under the watchful eye of Mr Haydn Jones. One would be put on at Christmas, generally ran for five nights, and attracted an audience which did not just include parents, as the production reached such a high standard. On top of this, another play would be arranged in the summer exclusively for parents. Since 1959, the school had also been producing its own magazine entitled 'Fanfare' which was published every July. Running to 60 pages, it was edited by Mr Haydn Jones.

WEDNESDAY, MARCH 27th

Mr Conduct, the Head of the Junior School, was granted permission to be absent for the afternoon, in order that he could lobby his Member of Parliament over the injustices of the proposed pay award, which was to be imposed by the Minister for Education.

APRIL

INTERMEDIATE

	P	W	D	L	F	A	PTS
MARSH HILL TECH	17	15	1	1	64	18	31
PAGET	16	12	1	3	84	28	25
HODGE HILL	13	9	1	3	60	14	19
SLADE	14	6	2	6	47	34	14
MOOR END	13	5	0	8	24	36	10
STOCKLAND GREEN	15	4	1	10	28	59	9
RILAND-BEDFORD	9	4	0	5	28	59	8
NECHELLS	15	3	2	10	31	57	8
ABBEY	11	3	0	8	30	72	6
BOLDMERE	7	0	0	7	2	45	0

UNDER 15'S
WINNERS LEA VILLAGE RUNNERS UP STOCKLAND GREEN

UNDER 14'S
WINNERS ALDERLEA RUNNERS UP HODGE HILL

UNDER 13'S
WINNERS PAGET RUNNERS UP MARSH HILL TECH

UNDER 12'S
WINNERS HODGE HILL RUNNERS UP ALDERLEA

SENIOR

	P	W	D	L	F	A	PTS
MARSH HILL TECH	13	12	0	1	55	11	24
STOCKLAND GREEN	14	11	0	3	46	26	22
PAGET	14	9	3	2	50	19	21
HODGE HILL	14	9	0	5	42	31	18
ABBEY	13	6	0	7	27	39	12
NECHELLS	14	5	0	9	36	38	10
MOOR END	14	4	1	9	30	51	9
SLADE	13	3	2	8	20	42	8
BOLDMERE	9	1	2	6	19	25	4
RILAND-BEDFORD	10	0	0	10	14	50	0

Top: Final Tables Erdington Schools' Football Leagues 1962/1963 Season.
Bottom: Secondary Boys' School Intermediate Football Team 1962/1963.

SENIOR LEAGUE 1963				
	P	W	L	PTS
STOCKLAND GREEN	5	5	0	15
SLADE	5	3	2	9
ABBEY CATHOLIC	5	3	2	9
MOOR END	4	2	2	6
PAGET	4	1	3	3
NECHELLS	5	0	5	0
INTERMEDIATE LEAGUE 1963				
	P	W	L	PTS
PAGET	5	4	1	12
SLADE	5	4	1	12
STOCKLAND GREEN	5	3	2	9
MOOR END	5	3	2	9
ABBEY CATHOLIC	5	1	4	3
NECHELLS	5	0	5	0

Final Tables Erdington Schools' Cricket League.

WEDNESDAY, MAY 29th

Today saw the Erdington schools' sports take place at Jaffray Road playing fields. The school succeeded in finishing as runners up for the Junior Girls' Shield, whilst G. Seeley, as winner of the long jump competition, was chosen as a representative of the school to participate in the Birmingham Schools' Sports Federation Championships.

FRIDAY, JULY 5th

The annual Junior School trip to Rhyl took place – this time only 91 children went.

JULY

The Secondary Boys' School had their leaving service this month at St. Martins in the Bull Ring. Arranged by the Head's brother, Sid Dawes, 32 leavers attended the service which lasted between an hour and an hour and a half.

THURSDAY, NOVEMBER 21st

The City of Birmingham Symphony Orchestra's piano quintet gave a concert to the Junior School.

THURSDAY, DECEMBER 12th to THURSDAY, DECEMBER 19th

Christmas parties were held on the first five days for the respective years in the Junior and Infant School; before the term closed with a carol concert on the nineteenth.

1964

TUESDAY, FEBRUARY 4th and 11th

Part one and two of the Junior Schools' leaving examination were held on these days.

FRIDAY, MARCH 20th

In the Schools' Handicrafts Exhibition, organised by the Erdington Rotary Club at the Erdington Y. M. C. A., the Junior School were awarded a prize for their group work in the Embroidery section.

WEDNESDAY, APRIL 1st

JUNIOR LEAGUE A	P	W	D	L	F	A	PTS
YENTON	16	13	2	1	44	15	28
ABBEY	16	12	1	3	43	13	25
COURT FARM	16	10	1	5	31	17	21
SLADE	16	8	1	7	31	29	17
NECHELLS	16	7	1	8	20	23	15
PAGET	16	4	4	8	26	36	12
GUNTER	15	4	3	8	24	32	11
BIRCHES GREEN	16	2	3	11	13	34	7
OSBORNE	15	3	0	12	11	44	6

ERDINGTON & SALTLEY LEAGUE SENIOR DIVISION 1	P	W	D	L	F	A	PTS
LEA VILLAGE	12	10	1	1	45	18	21
HODGE HILL	13	9	1	3	53	30	20
PARK HALL	11	6	0	5	43	33	12
STOCKLAND GREEN	10	5	1	4	30	29	11
MARSH HILL TECH	6	5	0	1	24	13	10
PAGET	11	4	2	5	27	18	10
LEIGH	11	0	1	10	25	68	1
ALSTON	11	0	1	10	18	56	1

ERDINGTON & SALTLEY LEAGUE SENIOR DIVISION 2	P	W	D	L	F	A	PTS
SLADE	13	10	1	2	49	21	21
LOXTON	14	9	2	3	49	23	20
ROSARY	10	6	1	3	47	30	13
BOLDMERE	12	6	0	6	48	46	12
MOOR END	14	4	2	8	37	62	10
RILAND-BEDFORD	13	4	1	8	21	39	9
ABBEY	13	3	2	8	44	49	8
NECHELLS	13	3	1	9	26	51	7

ERDINGTON & SALTLEY LEAGUE INTERMEDIATE DIVISION 1	P	W	D	L	F	A	PTS
HODGE HILL	13	13	0	0	62	13	26
MARSH HILL TECH	9	7	1	1	28	16	15
STOCKLAND GREEN	11	7	1	3	39	25	15
PAGET	11	5	0	6	37	29	10
ALSTON	13	4	1	8	25	55	9
LEA VILLAGE	12	3	1	8	29	44	7
PARK HALL	10	2	3	5	9	15	7
LEIGH	13	1	1	11	10	42	3

ERDINGTON & SALTLEY LEAGUE INTERMEDIATE DIVISION 2	P	W	D	L	F	A	PTS
LOXTON	13	11	1	1	53	15	23
SLADE	13	10	0	3	53	20	20
RILAND-BEDFORD	13	8	2	3	62	19	18
BOLDMERE	14	7	2	5	44	31	16
ALSTON	13	6	1	6	55	31	13
ROSARY	13	3	1	9	31	59	7
MOOR END	14	2	0	12	23	82	4
NECHELLS	14	1	1	12	18	82	3

SENIOR CUP
WINNERS KINGSHURST RUNNERS UP LOXTON

UNDER 14'S
WINNERS PAGET RUNNERS UP MARSH HILL TECH

Final Table Erdington Junior Schools' Football League 1963/1964 Season.
Final Tables Erdington and Saltley Schools' Football Leagues 1963/1964 Season.

MONDAY, APRIL 6th

As at today the Junior and Infant School roll stood at 550.

SATURDAY, MAY 9th

The Erdington Schools' Swimming Gala was held this evening. Both the boys and girls of the Junior School placed fourth.

WHIT SUNDAY, MAY 17th

Mr B. S. Reakes died in hospital this morning from heart disease. Tribute was paid to the work that he had done in the Junior School during his 13½ years of service. He was held in great esteem by parents and children alike. Under the Burnham award, he had been nominated for a new post as a Head of Department. Unfortunately, this had not been confirmed at the time of his death. However, the Education Committee did approve his appointment in June, backdating it to September of 1963.

TUESDAY, MAY 26th

Three classes of the Junior School attended the Drama Festival at the Midland Theatre Centre, entertaining the audience with their interpretation of the play *The Visitor.*

THURSDAY, OCTOBER 15th

The school was closed today, as it was to be used for the purposes of a polling station for the General Election.

FRIDAY, OCTOBER 16th

Thirty-six newly-appointed teachers from the Education Office visited the Junior School this morning for a lecture and discussion on science teaching. For some years, the school appeared to have been at the forefront of teaching in this subject for teachers from other schools, as well as students, had attended from time to time to observe the work in progress.

TUESDAY, OCTOBER 20th

Mr Conduct was absent today at Burton on Trent where he was lecturing at the Children's Book Festival.

THURSDAY, OCTOBER 22nd

A performance of *The Nightingale* was given to the Junior School by the players from the Theatre for Youth this morning.

WEDNESDAY, DECEMBER 9th

A television outside-broadcast team from the B.B.C. came in to film the children in charge of Mr E. Coe for the purposes of a sociological programme. The following day saw the start of the Christmas parties, culminating with the carol service on the seventeenth.

ERDINGTON SCHOOLS' LEAGUE	P	W	D	L	F	A	PTS
MARSH HILL 'B'	7	6	1	0	49	21	13
SALTLEY GRAMMAR SCHOOL 'B'	7	5	2	0	50	20	12
SHELDON HEATH 'B'	7	4	1	2	48	22	9
SLADE 'A'	7	3	1	3	37	33	7
ALDERLEA 'A'	6	2	1	3	34	26	5
ST.CHADS 'A'	4	1	0	3	10	30	2
MARSH HILL 'D'	5	0	0	5	10	40	0
ALDERLEA 'B'	5	0	0	5	3	47	0

ASTON SCHOOLS' LEAGUE	P	W	D	L	F	A	PTS
UPPER THOMAS 'A'	6	6	0	0	43	17	12
MARSH HILL 'C'	7	6	0	1	52	18	12
SUMMER LANE 'A'	6	4	0	2	38	22	8
NECHELLS PARK 'A'	5	3	1	1	29	21	7
SLADE 'B'	6	2	1	3	31	29	5
NECHELLS	6	1	1	4	24	36	3
SUMMER LANE 'B'	7	1	1	5	29	51	3
GOWER 'A'	7	0	0	7	14	56	0

Erdington and Aston Schools' Table Tennis Leagues, 1964.

SATURDAY, DECEMBER 19th

At this time the Boys' School was competing against other schools at table tennis, as can be seen from these tables, which show the positions immediately before the school broke up for Christmas.

1965

TUESDAY, FEBRUARY 2nd and 9th

The Junior Schools' leaving examination was held on these two days. A total of 69 pupils sat the tests.

THURSDAY, MARCH 4th

Owing to a blizzard, all members of staff were delayed and many children were late or absent.

TUESDAY, MARCH 9th

Mr Conduct visited the City of Birmingham Training College to lecture on the teaching of science in the classroom.

FRIDAY, MARCH 12th

Plans for the replacement of the Boys' School were now so well advanced that the Birmingham Education Committee had decided to commence work on the building of the new school in Marsh Lane in 1966 with completion in 1968. It had been decided that the new establishment would be known as the Erdington Boys' School, as to retain the name 'Slade' would cause confusion to arise. The local councillor for the Gravelly Hill ward, Miss Sheila Wright, said that it was most likely that the majority of parents would choose to send their children to the new site. However, she thought that those living in Aston might consider it too far for their sons to travel. The Headmaster, Mr Dawes, was already on record as having said that the existing school was quite inadequate for its purposes. At the time that the Boys' School moved, the Junior and Infant School, which was already suffering from the problem of inadequate space, was expected to extend itself to fill the vacant area.

WEDNESDAY, MARCH 31st
Road Safety certificates were presented to 64 children from the Junior School at the Town Hall this evening.

During the week, Mr Conduct had been away for three days taking the chair at the Junior Meeting of the British Association at Birmingham University.

APRIL

	P	W	D	L	F	A	PTS
YENTON	16	14	0	2	43	13	28
PAGET	15	12	1	2	55	16	25
NECHELLS	14	11	0	3	53	21	22
COURT FARM	14	5	4	5	23	20	14
ABBEY	16	4	4	8	29	33	12
HAWTHORN	15	4	3	8	26	28	11
SLADE	15	4	3	8	28	35	11
OSBORNE	14	3	2	9	18	48	8
GUNTER	13	0	1	12	2	63	1

Final Table Erdington Junior Schools' Football League.

FRIDAY, APRIL 30th
A missionary gave a lecture to the older junior children about Nigeria.

FRIDAY, JUNE 18th
During the evening a jumble sale was held in the Junior School to raise funds for sports equipment.

TUESDAY, JUNE 22nd
The school was closed today, this being the 750th anniversary of the adoption of the Magna Carta.

FRIDAY, JUNE 25th
The annual School Outing for the top four junior classes. Whereto but Rhyl!

WEDNESDAY, JUNE 30th and THURSDAY, JULY 1st
The top junior class presented *The King of Thebes* whilst the school choirs gave a concert for parents. This took place on the afternoon of the first day with an evening performance on the second.

TUESDAY, JULY 6th
An open day for parents was held in the Junior School. Around 200 parents attended.

FRIDAY, AUGUST 6th
The new premises for the Boys' School were not to be in Marsh Lane after all! Birmingham Education Committee had had a change of heart and the school was now to be resited on the playing fields adjoining Fentham Road Girls' School. In replying to the opposition of Alderman S. E. Dawes, Councillor N. T. Cook said that they had had to weigh in the balance the best educational interests of the children and the immediate loss of a particular playing field. On balance, they had decided that the educational opportunities afforded by siting the school on the playing fields outweighed the disadvantages occasioned by using the field.

THURSDAY, OCTOBER 14th
The Birkenhead Players visited the school to give a presentation of *Hansel and Gretel.*

THURSDAY, NOVEMBER 4th
Brooke Bond paid a visit today to give a showing of their film on the production of tea.

WEDNESDAY, NOVEMBER 10th
At the Bristol Cinema they were showing the film *The Greatest Story On Earth.* This film from the gospel was attended by one of the junior classes.

FRIDAY, DECEMBER 3rd
The brass section of the City of Birmingham Symphony Orchestra gave a concert this afternoon.

1966

WEDNESDAY, FEBRUARY 16th
A Birmingham City bus carrying a party of children to the swimming baths overturned in Slade Road. It had been in a collision with a saloon car and had toppled over onto its side in the gardens of 322 and 324 Slade Road. Fifteen of the thirty-three youngsters on the bus were taken to various hospitals in the city. Two of the children, as well as the driver of the car, were thought to have been more seriously injured. Susan Gauden, aged 11, of Clarence Road was travelling in the lower deck of the bus at the time of the crash. She described the incident thus: "It was nightmarish. Everyone was screaming as seats and glass came raining down on us."

WEDNESDAY, MARCH 30th
The Headmaster of the Junior School, Mr Conduct, was admitted to hospital today; and was expected to be away for some time.

FRIDAY, APRIL 29th
The Primary School was experiencing difficulty in accommodating the numbers of children that wished to attend. Turfpits and Court Farm were in the same situation.

Although Easter was now past, the school was still unable to accept an intake of reception-age children – known to educationalists as the 'rising fives' – because of a serious lack of accommodation. In 1965, Turfpits Lane had had to accept pupils wishing to attend Slade Road and nothing, it seemed, would change until the Boys' School moved elsewhere.

WEDNESDAY, MAY 25th
The Junior School was closed this afternoon for the Erdington District Schools' sports. The field events had taken place on Tuesday of the previous week.

FRIDAY, JUNE 3rd
Mrs E. P. Harkin, who was acting as Head Teacher of the Junior School during Mr Conduct's enforced absence, commented to the press on a resolution that had been placed before the Whitsun Conference of the National Association of Head Teachers by Birmingham representatives. It would appear that some local head teachers were looking for immediate steps to improve conditions in schools which had immigrant children. She stated that under twenty percent of the children attending the Primary School were immigrants, none of whom were causing particular problems, although she went on to say that any improvements would be most welcome.

WEDNESDAY, JULY 13th
The Junior School held a highly successful 'open evening' for parents.

WEDNESDAY, OCTOBER 12th
Two performances of *The Princess and the Drummer Boy* were enjoyably presented for the entertainment of the Primary School by the Theatre for Youth.

WEDNESDAY, OCTOBER 19th
A young lad was bitten on the leg by a dog in the playground before school started at nine o'clock. This was reported and a protest was sent to the owner of the dog.

WEDNESDAY, OCTOBER 26th
Another injury! This time one of the boys managed to trap his finger in a lavatory door. An ambulance was called to take him to the General Hospital as he had badly cut his finger, which required stitches.

MONDAY, NOVEMBER 14th
After an absence of over six months Mr Conduct returned to school, although he would initially work mornings only.

WEDNESDAY, DECEMBER 7th
The Infant department held an 'Open Afternoon' which was well attended by parents and friends.

MONDAY, DECEMBER 12th
As from today Mr Conduct resumed school full time.

WEDNESDAY, DECEMBER 14th
On the afternoons of the previous few days Christmas parties had been held for the various year groups in the Primary School. During the evening the fourth-year juniors had their own special party.

1967

FRIDAY, JANUARY 6th
Once again Councillor Ken Barton pressed Birmingham City Council to consider placing a pedestrian crossing outside the Junior School in Slade Road. This was the third time that a request had been made, previous ones having been turned down. Although there was a crossing warden, cars were travelling along the road too fast, resulting in a number of 'near misses' during past years. In March of 1966, Ken Barton had raised a petition concerning the crossing, but with disappointing results. The same thing had happened two years earlier. It was hoped that a different, more drastic approach, might bring results.

TUESDAY and FRIDAY, JANUARY 10th and 13th
A representative of British Railways talked to the infants and juniors about the electrification of the railways.

WEDNESDAY and THURSDAY, JANUARY 11th and 12th
Road Safety was an issue of which the children particularly needed to be reminded. Consequently, two police officers came to the school to talk to the infants and juniors on separate days about the subject.

FRIDAY and MONDAY, FEBRUARY 10th and 13th
Audio tests were given to children who were four to five years of age.

THURSDAY, FEBRUARY 16th
The police were back again. Once more road safety was the issue, with films on the subject being shown to the whole of the Primary School.

TUESDAY, FEBRUARY 28th and FRIDAY, MARCH 3rd.
Vision tests were carried out on new entrants to the reception classes.

WEDNESDAY, MARCH 22nd
Mr W. Davies, Head of the Mathematics department in the Primary School, left today to take up the position as Deputy Head at Wilkes Green Junior School.

THURSDAY, MARCH 23rd
The Boys' School, playing in the Erdington and Saltley Schools' Football League, were crowned champions of the second division of the senior competition. With 6 wins, 1 draw and 1 defeat, their 37 goals for and 14 goals against record just gave them the edge over St. Thomas', who finished with the same number of points, but a worse goal average.

EASTER
Most children would not be seen anywhere near a school during the holiday break but, over Easter, the playground. and hall of the school echoed to the laughter of children on Tuesday and Thursday mornings. More than 40 children attended a holiday playgroup which was held by the Erdington and District Inter Racial Council. Several members of the Council and the United Nations Association Youth Group ran this, the pilot scheme, which it was hoped would lead to another during the summer holiday.

Making friends easily is sometimes hard work, but these children who went to Slade Road School during the Easter holidays did not find it so. They attended a holiday playgroup held by the Erdington and District Inter-racial Council.

FRIDAY, APRIL 28th
The Primary School closed early this afternoon in order to allow the children to go home during the presentation and farewell party to Mr Geoffrey Conduct. He was retiring as Headteacher after 7 years and 8 months. During his teaching career, which had begun in Birmingham in 1928, he had been concerned in many educational enterprises, all of which he had undertaken with the benefit of both the child and teacher in mind. To him, the children not the rules had always come first. For example, when employed as Headmaster at Birches Green, he had given special teaching to children from visiting canal boats. After the end of the war he had begun studying child psychology in order to better understand children. In an attempt to bridge the gap between old and new methods of teaching he had, only two years previously, published a set of work cards on science, and had commenced on a similar set for mathematics. Because of his interest in science, Mr Conduct had been one of the officers in the West Midlands branch of the British Association for the Advancement of Science, which had for several years been running a science fair at Birmingham University, as well as many series of lectures for pupils. This year, some of the juniors from the school would be taking part in the science fair, displaying the results of a traffic census that they had been carrying out on Slade Road.

MONDAY, MAY 1st
Mr Terry Spinks assumed the Headship of the Primary School.

FRIDAY, JUNE 16th

The Secondary Boys' School was finding difficulty with the new teaching developments. Raising the school leaving age to sixteen was a controversial subject in itself, but they were discovering many difficulties in continuing or expanding the deployment of outgoing teaching. The main problems appeared to relate to financial and transport matters and, not having received any help from the authorities, they were endeavouring to struggle on alone in the hope that someone would come to their assistance. During the week, a party of 17 boys had stayed at a log cabin at Earlswood, that belonged to the Federation of Boys' Clubs. They were undergoing a life and leisure course and, during their stay, they were entirely self-supporting, looking after themselves, cooking their own meals, with two members of staff present in an advisory capacity only. Whilst they had been staying there, they had been visited by representatives of the Youth Hostelling Association; City Police Training Centre; Stonehouse Youth Club; National Savings Movement; Industrial Safety Association; Horne Brothers and the Marriage Guidance Council. The boys had been encouraged to join in discussions on all subjects and on the Wednesday had held an open night to many local councillors and visitors from Erdington, doing the catering and entertaining themselves. Mr Dawes, as well as many other heads, were anxious to develop these courses, which were an education both academically and socially, as soon as possible. However, the weekly course had cost each boy 25 shillings, with the staff having to provide private transport to and from Earlswood. It was hoped that another expedition would take place later in the summer, taking a whole class of boys who had been studying forestry. As well as learning about camping, they could, therefore, do some practical forest and nature study. Mr Dawes knew that it would be expensive, as a coach would have to be provided, but he was prepared to undertake the expense in the hope that the Education Department might provide a grant.

FRIDAY, JUNE 23rd

Staff and pupils combined to give a concert for the entertainment of the old people in the area at All Saints Church Hall. The vicar, Mr M. Charles, had encouraged the senior boys at the school to help the old people in the Gravelly Hill ward. and, as such, sixty elderly people were invited to the event. Under the direction of two masters, Mr T. Jones and Mr H. Griffiths, the boys sang solos, comedy songs and folk songs. Special items were added to the concert by Mr A. Jupp, who arranged the concert and gave an impersonation of the Prime Minister; and by David Roberts, a soloist and tap dancer. Amongst the songs from the choir were *Michael rowed the boat ashore, The Swanee River, We shall overcome*, and other well-known folk songs. The audience was provided with refreshments by some of the lady members of staff and the headmaster's wife, Mrs R. Dawes.

FRIDAY, JULY 28th

The Secondary Boys' School won all of the eight matches that they played in the senior division of the Erdington Schools' Cricket League and were, therefore, crowned outright winners. Mr K. Campbell, one of the sports masters, said that the main strength of the team

Secondary Boys' School – Old Age Pensioners' Concert, 1967.

was in its bowling, whilst the fielding was also extremely good under the direction of the captain, W. Arnold. The intermediate team also gave good performances throughout the season, winning six of their eight games, drawing one and losing one. Mr Campbell reckoned that the reason for the general attitude of the team being so good could have been to do with the fact that 50% of them were West Indians.

FRIDAY, OCTOBER 20th

47 years ago a young man left Erdington to make his home in Canada. Mr Alfred Evans, who had attended the school as a pupil fifty years earlier, paid a surprise visit, together with his wife. He toured the school to see what differences there were, but found that the building had not changed at all. The manual training classes and rooms were exactly where they had been when he was a pupil. The one big difference was that the school had now become a Secondary School whereas, in his day, it was simply the 'Big Boys' section.

(Left to Right) Mr Reg Dawes, Headmaster David Evans, Head Boy Alfred Evans, ex-pupil.

1968

MONDAY, JANUARY 1st

The Secondary Modern Boys' School moved to its new premises in Fentham Road.

FRIDAY, APRIL 19th

UNDER 15 DIVISION 1	P	W	D	L	F	A	PTS
PARK HALL	12	10	2	0	71	14	22
HODGE HILL	12	10	1	1	48	20	21
SLADE	12	6	2	4	45	32	14
ST.THOMAS'	12	4	1	7	43	52	9
STOCKLAND GREEN	12	3	0	9	35	48	6
BOLDMERE	12	3	0	9	37	51	6
PAGET ROAD	12	3	0	9	30	88	6
UNDER 14	P	W	D	L	F	A	PTS
PARK HALL	14	10	3	1	63	32	23
HODGE HILL	14	10	0	4	60	22	20
STOCKLAND GREEN	13	8	2	3	52	36	18
SLADE	14	7	2	5	59	35	16
BOLDMERE	14	6	0	8	34	37	12
CASTLE VALE	14	4	2	8	37	72	10
MARSH HILL 'B'	14	3	1	10	41	60	7
ST.THOMAS'	13	1	0	12	14	65	2
UNDER 13 DIVISION 1	P	W	D	L	F	A	PTS
ST.THOMAS'	14	11	2	1	70	7	24
HODGE HILL	14	12	0	2	85	24	24
SLADE	14	11	1	2	60	20	23
PAGET ROAD	14	6	1	7	62	47	13
PARK HALL	14	5	2	7	27	33	12
STOCKLAND GREEN	14	3	4	7	21	42	10
ROSARY	14	1	2	11	9	94	4
BOLDMERE	14	1	0	13	13	80	2

Final Tables Erdington and Saltley Schools' Football League 1967/1968 Season.

THURSDAY, OCTOBER 10th
At 4.10p.m. Miss Crooks, a teacher, was attacked by two children. The girl hit her; and then she and her brother set upon the teacher, kicking and bruising her legs. A cleaner, who came into the room, ended up being bitten. Before even entering the classroom, the girl had slapped a lad who was waiting outside. On the way out her brother punched the same lad twice in the stomach. The following day, both children were punished by being slapped themselves!

FRIDAY, OCTOBER 25th
Slade Road Secondary Boys' School officially ceased to exist today, as an opening ceremony was carried out at 2.30p.m. at the new school in Fentham Road. It would now be known as the Erdington Secondary Modern Boys' School and could accommodate 450 boys.

1969

THURSDAY, APRIL 3rd
In the Erdington Junior Schools' Football League, it was decided that no more matches would be played, the league champions and runners up being decided on the average points from games played. The South Division is shown on the next page, the other divisions being won by Hawthorn and Perry Common.

FRIDAY, JUNE 27th
Aware of the amount of damage being done by vandals on the motorway sites in the Erdington area, many local schools were faced with the task of impressing upon their pupils

the dangers of trespassing on the workings. To this end, the school launched an anti-vandal campaign aimed at both parents and children in the area. A number of posters, being copies of the motorway-vandalism story which appeared in the Erdington News, were put on display around the school, both inside and out. Parents and children were asked to read and take note.

SOUTH LEAGUE							
TOPCLIFFE	14	13	1	0	50	8	27
NECHELLS	13	9	3	1	39	7	21
COURT FARM	13	10	1	2	37	18	21
PAGET	12	5	1	6	18	16	11
SLADE	14	3	0	11	12	24	6
MANOR PARK	11	2	1	8	11	35	5
ASTON HALL	12	2	1	9	9	38	5
BIRCHES GREEN	12	1	2	9	16	39	4

Erdington Junior Schools' Football League, 1968/1969.

FRIDAY, JULY 18th

During the week parents, pupils and headteachers from schools all over the Erdington area visited Slade School, where a motorway exhibition was being staged. The exhibition, which centred on the Gravelly Hill interchange, was displayed to include all aspects of the school's work from craft to science. The school was very concerned that the children should feel the importance of the motorway, as well as expressing safety to them. The different aspects of the motorway had been divided amongst the pupils, some dealing with the materials used, whilst others had concerned themselves with the history of the roads and bridges Other children had been involved looking into the social links which the motorways made between people. Representatives of the contractors had done much to encourage the work; and had viewed the models and written work.

FRIDAY, SEPTEMBER 26th

Four ten-year-old children from the school were selected to take part in the annual B.B.C. television series, 'Young Scientists of the Year'. They were Christopher Fox, Timothy Cotton, Alan Lord and Jacqueline Stanley. The team was selected by the B.B.C.

Left: (Left to Right) Timothy Cotton; Christopher Fox; Alan Lord; Jacqueline Stanley
Right: (Left to Right) Jacqueline Stanley; Timothy Cotton; Alan Lord; Christopher Fox.

from the Birmingham Science Fair that had recently taken place at Birmingham University. Altogether twelve schools from all over the country had been invited to participate in the series. The school's project involved the collection of local geological samples which were then compared with the stones and rocks from other parts of the country. The samples were carefully washed, ground smooth and then lacquered, so that the markings could easily be seen. A great deal of help was given by Monk Ltd., one of the motorway contractors of Gravelly Hill, who supplied the children with geological samples from the underground stratas of rock. The heats were due to commence the following January, with two of the eventual finalists being invited as guests of Philips Electrical Ltd. to compete against other young scientists in the European Science Fair, which was to be held in Eindhoven in Holland.

THURSDAY, DECEMBER 18th
Many of the children from the school took part in an essay competition to decide what apparatus should be installed at the new Adventure Playground in Park Road.

Junior School Open Adventure Playground, 1969.

2.30
Young Scientists of the Year

What's a gribble, and how do you upset its appetite?
Why don't cranes fall over?
Do mice cross white lines?
What are tomorrow's scientists up to today?
A chance to find out as teams of schoolchildren from all over the country, compete in the second of four heats for the *Sunday Times* 'Science Fair' trophy. The winners will represent Great Britain at an international Science Fair in Holland.

Finding out the answers, pupils from
MANOR COURT SECONDARY SCHOOL, PORTSMOUTH
SLADE JUNIOR INFANTS SCHOOL, ERDINGTON, BIRMINGHAM
MARLBOROUGH SCHOOL, WOODSTOCK, OXFORDSHIRE
The Judges:
DR. M. PUGH THOMAS
PROFESSOR JOHN FREMLIN
DR. JOHN CARTHY
Presented by PADDY FEENY

Birmingham's tiny boffins

Three boys and a girl with an average age of 10 compete in the BBC1 **Young Scientists of the Year** programme on Sunday. 'They're the youngest of the young,' says the series' producer Alan Grimley. 'The average age of children taking part is nearer 15.'

The 10-year-olds come from Slade Junior Infant School at Erdington in Birmingham. They have delved into the mysteries of why cranes don't fall over and why bridges don't snap.

The answers are to be found in the complicated world of applied mechanics, but the tiny boffins of Birmingham tried another way – by playing with the real thing on an £8½-million construction site.

Young Scientists of the Year – Articles, 1970.

1970

SUNDAY, JANUARY 25th

Four pupils from the school took part in the B.B.C. television programme, 'Young Scientists of the Year', today when they competed against Marlborough Comprehensive School and Portsmouth Secondary School. The project had involved collecting local geological samples and comparing them with stones and rocks from other parts of the country. They had also wanted to know why cranes with such slender legs did not fall over; and had been taken around the site at Gravelly Hill to inspect the cranes that were operating there. It had originally grown out of the exhibition that had been held at the school in July on the work on the motorway. They eventually finished a creditable second in their heat with 195 points.

FRIDAY, JANUARY 30th

Aston Villa donated a trophy to the Erdington Junior Schools' Football Association.

SATURDAY, MARCH 21st

During the football season teachers had been striking and working to contract. Unfortunately, this toll had its effect, even though teams co-operated to ensure that most of the season's plans were fulfilled.

TUESDAY, JUNE 16th

Once again the issue of safety on Slade Road reared its head. On this occasion, the children from the school decided to go to the very top. Today, 40 of them, accompanied by Councillor W. Donaghy (Gravelly Hill), were welcomed by the Lord Mayor, Alderman Stanley Bleyer, in his parlour at the Council House. This was just one part of a four-part plan in an endeavour to obtain safety measures in Slade Road. They had previously sent individual letters to him, telling him about the dangers that existed on the road where the

A poem for the Lord Mayor

- by all of Class Five.
Slade J. and I. School

Parking

As I come to school at nine
It really is quite shocking
To see the cars parked in a line
On Slade Road, my view blocking.

I cannot safely cross the road,
The heavy lorries thunder past,
I cannot do my highway code,
Until these cars are moved at last.

Lord Mayor, could you help us please?
Breaks squeal and drivers curse,
As through the cars the children squeeze,
They will be hurt or worse!

If you painted yellow lines
Along one side of Slade,
The cars would heed these warning signs
And crossings could be safely made.

Our warden does the best he can
To see if all is clear
If, on parking here a ban
Was put, it would be safer here.

We know you'll do what you think best,
We're not just optimistic.
Not one of us would like to rest
A lifeless road statistic.

Left: Poem for the Lord Mayor, 1970. Right: Lord Mayor and children, 1970.

school was situated. On the same day, the Councillor had presented a petition, signed by 400 residents, to Birmingham City Council, demanding parking restrictions and a zebra crossing. He had conducted a survey after seeing a young boy killed in the road, as he did not want anything like it to happen again. The Lord Mayor was very sympathetic with their views, afterwards showing the children around the council chamber. At the meeting of the council, the petition was referred to the Public Works Department for consideration.

1971

JANUARY

Slade Road Nursery opened its doors for the first time – with six staff – in the buildings vacated by the Senior Boys' School at the top of Broomfield Road.

MONDAY, FEBRUARY 1st

New waiting restrictions came into force today along Slade Road, in response to the appeal made by the children eight months earlier. Mr Spinks thanked the Lord Mayor and the Council for answering the school's plea, particularly as previous requests appeared to have fallen on deaf ears. About 80% of the 600-plus children attending the school came from the other side of George Road; and had to weave their way between parked vehicles and moving traffic.

SATURDAY, MARCH 20th

As can be seen from the following end-of-season league table for the Erdington Junior Schools' Football League, Slade School were not the force that they once were.

NORTH LEAGUE

	P	W	D	L	F	A	PTS
YENTON	14	10	1	3	35	12	21
PERRY COMMON	14	8	2	4	43	21	18
ABBEY	14	8	2	4	47	21	18
PEGASUS	13	8	2	3	26	17	18
ERDINGTON HALL	13	5	3	5	26	27	13
MARSH HILL	13	4	2	7	15	22	10
ST MARY & ST JOHN	11	3	0	8	13	26	6
SLADE	12	0	0	12	3	49	0

Top Left: Slade School Nursery. Right: Junior School – Waiting restrictions lifted, 1971.
Bottom Left: Erdington Junior Schools' Football League, 1970/1971.

FRIDAY, MAY 28th

All was not doom and gloom on the sports front, however, for, at the Erdington Schools' Sports, the school finished as runners up to Osborne Road in the Open Boys' Championship, in the process winning the boys' high jump, as well as the 80 metres for third-year boys. In the girls' competition, the school only managed to win the high jump.

OCTOBER

Erdington Junior Schools' Football League, 1971/1972.

NORTH LEAGUE	P	W	D	L	F	A	PTS
YENTON	13	10	1	2	63	9	21
TOPCLIFFE	14	8	4	2	37	26	20
ERDINGTON HALL	13	7	2	4	31	22	16
ABBEY	12	7	1	4	46	21	15
PERRY COMMON	12	4	2	6	37	42	10
PEGASUS	12	3	3	6	23	34	9
SLADE	12	2	5	5	19	28	9
MARSH HILL	12	0	0	12	6	81	0

Erdington Junior Schools' Football League, 1971/1972.

1972

FRIDAY, MARCH 10th

This year saw a slight improvement in the school's fortunes whilst competing in the North Division of the Erdington Junior Schools' Football League.

FRIDAY, JUNE 16th

A three-year study of the hazards and social effects the gaining of Spaghetti Junction would have on the surrounding area, and the motorists who used it, was put on display at the school this week. More than 1,000 children had worked on the project. The infants had concentrated on safety aspects of the development, with emphasis on kerb drill and road care. This had resulted in the growth of probably Birmingham's largest 'Tufty Club'. In the meantime, the juniors had worked on the wider significance of the interchange to the area, its place in the country's communication system, and the social effects. The project had originally begun in 1969 when the first signs of Europe's most complex road interchange were emerging from the Gravelly Hill mud. The possibilities that such a scheme offered were realised and the site contractors were approached with a view to seeking their assistance. They were extremely helpful, allowing both parents and children to study the site as it progressed and

Top: Tracing the path of Spaghetti Junction on their model. Bottom: The infants with a model that they built of the first railway engine.

Junior School Football Team 1972/1973.

developed. This undoubtedly proved beneficial in satisfying that certain curiosity that children in particular have, so that they would resist the temptation to trespass on the site. With each year of the project's development the children entering the school were encouraged to take part in the construction of models and painting. It soon became an integral part of the active work, with teachers being given a free hand to teach the transport and safety aspects, its fields including Mathematics, Literature and Handicrafts. They studied the development of canals and railways, as well as roads, and, from there, broke down the specific fields. Terrific support was forthcoming from parents and helpers. The pupils' work had included scale models of the layout; instructions on how to get on and off the system; and a study of transport through the ages. Birmingham police praised the school for its efforts, and asked for part of the exhibition to be re-assembled for display during the 'Stay Alive' campaign, which would take place in March 1973. The exhibition had recently attracted over 200 visitors, including representatives of Monks, and pupils and staff from other schools in the area.

1973

FRIDAY, APRIL 13th

Yet again, it was not a very good year for the football team, as the Erdington Junior Schools' Football League concluded with Slade holding up the rest of the teams in their division.

NORTH LEAGUE	P	W	D	L	F	A	PTS
ERDINGTON HALL	14	10	3	1	46	15	23
PEGASUS	13	9	1	3	50	31	19
YENTON	13	8	2	3	46	18	18
PERRY COMMON	14	8	2	4	42	31	18
MARSH HILL	13	2	5	6	35	44	9
ABBEY	14	2	4	8	19	35	8
TOPCLIFFE	13	3	2	8	15	42	8
SLADE	14	1	3	10	10	47	5

Erdington Junior Schools' Football League, 1972/1973.

Left: Pansita Hutchinson tries by leaps and bounds to win for Slade Road.
Right: All the young 'star' athletes take a bow.

MONDAY, JULY 2nd
The search to find the athletic stars of the future took place at Salford Park Stadium, Gravelly Hill, this evening. Girls from eight Erdington Junior and Primary Schools were invited to compete in the annual Invitation Trophy Competition organised by Lozells Harriers. Schools taking part included Hawthorn, Osborne, Abbey, St Peter and Paul, St Mary and John, Sacred Heart, Marsh Hill and Slade. In the overall results, there was a tie for first place between Marsh Hill and Slade who both accumulated 61 points.

FRIDAY, SEPTEMBER 21st
The Erdington Junior Schools' football season was well under way, Slade having made their best start for several years with three successive victories, the latest a three goal to nothing win over Erdington Hall. Unfortunately, it was not set to continue, the school eventually dropping well down the final table.

1974

WEDNESDAY, JANUARY 9th
Today saw the arrival of 22 newly-admitted 5 year-olds.

TUESDAY and WEDNESDAY, APRIL 23rd and 24th
Easter having passed us by a further 10 infants, aged 5, joined the school.

TUESDAY and WEDNESDAY, SEPTEMBER 10th and 11th
The start of a new school year and the arrival of 41 infants, many of whom were not yet five years of age – they would reach that landmark between now and Christmas.

THURSDAY, OCTOBER 10th
General Election day, and the school was closed as was the customary practice. Elected as Member of Parliament for Erdington was Julius Silverman, the Labour candidate and sitting member, who had served the country for the previous 29 years.

1975

TUESDAY, WEDNESDAY and THURSDAY, JANUARY 7th, 8th and 9th
There were 43 newly-admitted infants over the three days, most of them short of their fifth birthdays.

SATURDAY, JUNE 7th
At the Erdington Carnival the school won the five-a-side schools' football tournament.

JULY
The end of the school year and 5 girls, who had passed the Grammar Schools' admission examination, left, four for the Erdington Girls' Grammar School and one for King Edward's, Handsworth.

WEDNESDAY, THURSDAY and FRIDAY, SEPTEMBER 3rd, 4th and 5th
27 infants started their first year at school today.

THURSDAY, NOVEMBER 20th
In a monthly competition open to all schools in the Sutton Coldfield and Birmingham areas, and organised by Birmingham City Council's 'Beacon' road safety magazine, the school was

Junior School – Road Safety Award, 1975.

adjudged the winners this month. The judges thought that the school had produced the best essays, paintings and models on the theme of 'road rage'. Nine-year-old Julia Rushby accepted a £5 voucher on behalf of the school from Birmingham's road safety officer. It was intended that the money would be spent on furthering road safety at the school.

1976

MARCH

House competitions were held in Mathematics, Spelling, Art, Gymnastics, Chess, Class Work and Courtesy during the month between the Knights, Queens, Bishops and Kings. A team was also taking part in a Law and Order competition against other schools. The latest result was a win by one point over Perry Beeches in the second round. By the end of the month, a new school magazine, 'Top Class', had been launched by Mr Rashid Ahmad, the teacher of class 1, the top class in the school.

The first Board of Editors comprised four of the children who were: Editor – Michael Foy, Sub. Editor – Beverley Myers, News Correspondent – Michael Davis, Sports Correspondent – Shane Ward. There was to be a small cover charge of one penny.

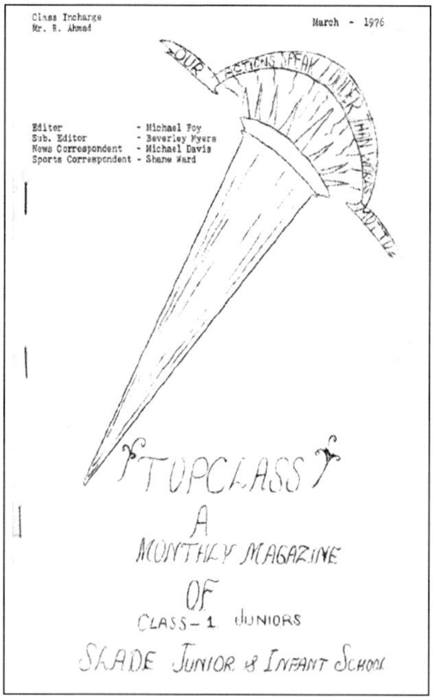

Top Class, School Magazine.

MONDAY, MARCH 8th

The school was converted to North Sea Gas over the following two days. In consequence, the children were given the time off.

WEDNESDAY, MARCH 17th
The 4-a-side football team travelled to West Bromwich Gala Baths to play in the finals of the Erdington 4-a-side competition. They lost to St Mary and John in the final and ended up with silver medals as runners up.

TUESDAY, MARCH 30th
A third-year netball competition was held at Perry Common Junior School this evening. The teams had to play seven matches of five minutes each. The result was a resounding win for Slade who won all of their matches scoring 17 goals with only 4 against. In the meantime, the senior netball squad, who played in blue leotards and orange skirts, remained unbeaten in the Erdington league.

An outing for the Junior School to the West Midlands Safari Park. In the lower picture, Mr Walpole is approaching the camera; Mr Spinks has his back to it, whilst the deputy head, Helen John, is directly to the left of Mr Spinks, c.1976/7.

FRIDAY, APRIL 2nd
This morning, the best House competition yet was staged. Girls and boys from every year in the Junior department took part. Each competitor did a short exhibition of floor work followed by a demonstration of their skills on the box. It was ably organised, the children enjoying every minute of it. The latest House positions showed that the Queens occupied first place with Knights, Bishops and Kings in that order.

WEDNESDAY, MAY 26th
It was Mr Holmes' birthday, the teacher of class 1J. Paul Cotter threw a flour bomb at him, which missed, sending flour everywhere; and covering lots of the other children. He was, then, given the task of sweeping up the mess!

JUNE
The whole school was suffering from a craze of selling raffle tickets, in order to win a free day out for their class.

FRIDAY, JUNE 25th
The annual school trip took place, this year affording the pupils a chance to visit Drayton Manor.

THURSDAY, SEPTEMBER 2nd
The school re-opened after the summer break, the cost of the school magazine increasing to two pence a copy.

FRIDAY, OCTOBER 8th
The produce, that had been brought into school for the Harvest Festival service, that had taken place on the previous day, was delivered to numerous local, old-age pensioners. The school received 30 letters of thanks.

THURSDAY, OCTOBER 21st
Another dreadful day for the school! On the evening that the school broke up for half term, Jane Snipe, a cheerful member of Infant Class 2 – remembered with a happy smile – was tragically killed in a traffic accident.

SATURDAY and SUNDAY, NOVEMBER 6th and 7th
Twenty children spent the weekend at the Children's Venture Centre at Grestone, Atherstone.

SATURDAY, NOVEMBER 13th
A Xmas Fair was held with a Father Christmas grotto.

SATURDAY, DECEMBER 4th
Twelve children joined in the carol singing at the Old Square in Birmingham City Centre.

TUESDAY, DECEMBER 14th
The caretaker discovered on his early-morning rounds that the school had been broken into. Virtually all the rooms in the school had been entered, the doors having been forced open. The police located the point of entry as a swinging window in the Infants' cloakroom, near to the headteacher's room. There were finger prints on the window frame and track-shoe prints on the window sill. Desks, cupboards and lockers had been broken into. Ice cream and jellies that were meant for the Christmas party had even been eaten! Any small change that had been left around had also been taken. The contents of desks and cupboards were scattered all over the place. Everywhere looked a proper mess! The perpetrators had then made their exit through the double doors by the front office at the north end of the corridor. The bolts had been pulled and the doors forced without too much difficulty. What was more, it meant that the school had remained open throughout the night! An urgent request had to made for repairs to be carried out. All the locks were restored and the doors reinforced within forty-eight hours, although the repairs to desks and cupboards had to wait until the New Year.

THURSDAY, DECEMBER 16th
The staff were still able to have their Christmas dinner, the school closing for the holidays the following day.

1977

TUESDAY, JANUARY 4th
A new caretaker started today. Mr Rose, who had been the assistant caretaker at Perry Common, had been selected from three applicants on November 10th. With the start of a new year, many of the staff had made New Year resolutions. Included amongst them, Mr Andy Hill had given up smoking again, but then found that he seemed to have had a permanent sore throat and congestion ever since. Mr Rashid Ahmad was likewise trying to give up smoking, but hadn't been very successful; and was now smoking more than ever. However, he felt a lot happier that he had been successful in making a resolution! Miss Sheila Staunton gave up tripe and onions. She did this every year but, as she detested them anyway, she was hardly going to break the resolution!

THURSDAY, MAY 5th
As the school was being used for the elections it was closed for the day. However, two pupils chose the occasion to interfere with the tyres of local cars. They were suitably rewarded by Mr Spinks!

MONDAY to FRIDAY, MAY 9th to 13th
Cycle proficiency tests took place at the school. On Monday the children's bikes were checked over by two policemen. On the next three days they rode around blocks in the playground making signals, besides showing how well they could control their bikes. On the final day, under supervision, they were allowed out onto Slade Road. They cycled up George Road and into Park Road before returning to the school. Most of the children passed and were rewarded with either badges or certificates.

TUESDAY, MAY 17th
The field events of the Erdington Junior Schools' Athletic Sports took place between twenty schools. Christopher Burgess was the school's only winner, finishing first in the long jump.

MONDAY, MAY 23rd
The athletic sports continued with the track competition. Derek Brown, Sonia Hemans and Lenora Laing all won their sprints, whilst the 3rd years took the relay. Later, in the 300 metres, Peter Cunningham won the boys' event, Linda Salmon courageously being beaten into second place in the girls' competition. Due to a great deal of effort, both the boys and girls were able to finish as runners up in their respective championships.

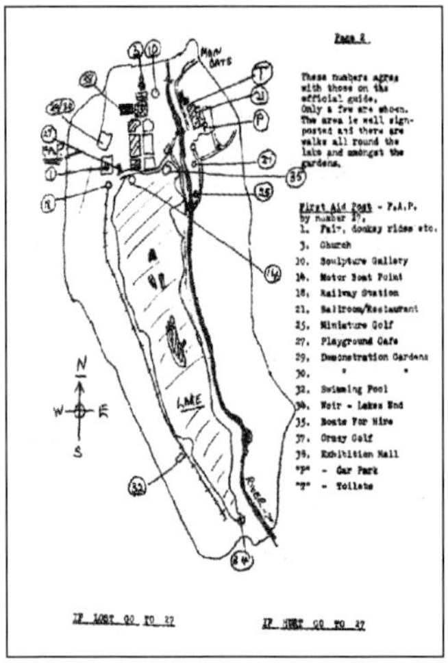

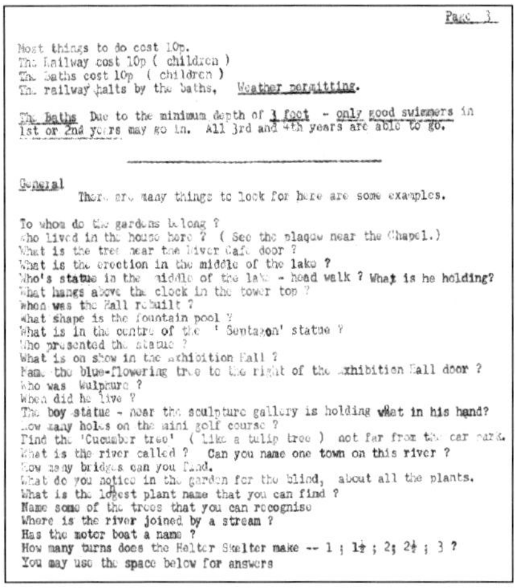
Page 3

Most things to do cost 10p.
The Railway cost 10p (children)
The baths cost 10p (children)
The railway halts by the baths, Weather permitting.

The Baths Due to the minimum depth of 3 foot - only good swimmers in 1st or 2nd years may go in. All 3rd and 4th years are able to go.

General
There are many things to look for here are some examples.

To whom do the gardens belong ?
Who lived in the house here ? (See the plaque near the Chapel.)
What is the tree near the River Cafe door ?
What is the erection in the middle of the lake ?
Who's statue in the middle of the lake - head walk ? What is he holding?
What hangs above the clock in the tower top ?
When was the Hall rebuilt ?
What shape is the fountain pool ?
What is in the centre of the ' Sentagon' statue ?
Who presented the statue ?
What is on show in the Exhibition Hall ?
Name the blue-flowering tree to the right of the Exhibition Hall door ?
Who was Wulphure ?
When did he live ?
The boy statue - near the sculpture gallery is holding what in his hand?
How many holes on the mini golf course ?
Find the 'Cucumber tree' (like a tulip tree) not far from the car park.
What is the river called ? Can you name one town on this river ?
How many bridges can you find.
What do you notice in the garden for the blind, about all the plants.
What is the longest plant name that you can find ?
Name some of the trees that you can recognise
Where is the river joined by a stream ?
Has the motor boat a name ?
How many turns does the Helter Skelter make -- 1 ; 1½ ; 2; 2½ ; 3 ?
You may use the space below for answers

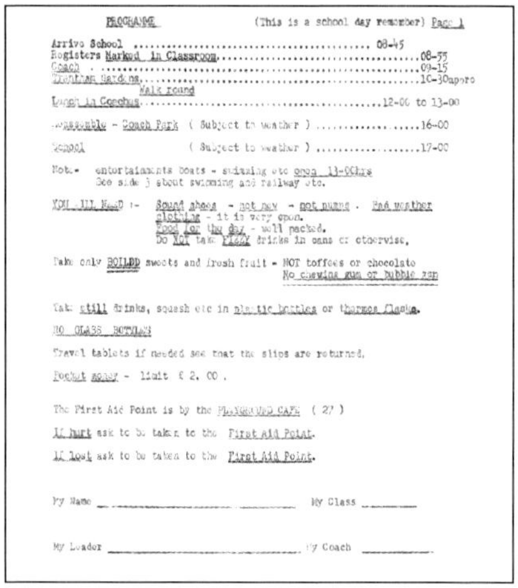
PROGRAMME (This is a school day remember) Page 1

Arrive School 08-45
Registers Marked in Classroom........................ 08-55
Coach 09-15
Trentham Gardens........................ 10-30appro
Walk round
Lunch in Coaches........................ 12-00 to 13-00
Reassemble - Coach Park (Subject to weather) 16-00
School (Subject to weather) 17-00

Note.- entertainments boats - swimming etc open 11-00hrs
See side 3 about swimming and railway etc.

YOU WILL NEED :- Sound shoes - not new - not pumps. Bad weather clothing - it is very open.
Food for the day - well packed.
Do NOT take FIZZY drinks in cans or otherwise,

Take only BOILED sweets and fresh fruit - NOT toffees or chocolate
No chewing gum or bubble gum

Take still drinks, squash etc in plastic bottles or thermos flasks.

NO GLASS BOTTLES

Travel tablets if needed see that the slips are returned.

Pocket money - limit £ 2. 00 .

The First Aid Point is by the PLAYGROUND CAFE (27)

If hurt ask to be taken to the First Aid Point.

If lost ask to be taken to the First Aid Point.

My Name ________ My Class ________

My Leader ________ My Coach ________

Trentham Gardens Trip Booklet, 1977.

FRIDAY, JUNE 17th

228 junior children, plus 18 adults, went on a trip to Trentham Gardens. They arrived at school at 8.45a.m., the registers being marked in their classrooms ten minutes later. At a quarter-past nine the coaches arrived and everyone boarded. The journey took approximately an hour and a quarter. Express instructions were given out to everyone as can be seen from the programme.

MONDAY to FRIDAY, JUNE 20th to 24th

A busy week! First, a party of 15 children together with Mr Holmes went to the Woodlands Camp for five days. On the Tuesday, the top and middle infants spent the day out at Weston

Park, whilst the nursery had an enjoyable day at Sutton Park. Come Thursday and it was the turn of the reception and younger infant classes to spend some time away from the school. They visited the Botanical Gardens.

TUESDAY and WEDNESDAY, JULY 12th and 13th
Parents' evenings. Attendances varied between 30% and 70%. Mrs Blewitt and her class performed Irish and English traditional dances so beautifully for the enjoyment of the parents.

FRIDAY, JULY 15th
A special Jubilee party, with sports for all, was held today, this being the occasion of the Queen's Silver Jubilee. The school had been especially decorated for the occasion. All the children had helped to put on a Jubilee display and exhibition, later being presented with their free souvenir mugs. There had also been a Jubilee Hat Parade along Slade Road. The staff had been extremely busy, involved as they were in a monster 'cook in' preparing the food for the Jubilee parties.

TUESDAY, JULY 19th
As there was little to choose between two of the junior classes, as far as the sale of raffle tickets was concerned, it was decided that both groups of children could enjoy their traditional 'free day-out'. One class went to the West Midlands Safari Park, whilst the other ventured to Twycross Zoo.

FRIDAY, JULY 22nd
The final day of term and three staff were fortunately leaving, as otherwise it would have been necessary to lose some anyway due to the falling intake. Furthermore, owing to the dictates of the economy, the L.E.A. had decided that primary schools could no longer employ needlework assistants, resulting in the loss of another two staff members.

THURSDAY, OCTOBER 6th
All the juniors and first and second-year infants attended the Harvest Festival service. In the afternoon, distribution of the collected produce began, concluding the following day.

FRIDAY, OCTOBER 7th
The previous day's distribution of food was finally completed during the morning. At four o'clock in the afternoon, the school held a cross-country run in Brookvale Park as part of the House competitions.

TUESDAY, NOVEMBER 1st
Miss Chamberlain and her team of dancers gave a display at Bordesley College. Sales of Remembrance Day poppies commenced.

SATURDAY, NOVEMBER 12th

The Christmas Fair was both crowded and successful. There were numerous stalls, including ones where you could buy clothes and groceries. Another offered the chance to win a teddy bear whilst cakes, tea, coffee, coke, hot dogs and ice cream were also available. A Christmas Grotto was provided where Father Christmas gave out presents to the children. On top of this, a lot of people had gone in for the Fancy Dress competition, many of them winning prizes for their efforts.

THURSDAY, DECEMBER 1st

Juniors from class 8 walked to Gravelly Hill railway station, where they caught the train to the city centre. On arrival, they walked around the shops before travelling back to school to write about their experiences.

1978

THURSDAY, JANUARY 5th

The school re-assembled in the new year to a cold building. All the staff had once again made New Year resolutions, although not many of them would be kept. Most had resolved to give up smoking or lose weight, but were finding it difficult to succeed.

SATURDAY and SUNDAY, JANUARY 21st and 22nd

Highball was a place where two schools went for a weekend. Fourteen children paid £2 for the privilege of spending their time walking through the countryside and playing games.

FEBRUARY

28 children received their free swimming passes.

WEDNESDAY, FEBRUARY 8th

A number of junior classes went to see *Star Wars* at the Gaumont Cinema.

MONDAY, FEBRUARY 20th

Although the school awoke to snow this morning, all the teachers were present and correct. Unfortunately, the boilers in the lower-junior school had failed to ignite. The temperature in that part of the building was only 47°F. Other rooms fed by it had managed to struggle up to 50°F. Emergency servicing restored the heating, but the building was cold all day.

TUESDAY, FEBRUARY 21st

Domestic hot water failure! The tanks were frozen.

FRIDAY, FEBRUARY 24th

The year seemed to have got off to a good start! Warnings were now received that the various trade unions were proposing action over meal-time duties and dinner-time activities. Those members in a union agreed to support any action that was requested.

WEDNESDAY, MARCH 8th

At Castle Vale Secondary School, a troupe performed Irish and Floral dancing. The judge was so impressed that they were invited to perform at Birmingham University.

MONDAY, MARCH 13th

All trade union members now refused to do any extra activities during dinner times. Only free meals came in and Mr Spinks (Head Teacher), Miss John (Deputy Head) and Miss Staunton covered for safety, together with the meal-time supervisors.

MONDAY, MAY 1st

Today, the school was closed owing to the granting of the new May Day Bank Holiday.

FRIDAY, JUNE 23rd

The annual school outing for the juniors. This year, after a week of preparations, in which trip booklets were prepared and issued, it was time to be off. The destination was Bourton on the Water, where the children explored the Model Village and the Bird Sanctuary. Although it was a rather damp day, a wonderful time was had by all.

WEDNESDAY, JULY 12th

A number of the junior children spent the afternoon at the Ice Rink in the city centre learning to skate.

The school was reasonably proficient at rounders. Having beaten St Mary and St John, Osborne, Nechells, Abbey and Birches Green, they found themselves in the finals of the tournament which were held at Spring Lane today. Beating St Margaret and St Mary put them in the final match against St Gerrards. However, they came up short by half a run and had to settle for the runners-up spot.

FRIDAY, JULY 21st

It was the close of another school year. Mr Rose, who had been considered a very good caretaker, was leaving. It was also time to say farewell to all the children who were leaving to go to secondary schools. During the year, House competitions had been held in football, cricket, netball, rounders, art, story writing, poetry, speech, chess, mathematics, religion and general knowledge. The result was a win for the Queens, followed by the Knights, Bishops and Kings in that order.

SEPTEMBER

All the children in class 9J were growing oak and laburnum trees. They hoped to start a forest!

THURSDAY, OCTOBER 5th

The usual Harvest Festival took place today with the distribution of parcels by the junior children during the following afternoon to local elderly residents.

WEDNESDAY, OCTOBER 25th
Parents' evening from 7p.m. until 9p.m.

MONDAY, NOVEMBER 6th
The school recommenced after the half-term holiday with the sale of Remembrance Day poppies.

MONDAY, DECEMBER 4th
The Seagull Theatre visited the school to perform a play called *Baron Bumble and the Giants*. This was laid on for all the children – juniors, infants and nursery.

FRIDAY, DECEMBER 8th
Councillor Mason spent the whole day at the school dressed as Father Christmas. Meanwhile, a post box had been erected in order that the children could send Christmas Cards around the school.

MONDAY, DECEMBER 18th
During the morning the staff entertained the children with a concert in which they were all involved. The following day, after the morning carol service, the afternoon was given over to parties.

1979

MONDAY, JANUARY 8th
The school re-opened after the Christmas holidays with a new caretaker, Mr Redding. As seemed all too usual, the heating was barely adequate, that in the infant hall having failed altogether.

FRIDAY, FEBRUARY 2nd
Slade met Hawthorn in the first match of the Law and Order competition. This took place in the main hall, where the audience – made up of two of the junior classes – was already seated, when the ten contestants – five from each team – came in. At the end of the first round Hawthorn had edged in front by three points. However, after much lip-biting and nail-tearing, by the end of the next round Slade had evened up the score. Now, came the moment of truth! The third round was to be the decider. Each 'team question' demanded a lot of thought and a good thirty-second discussion between the whole team, but, by the end of the round, Slade had won through by a clear 5 points. Afterwards, orange juice and biscuits were given out and both teams had a cheerful chat together.

MONDAY, FEBRUARY 5th
At 10.15a.m. there was a fire drill, which took three and a half minutes to clear and assemble everybody. Within nine minutes all the classes had been checked and cleared and permission given to return.

All the children in class 4J had written to the embassies of different countries, such as Mexico, Brazil, Colombia, Ghana, Jamaica, Austria and the U. S. S. R., with a view to finding out information for their topic on other countries.

WEDNESDAY, APRIL 4th
For the first time it was recorded that the infants had an Easter Bonnet Parade along Slade Road.

FRIDAY, MAY 11th
A break-in occurred at about seven o'clock in the evening, possibly with the use of a key. Subsequently, an outer door and the doors of three rooms were forced, as were the cupboards and teachers' desks within. Fire extinguishers were let off and garden tools were taken from near the kitchen in order to inflict further damage. The coin box of the payphone was vandalised and some small change taken, as well as approximately £5 from the tuck shop, and some other items. Within an hour and a half the break-in was discovered and the police informed. It later cost £6 to have the payphone repaired.

SATURDAY, MAY 19th
25 items of Art and Craft were selected to appear in a display that was to be held by the Rotary Club at the Y. M. C. A. Awards were given to five of the school's items.

FRIDAY, MAY 25th
During the summer mid-term break, three teachers accompanied 20 children to the Woodlands Camp, which was near to Aldridge and Streetly. They reported back safely on Sunday, June 3rd in time for school the following day.

WEDNESDAY, JUNE 20th
A large party of juniors and infants spent a very fine day on the annual school outing to Rhyl. They all walked up Hillaries Road in order to catch the train at Gravelly Hill railway station. On their arrival at Rhyl, they were shown the place, under a clock, where they were to meet up for the return journey. Many of the children enjoyed themselves at the funfair as well as on the beach. Quite a few children had never been to the seaside before and were very surprised to find that the sea tasted salty. Later, they spent time going round the shops choosing small gifts for family and friends before they all returned safely home.

FRIDAY, JUNE 22nd
A party of infants visited Twycross Zoo on the bus. They saw all the animals besides having rides on the donkeys and the miniature railway. It was a lovely day as they sat around having a picnic. Later on, they visited the gift shop where they spent the little money they had before boarding the bus for the homeward journey, tired but happy.

JULY

A group of children from Mr Ahmad's class entered the eye-care competition, organised by the Birmingham Opthalmic Information Council. Five girls walked away with awards, two of them coming first in the under 13s' category. Mandy Lareen and Susan Lewinson were each presented with shields. Mr Prime, a lecturer at Aston University, wrote to the school in the most glowing terms. His letter said that the illustrations in the dissertation were quite the best of the whole entry and would have done credit to a university student of opthalmic optics. The presentation of information was commendable, covering as it did many aspects of the visual system. He was extremely impressed!

FRIDAY, JULY 20th

The school closed for the main summer holiday. Altogether, four teachers had left, three of them at the end of term. Staff reductions were necessary for the new year beginning in September, but, fortunately, these had solved themselves.

MONDAY, SEPTEMBER 3rd

The school re-opened with 13½ staff in the juniors and infants and 3 in the nursery.

TUESDAY, SEPTEMBER 18th

After spending the first part of the morning in Sutton Park, where lunch was taken, a party of children went on to the Bookfair. At the fair was a chimp, who was wearing a T-shirt with the words 'chimps with everything' written across it. Whilst they were there, some of the children took the opportunity to join the Chipper Club.

THURSDAY, OCTOBER 11th

Harvest Festival was held this morning, following which 57 parcels were made up and distributed during the following day to elderly people in the area.

WEDNESDAY, OCTOBER 17th

Two classes visited the Avoncroft Museum, where they spent the day looking round the various buildings and artifacts.

MONDAY, NOVEMBER 5th

It was with great regret that the school learned that Michael Foy, the first chief editor of the school's magazine, Topclass, had died after a long illness.

WEDNESDAY, DECEMBER 12th

A concert was put on in which all of the junior children participated in some small way. Rehearsals had only started on December 4th, the stage being erected in the hall on the 7th and 8th, with dress rehearsals on the 10th and 11th. The concert was a sell out, tickets having to be rationed for the one and only performance.

Photographs of the teaching staff of the era. Left: Taken in the late 1970s, in the centre of the front row is Mr Spinks. Right: Front Row (Left to Right) Jeanne Jones; Janet Owens; Helen John; Andy Knipe; Andy Hill; Sally Forder; Iris Glasby. Back Row (Left to Right) Rashid Ahmad; Robert Walpole; Enid Greasley; Sheila Staunton; Ken Holmes; Rowford Bowditch, c.1982.

FRIDAY, DECEMBER 14th
Councillor Mason, dressed up as Father Christmas, spent the whole day at the school.

1980

MONDAY, JANUARY 7th
Because of rising costs the price of the school magazine was increased to 5p per copy.

FRIDAY, JANUARY 11th
In response to a bulletin of January 7th advising schools of the need to save 5% of their energy bill, Slade Primary School embarked on a project to see how energy savings could be made. This became part of a National Energy Competition.

MONDAY, FEBRUARY 4th
The younger children were treated to a visit from a Mr Johnson, who, for two years, had been visiting schools with different animals. This time he arrived with a toad, buzzard, chinchilla and Indian python.

WEDNESDAY, FEBRUARY 27th
A number of children had the opportunity to go to the pantomime at the Birmingham Hippodrome, where they saw *Babes in the Wood*.

MONDAY, MARCH 24th
The police visited the school to display their horses.

WEDNESDAY, MARCH 26th

The second Easter Bonnet Parade, during which the infants paraded their hats along Slade Road, took place.

THURSDAY, JUNE 5th

The school had reached the finals of the Law and Order competition by defeating both St Josephs and Chivenor. They played their final match against Abbey, who, on the day, proved too strong. Nevertheless, P. C. Killoch came to the school to present everyone who had competed with a certificate, and the school with a trophy as finalists.

SATURDAY, JUNE 7th

Over the previous few months the school had been involved in looking at energy savings under the guidance of Mr Andy Hill. As such, reporters from the Evening Mail, Birmingham Post and Junior Education visited the school, subsequent to which articles appeared in print. An interview was also taped for the children's programme *Playground* on Radio Two. Besides this, on March 23rd, some children had appeared on Ed Doolan's *Sunday Funday Show* on B.R.M.B. radio, immediately after he had interviewed David Soul. Nationally, an article had appeared in the Sunday Times colour magazine. The school reached the national quarter finals of the Department of Energy's competition before bowing out.

MONDAY, JUNE 30th

Once again it was time for the annual school trip. A special train was laid on by British Rail to take the staff, parents and 230 children to Barry. Unfortunately, it was an indescribably wet day, but, despite that, everyone had a great time and behaved themselves. The manager of the fun fair made a point of specially coming over to congratulate the school for being so well behaved!

WEDNESDAY, JULY 9th

During the evening the leavers had a special party. Every type of food imaginable was available as well as plenty of pop. There were games and records, with everyone having a lovely time.

SUNDAY, JULY 13th

Another break in! This time, the Hi-Fi Sound Centre was stolen along with two obsolescent tape recorders.

FRIDAY, JULY 18th

The last day of term and the school year. Although House competitions had been going on throughout the year, the rounders, cricket and general knowledge competitions had only taken place during the current week. The culmination was the presentation of the trophies to the winning houses on top of which the child, who had won the courtesy competition, would be named.

MONDAY, SEPTEMBER 1st

Most of the staff were in all day in preparation for the first day of school on Tuesday. Everywhere you looked the roof seemed to be leaking! It was so bad that the planned decorating had not started in many places. The parquet in the nursery had had to be relaid. The dining-hall floor had had to be repaired because of the leaks. The secretary's office had been painted but water was now coming in. Mr Spinks' room was, in fact, untenable! Two of the classrooms had been taken over by the painters and carpenters and would remain out of action until they had finished their work.

WEDNESDAY, SEPTEMBER 3rd

For the first time ever the new intake for infants was in single figures!

MONDAY, SEPTEMBER 15th

By now all the gutters around the school were being replaced. The old, cast-iron ones were corroded and on the point of collapse. From now on rooms were being vacated and classes resettled for window repairs and woodwork reparation. Each room was out of action for approximately three days at a time.

TUESDAY, OCTOBER 7th

New House names were chosen. One of the children had come up with the idea following a television programme that he had seen. In future, there would be three Houses called Falcons, Hawks and Eagles. A sign of déjà vu the Secondary Modern Boys' School, perhaps!

TUESDAY, OCTOBER 14th

Reverend Dodds from All Saints Church conducted the Harvest Festival service, which began at 9.30a.m. The infants had their own one for parents at 2 o'clock in the afternoon. The following day 58 food parcels were delivered to old-age pensioners in the area.

MONDAY, NOVEMBER 3rd

Repairs and redecoration work were still continuing, making it virtually impossible to find any available space for teaching when rooms were required to be vacated.

THURSDAY, NOVEMBER 20th

Today, a class of children went to Brookvale Park to plant 25 trees. There, they met the park-keeper and his assistants, who had already been digging the holes. Unfortunately, one of the holes was too small so they only ended up planting 24 after all. At the end of the ceremony they were presented with medals and certificates.

MONDAY, DECEMBER 1st

Up to date only about one fifth of the rooms in the school had been painted. Many rooms were being replastered for the second and third times as roofs, gutters and

Photographs of the School's editorial and reporting staff for 1981.

downpipes had still not been fully repaired. The library, infant hall, art and craft rooms had now been cleared for repairs and painting. It can't have helped that the caretaker, Mr Redding, was off on a course for five days. In at least twelve rooms the walls still remained wet!

FRIDAY, DECEMBER 5th
Mrs Forder had her purse stolen today. It was recovered seven days later in the grounds of Marsh Hill Secondary School, although there was no money in it by this time!

WEDNESDAY, DECEMBER 10th
The hall was filled for the Infant Nativity play to which parents were invited.

FRIDAY, DECEMBER 12th
Councillor Mason, once again in the guise of Father Christmas, spent the whole day at the school visiting up to 200 children.

TUESDAY, DECEMBER 16th
A Carol Service was held this morning at All Saints Church.

1981
TUESDAY, JANUARY 6th
The lunchtime hours were altered. In future the infants would finish at twelve noon, whilst the juniors would break for lunch half an hour later.

TUESDAY, JANUARY 20th
The magazine editors, together with Mr Ahmad, visited the Evening Mail to interview columnist, Maureen Messent, for the school magazine's 'Face to Face'. The children reckoned that she had 'pinched' her idea for a similar column from the school's magazine as their column had first appeared two to three years earlier.

Left: Interview with Bishop of Birmingham, 1981. Right: Interview with Clive Wilkinson, 1981.

WEDNESDAY, JANUARY 28th
The painters, who had left the site five weeks earlier, were now back! They were given a deferred Christmas treat of cakes and a glass of wine.

MONDAY, FEBRUARY 9th
The Bishop of Birmingham agreed to be interviewed for 'Face to Face'.

TUESDAY, FEBRUARY 24th
The school re-opened after half term to find the playground covered in ice; and in a very dangerous condition. There had been a blizzard on the Sunday. As the caretaker and staff were away, Mr Spinks spent all morning cutting paths across the playground where necessary.

WEDNESDAY, FEBRUARY 25th
Conditions had deteriorated so much that Mr Spinks had to treat the walkways with salt again. The snow and ice had brought down long stretches of the newly-erected plastic guttering all round the site. The painting and repair work, that had been going on for months, continued, such that the Art and Craft rooms were now not available for use.

SATURDAY, MARCH 7th
Highball Charity offered a number of places for children for the weekend, which the school was pleased to accept.

MONDAY, MARCH 23rd
On this occasion the editors of the school magazine met Clive Wilkinson in 'Face to Face'. At the time he was leader of the Labour Party on Birmingham City Council.

WEDNESDAY, APRIL 8th
A performance by the Seagull Theatre was given at the school.

FRIDAY, APRIL 10th
The school closed for the Easter break. Painting teams had come and gone; and there still remained a lot of plastering to be done! Mr Spinks had had to vacate his room once again as there was a serious roof leak. In fact, there were still quite a lot of roof leaks around the school. The painting was still only half-finished!

THURSDAY, MAY 14th
Mr Spinks had made a decision at the end of January to retire at the end of the school year; assuming his wife could likewise gain early retirement from her teaching position. A farewell dinner – part of an annual social occasion – was held by the Consortium Head Teachers at the Carvery in Four Oaks to which Mr Spinks was invited as a guest of honour.

THURSDAY, JUNE 4th
Exams started for the first, second and third-year juniors.

WEDNESDAY, JUNE 24th
A threat was made by the Trades Unions that, as from today, there would be no cover provided for absent staff.

WEDNESDAY, JULY 1st
The maintenance work was still continuing around the school. Furniture was being moved in and out of rooms as they were required. About three quarters of the work had now been finished.

FRIDAY, JULY 3rd
The juniors enjoyed a day out at Drayton Manor Park. The trip was very successful until the last few minutes when it decided to rain.

TUESDAY, JULY 7th
A large number of parents attended Parents' Evening, particularly to say goodbye to Mr Spinks.

THURSDAY, JULY 9th
Staff, past and present, as well as ex-colleagues from Upper Thomas Street, gathered to give Mr Spinks a cheery send off on the occasion of his retirement. The Lord Mayor and Lady Mayoress, Councillor and Mrs Barton, attended, together with representatives of the governors. The assembled company, totalling eighty-nine, enjoyed a generous meal and liquid refreshments. Subsequently, presentations were made by staff, parents and pupils, as well as numerous other members of staff and representatives of other schools.

There then followed a number of speeches, to which Mr Spinks replied, finding words difficult to come by. Mr Spinks, who was born on November 28th, 1917, initially went to school at Anthony Road – later known as Alum Rock School – in 1922. At the age of 9 he moved into the seniors with children as old as 14, until he passed the entrance examination for Saltley Grammar School, commencing there in 1928. Although he left in 1934 having completed both matriculation and higher certificate, it wasn't until 1936 that he decided to take up teaching, qualifying in 1938. After occupying several positions he eventually became the Head Teacher at Upper Thomas Street, before moving to Slade Road in 1967.

WEDNESDAY, SEPTEMBER 2nd
All members of staff attended for a staff meeting and distribution of stock under the direction of Miss Helen John, Deputy Head, who was acting as Head Teacher. Demons, Imps and Goblins were chosen as new House names.

MONDAY, SEPTEMBER 7th
A reception class intake of just one child!

THURSDAY, SEPTEMBER 24th
Mr Andy Knipe was chosen as the new Head Teacher and would commence his duties from January lst, 1982. Mrs McKay, who had ably, pleasantly, and with a quiet sense of humour, served as secretary of the school for many years, passed away. A requiem mass was held at the Abbey Church in Erdington on the following Monday, which was attended by virtually every member of staff.

WEDNESDAY, OCTOBER 7th
On the instructions of the Education Department the art room, infant hall and two infant classrooms were closed as an economy measure.

MONDAY, OCTOBER 12th
As a security and safety measure all entrances to the school were closed from today, excepting that in Slade Road.

FRIDAY, OCTOBER 16th
The Education Department had decided that further economy measures were required. In consequence, the needlework, library, and craft rooms were closed, although the library was now housed in another room in the main body of the school buildings.

TUESDAY, OCTOBER 20th
The Reverend Dodds conducted the Harvest Festival, following which 43 parcels were delivered to aged people in the area, many messages of thanks being received.

WEDNESDAY, NOVEMBER 11th
A further economy measure! One teacher now had to be redeployed from January 1st thus reducing the establishment. A few weeks later, Mrs J. Savage, Head of the Infant department, expressed an interest in a vacancy at Boldmere First School, which she obtained, so resolving the issue.

FRIDAY, NOVEMBER 20th
The caretaker, Mr Redding, discovered a break-in, which was duly reported to the police at 8.45a.m. this morning. A small amount of money had been taken from one of the junior classrooms, as well as a cassette recorder, and a further amount of money from the nursery.

MONDAY, DECEMBER 14th
The school had to be closed down for the day as there were frozen and burst pipes within the main building.

WEDNESDAY to FRIDAY, DECEMBER 16th to 18th
Wednesday saw a film show put on for all the junior, infant and nursery children, before a staff lunch, to which Mr Knipe, Reverend Dodds, Mr Spinks and many former members of staff were invited, took place. On the Thursday morning a carol service was held at All Saints Church, where all the junior and infant children participated. It was well attended by parents and parishioners. The afternoon was taken up with parties. Friday, the last day of the school term, saw Father Christmas visiting every one of the children, before the doors were closed at 3.30p.m. for the Christmas holidays.

1982

MONDAY, JANUARY 4th
It was with a mixture of apprehension, excitement and a sense of fulfilment that the new Head Teacher, Mr Andy Knipe, viewed his first day at Slade School, though these feelings would undoubtedly pass once the routine, everyday situation took hold. It didn't take long before the school suffered burst water pipes in the boys' toilets and the old library. Unfortunately for Mr Knipe the situation didn't improve any over the next two weeks. Friday saw a heavy fall of snow with only half the children putting in an appearance. Staff with long journeys were sent home as were children whose parents were at home. The school meals did not arrive until one o'clock. The following week started badly, all the outside toilets being frozen, whilst a radiator in the P. E. Hall burst. With no heat on the Tuesday, the nursery had to close. By Thursday, the water in the infant block was frozen; all but one set of toilets were out of action; another pipe had burst in the wash basin area near the hall and two more classrooms were without heat. The school was forced to close until the following Monday. All was not over, however, for, with an overnight thaw, the secretary's room flooded due to a burst pipe in the loft, there being extensive damage to the ceiling. Mr Knipe must have wondered what he had let himself in for!

Interview with Ron Saunders, 1982.

TUESDAY, JANUARY 26th
Four children visited the Aston Villa training ground in order to meet and interview the manager, Ron Saunders, for the school magazine's 'Face to Face' column.

MONDAY, MARCH 1st
A fire was started today in an out-building next to the old bike shed. Although it was easily dealt with by staff the fire brigade were called as a precautionary measure. The culprit was soon discovered and his parents informed.

FRIDAY, MARCH 5th
This afternoon an amusing incident took place when three of the children returned to the school after lunch with a St Bernard dog that they had found. Unable to trace the owner the dog was eventually taken to Queens Road Police Station. That is, when Mr Knipe was able to get it into his car!

TUESDAY, MARCH 16th
Sheikh Mubarak Ahmad, aged 72, the Imam of the London Mosque, accompanied by two colleagues, visited the school, where he addressed the children in assembly. Subsequently, he was interviewed for the school magazine's 'Face to Face' column before joining the staff for lunch.

Interview with Sheikh Mubarak Ahmed, 1982.

FRIDAY, MARCH 19th
During the afternoon a special Mothers' Day assembly was held. All the mothers attending were presented with a posy of flowers by their own children.

TUESDAY, MARCH 30th

It was found necessary to re-deploy another teacher! At a managers' meeting, it was decided that a nursery teacher would need to be asked to move to Banners Gate First School.

MONDAY, MAY 10th

Councillor Ken Barton, the Lord Mayor of Birmingham, paid a visit to the school today, speaking to the children in assembly. He was afterwards invited to be interviewed for the school magazine's 'Face to Face' column.

WEDNESDAY, MAY 26th

Many of the children from the junior classes took part in an athletics meeting with Osborne, Birches Green and Erdington Hall Schools. Slade School emerged as overall winners. Perhaps, on a more significant note, Aston Villa won the European Cup today.

MONDAY, JUNE 7th

For the second time in eighteen months the school was honoured with a visit by the Bishop of Birmingham. He spoke to the children about the work of Bishops before spending time visiting the nursery.

Top Left: Winners of the Plaza Cup for 1982, Jason Cook holds the trophy aloft.
Top Right: School magazine's editorial and reporting staff for 1982.
Bottom Left: Netball 1st team. Bottom Right: Football XI 1st. team, 1981/1982.

Stables, 1982.

SATURDAY, JUNE 12th

Today was the culmination of a lot of hard work as it was the occasion of the Erdington Festival. Besides organising a welly-whanging stall to raise funds for a proposed visit to Nethercott, entries were submitted for the Art exhibition. On the following day the choir took part in a local concert.

FRIDAY, JUNE 25th

Fifteen children, accompanied by Mr Knipe and Mr Hill, travelled with their families to the Stables Camping Centre at Bromsgrove for six nights, returning on Thursday, July 1st.

THURSDAY, JULY 15th

A most enjoyable and successful family evening was held at the school. Children invited their parents to come and see their work and some of the activities that they undertook each day. A book shop and tea room were laid on as added attractions.

SATURDAY, JULY 24th

Three days after the school closed for the summer holidays, Mr Knipe, who was 36 years of age, set off on a sponsored walk, in order to raise funds for 37 children to go on a visit to Nethercott Farm in Devon in May, 1983. His intention was to walk from Slade School to Nethercott Farm – a distance of 187½ miles – a journey he completed successfully on Monday, August 2nd. He hoped to raise half the cost for

Mr Knipe and Children, 1982.

each child, the other half being provided by the parents. He saw it as a way to help some of the pupils, whom he regarded as coming from disadvantaged homes, have a chance of experiencing country life.

TUESDAY, SEPTEMBER 7th

The day after the school opened following the summer break an occasional day was taken, so that a party of 180 children, accompanied by 40 parents, could visit Blackpool.

The trip had been arranged by the Birmingham Taxi Drivers' Association, in response to a request made by Councillor Ken Barton. There was no charge for the children or the adults. Meanwhile, all the staff attended for a staff meeting.

Taxi Drivers trip to Blackpool, 1982.

TUESDAY, OCTOBER 5th

Following the Harvest Festival service, gifts were distributed to elderly people in the neighbourhood, although some were retained for the children of Poland.

FRIDAY and MONDAY, OCTOBER 8th and 11th

The school was closed as there was no water supply, due to the district undergoing extensive maintenance to the water mains.

MONDAY, NOVEMBER 8th

The 37 children, who were to visit Nethercott Farm in 1983, spent today at Chapmans Hill Farm so that they could gain some experience of what to expect.

MONDAY, NOVEMBER 29th

28 children from the third and fourth-year juniors, accompanied by two teachers, set off for a five-day visit at Bell Heath Field Study Centre, returning safely on Friday of the same week.

Bell Heath, 1982.

1983

WEDNESDAY, FEBRUARY 9th

In order to raise funds for the school, all the children took part in a sponsored walk around the lake in Brookvale Park. Although the weather was fine, it was very cold. The younger children completed one lap, whilst the eldest achieved a total of five laps.

Top: School Football XI 1st team, 1983. Bottom: School Netball First team, 1983.

WEDNESDAY, FEBRUARY 23rd
Some computers were brought in from Newman College for the use of the children. It was intended that a representative from there would come in each Wednesday until the end of term, in order to help the children in their use.

SATURDAY, MARCH 26th
12 children went to stay for the weekend at the Highball Holiday Centre, near Malvern.

WEDNESDAY, APRIL 27th

Driver Higgs of British Rail visited the school in the morning to speak to the children about the dangers of playing on or near the railway tracks. As it happened he was a former scholar of Slade and promised to come and help with the 80th Birthday celebrations that were fairly imminent.

FRIDAY, MAY 13th

The culmination of numerous fund-raising efforts over the previous twelve months bore fruit today when 38 children, together with Mr Knipe and three other teachers, set off for a week's working experience at Nethercott Farm in Devon. They were to return on the following Friday, having undergone a 'once-in-a-lifetime' experience.

Nethercott Farm, May 1983.

SUNDAY, JUNE 12th
Mr Knipe, along with several pupils, took part in a 'Junction Jog'. This was one of the events organised in line with the Erdington Festival of this year.

TUESDAY, JUNE 14th
Another Erdington Festival event took place today, this time on school premises. An exhibition of Asian crafts was held in conjunction with the Erdington and Kingstanding Institute for Adult Education.

SATURDAY, JUNE 18th
Erdington Festival Carnival Day and the school had a float in the procession. They also had a cake stall in Rookery Park to raise funds, this time towards the school's 80th-Birthday celebrations.

THURSDAY, JUNE 30th
The school's foundation stone was laid 80 years ago today. In honour of that event the school held a party, to which former pupils, who had attended prior to 1943, were invited in the afternoon. An exhibition of photographs, school documents and other paraphernalia had been set up a few days in advance. The day began with an 'Edwardian morning' with the staff and many of the pupils dressed in the style of the period. Lessons in Scripture, Arithmetic, Poetry, Handwriting, Geography and Art were taught in the fashion of the times. Later, an 'Inspector' paid a visit – he was, in fact, the Head Teacher of Pegasus Junior and Infant School in disguise – during which two boys fainted from shock! In the afternoon current pupils showed the former pupils around, swapping experiences as they went. Amongst the guests were three former pupils who had attended on the school's opening day back in 1904, whilst a number of them had travelled from as far afield as Cornwall and Kent. Ted Allbeury, the author, and Harry Parkes, the former Aston Villa footballer – both ex-pupils – delighted the school by paying a visit. Altogether, the 150 guests had a marvellous time, enjoying a splendid tea and birthday cake, whilst happily reminiscing days gone by.

Top: 80th Birthday, 1983.
Centre: Nursery 80th Birthday, 1983.
Bottom: Taken in the upper playground, some of the younger children were especially dressed for the occasion.

At the eightieth birthday celebrations, wearing Edwardian costume, the children even did their sums in pounds, shillings and pence. They were encouraged to bring bread, cheese and an apple instead of their normal packed lunches of crisps and fizzy drinks by the Head, Mr Knipe (right), and his Deputy, Mr Hill (above).

MONDAY to THURSDAY, JULY 4th to 7th

8 pupils, accompanied by Mr and Mrs Knipe, went for a three nights' stay at the Stables Camping Centre at Blackwell. They travelled to Barnt Green by train from Gravelly Hill at a total cost of £7.50. For consenting parents of children who were taking part, there had already been an evening meeting – an opportunity to ask questions was provided – subsequent to half term to explain details of the camp organisation and activities programme. An exhibition of photographs taken at the previous year's camp had been on display at the school earlier. The cost to each child was £12, which included food, travel and insurance; there was a premium payable of £9 to the Municipal Mutual Insurance Limited; this covered all registered members participating in the school journey, as well as the Local Education Authority and the School's Governing Body. Whilst there, they took time out on the Wednesday to visit the Avoncroft Museum.

TUESDAY, JULY 19th

The Reverend Dodds paid his last visit to the school to take assembly, as he was moving to a new parish in Lincolnshire.

THURSDAY, SEPTEMBER 8th

Although a new school year had begun two days earlier, today saw 24 new children, aged 4, admitted to a newly-formed reception class. The new 'nursery' children were to be admitted on a gradual basis over the ensuing few weeks.

FRIDAY, NOVEMBER 18th
19 children, accompanied by Mr Knipe, Miss Morris and Miss Taylor, spent the weekend at the Stables Camping Centre at Blackwell. The centres were equipped to serve as a first-experience camping centre for children from Birmingham Junior Schools. As such they provided a selected environment for staff wishing to offer their pupils the advantages of camping experience, with the additional advantage of having help and advice readily available. The City of Birmingham Education Department undertook to provide all the basic essential equipment for a standing camp of 28/30 primary pupils and staff. Provided for pupils were Stormhaven ridge tents, karrimats, sleeping bags and sheet inner bags, whilst staff were given a frame tent and camp beds. Each group was responsible for its own catering and had to budget accordingly. Included on site were a water point, showers and washing facilities, flush toilets, an activities room, resources area, classroom, kitchen and emergency accommodation. Before each group visited they were provided with a comprehensive information booklet to help make their stay a pleasant one.

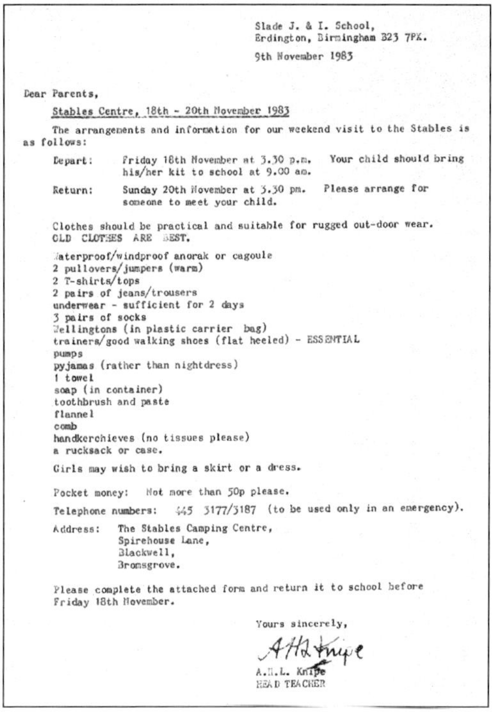

Slade J. & I. School,
Erdington, Birmingham B23 7PX.

9th November 1983

Dear Parents,

Stables Centre, 18th - 20th November 1983

The arrangements and information for our weekend visit to the Stables is as follows:

Depart: Friday 18th November at 3.30 p.m. Your child should bring his/her kit to school at 9.00 am.

Return: Sunday 20th November at 3.30 pm. Please arrange for someone to meet your child.

Clothes should be practical and suitable for rugged out-door wear.
OLD CLOTHES ARE BEST.

Waterproof/windproof anorak or cagoule
2 pullovers/jumpers (warm)
2 T-shirts/tops
2 pairs of jeans/trousers
underwear - sufficient for 2 days
3 pairs of socks
Wellingtons (in plastic carrier bag)
trainers/good walking shoes (flat heeled) - ESSENTIAL
pumps
pyjamas (rather than nightdress)
1 towel
soap (in container)
toothbrush and paste
flannel
comb
handkerchieves (no tissues please)
a rucksack or case.

Girls may wish to bring a skirt or a dress.

Pocket money: Not more than 50p please.

Telephone numbers: 445 3177/3187 (to be used only in an emergency).

Address: The Stables Camping Centre,
Spirehouse Lane,
Blackwell,
Bromsgrove.

Please complete the attached form and return it to school before Friday 18th November.

Yours sincerely,

A.H.L. Knipe
A.H.L. Knipe
HEAD TEACHER

Stables Centre Itinerary, 1983.

SATURDAY, NOVEMBER 19th
Although not discovered until Monday, it was thought that a break-in had occurred this evening, when a video recorder had been stolen.

MONDAY, DECEMBER 12th
During the afternoon the Parents' Association held a Toy Fayre when £80 was raised for school funds. This money was to go towards the cost of Christmas parties and presents.

FRIDAY, DECEMBER 16th to WEDNESDAY, DECEMBER 21st
On Friday morning the Winter Raffle Draw was made followed, in the afternoon, by Christmas parties for the reception and nursery children, to which Father Christmas was of course invited to come and give each of the children a present. The day was marred by an underground pipe fracturing in the resources room, causing steam to rise from the floor. Only the previous Friday the wall separating the Nursery play area from the gardens in

Hillside Road had blown down requiring attention. Tuesday saw the carol service having to be held in the hall, as heavy rain had ruled out the walk to All Saints Church. In the afternoon the Parents' Association organised a disco for the children. Wednesday, the last day of term, and a performance of *Oliver* was put on by the children in the Blue Group – juniors in years 5 and 6. Unfortunately, very few parents showed up, which was a pity as the singing was particularly good. The school then closed for the holidays at 3.20p.m.

1984

TUESDAY, FEBRUARY 7th

Although a lot of work had been carried out at the school over the previous two years, it would appear that all was still not right. It was noted today that the general state of the building was poor, there being many minor repairs required. Furthermore, of the 37 toilets available for children's use, only 3 had a bolt on the door, a seat and a working flush. Mr Knipe believed that the local authority seemed unable to respond!

MONDAY, FEBRUARY 27th

The school was given its first computer, an R. M. L. 480 Z.

FRIDAY, MARCH 16th

It was felt rather a shame that the nursery kitchen should be forced to close today, with the loss of two kitchen staff.

SATURDAY, MARCH 17th

The school team qualified for the finals of the Sports Argus 4-a-side football tournament to be held at Wyndley Leisure Centre today. They reached the semi-final, but lost to the eventual winners, St Peter and St Paul.

FRIDAY, MARCH 30th

A special Mothers' Day assembly was held this morning. All mothers were invited and flowers were given to the 80 who attended.

FRIDAY, APRIL 13th

The last day of a long term. A musical play, *Will Wanderer's Win*, was performed by the older juniors; whilst the infants held their Easter Hat Parade, judged by the lollipop lady. Over the previous few months there had been discussions about the development of community activities at the school. There were now English classes for adults; youth-training-scheme classes; Holy Koran classes for Muslim children; a play centre; and a keep fit class with Bianca, which took place every Wednesday between 2.30 and 3.15 in the afternoon. Ideas for the future included meals for the elderly; a library; children's activities; adult education and social groups. Meanwhile, the Parents' Association had been extremely busy raising money for school funds. Altogether, about £240 had so far been raised. They were also opening a new and nearly-new shop at the school, which was to be open between nine and ten o'clock each morning,

WEDNESDAY, MAY 9th

Members of the N.U.T. held a one-day strike in support of the teachers' pay claim. Only three classes – Reception, Second-year juniors and Fourth-year juniors – were in school today.

MONDAY, MAY 21st

Mr Walpole, Miss Morris and Miss Johnson accompanied twenty-five children on a week's visit to the Maypool Youth Hostel in Devon. They returned at a quarter to four on Friday afternoon, having spent an enjoyable week there.

SATURDAY, JUNE 16th

The school entered a float, decorated as an Edwardian classroom, in the Erdington Carnival procession. A cake stall was also provided at the carnival in Rookery Park.

TUESDAY, JUNE 26th

At 3.30p.m. the first staff meeting of the term was held. This was the first one that it had been possible to hold, due to the industrial action of the N.U.T. and N.A.S./U.W.T. members. Mr Knipe hoped that there would be no further disruption on this score.

TUESDAY, JULY 10th

Eighteen children, accompanied by Mr Hill and Miss Staunton, set off for three nights' camping at Bell Heath; whilst children from the Red Group paid a visit to the Botanical Gardens. Only a few weeks earlier parents of children in the 2nd and 3rd years had been invited to join the camp at Bell Heath for an inclusive cost of £12, as the school had been unable to raise sufficient numbers for an intended visit to Nethercott in May of the following year. Children were expected to arrive at school at 9a.m. as usual and assemble in the hall with all their kit suitably packed, a waterproof being readily available. They then travelled by coach to Bell Heath. The milkman had been notified by the Field Study Centre of their visit and would drive up onto the football pitch each morning between 9 and 10, in order to sell them their daily milk and bread. Anything else that might be required could be obtained from the local shops, the nearest of which was a mile and a half away in Romsley. Rota and tent lists were drawn up and the children worked and played hard until it was time to return during the Friday afternoon.

THURSDAY, JULY 19th

The school cricket team became champions of Erdington, as well as winning the softball championship.

THURSDAY, SEPTEMBER 6th

27 new children were scheduled for admission, although not all of them turned up. Today was the Festival of Eid, resulting in many Muslim children – particularly the older ones – being absent.

MONDAY, OCTOBER 1st
At the start of the new term a group, calling themselves Action Sport, started organising a number of activities for parents and others in the community. As a special introductory offer all sessions were free until November, when a fee of 20p would be charged for each session. Already established was an outdoor Adventure Group, whilst a Self-Defence course for women was due to be added imminently. Their programme of events for the week was as follows:

Monday: 9.00–10.00 Badminton Coaching in the Playground Hall. 13.00–15.00 Indoor Bowls in the Community Hall.

Tuesday, Wednesday, Thursday and Friday: 9.00–9.40; 9.40–10.20; 11.00–11.40. Recreational Badminton with 40-minute slots available for booking in the Playground Hall.

Wednesday: 10.00–11.00 Get Fit for the over 50s in the Community Hall.

Thursday: 13.30–15.30 Darts, Bowls, Pool and Table Tennis for the unemployed and others in the Community Hall.

The school itself had an active Gymnastics club, whilst the Computer and Bird Watching clubs were planned to start up after half term.

FRIDAY, OCTOBER 5th
The boys and girls in the Junior department enjoyed a treat today, being shown the Walt Disney film *The Love Bug*.

SATURDAY, OCTOBER 13th
A party of twenty-five children travelled to Liverpool to watch Everton play Aston Villa. An opportunity was also afforded for the school football team to play a match against a school from there. This was part of the 'Matchmates' programme initiated by the Mayor of Stoke on Trent. Unfortunately, the Liverpool school, Gilmour, were too strong, winning easily by seven goals to nil.

WEDNESDAY, NOVEMBER 14th
Officers from the Road Safety Unit, together with employees of the West Bromwich Building Society, performed a play for pupils of the Junior classes on the subject of road safety.

FRIDAY, DECEMBER 14th
Simone Francis must have been especially pleased today as she had won first prize, an electronic organ, in the school's winter draw.

Photographs of the teaching staff c.1983/1984.

4 class photographs c.1984.

TUESDAY, DECEMBER 18th
Father Christmas paid the school a visit in the guise of Walter Talboys, an ex-pupil of the school.

THURSDAY, DECEMBER 20th
The last day before the school broke up for the Christmas holidays. To the immense pleasure of the children – who thoroughly enjoyed it – the staff put on the pantomime *Cinderella*.

1985
MONDAY and TUESDAY, JANUARY 21st and 22nd
All Junior and Infant classes were suspended, as every one of the toilets was frozen.

FRIDAY, FEBRUARY 8th
Discussions commenced concerning the possibility of opening a Neighbourhood Office on the site.

MONDAY to FRIDAY, FEBRUARY 11th to 15th
Due to heavy snow and appallingly low temperatures – the toilets were frozen once again! – the whole school, including the Nursery, closed for the week. Letters had to be sent out

to parents at the end of the week informing them that, in any case, the school would be closed for half term from the 16th to the 24th inclusive.

MONDAY, FEBRUARY 25th
Returning to school after the lengthy vacation, it was discovered that, in the meantime, someone had broken in and stolen the computer, monitor, tape and associated software supplied by the Education Department. It was recognised at the time that the computer could not be replaced for many months. However, the school was not to be downhearted, realising that its loss could not change Slade from being anything other than a good school. The quality of the school was the spirit of the people within and, as was said at the time: "You can't steal people's spirits."

FRIDAY, MARCH 29th
The last day of term before the school broke up for the Easter holidays. During the morning there was the usual Easter Bonnet Parade, followed by a 'Paint an Egg' competition. The day culminated in the afternoon with entertainment laid on in the form of a magician.

WEDNESDAY, APRIL 17th
In order to raise much-needed funds, a sponsored walk was held around Brookvale Park. The children did the walking, the teachers just watched!

THURSDAY, MAY 2nd
Three teachers, including Mr Knipe, accompanied 15 children on a Youth Hostel holiday to Dorset. The cost was £30 for four nights. Everyone returned safely the following Bank Holiday Monday.

FRIDAY, MAY 10th
The football season had finally come to an end with Slade emerging as runners up in the Erdington Junior Schools' Football League.

THURSDAY, JUNE 27th
A special Congratulations Assembly was held this morning, in order that all the work in connection with the children's Eid project could be displayed. Many of the school's Muslim children wore their Eid clothes for the occasion, which was attended by a large number of parents.

FRIDAY, JULY 19th
This year, the school cricket team had to be content with sharing the Erdington Schools' Cricket Championship with Pegasus J. and I. School of Castle Vale.

THURSDAY, SEPTEMBER 5th
12 '4 plus' children were admitted today. The other two-thirds of the intake would start on the following Monday and Tuesday.

MONDAY, SEPTEMBER 9th
Work on the Neighbourhood Office, which was to be situated in the block between the Junior Hall and the old Secondary Boys' School, commenced today.

TUESDAY, OCTOBER 22nd
A half-day strike by members of the N.U.T. meant that four classes were sent home after dinner.

MONDAY to FRIDAY, NOVEMBER 11th to 15th
'Road Safety Week'. Special attention was given to this subject, particularly where nursery and infant children were involved. On Wednesday the school showed a film on road safety to Asian parents, there being a particularly good attendance.

MONDAY, DECEMBER 2nd
Re-decoration work commenced, which included the Nursery office and staffroom, as well as the Head Teacher's and secretary's rooms.

MONDAY, DECEMBER 9th
38 pupils from three of the junior classes, accompanied by two teachers, spent the week at the Bell Heath Field Study Centre.

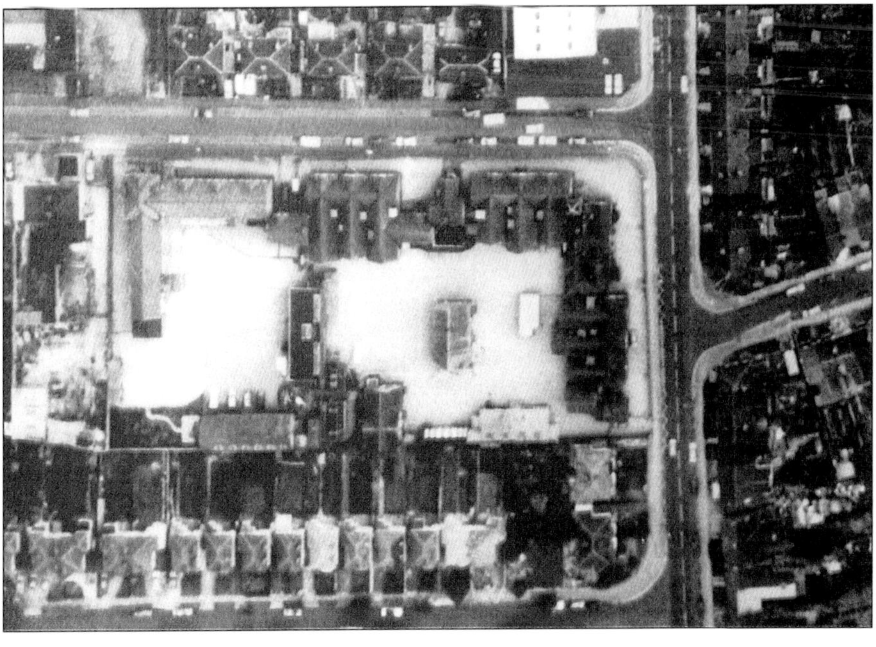

An overhead view of the school c.1980s. The school is bordered by Broomfield Road (top), Slade Road (right) and Hillside Road (bottom).

WEDNESDAY, DECEMBER 11th
The work on the new Neighbourhood Office was now completed and it opened to the public today.

1986

WEDNESDAY, FEBRUARY 5th
24 children went to a pantomime at the Alexandra Theatre.

FRIDAY, FEBRUARY 7th
The school closed for half term little realising that it would not open again for a further three weeks.

MONDAY, FEBRUARY 17th
In consequence of the toilets being frozen once again due to the extremely cold weather, the school was forced to remain closed following half term. A staff meeting was held during the morning.

WEDNESDAY, FEBRUARY 19th
A second staff meeting took place to discuss Music and Science. In the meantime all the staff were in attendance working on a variety of projects aimed at improving the school environment.

FRIDAY, FEBRUARY 21st
Plumbers had by now repaired all the burst pipes and, although the weather was cold, it was hoped to open on the following Monday.

MONDAY, FEBRUARY 24th
Further low temperatures resulted in all the toilets freezing once again! Consequently, the school remained closed.

WEDNESDAY, FEBRUARY 26th
Although the school was closed to pupils, a Parents' Day was held. Not surprisingly, there was a poor turnout. Portable heaters, fuelled by propane gas, had now been installed in the toilets in order to thaw them out. Unfortunately, one of them leaked and caught fire, resulting in one toilet door and the roof of the Infant toilets being damaged. The fire brigade had to be called out to extinguish the blaze, the water used turning the playground into a skating rink!

MONDAY, MARCH 3rd
At last the weather had shown an improvement and the school was able to re-open, the heaters appearing to do their job.

TUESDAY, JUNE 3rd
The first evening staff meeting for over twelve months was held. Their absence was due entirely to the industrial dispute over teachers' pay and conditions.

MONDAY, JUNE 16th
On January 14th of this year Mr Knipe had attended a meeting at the Education Department to discuss toilet provision. At last – and some would say long overdue! – work commenced on the new indoor toilets.

THURSDAY, JUNE 19th
A Parents' Evening – the first for over a year – was held. Industrial action had made it impossible for these worthwhile occasions to take place. The evening was well attended by parents.

TUESDAY, JUNE 24th
During the year the pupils had been corresponding with pupils from St Francis School, Bournville. Today, 30 infants and 40 third and fourth-year juniors, accompanied by their teachers, came to meet their Slade penpals.

WEDNESDAY, JUNE 25th
With two teachers and a former pupil in attendance, 20 children went off for a five-day Youth Hostelling holiday at Harlech. They all returned safely on the Sunday.

WEDNESDAY and THURSDAY, JULY 2nd and 3rd
A return visit was paid by the infants and juniors to St Francis School in Bournville to meet up again with their penpals.

FRIDAY, JULY 18th
The last day of the school year concluded with a Staff versus Pupils rounders match.

TUESDAY, SEPTEMBER 30th
Work on the new indoor toilets was at last finished, after a long, hard-fought battle had been waged to obtain this necessary provision. They were attractively finished and now the children had to play their part in maintaining their appearance. All in all the school looked splendid, reflecting the commitment of many of the staff and its pupils.

THURSDAY, OCTOBER 2nd
A meeting was called during the afternoon for all parents to attend, in order to discuss ways in which the school and parents could aid children's learning. 32 families were represented.

WEDNESDAY, OCTOBER 15th
An Autumn Fair was held this afternoon to raise funds towards the cost of Christmas presents for the children. A sum just in excess of £100 was collected.

MONDAY, NOVEMBER 3rd
Re-opening after half term the first School Council meeting was held in the afternoon. The Council consisted of 10 elected pupils who gave consideration to the many aspects and issues of school life which directly concerned them.

FRIDAY, DECEMBER 12th
The customary Winter Draw took place this morning. It had raised £150 towards Christmas activities.

THURSDAY, DECEMBER 18th
What a shock! During the morning, the school received a warning that there was a bomb on the premises. The police were called and it was discovered that a neighbouring school in the area had received a similar call. Fortunately, it was only a hoax and didn't spoil the Christmas festivities. The infants were able to perform *Little Red Riding Hood* for the parents and the rest of the children: whilst the 'bomb scare' didn't deter Father Christmas from paying a flying visit to give every child a present.

Daisy Darby, photographed with Blue 2, in the same position that her class was photographed 82 years earlier – see 1905 photograph (she is the girl who is moving).

1987

WEDNESDAY, JANUARY 14th

With a very heavy fall of snow taking place, many schools closed at midday, although Slade remained open until 3.20p.m. As more heavy falls were forecast, however, it was decided to close down until the following Monday.

THURSDAY, MARCH 19th

Members of the N.U.T. and N.A.S./U.W.T. staged a half-day strike in protest against the loss of negotiating rights. Six teachers were absent, the rest of the school working normally.

TUESDAY, APRIL 7th

The results of the opinion polls concerning school uniform were published by Mr Knipe today. 69% of teachers were for school uniform, whilst – maybe surprisingly – 64% of the pupils were in favour. It now rested on a meeting to take place on May 12th, when the parents would be given the final say.

MONDAY, APRIL 13th

Mr Knipe, two teachers, and 27 children visited the Sharpness Centre, where they spent an enjoyable four days.

THURSDAY, APRIL 16th

The school closed today for the Easter holidays. The House competitions were still going strong, although the names had changed, reverting to ones that had been used in earlier years. The Eagles led with 2, 132 points, whilst the Falcons and Hawks pecked at their heels with 2, 094 and 2, 036 points respectively. Equally, the annual Easter Hat Parade along Slade Road was still something to be looked forward to with the parade starting from the school at 11.00a.m.

TUESDAY, MAY 12th

Approximately 40 parents turned up to the meeting called to discuss the issue of school uniform. Following a fashion parade, Mr Knipe gave a talk on the subject. As most of the parents were in favour, a group was chosen to consider the type, colour and cost.

THURSDAY, MAY 14th

As part of the Canalcade Festival children from two classes visited the canal and Science Museum. One lad somehow managed to fall in, but was able to climb out easily. Dry clothes had to be taken to the museum and an anti-tetanus injection given. However, he appeared none the worse for his experience.

MONDAY, JUNE 1st

The school retained the Erdington Junior Schools' six-a-side cricket trophy, winning all their three matches, which took place against Court Farm, Pegasus and Birches Green. Only five overs were permitted in each game and, on each occasion, Slade passed the opposition's total for the loss of only one wicket.

WEDNESDAY, JUNE 24th

Accompanied by two teachers, a former pupil, and a parent, a group of 24 children commenced a Youth Hostel trip to West Wales. Despite rather poor weather everyone seemed to enjoy the holiday. The sea trip to Skomer turned out to be the sunniest day, when most managed a few minutes in the sea. The party returned safely on the Sunday.

WEDNESDAY, JULY 8th

In the Erdington Junior Schools' hardball cricket knockout final, the school put behind them any disappointment following their failure to win through to the final of the Warwickshire Softball Cricket Competition, which had taken place at Edgbaston. Against Birches Green, they were on top throughout. Put in to bat, Birches Green were soon struggling for runs, a workmanlike performance by the Slade bowlers having them all back in the pavilion for 31. Majid Aziz, the captain, and Shahad Fazal were hardly troubled by the bowlers and, except for an unfortunate run out, would undoubtedly have knocked the runs off easily. As it was, Rahim Abdul came in to finish off the job, Slade scoring 33 runs for the loss of one wicket and winning the cup for the second year in succession.

WEDNESDAY, JULY 15th

A family evening produced an excellent turnout of parents – around 80% made the effort – during which the new uniform was on display.

FRIDAY, NOVEMBER 13th

Not a very good day today! Two fourth-year pupils failed to attend school this morning, choosing to go shoplifting instead. Although the police were involved, the children were fortunate that no prosecution took place.

1988

SATURDAY, JANUARY 23rd

Daniel Douglas competed at the Birmingham table tennis finals. His first matches were against pupils who attended a primary school in Northfield. After some anxious moments, he came through unscathed to reach the semi-finals. He, then, had to win a hard-fought game against someone from his own table tennis club in order to reach the final. Having succeeded, the final was something of an anti-climax with Daniel easily emerging as the victor.

MONDAY, JANUARY 25th

The School Council held its second meeting of the year at 2.45p.m. On the agenda for discussion were the following points:

1) A School Bag. 2) A School Bank. 3) Urgent repairs to the 4th-year stockroom, a sink for the 4th years and the removal of the Infant toilets. 4) It would be a good idea if, when voting for members of the School Council, Asian children voted for English children and they voted for Asians.

FRIDAY, FEBRUARY 5th
In aid of Comic Relief, several fund-raising events were staged, resulting in £23.46 being raised.

MONDAY, FEBRUARY 15th
On a mild and sunny day, the school was treated to a glimpse of H.R.H. Princess Diana when she visited the Slade Road Drug Centre. The children assembled on the roadside to wave, several parents and staff being given the opportunity to shake hands with her.

MONDAY, JULY 18th
24 pupils, 2 staff, 2 parents and one helper set off for a Youth Hostel holiday at Penmaenmaior. They returned safely on the 22nd, the final day of term, Mr Knipe having joined them two days earlier.

THURSDAY, SEPTEMBER 22nd
The 'School Olympics' were held this afternoon. Many parents attended, more than 100 gold, silver and bronze medals being awarded.

MONDAY, OCTOBER 3rd
A sponsored 'Marathon of Marathons' was held in Brookvale Park. The intention was for the children to attempt 26 laps of the park. In the end, some actually managed 8 laps, whilst others struggled to complete one.

THURSDAY, NOVEMBER 17th
Interviews were held this morning for the vacancy of caretaker which had now arisen. Ken Stanton was appointed. He started his duties the following year on Monday, January 30th.

Princess Diana Visit, 1988.

1989

MONDAY, JANUARY 9th

On the day that the school opened for the start of a new term, 30 pupils accompanied by two teachers set off for a week at Bell Heath Field Study Centre.

MONDAY, JANUARY 23rd

Kate Bachelor commenced her duties as organiser of Homestart.

FRIDAY, MARCH 10th

Many fund-raising activities took place, this being Red Nose Day. £188.74 was collected.

THURSDAY, MARCH 23rd

Earlier in the day, before the school closed for the Easter holidays at 2p.m., the infants paraded their hats up and down Slade Road. There then followed an egg-rolling competition down the playground whilst, in the hall, egg decorating and mobile competitions were judged.

THURSDAY, MAY 25th

A most successful fire practice with the school cleared in less than two minutes.

THURSDAY, JUNE 15th

Due to the European elections, the school closed for the day as it was being used as a polling station. That is, all but for the Nursery, which worked normally. However, a number of educational visits were arranged to coincide with the event. The Blue group went to Sutton Park, the Yellow group visited Smestow Water Mill, whilst the Red group spent the day at home.

SATURDAY, JULY 8th

The Centenary Street Party was held in the afternoon. Unfortunately, the weather forced everyone, including the 150 children who turned up, into the hall. The success of the event owed much to the unstinting efforts of a nucleus of parents who had spent several weeks making the arrangements.

WEDNESDAY, SEPTEMBER 13th

The official launch of 'Homestart' in Birmingham of which Stockland Green Homestart was the 100th such national scheme. Homestart is a registered charity which supports pre-school children in their own home. They also run family-group sessions. Margaret Harrison, who initiated the concept, and Mr Knipe addressed the meeting, whilst the Lord Mayor, Councillor Fred Chapman, added his weight to the proceedings.

FRIDAY, OCTOBER 20th

36 children and 4 staff – Mr Knipe, Miss Duckles, Mr Walpole and Miss Carter – went away for a week at Nethercott, a working farm in Devon, run by the children's author Michael

Nethercott, 1989.

Morpurgo. A film, directed by Terry Steele of Central Television with Joanna Lumley as narrator, recorded the event, which was sponsored by B. P. Up at 7a.m., the children found themselves feeding and mucking out the various animals before breakfast. Then, it was more work until midday, when they spent half an hour in the classroom before dinner. Besides the outdoor tasks, they found themselves laying tables and cleaning rooms, although some free time was allotted each day. Before bedtime, Michael Morpurgo would read them a story – once, it was one he hadn't even finished writing. At different times of the week they found themselves being filmed by the camera crew until, at last, it was time for them to return home – a journey that took eight and a half hours on the coach. They arrived back safely as the school closed for half term.

MONDAY and WEDNESDAY, NOVEMBER 6th and 8th
Filming for the 'Nethercott' video continued with shots being taken at school. They proved to be more involved than anticipated, but it was the end result that counted.

WEDNESDAY, NOVEMBER 22nd
A number of children took time out to visit the Central Television studios, in order to record the theme music for the 'Nethercott' video.

1990
THURSDAY, JANUARY 11th
This evening, the Nethercott film 'A week, a world, a way' was shown to parents. It was exceptionally well made and credit for its success must not only go to the children of the school, but to Farms for City Children.

FRIDAY, MARCH 23rd
A special assembly was held this afternoon to celebrate Pakistan Independence Day.

TUESDAY, MARCH 27th
A representative group of 10 children accompanied Mr Knipe and Miss Carter to London. The purpose was the official launch of 'A week, a world, a way' held at Britannic House.

MONDAY, APRIL 30th
During the afternoon an Eid party was held for all parents and children. There was an excellent response from the mothers of Muslim children at the school who prepared all the food.

TUESDAY, JUNE 5th
The school hosted the filming of the Late Show for B.B.C.2. The programme considered the re-designing of Spaghetti Junction which came of age this year.

MONDAY, JULY 2nd
This evening, the Governors held a special meeting to consider the suspension of a pupil, whose behaviour had become so disruptive that the learning opportunities for other children were most seriously affected. The Governors decided upon a permanent exclusion, the first one for well over ten years. Eleven days later, the Education Department upheld the exclusion order of the ten-year-old.

TUESDAY, SEPTEMBER 4th
The start of a new term and with it a subtle change. During the Autumn term, Mr Knipe, the Head Teacher, and Mr Hill, his Deputy, would exchange roles.

TUESDAY, SEPTEMBER 25th
The children made Tetra-tetra flexagons as part of a city-wide Maths Roadshow. It was hoped that the efforts of many Birmingham schools would ensure an entry in the Guinness Book of Records.

Left: Mrs Greasley with Yellow 2. Right: Mr Hill (left) and Mr Knipe (right) with Blue 6.

1991

THURSDAY, JANUARY 17th

A representative from 'services finance' visited the school to discuss the budget. It would appear that there was an underspend of approximately £16,000, mainly in respect of the cover budget. The school was authorised to spend the money on equipment, tools and materials, enabling them to obtain much needed resources.

FRIDAY, FEBRUARY 8th

Due to a heavy fall of snow, the school was forced to close for the day.

TUESDAY, FEBRUARY 12th

Pupils from years 5 and 6 went skiing at the Ackers. There was real snow on the artificial slope!

FRIDAY, MARCH 22nd

Mr Knipe, Mr Hill and three other adults took 38 pupils for a week's visit to Treginnis, a working farm in west Wales. They returned on the following Thursday just in time for the Easter holiday.

MONDAY, MAY 20th

The demolition of the old project block (woodwork room) commenced.

TUESDAY and WEDNESDAY, JUNE 4th and 5th

Members of the Royal Ballet visited for the first time to work with pupils from the Red, Yellow and Blue groups.

Monday, April 29th, and the infants are working hard in the Red Group.

THURSDAY, JUNE 20th
A detailed survey of the building took place, so that a full report could be compiled prior to the school receiving a full delegated budget in April 1992.

MONDAY, JUNE 24th
Some of the older juniors enjoyed a day out at the Outdoor Education Centre, where the activities included campcraft and the climbing wall.

WEDNESDAY, JULY 3rd
Accompanied by teachers and parents, the younger juniors went for a day out at Barry Island.

MONDAY, SEPTEMBER 2nd
The new school year began with a School Conference, to which all employees, governors and representatives from the community were invited. Mr Knipe gave a talk entitled '1992 and all that' intended to outline the consequences of a delegated budget and pupil admissions.

TUESDAY, OCTOBER 15th
As part of the Birmingham Education Festival, pupils from Blue 6 took part in a Maths Orienteering Competition at Cannon Hill Park.

FRIDAY, OCTOBER 25th
The previous half term had been a particularly difficult one with all the improvements taking place to the building. All four of the boilers were being replaced, this work now nearing completion. A section of roof was also in need of replacement and, as a consequence, four classes had been displaced and a section of the playground cordoned off. It would be late November before the work was completed; and it was then planned for the exterior paintwork to be renewed.

FRIDAY, NOVEMBER 29th
The re-roofing was now complete. However, due to the extensive dust and dirt caused by the exercise, the school closed for the day, so that thorough cleaning could take place.

1992

THURSDAY, FEBRUARY 20th
Mr Knipe attended a second interview for the position of Head Teacher at a new school in Aston for which he learnt that he had been successful. He would leave at the end of the current term.

TUESDAY, APRIL 7th
A special assembly was held this morning, the last but one day of term, to say farewell to Mr Andy Knipe. He was presented with a cordless telephone by children and their parents. Later in the day, he was to attend the opening of his new school – to be known as Mansfield

Green – by the Duchess of Gloucester. In the evening, a party was organised by the staff at which he was presented with a camping fridge as a farewell present. In his last comments, he was obviously pleased and excited at the prospect of his new challenge, but still held a feeling of commitment to Slade, which he regarded as a very challenging and exciting school to work in. He considered that we had all strived collectively to build relationships, which were founded on respect and regard for each other. The children, he thought, had always been friendly, often needy, sometimes naughty and rarely calm, the various ethnic groups within the school adding to the task. However, he thanked everyone sincerely and wished them all the best in their collective pursuit of achievement.

MONDAY, APRIL 27th
A new term and, in the interim, Mr Andy Hill would act as Head with Miss Sheila Staunton his Deputy, until the vacant Headship had been filled.

FRIDAY, MAY 1st
The recently formed 'Staff Band' played together for the first time in assembly this morning. This certainly surprised and intrigued the children, who clapped spontaneously and appreciatively at the performance.

THURSDAY, JUNE 11th
The Head of Bournville Infants accepted an offer from the school of £50 for 16 double desks and 32 chairs.

TUESDAY, JUNE 23rd
350 children and parents had a wonderful day out at Barry Island. Andy Knipe took the day off from Mansfield Green especially to be with everyone.

MONDAY, JUNE 29th
A short list of candidates attended for their second interviews for the position of Headship at the school. It was learnt that Andy Sewell from Springfield was to be appointed, though he wouldn't start until January 1993.

THURSDAY, JULY 2nd
The annual Parents' Meeting proved lively with several issues being raised for debate. These included homework, the induction of reception children, and the need for the school to communicate more in community languages other than English. Because the meeting went on longer than anticipated, there was little time left, following the closure, for the parents to go and view their children's work.

SATURDAY, JULY 4th
The Parents' Association was now known as the 'Friends of Slade', and as such had organised a Car Boot Sale/Summer Fayre. Despite the complexity of the arrangements, it had been

extremely well organised. Unfortunately, they didn't have any control over the weather, heavy rain resulting in the event finishing early.

MONDAY, JULY 6th
From today until Thursday, a mixed group of 32 children from years 3, 4 and 5 camped out at the Stables. The weather was very kind, enabling them to swim and play games in both the daylight hours as well as after dark. During their time there, they were able to spend a day out at the Avoncroft Buildings Museum.

WEDNESDAY, SEPTEMBER 2nd
Today was to have been a teacher day. This had had to be cancelled, however, following an inspection of the school premises a few days earlier. Decorating had only just been concluded and the clean-up during the summer holiday had been disrupted due to staffing problems. As such, it was felt that opening after the holiday should be delayed until the following Monday. The staff were asked to help with the cleaning, which they ably did until it was completed on Friday morning.

FRIDAY, OCTOBER 16th
34 children went off to spend a week at Nethercott, together with four members of the teaching staff. Over the previous three weeks it had been necessary to organise some sponsored events, such as a swim and a walk, in order to raise much-needed extra funds. The children got to know the people on the farm, helping out with various chores, such as mucking out. They learnt how to use the milking apparatus and generally discovered what life on a farm was like. They had to clean up after themselves and be in bed by 9.30p.m., which might not have suited all of them, as it was hard to get to sleep because of the noise at times. The party returned at 5.30p.m. the following Wednesday, two hours after the school had broken up for half term.

WEDNESDAY, DECEMBER 9th
The Christmas concert played to an overfull house, but still managed to finish on time, as all the acts kept to their planned routines. The piano had been specially tuned, at a cost of £22, only two weeks earlier. The audience seemed to really enjoy themselves as did the children. To help out, the Friends of Slade had organised a crêche, so that the parents could thoroughly relax.

FRIDAY, DECEMBER 18th
During the morning session, Father Christmas paid a surprise visit to the school. He bore a striking resemblance to Mr Andy Knipe, particularly when asked to confirm that his favourite football team was West Bromwich Albion.

1993

MONDAY, FEBRUARY 1st
30 children from the Yellow Group (Year 4) spent the week, accompanied by three teaching staff, at the Bell Heath Environmental Study Centre near Worcester.

Considering the staff at the study centre were all ill, everyone coped very well, a fine time being had by all. The children spent a day out at Worcester looking at places of historical interest, besides going fishing, when they saw stickle backs, water scorpions and water snails, as well as fish. They went on a picnic, to a disco and played bingo during their spare time.

WEDNESDAY, MARCH 31st

During the football season the school succeeded in winning most of the trophies on offer in the Erdington Junior Schools' Football League. They won the Villa Cup going undefeated in their four matches, the Midweek League, the H.M.S. Progress Shield – they lost in the semi-final of the competition proper going out 7–6 on penalties – and the Perry Common Saturday League, where they finished with a record of W. 10 D. 2 L. 1 scoring 58 goals to their opponents 24. They also took the 6-a-side cup and the 4-a-side cup, in the latter progressing, by winning the Birmingham competition to the Midlands finals in West Bromwich, where they were the outstanding team on the first semi-final night. However, they were unable to sustain their form the following day and bowed out. Four boys played for Erdington whilst three turned out for Birmingham.

JUNE

For the first time the Erdington Junior Schools' area sports meeting was held at Wyndley Leisure Centre. Due to wins in three of the 90-metre sprints, the boys' and girls' 600 metres, the boys' throwing and the 100-metre boys' relay, the school was able to finish the day as joint winners with Marsh Hill.

Eloise Harvey wins the girls' 600 metres.

FRIDAY, JULY 16th
Today, by defeating St. Mary and John, the school became Erdington Junior Schools' cricket champions, going undefeated all season. In their first game, they had scored 55 runs dismissing the Abbey for a paltry 9. A tougher match followed against St. Peter and Paul, the school making 60 runs before bowling them all out for 38. Further wins against Birches Green and Pegasus set up the triumph.

TUESDAY, AUGUST 31st
Miss Sheila Staunton retired, aged 51, having spent 28 years at the school. Educated in Ledbury, she spent two years at Aston Hall School before joining Slade School on September lst, 1965.

SEPTEMBER
The children returned after the summer break to find that the stockroom at the bottom of the playground had disappeared in the interim. The infant hall had already been demolished earlier to leave the playground looking bigger than ever.

DECEMBER
For a period of eight weeks the new library had to be used as a classroom, as the Infant department were having a new roof installed. Everyone needed to take great care to keep away from the area, both at the front and rear of the building.

1994

Early in the year and an overhead shot of the school. The hall and the stockroom are no longer there, but the outside toilets bordering the near wall between the year 5/6 and year 6 classrooms can still be seen.

A view of the library taken three years later.

FEBRUARY
Friends of Slade contributed towards a display cabinet which was placed in the entrance hall where the school could proudly display their trophies.

FRIDAY, MARCH 4th
Michael Morpurgo visited the school today in order to officially open the new library Whilst there he read one of his stories to the children entitled *The White Stag.*

MONDAY, MARCH 21st
Over the previous few weeks the children had been collecting for the N.S.P.C.C. A total of £733.09 was handed over today.

MONDAY, JULY 4th
Celebrations were held today to commemorate the school's ninetieth birthday During the morning, every class put on a play with themes based on different decades of the twentieth century. Blue 6 started the proceedings off with an item based on an interview with Daisy Darby – she was an ex-pupil of the school who had started on its opening day – quickly followed by Blue 5/6 and Blue 5, whose plays were about the First World War and General Strike respectively. Gradually moving down the school class by class the items approached the current day, until the nursery concluded with their Robot Dance. Everything was repeated the following day in order to enable as many people to see it as possible. Mr Sewell and Mr Hill were dressed in long smocks with felt-tipped lines for moustaches. All the children thought they looked very funny! A number of ex-pupils came along, the older

juniors showing them around and talking to them about how the school had changed. The afternoon arrived and with it a fair in the top playground. On offer were bouncy castles, balloons, juggling and refreshments, whilst in the Community Rooms computer games and snooker were all the rage. Finally, the day was over and the school had to go back to the more mundane but important tasks of teaching and learning.

1995

FRIDAY, MARCH 31st to FRIDAY, APRIL 7th

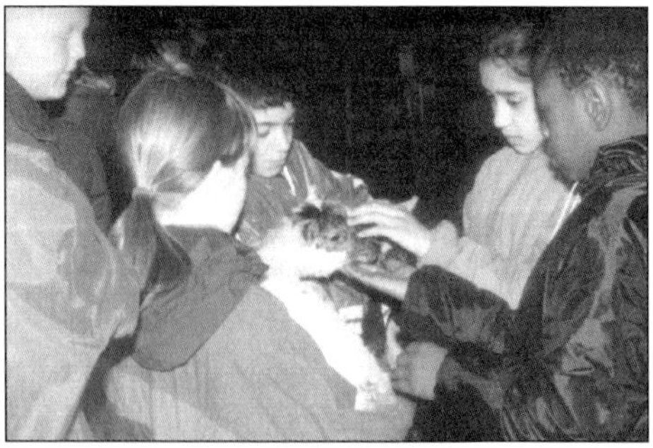

A visit to Treginnis Farm.

JULY

The cricket team played very well winning the Erdington Junior Schools' Softball League, in the process getting through to play at Edgbaston, where, unfortunately, they lost all their three games. In the Erdington Junior Schools' Hardball League, the school won the championship.

DECEMBER

Afza Hussain and Sadia Mahmood organised a collection of cards for the Blue Peter appeal. Posters were put up around the school and the collection went on for a period of three months.

1996

MONDAY, FEBRUARY 26th to FRIDAY, MARCH 1st

Energy Conservation Week, and the whole of the school were learning not just how to save it, but conducting experiments as well. The temperatures were checked in different parts of all the classrooms. In Blue 5/6 a chart was even drawn up to show where all the heat went. Some classes made water wheels, whilst another experimented with the harnessing of solar energy as a means of investigating sources of renewable energy. Others made sure that all the taps and lights were turned off. Meanwhile, the infants were baking carrot cakes to find out which was the most efficient method of making them. The children of Blue 5 chose to look at the burning of fuels and the transference of energy, conducting a variety of experiments to understand what took place. It was hoped that the message of saving would be remembered in years to come.

SLADE NEWS

March 1996 | Spring Edition

ENERGY SPECIAL

SLADE SCHOOL'S ENERGY CONSERVATION WEEK

FULL DETAILS INSIDE

Slade School have been learning about energy. We have just had an energy conservation week. All the classes have being doing experiments and learning how to save energy for future generations. The younger children have been cooking and looking out for energy being wasted.

Special Visitors

We have had special visitors coming into school. Mrs Blundy from the M.E.B has been to every class to tell them about electrical energy. Mr Postins, Energy Officer for the City of Birmingham took an assembly about energy saving. Mrs Fenoughty from City Support Services and Mrs Barham from ESSO brought in work packs and sheets for us to use.

DON'T LEAVE THE WINDOWS OPEN

Save Energy At School .... Save Energy At Home .... Save Money .... Save Our Environment

Slade News Frontispiece, 1996.

Top Left: Eyam, 1996. Top Right: Spring and Norman Goodwin, Stationmaster, looks after Mrs Hartley (right) and her class of children as they wait to board the train. Bottom: Sutton Park Aeroplane Crash, 1997.

THURSDAY, MARCH 7th

Today, the older juniors of the Blue Group went out for the day by coach to Eyam, a place struck down by the plague in 1664. They walked round the village where they saw many interesting artifacts. There was an oven for roasting sheep and a stone water trough for people to wash in; then they went through a number of fields and two kissing gates to have their lunch. Subsequently, they visited the church where some of the children prayed before most of them stopped at the shop to buy souvenirs, until it became time to return back to school on the coach.

FRIDAY, JUNE 28th

A major police incident in Sutton Park! An aeroplane crashes and the school, together with schools from other areas, help the police and rescue services to tackle it!

OCTOBER

Nethercott Farm in Devon was invaded once again by children from Slade School. On this occasion 36 of them spent an enjoyable but tiring time at the farm. Everyone had to be up before dawn in time to start the first job of the day at 7.30a.m. – before they'd even had breakfast! One of the main jobs was to clean the dairy – this meant sweeping up the cows' muck and it smelt! Day jobs included feeding the animals and moving the sheep between the fields. The last job of the day was after tea, but there were lots of breaks. There were two walks, one around the farm and the other to the village of Haverleigh. Unfortunately, on one occasion, one of the lads even managed to fall into the River Torridge. The farmhouse itself is rather old, but large and comfortable with polished oak stairs and a wood-panelled dining room. There were nine dormitories in which the children slept; three other rooms were provided, one for reading and resting, another for games and the last for changing into wellingtons. At the end of the week, the children had to say their sad goodbyes.

1997

A last look and a farewell to the Community Centre which was originally used by the Secondary Boys' School for classrooms.

THURSDAY, JANUARY 16th

The 37-seater coach driven by Mr Walpole, a teacher at the school, broke down for the second time in six days. On the first occasion it was coming back from cricket coaching at Edgbaston; on the second from the Buddhist Centre. The coach, previously used by the navy, was built in 1978. It was purchased for £4,500 by the Cherry Orchard Boys' Club – a youth club run by Mr Walpole initially on school premises – about nine years earlier. It was frequently used to ferry children to various events as Mr Walpole was a qualified bus driver. It would appear that someone had put water and soil in the fuel tank; even a firework was found! It cost £600 to repair, money that could have been spent more judiciously elsewhere.

TUESDAY, MARCH 25th

The end of the Easter term had arrived and with it the annual Infants' Easter Hat Parade, which took the same form as in previous years with the children parading their hats up and down Slade Road. They were escorted as far as Hunton Hill, where they made their way over the pedestrian crossing, returning on the other side, before recrossing at the lights opposite the school. Some children had made their hats at home whilst the remainder were fashioned in the classroom. Once morning break was over it was now the turn of the juniors to have their fun, which took the form of an egg-rolling competition. All the children brought a chair out to sit on, forming an inverted V up the playground. This was definitely one 'sport' where a sloping playground helped!

Easter Hat Parade. Egg Rolling, 1997.

MARCH
The school's football season ended with some success. They finished as runners up in the Perry Common Saturday League, just being overtaken for the title at the death. However, the girls fared even better. In the finals of the 4-a-side competition, contested indoors at Kingsbury School, they drew 1–1 with both of the other schools, not enough to secure them the title, unfortunately; but in the girls' 6-a-side competition – played on the Yenton Playing Fields – it was a different matter! In their three games they never conceded a goal! Wins of 5–0 against St. Gerards, 3–0 over Chivenor and 2–0 against Abbey gave them the title.

APRIL
Mr Robert Walpole, although only in his fifties, chose to retire early, having completed twenty-seven years of service with the school. He would, however, continue to work at the school over the following years as a supply teacher. He has also continued to place the coach at the service of the school, as well as being involved in the sports activities of the Erdington Primary Schools' Sports Association.

THURSDAY, JUNE 19th
The annual athletic sports of the Erdington Primary Schools were held at the Wyndley Leisure Centre in Sutton Coldfield this afternoon. The school performed extremely well winning not only the small schools' championship but the overall competition as well.

FRIDAY, JULY 4th
The summer fair raised over £500.

WEDNESDAY, JULY 23rd
The last day of the school year and two more long-standing members of staff departed – secretary, Mrs Iris Glasby, after 25 years, and Mrs Enid Greasley, a teacher, after thirty.

SUNDAY to WEDNESDAY, OCTOBER 12th to 15th
An outdoor education trip to the Kingswood Centre once again for a number of the children from the Blue Group. There were numerous activities which included Quad Bikes – small four-wheeled motorbikes; Aeroball – a game for up to four people which involved bouncing on a trampoline whilst trying to throw a ball into your opponent's net; and Archery. What, with snorkelling, climbing, go-karts and an outdoor initiative test, there was certainly a lot to do. Fuelled with egg, bacon, beans and chips, the children were involved with a project in the Computer Room – after they'd cleaned all the mud off themselves from outside, of course! All in all they had a thoroughly good time.

WEDNESDAY, DECEMBER 17th
Santa sledged around Slade this evening. A number of children, under the guidance of family, friends and helpers made their way around the local streets in the area raising money, a total of £246.96 being collected and shared between the school and the Rotary

Left: Santa Sledges around Slade, 1997. Right: Ofsted Team, 1998.

Club of Erdington, who had assisted with the provision of their sleigh. One lady from Marsh Lane gave them £5 for especially going out of their way to pay a visit to her house.

1998

MONDAY to FRIDAY, FEBRUARY 9th to 13th

It was a thumbs up when the school enjoyed a visit from the Ofsted inspection team – pictured above – this week. The school was considered to have many strengths and few weaknesses, the pupils having good attitudes to work and responding well during lessons. The teachers were generally praised for their teaching, the school being considered 'good value for money'.

MARCH

The girls' six-a-side football team had some success when they won the Erdington Primary Schools' championship going undefeated whilst maintaining a clean scoresheet throughout. They went on to play in the West Midlands competition at Wolverhampton, but failed to make the semi-finals winning only one of their four matches.

Girls' six-a-side.

FRIDAY, MAY 8th

Over the previous few weeks the children had been collecting for the N.S.P.C.C. Today, a total of £810 was handed over.

School football XI.

THURSDAY, MAY 21st

Some weeks earlier in April major work had started on building a new sewer across Erdington. As such, children were told that they must cross Slade Road by the pelican crossing outside the school and back again at the temporary lights on the other side of A.T.S., because of the work going on at the corner of Broomfield Road. In order that parents could have more information about the impact, a consultation was arranged to take place at the school with staff from Severn Trent, who would be displaying maps and photographs showing the extent of the work. A competition was organised to give a name to the giant tunnelling machine that would cut through the ground and, today, near Brookvale Park, ten-year-old Zakia Zaman unveiled 'Slade the Blade'. She also won a family ticket to the Sea Life Centre besides securing a conservation area for the school.

Slade the Blade, 1998.

THURSDAY and FRIDAY, JULY 9th and 10th

The Life Education Caravan visited the school, as it would do for years to come, locating in Broomfield Road. Children were given the opportunity to learn about healthy lifestyles in this special multi-media resource.

Concert – Empire and the Nightingale, 1998.

THURSDAY, JULY 16th
Prizegiving this evening during which the older juniors performed *The Emperor and the Nightingale.*

WEDNESDAY, JULY 22nd
The school closed for the summer holidays at 2p.m. Congratulations were in order for the cricket team had won the Erdington Primary Schools' cricket league.

THURSDAY, SEPTEMBER 3rd
Another school year commenced. For the previous twelve months the school had been involved in the National Numeracy Project with the aim of developing the children's mathematical skills. At the start in 1997 the children in Years 1, 2 and 4 had been tested. A year later and they were tested again. The result was an average 10% gain. Now, they were looking forward to starting the Literacy Strategy.

Arts Week, 1998.

Pizza Express, 1998.

MONDAY to FRIDAY, OCTOBER 19th to 23rd
As part of the Birmingham Year of the Arts, an 'Arts Week' was held with the theme of celebrations. Opportunities were given to take part in a variety of creative-arts activities, which included Asian and African dance and music.

THURSDAY, DECEMBER 3rd
As part of Design and Technology, classes from the Blue Group visited Pizza Express in Sutton Coldfield in order to learn how to make pizzas. Having studied the experts they returned to school where they designed and made their own pizzas and packaging.

THURSDAY, DECEMBER 17th

Christmas Assembly.

Nursery Christmas Concert, 1998.

FRIDAY, DECEMBER 18th
Now it was the turn of the nursery and reception to get in on the act performing their own versions of Christmas – the Nursery with the Nativity (above); and Reception with a more up-to-date look at Christmas.

TUESDAY, DECEMBER 22nd
The school broke up at 2p.m. for the Christmas vacation. Instead of sending each other Christmas cards, the staff had decided to save up the money that they would otherwise have spent and give it to charity. £52 was forwarded on to the Birmingham City Mission.

1999
THURSDAY, JANUARY 7th
School re-opened after the break. Tokens were available with Walkers Crisps, the Sun and the Sunday Times whereby free books could be obtained for schools. Parents and children were encouraged to save these so that as many free books as possible could be obtained.

FRIDAY, JANUARY 22nd
Class parties were held during the afternoon to celebrate the Muslim festival of Eid.

FRIDAY, JULY 2nd
At the Summer Fair held this afternoon the school raised £733.77.

SEPTEMBER
Back in January, the school started out with the intention of collecting 10,000 tokens in their effort to obtain free books for the school. By the closing date they had collected an

amazing 37,000 which meant that they received 100 free books for their efforts. Two classes – B6 and Y3/4 – shared a day out at Cannon Hill Park in recognition of there having collected the most tokens of any of the classes. Now, the children were being encouraged to collect Nestle tokens as every one was worth 10p. This would be put towards the purchase of PE, music and computer equipment.

The school was also proud to learn that they had achieved record results in the SATs examinations that had been taken some months earlier. Results were now to hand and showed a 15% rise at Key Stage 1 and 7% at Key Stage 2.

SATURDAY, OCTOBER 16th
After the huge success with the 'free books for schools' venture, it was now decided to embark on a 'free maths equipment for schools'. From today until June 2000 over 5 billion tokens could be collected from McVities biscuits and cakes, the Mirror and Sunday Mirror, the People, Hula Hoops and Skips. It was hoped to collect sufficient tokens to provide the school with computer software, compasses and protractors.

MONDAY to WEDNESDAY, OCTOBER 18th to 20th
Arts Week and there were lots of activities taking place. What with music education workshops, shadow-making puppets, juggling, plate-spinning, dance, puppet story-telling, 3D work and printing, it was certainly a very enjoyable few days.

FRIDAY, DECEMBER 3rd
Taking place between 3.30p.m. and 5p.m., the school's Christmas Fair raised £608.96

WEDNESDAY and THURSDAY, DECEMBER 15th and 16th
The Christmas concert was put on for parents, but, unfortunately, not very many turned up to the morning performance on Wednesday. However, there was a full house on Thursday afternoon.

Christmas Concert, 1999.

THURSDAY, DECEMBER 16th

For the third year in succession 'Friends of Slade' organised a Christmas Sleigh Ride around the local streets during the evening. Taking the same form as in previous years, it raised £291.40, which was split equally between the Erdington Rotary Club and the 'Friends of Slade', who would use the money collected for the benefit of the children at the school.

2000

JANUARY

An after-school club commenced, which was situated in a room next to the Neighbourhood Office. Starting at 3.15p.m. each afternoon, there were initially two charges – £3 per session up to 5p.m. and £4.50 should children not be collected until 6p.m.

MONDAY, JANUARY 31st

There have always been problems with head lice in schools. 'Friends of Slade' took action today, launching a special 'Bug Busters' kit which would be supplied to all children attending the school.

TUESDAY, FEBRUARY 8th

Robin Corbett, M.P. for Erdington, paid a visit to the school this morning in order to present the Investors in People award, received here by Mr Sewell, the Head Teacher. Whilst there, he was also able to hand over the trophy that had been won by the girls' 4-a-side football team, who had once again been crowned champions of Erdington.

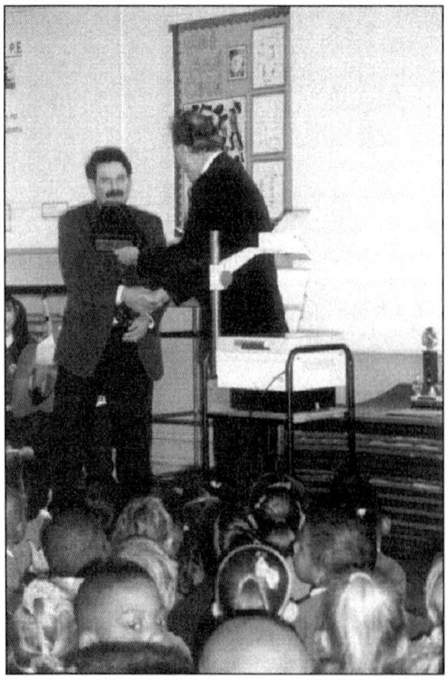

Investors in People Award, 2000.

Severn Trent New Garden, 2000.

APRIL
The new garden, sponsored by Severn Trent, and situated on the Hillside Road side of the school between the Blue 5/6 and Blue 6 classrooms, was planted up this month.

TUESDAY, APRIL 11th
At a special assembly this morning, Father David of All Saints Church was presented with various gifts on the occasion of his moving on to another parish.

MONDAY, JUNE 26th
Once again, the school's annual sports day took place at the Magnet Centre. During the afternoon numerous events were put on for the benefit of the children.

These included skipping, sack, running and relay races with the children representing their own house teams. In the end, the Tigers triumphed over the Panthers with the Lions and Jaguars occupying the minor positions.

Sports Day, 2000.

THURSDAY, JULY 13th

The school's new ICT suite was officially opened by Chief Education Officer, Professor Tim Brighouse, this morning. Both the outside corridor and the room itself had been designed and painted by members of the ancillary staff.

New ICT Suite, 2000.

TUESDAY, JULY 18th

Summer Concert. Cast of Pied Piper.

THURSDAY, JULY 20th
The last day of term and the children of Year 5 learnt that they had been awarded the overall runners-up place in the competition 'Caring is Cool' organised by the police, although one of the entries had actually placed first in the Year 5 category. They had just missed out on the first prize which was a trip in a helicopter! They had had to decide which aspect of their community they disliked most and design a poster or leaflet around it.

SEPTEMBER
Starting back to school after the summer holidays, a huge 'thank you' was due to all the children who had been collecting 'free books for schools' tokens. Over the previous twelve months an amazing 51, 562 had been collected. In consequence the school received 239 books, which consisted of dictionaries, big books, library and reading books. Blue 5 managed to collect the most tokens with 6,800.

It was also pleasing to notice how smart the children looked in their school uniform. However, there was an enormous amount of unclaimed and unidentified clothing in lost property. How did the children manage to lose so much; and not know that they'd lost it!

Early into the Autumn term and a morning playtime, which started at 10.30a.m. and lasted for fifteen minutes.

Playground Playtime, 2000.

THURSDAY, OCTOBER 12th
Children from the Green Group led a special Harvest Assembly this morning. Donations of

food in the form of tins, packets and fruit had been brought in during the previous few days; and were made up into parcels, which were given to the Birmingham City Mission for the Homeless.

THURSDAY, OCTOBER 19th
Meningitis jabs for children from year 1 to year 5 took place today, provided parents had first completed a consent form. Where Year 1 and 2 children were concerned, parents had to be present otherwise the injection could not take place.

TUESDAY, NOVEMBER 7th
A whole-school dental inspection took place.

THURSDAY, DECEMBER 7th
30 children from the Yellow Group went to the Old Rep to see a performance of *Charlotte's Web*.

TUESDAY, DECEMBER 12th
Now it was the turn of the Green Group to visit the theatre. Thirty of them saw *Rumpelstiltskin* this afternoon.

THURSDAY, DECEMBER 14th
This morning, at 9.30a.m., the children from the Yellow Group performed a musical production entitled *Michaelmas Mouse* – a Christmas story with a difference – for the benefit of those parents who were able to attend, as well as for the rest of the school.

FRIDAY, DECEMBER 15th
A Christmas fun day was organised for all the children. There was face painting, a bouncy castle, refreshments and lots of other fun activities for the children to participate in. There was even a lucky teddy stall. The day ended with the Friends of Slade having raised £708.07.

TUESDAY, DECEMBER 19th
Having dressed up for their Christmas party on the previous day, it was now the turn of the nursery children to dress up again – this time for their concert in the Nursery Hall. As appeared to be customary on these occasions, parents packed the hall to overflowing. It was standing room only!

2001

FRIDAY, JANUARY 5th
On the second day into a new school term, it was the turn of the children from the Blue Group to go to the pantomime this afternoon. Thirty of them went to see Leslie Grantham in *Peter Pan* at the Alexandra.

MONDAY, FEBRUARY 26th
Bags in the school colours, purchased by the Friends of Slade, were given out to all the children, so that items such as homework could be transported more easily between home and school. On leaving the school for good these were expected to be returned for use by new children.

THURSDAY, MARCH 1st
The school's annual charity appeal was held this morning – this one on behalf of the N.S.P.C.C. A few weeks later, shortly before Easter, the children were able to hand over £878.25, which they had managed to raise.

FRIDAY, MARCH 2nd
Eid parties were held during the afternoon.

SATURDAY, MARCH 3rd
During the previous few weeks the roof spaces in the Green and Yellow Groups' classes were being filled in. This was now completed.

THURSDAY, MARCH 15th
The photographer came into school this morning as he had done for many years past. Family portraits were taken at 9a.m., followed by individual children's photographs. Finally, a photograph was taken of every class, of which Blue 5/6 (top) and Blue 6 (bottom) respectively are shown alongside.

Classes, 2001.

FRIDAY, MARCH 16th
Today was Red Nose Day for Comic Relief. Despite one Yellow Group class disappearing to the Art Gallery and the Blue Group enjoying an Egyptian Day, the school still managed to raise £158.66 for charitable causes.

MONDAY, MARCH 26th
The Nursery Hall was closed for use for assemblies and physical education until further notice, as children were experiencing splinters from the parquet floor.

THURSDAY, MARCH 29th
Draughtproofing of the windows around the school started today.

FRIDAY, APRIL 6th
School closed for the Easter holidays with the annual Hat Parade up and down Slade Road, before re-opening again on St. Georges Day.

MONDAY, MAY 14th
All the Year 6 children took their SATs tests commencing today; and continuing until Friday.

MONDAY, MAY 21st to FRIDAY, MAY 25th
The whole week was given over to Arts.

THURSDAY and FRIDAY, JUNE 14th and 15th
The three Blue Group classes produced a C. D. entitled *Our World*, with the assistance of a Mr Peter Churchill, who brought in many and varied instruments as well as a recording system. Based on the theme of the environment, three pieces of music were produced – the jungle, the city and space. The instruments were not those normally associated with an orchestra, but those that had been made by different tribes or cultures across the world. All the children had a chance to participate in writing the words of a song and playing different instruments, as well as designing a cover for the compact disc. After it had been produced they had an opportunity to purchase a copy of their own.

MONDAY, JUNE 18th
The school held its annual sports day once again at the Magnet Centre, at the end of Park Approach, with the agreement of the current owners, the Greek Cypriot community. The older juniors walked to and from the school whilst the younger children were taken there and back by bus. Just under a hundred parents, relatives and friends turned up to watch the events, which involved both running and various forms of obstacle races. At the end of the afternoon the result was declared a tie between the Jaguars and the Lions, two of the four houses being represented by the children.

FRIDAY, JULY 6th
Following the success of the Christmas Fun Day, it was decided to hold another Fun Day instead of the customary Summer Fair. The children needed to bring spending money with them as there were lots of fun activities to enjoy throughout the day. It was another success with over £700 being raised.

During the afternoon a number of children went off to participate in the Erdington Primary Schools' sports at Wyndley Leisure Centre. There was no success, however, this year, although it was a close-run thing before the school finished in third place.

THURSDAY, JULY 12th
Tonight was an evening for the children to both enjoy themselves as well as receive the congratulations of the assembled audience. At 7p.m. it was time for the annual prizegiving

and a performance of the *Emerald Crown* – a musical which was based on the topical theme of environmental protection – given by the children from years 5 and 6.

TUESDAY, SEPTEMBER 4th
School re-opened after the summer holiday, during which a major refurbishment had been the complete replacement of both hall floors. The school was also working in partnership with the Education Welfare Service to raise attendance and punctuality across the whole school. Each week, the best class would be congratulated for achieving the fewest lates, a certificate being awarded in the form of an Early Bird certificate. Congratulations were also due to 6 children who had achieved 100% attendance during the previous school year.

FRIDAY, SEPTEMBER 7th
Science year was launched today at 11a.m., when 559, 493 children across the country, including those from Slade, jumped in the air for a minute in order to try and cause a mini-earthquake!

Concert – Emerald Crown, 2001.

MONDAY, SEPTEMBER 17th
As at this morning the number of children on the roll stood at 283, a reduction of 5 compared to the previous year's figures.

THURSDAY, OCTOBER 18th
A special Harvest assembly was held at 9.15a.m. Since Monday children had been asked to bring in donations of food and fruit, which would be made up into food parcels, and then distributed to the homeless via local charities. The new vicar of All Saints, Gregg Mensingh, came in to take the assembly and receive the gifts of food.

THURSDAY, NOVEMBER 15th
Inspire Workshops started today with a different year group being involved each week. Every child brought a parent or relative along with a view to making maths games, which could be used at home. With tea and coffee available, as well as prizes, it started at 9a.m. and lasted for two hours. The workshop was a light-hearted way to help families and children think about maths.

WEDNESDAY, DECEMBER 5th
Thirty children from the Yellow Group visited the Old Rep to see a production of *James and the Giant Peach* this afternoon.

WEDNESDAY, DECEMBER 12th
Now it was the turn of the infants to go to the theatre – this time the Crescent to see *Honk*.

THURSDAY, DECEMBER 13th
Reflector kits were issued to all the children, courtesy of the Nationwide Building Society. How many of the children will wear them is, of course, debatable!

FRIDAY, DECEMBER 14th
Lessons were suspended for the day, as all the children enjoyed a special Fun Day, during which many exciting activities were laid on. It was a great success, over £800 being raised. During the day, Father Christmas paid his customary visit, presenting every child with a present.

Blue 5, with Miss Heath, taken in their own classroom a few weeks before Christmas.

FRIDAY, DECEMBER 21st
School closed for the Christmas holiday at 2p.m. On the 18th the nursery and reception children had performed a nativity play and sung Christmas songs, before holding their combined Christmas/Eid parties the following day. Meanwhile, on the morning of the 19th, the Yellow Group children had put on a musical entitled *Do you believe in Father Christmas* in the main hall to which all parents were welcome to attend. The Yellow Group children, together with the children from the Blue and Green Groups, then held their parties the following afternoon.

2002
THURSDAY, JANUARY 10th
Two days after the school had re-opened following the Christmas holidays, and 40 Blue Group children had the opportunity to visit the Birmingham Hippodrome to see the pantomime *Dick Whittington* starring Brian Conley.

WEDNESDAY, FEBRUARY 20th
The week after half term and the Nursery and Yellow Group children visited the Life Education caravan in Broomfield Road. Meanwhile, a number of children from the Green Group were given the chance to go to the Nature Centre, whilst, at that morning's assembly, the rest of the school – those children in Years 4, 5 or 6 – were invited to consider joining

up with the Children's University. They had to complete the form and return it as soon as possible, because places were extremely limited. The Children's University Pop Programme was being run at the school every Saturday morning between 10 and 12, March 2nd to 23rd inclusive. Children had the opportunity to not only have fun with their friends, but to learn something new – Art, Music and I. C. T. – and all connected with popular music.

THURSDAY, FEBRUARY 28th
Today saw the launch of this year's children's charity appeal. The message went out for Barnardos and the children were subsequently forthcoming to the tune of £812.58.

THURSDAY, MARCH 14th
The school photographer called today, taking numerous photographs of which Blue 6 (right), with Miss Bayliss, is one example. These were available at a cost of £4.50 each.

Top: Class, 2002. Bottom: Mrs Janet Owens, who is both a former pupil and a teacher at the school, leads the procession.

TUESDAY, MARCH 26th
The last day of term before the school broke up for the Easter holidays. Fortunately, it was a fine day so there was no problem in holding the Easter Hat Parade. At 9.30a.m. the infants assembled outside the school before taking the traditional walk as far as Hunton Hill, where they crossed to the other side, thence to return to the school via the pelican crossing outside.

MONDAY, APRIL 15th
It was learned that, since the introduction of the Early Bird scheme at the beginning of the school year, lates had been reduced by 50%.

Starting today, as an adjunct to the After-School Club that had commenced in January 2000, was a Before-School Club. This was run on the same lines and enabled responsible parents to safely leave their children when they needed to be somewhere else before school started for the day. The club had a limit of 24 places, the cost being £2 for the hour between 8 and 9 o'clock.

MONDAY, APRIL 22nd
Stricken by a tracheal infection, Mr Andy Sewell, the Head Teacher, found himself unable to attend school for the following 4 weeks.

WEDNESDAY, MAY 1st
For the next seven school weeks, each of the seven classes of children, that had not already been given an opportunity to be involved in the Inspire Workshops, that had commenced in November of last year, were given their chance to make a maths game.

THURSDAY, MAY 2nd
The school closed for the local Council elections.

MONDAY to WEDNESDAY, MAY 20th to 22nd
Children from the Blue Group – Years 5 and 6 – spent an enjoyable, but tiring 3 days at the Kingswood Centre in Staffordshire. Children slept in centrally-heated dormitories, being supervised at all times by both Kingswood staff as well as staff who had accompanied them from the school. The centre gave them a unique opportunity to take part in a range of adventurous activities, which included archery, aeroball, climbing, quad bikes, team games and problem solving. In addition, they were also able to use the suite of computers in order to develop their skills in information technology. Commenting afterwards, the children said that they had liked all the activities, which they had found to be great fun. They had enjoyed learning new skills, besides which the food was great and the dormitories warm and cosy. A further course had now been booked for November for children who were currently in years 4 and 5 at a cost of £60 per child, which included transport, full board and accommodation, as well as tuition fees and other related costs.

SATURDAY, JUNE 15th
The day was only half an hour old when the fire service received a call from a local resident, who had seen flames and smoke emanating from the school. Someone had smashed the window of the resources room in Broomfield Road and thrown some lighted paper into it. The Erdington fire service were quick to respond and, in consequence, were able to contain the fire to the one room. There was a considerable amount of smoke and heat damage to the room, which was used for the storage of exercise books, paper and paints, as well as craft and resource materials for the various subjects. Both photocopiers also suffered damage. Adjoining rooms, which included the staff room and three classrooms, suffered some problems with smoke, but, fortunately, only the staff room was put out of commission. The staff had to repair to the library until conditions were improved. Meanwhile, the support staff had sorted out what could be saved and had placed this into a large container that had been especially provided for the purpose. It was now up to workmen to restore the building to its former unspoilt condition.

Ten o'clock in the morning and the Children's University were holding another module at the school until two o'clock in the afternoon. Children were given the chance to be a step ahead of the rest by learning a modern foreign language; and have fun as well! The following week would see an opportunity to use their imaginations artistically; become an artist; have fun with paints; or even make things.

TUESDAY, JUNE 25th

Today saw all the children completing a survey form into bullying and its effects. They were asked a substantial number of questions in complete anonymity, so that they could feel free to answer with total honesty what effect, if any, bullying might be having on them. The results of the survey would give the school the chance to proactively address any problems in the best way possible.

MONDAY, JULY 1st

The school held its annual sports day once again at the Magnet Centre this afternoon for the infants and juniors. The nursery and reception had held their own sports the previous Thursday on school premises. The afternoon was cool and overcast, showers punctuating the events, such that the races had to be rushed through with due expediency before the heavens really opened up. After holding up the other three teams two years ago, the Jaguars, with 194 points, won by a considerable margin for the second year in succession. Next came the Tigers with 156, the Lions and Panthers fighting it out to avoid the bottom place, the former eventually securing third place by just four points with 130.

THURSDAY, JULY 11th

One week before the end of term – and the school year – it was time for the annual concert and awards' evening, which began at 7p.m., tickets having to be reserved. During the afternoon an opportunity had been given for other parents to see the concert, the dress rehearsal having taken place the previous day. An excellent 45-minute show was put on, the children having practised their songs and dancing routines for many weeks past.

Concert Programme – Wilbur and the Web, 2002.

MONDAY, JULY 15th

The school had its annual canteen inspection this morning. As was usual, the Environmental Health Department turned up without warning to carry out the check, once again giving the school a clean bill of health.

TUESDAY, JULY 16th

Summer Fun Day and £768 was raised from all the activities.

AUGUST

Work started on the new toilet provisions – intended to ensure that all the children in the school could reach a toilet without having to go outside at all. Those for Blue 5 and Blue 5/6 were placed at either end of the classrooms, their stockrooms being closed off as the work was in progress to convert them; that for Blue 6 would be in the old air-raid shelter, attached to the side of the building, a hole having to be knocked through the adjoining wall. Meanwhile, a corridor had been built alongside the old staffroom, work going ahead – albeit slowly – to effect the changes necessary to the burnt-out resources centre. Many months would elapse until everything was complete. In the meantime, the library had to accommodate the staff and some of the maths groups, whilst still providing a haven for booklovers!

Concert – Wilbur and the Web, 2002.

MONDAY to WEDNESDAY, SEPTEMBER 23rd To 25th

Each of the three Blue Group classes visited the Stables Camping Centre at Blackwell for a day on the 'school coach', which was driven by Mr Walpole. Whilst there, they had a tremendous time trying out various disciplines. There were woodland paths to be explored,

Stables Centre, 2002.

map reading and orienteering skills to be learned, as well as trusting a partner to lead them blindfolded along a rope trail, that was called the Nightline.

MONDAY and TUESDAY,
SEPTEMBER 30th and OCTOBER 1st
A team of inspectors from the L.E.A. paid a visit, at the school's request, to carry out a mini-inspection, in order to determine the school's weaknesses, so that these could be addressed: it was realised that it had been over four years since the last Ofsted inspection, and another one must be imminent.

LEA Inspection Team, 2002.

TUESDAY, OCTOBER 15th
The Reverend Gregg Mensingh of All Saints Church came into school this morning to take the Harvest assembly and receive gifts of tinned and packeted foodstuffs from the children. Mr Sewell later took these to the Birmingham City Mission where they would be used to help and support their ongoing work amongst the homeless, elderly and needy families with whom they were in contact.

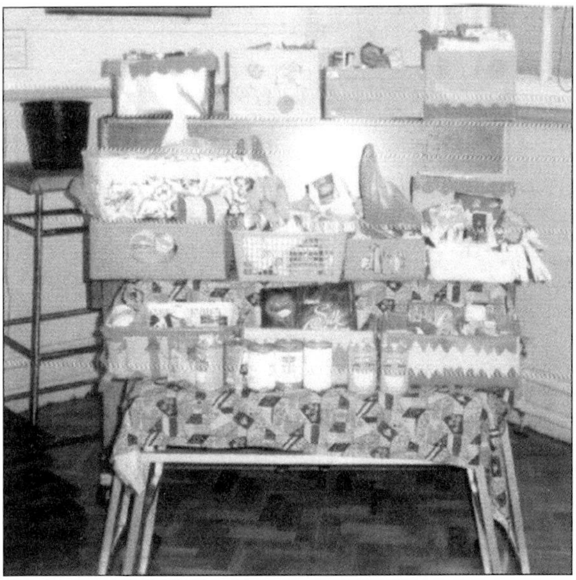

The Reverend Gregg Mensingh addresses the children at the morning assembly to the left, whilst above is a display of some of the items that the children brought in.

WEDNESDAY, NOVEMBER 13th

This morning saw a visit from the Birmingham Hippodrome Pantomime Roadshow. Not only the children, but many members of the staff, almost split their sides with laughing as 'Tracey' – played by Nigel Ellacott – and 'Sharon' – played by Andrew Ryan – entertained them before morning break. Having used the Kids Club room alongside the Neighbourhood Office to change, one can only imagine what the staff and clients must have made of it all! After break the children returned to the main hall to learn more about the secrets of a successful pantomime, some of them having an opportunity to dress up as some of the characters, before it was time for the dinner ladies to set up the hall for lunch.

MONDAY to WEDNESDAY, NOVEMBER 25th to 27th

At 1.30p.m. thirty children set out for Kingswood – for some of them it was their second visit of the year – where they spent two nights and three days, before returning on the Wednesday afternoon as school was concluding for the day.

THURSDAY, DECEMBER 12th

The stage awaits Mary and Joseph and the remainder of the cast of the concert put on by the Nursery this morning. Meanwhile, in the main hall, the children from the various classes were given time to enjoy themselves on the Christmas Fun Day, which raised £666.

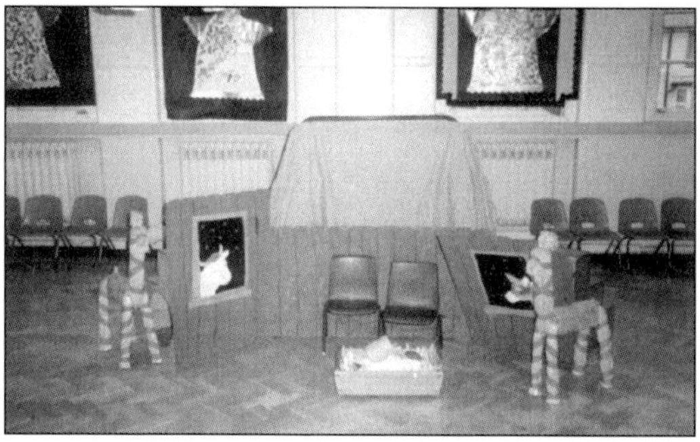

Nursery Christmas Concert, 2002.

WEDNESDAY, DECEMBER 18th

Two days before the school closed for the Christmas holidays – not to return until Wednesday, January 8th – and the day after thirty children from the Blue Group had been to the theatre to see the *Arabian Nights*, the Yellow Group put on their Christmas concert entitled *It's a Miracle* for the parents this morning.

Christmas Concert – It's a Miracle, 2002.

2003

WEDNESDAY, JANUARY 8th

Returning to school this morning, the children from the Blue and Yellow groups found themselves being entertained by a MADman. On this occasion the man was quite sane, explaining to them how it was possible to learn lots of facts and information more easily. They were surprised at how they were able to learn the names of the countries in the E. E. C., as well as Japanese numbers, off by heart, with just a little tuition. The MADman was *making a difference*.

Meanwhile, all the infants had the chance of enjoying free fruit each week from now on, courtesy of an initiative from the Government. Across the city, 47630 four to six year olds in 278 schools benefited each day from the School Fruit Pilot programme, which was backed by the lottery's New Opportunities Fund. The city was part of a £10 million West Midlands scheme, launched in November 2001, which saw over 1.1 million pieces of fruit handed over each week.

WEDNESDAY, JANUARY 15th to FRIDAY, JANUARY 17th
The Life Education Caravan visited again, giving all the children in the school the opportunity to understand what a healthy life was all about.
Whilst all this was going on, Year 6 pupils went skiing and rock climbing at the Ackers on Thursday, Year 5 children spending the day out on Friday on Cannock Chase.

MONDAY, JANUARY 20th
At last, the work that had started during the previous summer holiday was completed! The new staffroom was now available, as was the new resources centre, the two having swapped positions with each other. Up above the staffroom had been built another room, reached by a metal, spiral staircase, which could be used as an additional teaching resource for pupils.

MONDAY, FEBRUARY 10th
Today, work started to replace the roof over the main hall and library. Scaffolding had been erected over the previous few days.

TUESDAY, FEBRUARY 11th
The Kids Club was subject to an Ofsted inspection this afternoon. It passed with flying colours.

MONDAY, MARCH 3rd
The Ofsted inspection team – pictured to the right – arrived this morning – 8 of them to be exact for a period of three and a half days. The result – a failure and special measures! Despite having had a trial run with the LEA only six months earlier. The school's SATs results – although there had been a good improvement, many new initiatives having been introduced – had not reached the Government's targets, so that can't have helped matters.

However, two months later, and the D. of E. awarded the school a certificate, and over £8,000 to be shared amongst the staff for these significant improvements!

Ofsted Team, 2003.

Still, the school has had to accept the outcome, and has to endeavour to convince Ofsted during the months ahead of significant improvements.

WEDNESDAY, APRIL 16th

The last day of what had been a rather difficult term, and it was time to break up for Easter. First off, the children from the infants held their annual Hat Parade, leaving the school buildings at 9.30a.m. to a cheery send-off from the nursery; and what a lovely day it was too – a gorgeously hot sunny morning! A walk up Slade Road to Hunton Hill, and back again on the other side of the road. Surely better than lessons! Now, it was ten o'clock and a morning assembly at which the infants had a chance to show off their creations to the rest of the school; and receive their congratulations. Then, it was time to present Easter eggs to those children from the junior classes, who had produced decorated eggs, that had been judged by staff from Homestart earlier in the morning. It was also an opportunity to say 'goodbye' to Mr Andy Hill, the Deputy Head Teacher, who had decided to take early retirement after 27 years at the school. Although not yet sixty – the rules concerning the early retirement of teachers were changed a few years earlier because so many of them were leaving – he had been considering the matter for a few months, and was able to negotiate a suitable retirement package. Still, it must have come as something of a shock to many of the staff and children who had known him, as it was only announced two days prior to his departure. Children from all the classes in the school gave him cards that they had made as well as presents. With the end of assembly the children were released to the playground for their fifteen minutes' morning break, until it became time for them to bring out their chairs and line them up in the customary fashion down the playground. It was now time for the egg-rolling competition! With that over and done with by midday, the staff retired to the staffroom for the usual end-of-term buffet. Subsequently, Mr Hill was presented with some garden furniture – it would be delivered to his home later on – that the staff had bought

The nursery (above) waves off the annual Easter Hat Parade (right).

for him as a going-away gift. He had started at the school in January of 1976 and had worked at four schools before he came to Slade. Also leaving after more than thirty-two years in the Nursery – she had started at the end of 1970 – was Mrs Jan Rushton. She had chosen to leave, having been away ill for the previous twelve months.

MONDAY, MAY 19th
Twelve pupils from year six were appointed as prefects, a rota being drawn up for each day to enable them to carry out their required duties.

MONDAY, JUNE 2nd
Work commenced on the disability ramp at the main entrance to the school, as well as the entrance hatch at reception. Upgrading of the female staff's toilet provision also got underway.

WEDNESDAY, SEPTEMBER 3rd
Opening after the long summer holiday, returning children could not help but notice the changes around the school. Not only had the walls of the corridors been painted a welcoming yellow, new carpeting had been laid, whilst new doors had also been installed.

THURSDAY, SEPTEMBER 4th
Today, it was announced that it would no longer be acceptable for crisps to be brought into school.

MONDAY, SEPTEMBER 8th
Toni-Ann Byfield came to Slade School in November of 2002. She settled in well, made friends, and was a well-liked member of the school community, until she left in June of this year to go and live with her 'aunt' in London. Today, a few hours after returning from a shopping trip, 7-year-old Toni-Ann died, the result of a Yardie-style killing. A gunman fatally shot her father Bertram, a convicted drug dealer, before turning the gun on the fleeing Toni-Ann, cruelly murdering the young girl with a single shot to her back. A number of arrests were made over the subsequent weeks, leading eventually to a man being convicted in 2006. A book of condolence was subsequently raised.

MONDAY, SEPTEMBER 22nd
As part of the school's constant striving to improve and promote a positive ethos 16 new prefects were appointed for the year. The children had been chosen by interview, before nominating a Head Girl, Amy Isaac, and Head Boy, Jamie Cooper. The prefects had a supportive role to play at dinner times and play times, wearing their badges and hats with pride. They provided a helping hand, showing younger children how to play nice games, as well as taking children to first aid. As role models for the other children in the school, they would be given the opportunity to show visitors around or perform other responsible duties.

MONDAY, NOVEMBER 3rd

The school opened following half-term with a change to the timetable. In future the juniors would break for an hour's lunch at 12.15. However, their afternoon break would disappear as a result. Mornings would now be given over to the sole teaching of numeracy and literacy, all other lessons taking place during the two-hour afternoon session.

WEDNESDAY, NOVEMBER 26th

The family of Toni-Ann Byfield attended an assembly at the school this morning, in order to witness the unveiling of a 'Buddy Bench' in memory of Toni-Ann. This was placed adjacent to the entrance to the vault, immediately below the door that led into the year 2 classroom of the Green group.

Toni-Ann Byfield 'Buddy Bench', 2003.

2004

THURSDAY and FRIDAY, JANUARY 22nd and 23rd

Ofsted called to check on the progress that had been made to turn the school around since its failure early last year. They expressed themselves well-satisfied and would not be returning until the autumn term.

MONDAY, FEBRUARY 23rd

During the night, a burglary took place when the overhead projectors were stolen from the classrooms of Blue 5/6 and Blue 6. The entry point appeared obvious in Blue 5/6 where a window lay smashed and torn out from its fixings. However, there was no sign of a break-in in the classroom of Blue 6, and one is left to wonder how the thieves gained access! It was somewhat illuminating that the projector in Blue 5 had not been taken. Perhaps it had something to do with the fact that it had not worked since its installation at the beginning of the school year! At roughly the same time as the burglary took place, the son of the caretaker, Mr Stanton, was coincidentally attacked and robbed directly opposite the school on the corner of Hillaries Road.

THURSDAY, MARCH 4th

At a special assembly this morning an opportunity was given to the National Children's Homes – it was their turn on the rota system this year – to speak to the children about the work that they carried out. In response to their appeal, a sum of £573.03 was subsequently raised.

FRIDAY, MARCH 12th

Congratulations Assemblies were held on every Friday of the school year, in order to present those children, who had earned a certificate or other honour, to the rest of the school, so that they could be rewarded with praise for their efforts. Their parents or guardians were given an opportunity to attend, and feel pride at their child's attainments. This morning, ten children were brought forward to receive acclaim, who had been nominated and chosen by their peers to sit on the newly-formed School Council. There had previously been a School Council formed in 1986, but this had faded away some years earlier. Two children – a boy and a girl – were chosen from Year 2 to Year 6 inclusive.

FRIDAY, JULY 2nd

Although the school's official birthday was not until Sunday, it was celebrated today. A concert was put on this morning at 9.45a.m. to which ex-pupils, friends, teachers and governors were invited. After both of the school's choirs had sung – the Blue Group Choir with *Silver Lining; World in Union; Sin Je Je* and the Yellow Group Choir with *Baby one, two, three; Sing All Together* – it was time for each class to perform their party piece, starting with Blue 6, and ending with the Nursery singing Happy Birthday to the school. Each class portrayed a specific period from the previous 100 years, acknowledging an event that had occurred in each year of the decade that they were representing – the children were dressed appropriately, many in costumes of the period they were portraying. Obviously, some classes had a better deal than others, especially with the choice of music that they were afforded – notably Blue 5 with *The Charleston* from the 1920s; Yellow 3 with *Rock and Roll* from the 1950s; and Green 2 with the 1960s and *The Beatles*. The whole performance lasted an hour and a half, each class being enthusiastically applauded on finishing their act. Afterwards, the audience were invited to partake of refreshments before the birthday cake was cut at a quarter to twelve. Some of the ex-pupils later recorded their comments as follows:

> "Absolutely fantastic. Everyone must have worked so hard!"
> "A super morning. Much work involved!! Many thanks."
> "Thank you for leaving me with more happy memories of Slade School."
> "A great concert. Impressed with all we saw and heard. Many thanks to all involved."
> "Excellent morning out. Great concert and lovely to meet old friends."
> "Very enjoyable. A day to remember."
> "Really enjoyable trip down memory lane."
> "The most memorable experience of late. Many thanks."

In the afternoon, the juniors were treated to a magic show whilst the reception classes and the infants enjoyed Punch and Judy, before each class had its own party to end the day.

Miss Bayliss with Blue 6, (1900s).

Blue 5/6, (1910s).

Mrs Sturgess with Blue 5, (1920s).

Mr Kanyua with Yellow 4, (1930s).

Mrs McKernon (left) Mrs Massie (right) and Yellow 3/4, (1940s).

Miss Tobin (centre) Mrs Bagshaw (right) and Yellow 3, (1950s).

Miss Carolan and Green 2, (1960s).

Mrs Hartley and Green 1/2, (1970s).

Miss Forgham (right) Mrs Verma (left) and Green 1, (1980s).

(Left to Right) Mrs Nicholls, Mrs Baht, Mrs Kite, and far right, Mrs Ogier and Reception, (1990s).

(Left to Right) Mrs Owens, Mrs Morris, Mrs Droch, Mrs John and Nursery, (2000s).

Mr Sewell cuts the birthday cake.

Appendix 1.
GENERAL HISTORY

1903	June 30th	Foundation stone laid.
1904	July 4th	Separate Infant and Mixed Schools open.
1906	September 6th	New building opens. Mixed School becomes separate Girls' and Boys' Schools.
1910	September 1st	Further new buildings open. There are now 4 departments – Girls', Boys', Infants', and new Junior Mixed, as well as a new Assembly Hall.
1915	June 11th	The Junior Department ceases to exist. There are now once again only Infants', Girls' and Boys' Departments.
1931	July 22nd	The Girls' Department ceases to exist.
	August 24th	The school re-opens with departments for Infants, Senior Boys and Junior Mixed.
1941	May 5th	The Infants and Juniors merge to become The Slade Primary School.
1945	September	The Senior Boys' School becomes a totally separate school to be known as the Slade Boys' County Modern School.
1968	January 1st	Slade Secondary Modern Boys' School move to their new premises in Fentham Road.
	October 18th	Slade Secondary Modern Boys' School officially ceases to exist. At an opening ceremony it is re-named the Erdington Secondary Modern Boys' School.
1971	January	A new Nursery department opens. The school now caters for Junior, Infant and Nursery children.

Appendix 2.
HEAD TEACHERS

1904–1906	Mr Henry Page	Mixed School
1904–1931	Miss Nellie M. Bryan	Infants
1906–1921	Mr Henry Page	Boys' School
1906–1931	Miss Clara A. Baum	Girls' School
1910–1914	Miss Alice B. Horne	Junior School
1913–1920	Mr William Shelton	Evening School
1914–1915	Miss Kate Smith	Junior School
1920–1942	Mr Valentine W. G. Thomas	Evening School
1921–1931	Mr Edmund W. Jones	Boys' School
1931–1936	Mr Edmund W. Jones	Senior Boys' School
1931–1941	Mr Charley Gooding Clarke	Junior School
1932–1941	Miss G. M. Freeling	Infants
1936–1950	Mr H. Caddick	Senior Boys' School
1941–1959	Mr Charley Gooding Clarke	Junior and Infants' School
1950–1954	Mr W. H. Griffin	County Modern Boys' School
1954–1956	Mr W. Barnett	County Modern Boys' School
1956–1968	Mr Reg. Dawes	County Modern Boys' School, later Secondary Modern Boys' School
1959–1967	Mr Geoffrey N. Conduct	Junior and Infants' School
1967–1971	Mr Terry Spinks	Junior and Infants' School
1971–1981	Mr Terry Spinks	Junior and Infants' School and Nursery
1982–1992	Mr Andy Knipe	Junior and Infants' School and Nursery
1993–	Mr Andy Sewell	Junior and Infants' School and Nursery

Appendix 3.
SPORTS SUCCESSES

1909	Winners ½ mile school team race Erdington Charity Sports
1911	Winners ½ mile school team race Erdington Charity Sports
1912	Winners Aston Schools' Football Challenge Shield
1913	Winner Erdington Schoolboys' Swimming Championship – Paget Evans Cup – Dennett
1914	Runner Up Erdington Schoolboys' Swimming Championship – Marston
1915	Winners North Birmingham Schools' Netball Shield
1916	Winners North Birmingham Schools' Netball Shield
1917	Winners Aston Schools' Football League
	Runners Up Aston Schools' Football Challenge Shield
	Winners North Birmingham Schools' Netball Shield
1918	Winners Aston Schools' Football Challenge Shield
	Runners Up Aston Schools' Football League
	Runners Up H.M.S. Birmingham Football Shield
1919	Winners North Birmingham Schools' Football League
	Runners Up North Birmingham Schools' Cricket League South
1920	Runners Up North Birmingham Schools' Football Challenge Shield
	Runners Up North Birmingham Schools' Football League
	Winners North Birmingham Schools' Sports Shield for Boys
	3rd Place Erdington Schools' Swimming Championship – J Law
1921	Runners Up Erdington Schools' Football League
	Winners Erdington Schools' Athletic Sports for Boys – Wiggins-Davies Shield
	2nd Place Team Erdington Schools' Swimming Championship Race
1922	Winners Erdington Schools' Football League
	Runners Up Erdington Schools' Athletic Sports for Girls
1923	Winners Erdington Schools' Netball Championship
	Winners Erdington Schools' Athletic Sports for Girls – Yenton Shield
	Runners Up Erdington Schools' Athletic Sports for Boys

1924	Winners Erdington Schools' Netball Championship
	Winners Erdington Schools' Athletic Sports for Girls – Yenton Shield
1925	Winners Erdington Schools' Netball Championship
	Winners Erdington Schools' Football League
	Winners Erdington Schools' Junior Football Cup
	2nd & 4th Places Schoolboys' Event opening new Erdington Swimming Baths
	Runners Up Erdington Schools' Athletic Sports for Girls
1926	Winners Erdington Schools' Junior Football Cup
	Winners Erdington Schools' Junior Cricket League
	Runners Up Erdington Schools' Athletic Sports for Boys
	Runners Up Erdington Schools' Athletic Sports for Girls
	Winners Erdington Schools' Swimming Relay Championship for Girls
1927	Winners Erdington Schools' Football League Division 1
	Winners Erdington Schools' Football League Division 2
	Runners Up Erdington Schools' Athletic Sports for Girls
	Winners Erdington Schools' Cricket League
	Winners Erdington Schools' Swimming Relay Championship for Girls
1928	Winners Erdington Schools' Athletic Sports for Boys – Wiggins-Davies Shield
	Winners Erdington Schools' Athletic Sports for Girls – Yenton Shield
	Winners Erdington Schools' Cricket League
	Runners Up Erdington Schools' Swimming Championship for Girls
1929	Runners Up Erdington Schools' Athletic Sports for Boys
	Runners Up Erdington Schools' Athletic Sports for Girls
	Winners Erdington Schools' Netball Championship
	Joint Winners Erdington Schools' Cricket League
	Runners Up Erdington Schools' Swimming Relay Championship for Girls
1930	Joint Winners Erdington Schools' Swimming Championship for Boys
	Winner Erdington Schools' 2 lengths Swimming Championship for Boys – R Turner
1931	Runners Up Erdington Schools' Junior Football Cup
1932	Runners Up Erdington Schools' Junior Football Cup
	Winners Erdington Schools' Athletic Sports for Junior Girls
	Runners Up Erdington Schools' Cricket League
1933	Runners Up Erdington Schools' Intermediate Football Cup
	Winners Erdington Schools' Athletic Sports for Junior Girls
	Winners Erdington Schools' Athletic Sports for Junior Boys
	Joint Winners Erdington Schools' Swimming Championship for Junior Girls
	Runners Up Erdington Schools' Swimming Championship for Junior Boys
1934	Winners Erdington Schools' Junior Football Cup
	Winners Erdington Schools' Athletic Sports for Junior Mixed

	Runners Up Erdington Schools' Cricket League
	Runners Up Erdington Schools' Junior Cricket League
1935	Winners Erdington Schools' Athletic Sports for Junior Mixed
	Winners Erdington Schools' Swimming Championship for Senior Boys
	Winners Erdington Schools' Swimming Championship for Junior Girls
1936	Runners Up Erdington Schools' Football League
	Runners Up Erdington Schools' Intermediate Football Cup
	Winners Erdington Schools' Junior Football Cup
	Winners Erdington Schools' Athletic Sports for Senior Boys – Wiggins-Davies Shield
	Runners Up Erdington Schools' Cricket League
	Runners Up Erdington Schools' Intermediate Cricket Cup
1937	Runners Up Erdington Schools' Athletic Sports for Junior Girls
	Runners Up Erdington Schools' Junior Cricket League
	Runners Up Erdington Schools' Intermediate Cricket Cup
1938	Winners Erdington Schools' Reserve Football League
	Winners Erdington Schools' Intermediate Football Cup
	Runners Up Erdington Schools' Junior Football Cup
	Runners Up Erdington Schools' Intermediate Cricket Cup
1939	Runners Up Erdington Schools' Football League
	Winners Erdington Schools' Cricket League
	Runners Up Erdington Schools' Athletic Sports for Senior Boys
	Winners Erdington Schools' Athletic Sports for Junior Boys
1940–1945	Erdington Schools' Sports suspended for duration of World War Two
1946	Joint Winners Erdington Schools' Athletic Sports for Junior Girls
	Runners Up Erdington Schools' Athletic Sports for Senior Boys
1947	Winners H.M.S. Birmingham Football Shield
	Winners Erdington Schools' Junior Football League
	Runners Up Erdington Schools' Football League 'A' Division
	Runners Up Erdington Schools' Football League 'B' Division
	Runners Up Erdington Schools' Athletic Sports for Junior Girls
	Joint Winners Erdington Schools' Swimming Championship for Junior Girls
1948	Winners Erdington Schools' Junior Cricket League
	Runners Up Erdington Schools' Intermediate Cricket League
	Winners Erdington Schools' Athletic Sports for Junior Boys
	Winners Erdington Schools' Swimming Championship for Senior Boys
1949	Joint Winners Erdington Schools' Junior Football Cup
	Winners Erdington Schools' Cricket League
	Runners Up Erdington Schools' Intermediate Cricket League
	Runners Up Erdington Schools' Junior Cricket League North
	Winners Erdington Schools' Athletic Sports for Junior Girls
	Winners Erdington Schools' Swimming Championship for Junior Girls

1950	Winners Erdington Schools' Football League
	Winners Erdington Schools' Football Cup – Oldroyd-Wedd Trophy
	Runners Up Erdington Schools' Intermediate Football League
	Runners Up Erdington Schools' Intermediate Football Cup
	Joint Winners Erdington Schools' Cricket League
	Runners Up Erdington Schools' Intermediate Cricket League
	Winners Erdington Schools' Athletic Sports for Junior Boys
	Runners Up Erdington Schools' Athletic Sports for Junior Girls
1951	Winners Erdington Schools' Intermediate Football League
	Winners Erdington Schools' Intermediate Football Cup
	Runners Up Erdington Schools' Athletic Sports for Senior Boys
	Winners 400 yards relay race for schoolboys – Fisher and Ludlows annual sports
1952	Runners Up Erdington Schools' Football League
	Runners Up Erdington Schools' Football Cup
	Runners Up Erdington Schools' Intermediate Football League
	Runners Up Erdington Schools' Intermediate Football Cup
	Runners Up Erdington Schools' Junior Football Cup
	Winners Erdington Schools' Swimming Championship for Junior Boys
1953	Winners Erdington Schools' Football League
1954	Winners Erdington Schools' Football League
	Joint Winners Erdington Schools' Swimming Championship for Senior Boys
	Runners Up Erdington Schools' Athletic Sports for Junior girls
1955	Runners Up Erdington Schools' Football League
	Runners Up Erdington Schools' Athletic Sports for Junior Boys
1957	Winners Erdington Schools' Athletic Sports for Senior Boys – Wiggins-Davies Shield
1959	Winners Erdington Schools' Intermediate Football League
	Runners Up Erdington Schools' Junior Football League 'C' Division
	Runners Up Erdington Schools Junior Football Cup
1962	Winners Erdington Schools' Junior Football League 'B' Division
	Runners Up Erdington Schools' Junior 7-a-side Football Cup
1963	Runners Up Erdington Schools' Junior Football League 'A' Division
	Runners Up Erdington Schools' Cricket League
	Joint Winners Erdington Schools' Intermediate Cricket League
	Runners Up Erdington Schools' Athletic Sports for Junior Girls
1964	Winners Erdington & Saltley Schools' Football League Division 2
	Runners Up Erdington & Saltley Schools' Intermediate Football League Division 2
1967	Winners Erdington & Saltley Schools' Football League Division 2
	Winners Erdington Schools' Cricket League
	Winners Erdington Schools' Intermediate Cricket League

1971	Runners Up Erdington Junior Schools' Athletic Sports for Boys
1973	Joint Winners Lozells Harriers Invitation Trophy Meeting
1975	Winners Erdington Carnival 5-a-side Schools' Football Tournament
1976	Runners Up Erdington Junior Schools' 4-a-side Football Cup
	Winners 3rd Years' Netball Tournament at Perry Common
1977	Runners Up Erdington Junior Schools' 4-a-side Football Cup
	Runners Up Erdington Junior Schools' Athletic Sports for Girls and Boys
1978	Runners Up Erdington Junior Schools' Rounders Championship
1982	Winners Erdington Junior Schools' Athletic Sports
	Winners Erdington Junior Schools' Football Cup – Plaza Cup
1984	Winners Erdington Junior Schools' Cricket League
	Winners Erdington Junior Schools' Softball Championship
1985	Runners Up Erdington Junior Schools' Football League
	Joint Winners Erdington Junior Schools' Cricket League
1986	Winners Erdington Junior Schools' 6-a-side Knockout Cup
1987	Winners Erdington Junior Schools' 6-a-side Knockout Cup
	Winners Erdington Junior Schools' Cricket Knockout Cup
	Beaten Finalists Warwickshire Softball Cricket Competition
1988	Winner Birmingham Table Tennis Final – Daniel Douglas
1993	Winners Erdington Junior Schools' Football – Villa Cup
	Winners Erdington Junior Schools' Football Saturday League
	Winners Erdington Junior Schools' Football Midweek League
	Winners Erdington Junior Schools' 6-a-side Football Cup
	Winners Erdington Junior Schools' 4-a-side Football Cup
	Winners Erdington Schools' H.M.S. Birmingham Progress Shield
	Runners Up Erdington Junior Schools' 4-a-side Football Cup for Girls
	Joint Winners Erdington Junior Schools' Athletic Sports
	Winners Erdington Junior Schools' Cricket League
1994	Winner Erdington Junior Schools' Swimming Gala – Michael Carlisle
1995	Winners Erdington Junior Schools' Softball Cricket League
	Winners Erdington Junior Schools' Cricket League
1997	Winners Erdington Junior Schools' 6-a-side Football Cup for Girls
	Runners Up Erdington Junior Schools' 4-a-side Football Cup for Girls
	Runners Up Erdington Junior Schools' Football Saturday League
	Winners Erdington Junior Schools' Athletic Sports – Small Schools & Overall
1998	Runners Up Erdington Junior Schools' 4-a-side Football Cup for Girls
	Winners Erdington Junior Schools' 6-a-side Football Cup for Girls
	Runners Up Erdington Junior Schools' Athletic Sports – Small Schools
	Winners Erdington Junior Schools' Cricket league
1999	Winners Erdington Junior Schools' Football League for Second Teams
	Runners Up Erdington Junior Schools' 4-a-side Football Cup for Girls

2000	Winners Erdington Junior Schools' 4-a-side Football Cup for Girls
	Runners Up Birmingham Junior Schools' 7-a-side Football Championship
2001	Runners Up Erdington Junior Schools' 8-a-side Football Championship for Girls
	Winners Tops Community Hockey Competition – Wyndley Leisure Centre

Appendix 4.
MUSIC SUCCESSES

1921	Friday, April 29th	1st Cantata class for Public Elementary Girls' School Choirs in Birmingham Midland Competition Festival
1922	Wednesday, May 10th	1st Children's International Dances for 7–17 year olds at a school in the Midland Counties Midland Competition Festival
	Saturday, May 13th	2nd Public Elementary Girls' School Choirs in Birmingham Midland Competition Festival
1923	Wednesday, May 2nd	1st Children's International Dances for 7–17 year olds at a school in the Midland Counties Midland Competition Festival
	Thursday, May 3rd	1st Cantata class for Public Elementary Girls' School Choirs in Birmingham Midland Competition Festival
1924	Tuesday, May 20th	1st equal Junior Choirs of 30–40 children under 11 years of age at a Public Elementary School in Birmingham Winners Harding Challenge Shield Midland Competition Festival
	Wednesday, May 21st	1st Cantata class for Public Elementary School Choirs in Birmingham of 25–35 scholars Winners Daily News Challenge Shield Midland Competition Festival
1925	Wednesday, May 13th	2nd equal International Dances for 12–17 year olds of not less than 4 at a school in the Midland Counties Midland Competition Festival
	Friday, May 15th	2nd Cantata class for Public Elementary Girls' School Choirs in Birmingham Midland Competition Festival

	Saturday, May 16th	1st Junior Choirs under 11 years of age at a Public Elementary School in Birmingham Midland Competition Festival
1926	Wednesday, April 28th	2nd Cantata class for Public Elementary School Choirs in Birmingham of 25–35 scholars Midland Competition Festival
1927	Friday, May 13th	1st Public Elementary Girls' School Choirs in the Midland Counties Midland Competition Festival
	Saturday, May 14th	2nd Junior Choirs under 11 years of age at a Public Elementary School in Birmingham 2nd Cantata class Public Elementary School Choirs in Birmingham Midland Competition Festival
1928	Tuesday, May 8th	2nd National Dances for 11–14 year olds of not less than 6 at a school in the Midland Counties Midland Competition Festival
	Friday, May 11th	2nd Public Elementary Girls' School Choirs in the Midland Counties Midland Competition Festival
	Saturday, May 12th	1st Junior Choirs under 11 years of age at a Public Elementary School in Birmingham Winners Harding Challenge Shield 2nd Junior Choirs under 11 years of age at a Public Elementary School in Birmingham 2nd Cantata class Public Elementary School Choirs in Birmingham Midland Competition Festival
1929	Saturday, May 4th	1st Public Elementary Girls' School Choirs in the Midland Counties 1st Cantata class Public Elementary Girls' School Choirs in Birmingham Midland Competition Festival
1930	Thursday, May 15th	2nd National Dances for 11–14 year olds of not less than 6 at a school in the Midland Counties Midland Competition Festival
	Saturday, May 17th	2nd Public Elementary Girls' School Choirs in the Midland Counties Midland Competition Festival

INDEX

B

N